The Deal Decade

The Deal Decade

What Takeovers and Leveraged Buyouts Mean for Corporate Governance

MARGARET M. BLAIR
editor

The Brookings Institution
Washington, D.C.

Copyright © 1993 by

THE BROOKINGS INSTITUTION

1775 Massachusetts Avenue, N.W., Washington, D.C. 20036

Library of Congress Cataloging-in Publication Data

The deal decade: what takeovers and leveraged buyouts mean for
  corporate governance / Margaret M. Blair, editor.
  p.   cm.
  Includes bibliographical references and index.
  ISBN 0-8157-0946-3 (bound)—ISBN 0-8157-0945-5 (pbk.)
  1. Consolidation and merger of corporations.   2. Corporate
governance.   3. Industrial management.   I. Blair, Margaret M.,
1950–   .
HG4028.M4U53   1993
338.8′3—dc20   92-39450
                                                        CIP

9 8 7 6 5 4 3 2 1

The paper in this publication meets the minimum requirements of the
American National Standard for Information Sciences—Permanence
of Paper for Printed Library Materials, ANSI Z39.48-1984.

Foreword

During the 1980s an unprecedented wave of corporate takeovers, leveraged buyouts, and refinancings roiled financial markets in the United States. In ten years the nonfinancial corporate sector added $1.84 trillion in debt. Companies with a total value of $1.16 trillion were taken private or acquired in mergers. Yet by the early 1990s the wave of restructurings had ebbed almost as suddenly as it had arisen.

The extraordinary activity raised significant questions. Why did the restructurings occur—and why then? What were the mechanisms of the buyouts and how were they used? And who should control this country's largest corporations?

This book tries to answer some of those questions. From widely varying perspectives, the contributors examine how the surge of takeovers and restructurings changed the performance of corporations and altered relations between corporate management and the financial markets. The nine studies and their attendant comments examine the argument that takeovers and debt contracts were used to restrain managerial empire building. They consider the economic and institutional conditions that may have encouraged restructuring. And they assess how well the companies have done since being taken over. Although the conclusions are not unanimous, the authors do illuminate the causes of the restructurings, their effects, good and ill, on the country's political and economic environment, and the changes that have occurred in corporate governance.

Early drafts of the papers in this book were presented to a 1991 conference at the Brookings Institution attended by economists and legal scholars, lawyers, corporate executives, and investment bankers. Some of the comments and reactions to the conference papers were incorporated in subsequent drafts, and some are included in this volume as general comments on each paper.

James Schneider edited the manuscript with the aid of Patricia Dewey and Caroline Lalire. Laura Kelly verified its factual content, Susan Woollen prepared it for typesetting, Carlotta Ribar proofread it, and Rhonda Holland compiled the index. Irene Coray provided valuable secretarial assistance throughout the project, and Kathleen M. Bucholz, Diane Maranis, Valerie M. Owens, Evelyn M. E. Taylor, and Anita G. Whitlock helped with corrections and amendments to the transcript.

Funding for this project was provided in part by the Boston University Manufacturers Roundtable and the Brookings Center for Economic Progress and Employment, whose supporters include Donald S. Perkins, American Express Philanthropic Program, AT&T Foundation, The Chase Manhattan Bank, N.A., Cummins Engine Foundation, Ford Motor Company Fund, Hewlett-Packard Company, Morgan Stanley & Company, Motorola Foundation, Springs Industries, Union Carbide Corporation, Warner-Lambert Company, Xerox Corporation, Aetna Life and Casualty Company, The Ford Foundation, General Electric Foundation, The Prudential Foundation, Alfred P. Sloan Foundation, Institute for International Economic Studies, and Alex C. Walker Educational and Charitable Trust.

The views expressed here are those of the authors and should not be ascribed to the trustees, officers, or staff members of the Brookings Institution.

BRUCE K. MAC LAURY
President

Washington D.C.
December 1992

Contents

Financial Restructuring and the Debate about Corporate
Governance   1
Margaret M. Blair

Theories of Optimal Capital Structure: A Managerial
Discretion Perspective   19
Oliver Hart

    Comment by Paul R. Samuelson   43
    General Discussion   47

Routines, Cash Flows, and Unconventional Assets:
Corporate Change in the 1980s   55
Sidney G. Winter

    Comment by Gordon Donaldson   80
    Comment by John C. Coffee, Jr.   82
    General Discussion   88

Industry-Level Indicators of Free Cash Flow   99
Margaret M. Blair and Martha A. Schary

    Comment by George N. Hatsopoulos   136
    Comment by Stewart C. Myers   137
    General Discussion   140

Industry-Level Pressures to Restructure   149
Margaret M. Blair and Martha A. Schary

    Comment by Darius Gaskins   191
    Comment by Dennis C. Mueller   193
    General Discussion   196

Decade of Debt: Lessons from LBOs in the 1980s   205
William F. Long and David J. Ravenscraft

    Comment by Carl Ferenbach   225
    Comment by Frank Lichtenberg   230
    General Discussion   234

Corporate Restructuring in the Chemicals Industry   239
Sarah J. Lane

    Comment by F. M. Scherer   273
    Comment by Philip K. Verleger, Jr.   277

Financing Acquisitions in the Late 1980s:
Sources and Forms of Capital   289
Peter Tufano

    Comment by Robert Vishny   306
    Comment by Robert Johnson   309
    General Discussion   313

Takeover Politics   321
Mark J. Roe

    Comment by Martin Lipton   353
    Comment by Ronald J. Gilson   357
    General Discussion   363

Conference Participants   381

Index   385

Tables

4-1. Cash Generation Rate and Net Returns to Capital (SQZ), by
     Industry State   104
4-2. Industrial Chemicals Industry Data for Cost-of-Capital
     Calculation, 1971–89   105
4-3. Calculation of Free Cash Flow, Industrial Chemicals Industry,
     1971–89   108
4-4. U.S. Aggregate Data for Cost-of-Capital Calculation, 1977–89   112
4-5. U.S. Aggregate Data, Free Cash Flow Variables, 1977–89   113
4-6. Mean Industry Values for Indicators of Free Cash Flow and
     Components, Eighteen Industries, 1971–89   117
4-7. Frequency Distribution for Year-to-Year Changes in Operating
     Profit Rate, Cost of Capital, and Capital Squeeze, Seventy-One
     Industries, 1979–89   127
4-A1. Selected Industries in DATA1, by Level of Merger Activity   131
4-A2. Depreciation Tax Shield Components, 1970–89   134
4-A3. Depreciation Tax Shield Value, 1971–89   135
4-A4. Maximum Taxation of Returns from Investments Totally Financed
     by Debt and Totally Financed by Equity, 1980, 1982, 1987   137

Contents

5-1. Financial Restructuring Events, by Type, 1979–89   153

5-2. Asset Size of Restructuring Firms, by Type of Restructuring, Selected Periods, 1979–89   155

5-3. Debt-to-Assets Ratios of Restructuring Firms Relative to Their Industry, by Type of Restructuring, Selected Periods, 1979–89   158

5-4. Real Growth Rate of Assets before and after Restructuring, by Type of Restructuring, Selected Periods, 1979–89   162

5-5. Mean and 90th Percentile of Industry Restructuring Rates, by Type of Event, 1979–89   168

5-6. Real Interest Rates, 1955–89   170

5-7. Indicators of Tax Policy Effects, 1970–89   174

5-8. Determinants of Financial Restructuring Activity, 1979–89   177

5-9. Determinants of Private Buyout Activity, 1979–89   180

5-10. Determinants of Junk Bond Activity, 1979–89   181

5-11. Determinants of Leveraged Restructuring Activity, 1979–89   182

5-A1. Industry Definitions   189

6-1. Characteristics of Whole-Company Leveraged Buyouts   210

6-2. Whole-Company, QFR, Matched One-Year Pre- and Postbuyout Sample, 1981–87   214

6-3. Whole and Divisional, LRD, Matched One-Year Pre- and Postbuyout Sample   218

7-1. Percentage of Mergers and Acquisitions in Industrial Chemicals Manufacturing Relative to All Manufacturing, 1979–87   242

7-2. Value of Mergers and Acquisitions in Industrial Chemicals Manufacturing and All Manufacturing, 1979–87   243

7-3. Firms, Plants, and Products in Data Set, 1978–88   244

7-4. Indicators of U.S. Chemicals Industry Performance, 1979–90   246

7-5. Average Capacity Changes, by Type, 1979–89   248

7-6. Capacity Changes after Ownership Change, 1979–88   250

7-7. Divestitures in Chemicals Manufacturing and All Manufacturing, 1979–87   252

7-8. Horizontal Mergers and Acquisitions in Industrial Chemicals Manufacturing and All Manufacturing, 1979–87   254

7-9. Industrial Chemicals Manufacturing Production Trends, 1978–88   257

7-10. Acquisitions by Foreign Firms and Foreign Firms as Targets, U.S. Industrial Chemicals Companies and All Manufacturing Companies, 1979–87   258

7-11. Percentage Capacity Changes in Chemicals Manufacturing, by Product, 1978–88   262

7-12. Major Restructuring Events, 1979–91   270

8-1.   Mergers, Leveraged Buyouts, and Other Acquisitions Valued at
       $50 Million and More, 1987–89   290

8-2.   External Financing Supplied to U.S. Acquirers and to All
       Nonacquirers, 1987–89   292

8-3.   Loans and Debt Securities Issued to Finance Acquisitions,
       by Type, 1987–89   293

8-4.   Distribution of Acquirers' Public Offerings of Tailored Securities,
       by Type, 1985–89   295

8-5.   Financing Characteristics of LBOs and Other Acquisitions,
       1985–89   297

8-6.   Characteristics of Large Firms That Issued Public Debt Securities
       to Finance an LBO, by Type of Debt, 1987–89   302

8-A1. Standard and Tailored Securities Issued in U.S. Public Markets,
       1985–89   306

Figures

1-1.   Aggregate Operating Profit and Cost of Capital, Nonfinancial
       Firms, 1977–89   4

2-1.   Investment Decision   21

2-2.   Liquidation Decision   30

2-3.   Liquidation Decision with Uncertainty   31

2-4.   Investment Decision with Uncertainty   34

2-5.   Recapitalization Decision in Face of Hostile Bid   38

2-6.   Liquidation versus Continuation in Good and Bad States   39

2-7.   Recapitalization Decision with Hostile Bid and Uncertainty   40

3-1.   Value of Hypothetical Firm at Various Interest Rates   68

3-2.   Value of Hypothetical Firm, Difference between Fadeaway and
       Continuation Strategies   69

4-1.   U.S. Cost of Capital, Five Estimates, Selected Years, 1970–89   115

4-2.   Frequency Distribution of Cost of Capital, 1971–89   119

4-3.   Frequency Distribution of Operating Profits, 1971–89   120

4-4.   Frequency Distribution of Squeeze on Capital, 1971–89   122

4-5.   Operating Profit Rates and Cost of Capital, Three Industries,
       1971–89   123

4-6.   Frequency Distribution of Cash Generation Rate, 1971–89   125

5-1.   Aggregate Debt-to-Assets Ratios, Restructuring and
       Nonrestructuring Firms, 1979–90   156

Contents

5-2.	Incidence of Private Buyouts, by Value (1982 Dollars) and Industry Sector, 1979–89	165
5-3.	Incidence of Junk Bond Events, by Value (1982 Dollars) and Industry Sector, 1979–89	166
5-4.	Incidence of Leveraged Restructuring Events, by Value (1982 Dollars) and Industry Sector, 1979–89	167
7-1.	Capacity Changes, 1979–90, by Four Levels of Production Growth, 1979–84	264
7-2.	Proportion of Firms Producing Product in 1978 That Were Still Producing It in 1988, by Four Levels of Production Growth, 1979–84	265
7-3.	Junk Bond Issuances and Leveraged Restructurings, 1980–89	267
7-4.	Industrial Chemical Company Ratios of Long-Term Debt to Total Assets (Book Value), 1979–90	268

The Deal Decade

Financial Restructuring and the Debate about Corporate Governance

Margaret M. Blair

U.S. COMPANIES are still reeling from the leveraged buyouts, takeovers, junk bonds, recapitalizations, and other financial restructuring transactions that reshaped the corporate sector in the 1980s. This book discusses how those transactions affected the performance of corporations and altered the relationship between corporate management and the financial markets. Nine scholars contributed studies of the restructuring phenomenon. In addition, scholars, investment bankers, corporate executives, lawyers, and other participants in the decade's financial restructuring activity discussed and critiqued early drafts at a conference sponsored by Brookings.

It would be easy—but dangerous—to draw quick conclusions about the impact financial restructuring has had on corporate performance. The corporate sector increased its debt levels dramatically in the 1980s, pushing aggregate leverage (on a book-value basis) to record levels. Partly as a consequence, more large companies have faced financial distress in the past few years than at any time since the Great Depression. And along with the load of debt came cutbacks in spending on investment and on research and development, stagnation in blue-collar pay, reductions in white-collar employment, and increased plant closings and layoffs. Many companies and industries also steadily lost ground to foreign competitors in domestic and international markets.

But at the same time, the growth rate of productivity in manufacturing (where much of the financial restructuring was concentrated, at least in the early part of the 1980s) increased sharply from its lows of the mid-1970s. The stock market rose dramatically, perhaps because financial markets considered corporations' prospects of profits greatly improved, at least relative to the doldrums of the late 1970s and early 1980s. Finally, executive compensation packages soared, widening the spread between executive pay and the pay of average workers.

1

Were takeovers and financial restructurings, then, a good or bad development for the U.S. economy? Framing the question in this simplistic way may be misleading. Restructuring seems to have been good for some companies, bad for others. Moreover, the connection between restructuring and changes in corporate performance is not always clear. But most important, the financial restructuring activity partly reflected a breakdown in the social consensus about what constitutes good corporate performance. At the root of the activity was a dispute over who should control large public corporations, what their goals should be, and to whom the organizations and their managers should be accountable.

Corporate performance should be assessed in many ways. Are companies providing an adequate return to shareholders and other investors? Are they gaining or losing market share? Are they contributing to overall growth in productivity? Are they developing new products and staying at the forefront of technological developments in their industries? Are they providing good jobs, jobs that provide stability and prosperity in their communities? Are corporate executives compensated reasonably and held accountable for their firm's performance in all of these areas?

A problem this book addresses is that these laudable goals were not all compatible in the 1980s. Restructuring was largely fueled by the conflict among managers, financial institutions, and shareholders over whose interests should take precedence. This conflict has not been resolved and will continue to influence the business climate of the 1990s, even though the financial restructuring activity itself has died out.

This book thus tackles many matters. Why did long-dormant questions about corporate performance and corporate governance surface in the 1980s? Why did they manifest themselves in takeovers and financial restructurings? Were the increased use of debt, the rapid pace of innovation in financial markets, and the explosion in takeover activity independent phenomena or were they related? And if related, which caused which? Finally, why did the impulse to restructure subside without having resolved the controversies that underlay it?

Why Financial Markets Wanted to "Reform" Corporations

To begin with, why did all these matters come to a head in the 1980s? Theories, popular and scholarly, have abounded:

—Takeovers were a mechanism for disassembling the conglomerates that were created during the previous takeover wave.

—Firms were leveraged up because they had high market values and stable cash flows and could handle more debt.

—Provisions in the tax code made debt more attractive than equity for many corporations.

—Innovations in financial instruments made it possible to carry out deals that could not have been completed before.

—Greedy financial manipulators were behind the whole process.

Although they are frequently argued, none of these causes seems adequate by itself to explain the phenomenon, and the authors in this book find little evidence to support any of them. Instead, the authors present a more complex theory. First, takeovers and financial restructurings were devices the financial markets used to discipline corporate managers and pressure them to increase cash flows and to pay out more money to shareholders and other investors.[1]

Second, the rationale for applying this discipline is most compelling when firms have free cash flow, defined as cash flow in excess of that needed to fund investment opportunities.[2]

Finally, the return on investment required by the financial markets (the "cost of capital") rose to unusually high levels in the 1980s. Real interest rates on government securities and other safe financial instruments, which had hovered between zero and 2 percent since the mid-1950s, rose to 6 to 8 percent in the mid-1980s, driving up the returns investors required for risky investments such as corporate stocks. Meanwhile, the returns to capital earned by firms in many industries were low during the 1970s and declined even further in the recession of 1981–82. Thus in the late 1970s and early 1980s, important goals of publicly traded corporations—growth, competitiveness, good jobs with good pay and benefits, and high returns to investors—began to come into direct conflict for the first time since the end of World War II.

Measures of the aggregate operating profit rate of the corporate sector and the aggregate cost of capital are developed by Margaret Blair and Martha Schary in one essay for this book. These are plotted in figure 1-1, which shows the aggregate operating profit rate measured as the gross cash flows of the nonfinancial corporate sector (revenues minus operating costs) divided by the book value of assets. The aggregate cost of capital is a more complex calculation that measures the return required to compensate investors for taxes, economic depreciation, and the opportunity cost of funds.[3] The difference between these two measures was unusually small in the 1980s and in some years the profit rate was less than the cost of capital. Thus many firms could no longer fulfill broad

Figure 1-1. Aggregate Operating Profit and Cost of Capital, Nonfinancial Firms, 1977-89

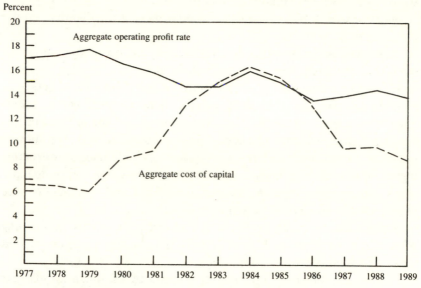

Source: Author's calculations from Compustat.

social goals and still provide investors with an adequate return.[4] In fact, the increase in the cost of capital changed the definition of what constituted good performance for many firms, especially those in industries with weak investment opportunities, and triggered a dispute over whether these companies should retain cash for reinvestment or speed up the rate at which they paid it out to investors.

The pressure on net returns (the difference between operating profits and the cost of capital) varied significantly across industries. But where it was greatest, investors had a strong incentive to try to force changes in corporate management in hopes of making returns commensurate with the opportunity costs. In the early part of the decade, tender offers, hostile takeovers, and leveraged buyouts emerged as the weapons of choice for attacking the status quo. The raiders and takeover specialists were able to carry out these kinds of deals because they convinced large financial institutions, eager for higher returns, to supply them with funds. Potential target firms often fought off unwanted takeovers by embarking on stock buyback programs or otherwise providing improved payouts to shareholders. Some firms financed these payouts with current cash flows, but many others used borrowed money. The extreme version of this kind of restructuring was the leveraged buyout, in which a private investor group borrowed funds to buy out public shareholders completely and take the firm private.

The popular rhetoric and academic arguments used to justify takeovers and financial restructurings were filled with implications or accusations that the target firms were poorly managed, and early empirical work showed that shareholders of target firms were, in fact, made wealthier by takeovers.[5] In some cases, of course, the required improvements in returns to investors could be achieved by eliminating corporate jets or other executive perquisites or by reducing inventories, cutting energy consumption or error rates, or making delivery systems more efficient. But in many cases improved returns could be achieved only by obtaining concessions from suppliers or customers, reducing the amount of taxes paid, extracting wage concessions, or cutting white-collar corporate staff. Or they could come from reducing investment. In other words, the improved returns to shareholders had to be achieved at the expense of other social goals of the corporations. The social benefit of cutting back on investment is questionable, but even if it were not socially beneficial, the shareholders of the target firm would benefit.

The case in which shareholder wealth is increased by reducing investment is examined in several of the essays of this book. This case is central to the free cash flow argument, which says that takeovers targeted firms that have significant cash flow from past investment but a dearth of attractive new investment opportunities. In somewhat more technical terms, these firms have high average returns on investments made in the past, but the net marginal returns from new ones are too low to justify continued investment.

In the context of high opportunity costs of capital and widespread free cash flow in the 1980s, the specific sin of management that the financial markets were eager to correct was managers' tendency to build empires— that is, to overinvest.[6] For thirty years after World War II, investment opportunities were good enough in general, and the opportunity cost of capital was low enough, that financial interests did not try to interfere with strategies to retain and reinvest. But in the sustained period of high real interest rates of the 1980s, investors began contesting these strategies and demanding higher returns.[7]

How Management Responded

In the initial round of takeover attempts, managers of big, old-line companies felt threatened, cried foul, and accused the raiders of forcing them to increase short-term profits at the expense of the long-run health of their companies. They scrambled to erect whatever barriers they could to protect themselves from unwanted takeovers. At the same time, many of them undertook serious internal studies to see how they could improve returns to shareholders.

Some of the early takeover entrepreneurs discovered that they could make a lot of money by buying companies and reorganizing their capital structures—their mix of debt and equity. The new, highly leveraged capital structures were intended to provide managements with both the stick and the carrot needed to force belt tightening and enhance returns. This was a new idea. The traditional way of viewing debt and equity was simply as alternative means of raising capital, albeit with different costs and risks. But in the 1980s these instruments came also to be regarded as ways the suppliers of capital could influence more directly or control the decisions made by managers. In particular, debt contracts put management at risk of losing control to the creditors if the firm failed to meet its contractual obligations to service its debt or to maintain its liquidity ratios. Subsequent research has supported the contention that large increases in leverage, even without a change of control, can lead to significant changes in performance.[8]

The money made by financial entrepreneurs in the early deals encouraged a tremendous expansion in deal making. Investment bankers and Wall Street law firms added staff, attracting the brightest graduates of the best schools and MBA programs. These whiz kids developed dozens of new financial instruments. The social stigma attached to debt faded, and parts of the financial sector were deregulated, allowing certain financial institutions more freedom to pursue high-return, high-risk investments. As a consequence, money poured into special funds to finance leveraged buyouts.

As the decade proceeded, buyouts and financial restructuring activity accelerated and, many observers allege, the deals became larger and riskier, with less compelling financial logic behind them.[9] The use of leverage was pushed to such extremes that large, highly visible firms began collapsing under the weight of their debts. Financial markets finally panicked, and funding for junk bonds and leveraged buyouts dried up. By 1990 the deal-making decade had ended. Now leverage ratios are being reduced as firms issue new equity in record amounts to refinance their debt.

But the Pandora's box of who will have control of corporations cannot easily be closed. Shareholder coalitions and large institutional investors learned to pull the levers of power within corporations in the 1980s and, in the name of improving "accountability," continue to lobby for regulatory changes that will give them even more influence. Management, with the support of labor, has fought back by pressing state legislatures to pass laws to protect managers who pursue goals other than maximizing share value. This tug of war between financial interests and other corporate constituencies—labor (including retirees), management, customers, and communities—will continue in the 1990s because the question of whose interests corporations are to serve, and with what priorities, has not been answered, or even adequately acknowledged.

Summary of Arguments and Evidence

The foregoing interpretation is partly conjectural, but it provides a coherent framework for considering a growing body of empirical evidence that attempts to explain the wave of corporate restructurings in the 1980s. Parts of the story had been outlined before research began on the studies in this book, and it was hoped that the studies would further illuminate the nature and timing of the restructuring activity.

The studies include two theoretical papers, five empirical papers, and an essay on legal and political developments that shaped the takeover decade. The first theoretical paper examines the argument that debt contracts can constrain the behavior of managers in ways that increase the value of the firm. The second shows how high real interest rates affect the capital budgeting decisions and investment strategies of corporations. The legal essay traces political and institutional forces that may have encouraged takeovers in the early 1980s and the elements that came into play late in the decade to make takeovers harder to accomplish. The five empirical papers examine the kinds of instruments devised in the late 1980s to finance acquisitions, develop measures of the cost and returns to capital at the industry level and test whether the costs and returns were related to financial restructuring, track the performance of firms that were taken private in highly leveraged transactions, and follow the complex changes wrought by restructuring in one industry. These five papers are all based on original data.

The authors' interpretations generally agree with the story outlined earlier, but they are richer and more complex. When each piece of the story was examined under the microscope, internal contradictions and conflicting evidence were often revealed. What follows, then, should be read as a dialogue. The findings of the scholars are presented, and then other scholars, observers, and corporate and financial executives respond with their own reactions, interpretations, and questions about the arguments and evidence presented.

Oliver Hart begins with a stylized model that examines the relationship between capital structure and corporate governance. Until very recently, the literature on optimal capital structure focused on taxes, the risk of bankruptcy, and asymmetric information (for example, that corporate insiders know things outside lenders and investors do not know) as the primary determinants of capital structure. Hart stresses the importance of the potential conflict of interest between a firm's managers and its outside security holders. The model highlights the monitoring and enforcing function of debt, especially senior debt.[10]

Hart contends that if corporate executives could be absolutely and unequivocally relied on to choose investments and set policy in ways that maximize the value of a firm, senior debt would never be used because it could inhibit the ability of the firm to make profitable new investments and could introduce the potential for premature bankruptcy or liquidation. Junior debt would not impose these same costs because the firm, faced with financial distress or unfunded investment opportunities, could always issue additional debt that would be senior to the existing junior debt. That senior debt is used in the real world can only be explained, Hart says, if managers are considered likely to abuse their power in a way detrimental to investors. The constraints imposed by senior debt help prevent managers from misusing corporate resources, a benefit that offsets the potential costs of these contracts.

Hart provides a structured theoretical basis for the argument that high leverage can improve a firm's performance by imposing discipline on managers, a contention that has previously been argued much more loosely. But Hart's model turns out to be more limited in explaining leveraged restructuring than might be expected. In the first place, his work provides a "discipline" explanation only for senior debt. And yet, as Peter Tufano shows in his paper, a great many innovative financial tools used in the deals of the late 1980s were more like the junior debt of Hart's model in that they were designed specifically to give corporate managers flexibility. Moreover, Hart's model cannot by itself explain all observed choices of capital structure or governance arrangements.[11]

One implication of Hart's model that bears on the free cash flow theory is that the optimal balance between senior debt, on the one hand, and equity or junior debt, on the other, depends on whether the expected future profits come more from past investments or from new ones. Hart finds that as the share of expected profits from new investments becomes smaller, the optimal capital structure shifts to favor senior debt. This finding is consistent with the free cash flow argument as an explanation for leveraged restructuring: as returns from new investment opportunities decrease relative to returns from past investments, debt becomes more important in disciplining management, and the optimal capital mix uses more debt contracts.

Peter Tufano examines the kinds of debt contracts and other securities used in the late 1980s. He shows that acquirers and investor groups financing leveraged buyouts were more likely than nonacquirers to raise funds in the private markets, issue debt securities, and make use of certain custom-designed securities. In particular, although junk bonds represented only a small fraction of total acquisition financing, half of all junk bonds issued were used to finance or refinance acquisitions. And this share increased from 35 percent in 1985 to 65 percent in 1989.

The share of public offerings that involved some innovative feature grew from 20 percent in 1985 to nearly 40 percent in 1989. Among these "tailored" securities, "reduced cash flow" instruments, which include zero coupon bonds, zero/step bonds, increasing rate bonds, and payment-in-kind (PIK) instruments, were much more likely to be used to finance acquisitions, especially leveraged buyouts, than for other corporate purposes. They were designed to provide cash flow flexibility in the years immediately following the transaction.

Were these instruments used simply because they were a cheap source of funds for issuers, given their risk? Although a number of conference participants believed so, Tufano argues against that interpretation. The fact that subsequent default rates on junk bonds in general were high does not prove that investors were overly optimistic in buying them: to argue that way would be ex post reasoning. Moreover, if they were such a cheap source of funds, why didn't everybody try to use them? The fact that acquirers used these instruments much more often than nonacquirers did, and issuers that were financing leveraged buyouts used them more often than other acquirers, suggests that acquirers needed cash flow flexibility and were willing to pay for it. Tufano also notes that a variety of similar instruments have existed for years and have been used by firms in financial distress.

But if the purpose of the tailored instruments was to buy cash flow flexibility, wouldn't that be evidence against the argument that the buyouts were an attempt to impose cash flow discipline on management? In response to Tufano, Robert Vishny notes that reduced cash flow instruments were typically issued as part of a total financing package, the other components of which often included a large amount of funding from banks and private placements. The total package might provide more flexibility in the early years. But in the longer term, these packages required large increases in cash flow to support the debt, while in the interim, responsibility for monitoring the firm to be sure that cash flow projections were being met was shifted to the banks and large financial institutions that had put up the privately placed capital. Set in context, then, the use of reduced cash flow securities to finance buyouts and takeovers may still be considered consistent with cash flow discipline as an explanation for takeovers and financial restructurings.

Three papers explore the idea that the rise in the cost of capital and the consequent reduction in profitable investment opportunities may have generated the wave of financial restructurings. Sidney Winter argues that the existence of high real interest rates in the 1980s reconciles the views of both the critics and proponents of takeovers and financial restructurings. Both view these transactions as ways to force firms to focus more on short-term cash flow and to cut back expenditures of all types. But while such cutbacks are viewed with alarm by the critics, they are considered streamlining by advocates, an "exemplary case of capital market discipline," as Winter says. In the context of high real interest rates, which reduce the value of any spending that has a long-term payout, both sides may be right.

Winter considers a model of corporate investment decisions that specifically takes account of resources devoted to what he calls unconventional assets. These include internal coordination, organizational routines, corporate reputation, and job-specific worker training. Unconventional assets may be the product of experience and a history of doing things a certain way. Although unconventional assets are not recognized as assets by traditional accounting systems, to build or maintain them clearly requires some investment of resources. But investments in unconventional assets are often hidden in other costs and may be confused with truly wasteful expenditures that add no value to the firm.

Using a simple simulation model, Winter shows how the presence of unconventional assets influences the response of firms to a substantial rise in the discount rate used to value their long-term cash flows. A rise in the discount rate encourages firms to disinvest by allowing existing assets to depreciate. Winter calls this a "fadeaway" strategy. When the discount rate is high, a fadeaway strategy is more attractive than a continuation strategy the higher that a firm's fixed costs (depreciation, for example) are relative to its variable costs, the larger its capital stock is, and the more unconventional assets it has relative to conventional assets.

In two companion papers, Margaret Blair and Martha Schary examine the cost of capital, the returns to capital, and the rate of cash generation in seventy-one industries during the 1980s. They show that the cost of capital rose dramatically in most industries, while operating profits fell in many. Together, these forces often made investment opportunities much less attractive. The authors also show that the rate of cash generation declined somewhat, but the deterioration in investment opportunities—measured by the difference between operating profits and the cost of capital—was much greater. Taken together, these findings suggest that free cash flow was very common in the 1980s.

Although the squeeze on investment opportunities was general, it affected some industries more than others. If the free cash flow hypothesis is correct, takeovers and financial restructurings should have been concentrated in those industries in which investment opportunities were squeezed the most but cash generation remained high. In their second paper, Blair and Schary assemble data on three kinds of financial restructuring transactions: private buyouts of public companies, junk bond issues, and large increases in leverage. They show that restructuring transactions disproportionately involved manufacturing firms. Consistent with Winter's argument that the 1980s restructurings put disinvestment policies in place in many companies, Blair and Schary find that the transactions they examine marked turning points for firms, after which their rates of asset growth slowed significantly or declined.

Most important, the pace of restructurings across industries was related to reduced investment opportunities, as measured by the difference between the returns to capital and the cost of capital. The strength of this finding varied for different kinds of restructuring and different periods, however. The best case that restructuring was driven by free cash flow can be made for private buyouts and junk bond issues before 1986. These events were concentrated in slowly growing, low-technology industries that were generating large amounts of cash but had low net returns. For the years after 1986, none of the theories examined help very much to explain financial restructuring. One interpretation of this finding is that restructuring took on a life of its own.

William Long and David Ravenscraft study the characteristics and pre- and postbuyout performance of companies that went private in the 1980s. By linking their transaction-level data to confidential firm-level data at the Bureau of the Census, they tap into much more information about these firms than previous researchers have had available. They show that, on average, companies taken private were 30 percent management owned before the buyout and that acquisitions and divestitures made by these firms just before or just after the buyout represented a relatively small proportion of their assets. These findings suggest that buyouts of whole companies were not driven primarily by the need to improve managerial incentives by making managers owners. Nor were they caused by the need to sell off assets.

The authors compare the performance of buyouts that occurred in 1981–84 with those in 1985–87. The earlier deals involved smaller, more closely held companies, premiums paid for the companies were lower, and on average the ratio of cash flow to sales increased 20 percent after the buyout. Later deals failed to result in improved ratios of cash flow to sales. Long and Ravenscraft also find that manufacturing firms that were bought out improved their operating performance on average 15 percent relative to other firms in the same industry. Nonmanufacturing firms bought out had declines of 5 percent relative to other firms in the same industry. Mining, wholesaling, and retailing are, however, the only non-manufacturing sectors the authors are able to look at with their data.

The combined evidence from Tufano, Blair and Schary, and Long and Ravenscraft suggests that, as the decade went on, financial restructuring involved more and larger firms and greater reliance on debt instruments, particularly junk bonds. Premiums grew, management involvement decreased, improvement in cash flow performance dwindled, and tax savings increased. What started as a rational exercise in restructuring firms in slow-growing and declining industries—particularly manufacturing—seems to have become a fad driven by the machinery invented to facilitate the deals and was possibly encouraged by tax changes. The later deals involved more firms where the potential benefit was smaller, and more firms outside manufacturing, where the rationale of free cash flow may never have been as strong. Nonetheless, deals throughout the decade resulted in reduced capital spending and slower growth rates for the firms involved.

Sarah Lane presents a detailed case study of industrial chemicals, an industry that experienced an unusually high incidence of takeovers, divestitures, and financial restructurings in the 1980s. She examines these transactions in the context of industry-specific events affecting input and output prices, competition, and product demand, and considers the public record regarding the motives and rationales of individual companies involved. Her work reaffirms that restructuring takes many forms and involves complex causes and effects.

Early in the 1980s, manufacturers of industrial chemicals shut down production of key commodities in some plants and reduced capacity in other plants because of overbuilding in the 1970s and a collapse in demand during the recession of 1981–82. A few years later, many plants changed ownership. Lane shows that most reductions in plant capacity were achieved before rather than after units were sold, which contradicts the idea that changes in control are somehow necessary to achieve consolidation. And contrary to popular assertions that firms were dismantling their conglomerate structures and refocusing on core businesses, large chemical companies sold off core businesses and acquired other firms that produce specialty chemicals with higher value added.

One striking feature of restructuring in the industry was that small, closely held, often highly leveraged firms emerged to specialize in producing the commodity chemicals. Many were first formed through leveraged buyouts of units sold by large companies. Lane argues, and discussant Philip Verleger agrees, that these restructuring transactions occurred because the large public companies wanted to bail out of commodity businesses in the middle of the decade. Commodity businesses are cyclical, and they were in the doldrums of a cyclical trough.

But neither Lane nor Verleger satisfactorily explains why new companies would enter the business at that time, since firms that specialize in commodities are even more vulnerable to cyclical swings than larger, more diversified companies. One possibility is that commodity chemicals manufacturers are a classic illustration of free cash flow theory. These companies typically have a large base of capital investment in place generating cash but very limited opportunities for innovation or growth. Thus they are in precisely the kind of industry that the theory claims would be best managed by smaller, highly leveraged, closely held firms that can focus on operational control and cost cutting, although, again, such firms do not seem well positioned to weather strong business downturns. Large, well-capitalized, publicly traded firms may be better vehicles for more research- or marketing-intensive business. But this hypothesis is weakened by the fact that many of the new firms reverted to their old form by going public again through stock issues or by being acquired by foreign buyers.

In the final essay of the book, Mark Roe describes the institutional and political conditions that first encouraged takeovers and then supported attempts by state legislatures and courts to prohibit them. Before the 1980s, Roe contends, managers of large U.S. public companies had a great deal of autonomy. First, the common stock of most firms was widely distributed among shareholders who were small relative to the size of the companies. Second, financial institutions in the United States have always had relatively little power to influence the managements of the companies in their portfolios. This limitation of power is by design, Roe argues. The structure of the financial sector in the United States has always been fractured—insurance separated from banking, and banking separated from brokerage and from investment banking, for example— and regulations have prevented financial institutions from holding large blocks of equity in nonfinancial operating companies.

Managerial autonomy was greatly threatened by raiders in the early 1980s, however, and despite widespread public suspicion of takeovers, regulatory and judicial bodies at the federal level declined to stop or even restrict the buyouts. The Securities and Exchange Commission was ideologically committed to letting the market take its course, and the Supreme Court struck down crucial state antitakeover statutes. Business leaders then carried their complaints to Congress, which held a lot of hearings but ultimately refused to do much. The business leaders then turned to the states. Managers at potential targets tried new tactics— poison pills, for example—that gave them the upper hand in takeover attempts, and state courts upheld many of these tactics. State legislatures were strongly influenced by managers and labor as well as by popular mistrust of takeovers and were loath to upset these court decisions. Thus the history of corporate law in the decade can be read as an attempt by corporate managers to win back their traditional autonomy through the courts and legislatures.

By the end of the 1980s, more than forty states had passed new antitakeover laws. In the state most important for purposes of corporate law, the Delaware Supreme Court seemed to rule in *Paramount Communications* v. *Time Inc.* that the managers of a target company could justify refusing to acquiesce to a takeover if they merely had a business plan in place that contemplated the company as an independent firm. This ruling, combined with statutes passed in twenty-nine states that specifically authorized corporate directors to consider the interests of constituents other than shareholders in deciding about takeover offers or setting other corporate policies, has, for now at least, tilted the scales of corporate governance back toward managerial autonomy.

Lessons and Conclusions

Two questions not explicitly pursued in this book are how much changes in the tax code stimulated financial restructuring and whether large institutional investors encouraged the takeover activity. The influence of tax laws has been treated extensively in previous studies, most of which have concluded that they played only a small role, if any.[12] The growing influence of large financial institutions, mentioned repeatedly by participants at the Brookings conference, has been studied very little. Historically, these institutions have been very passive in corporate governance, but they are likely to be more assertive in the years ahead. Thus research into the ways that institutional investors can, and should, influence corporate performance is becoming a priority.

The lessons provided by the corporate restructurings of the 1980s that can be taken from this book include the following.

—Not all financial restructuring transactions are alike. Some takeovers, private buyouts, and leveraged restructurings, especially the earliest deals, have led to improved operating performance for the target firms. But later in the 1980s, the rationale for a great many deals was probably weak to begin with, and restructuring failed to improve performance. In addition, the restructured firms were left too weak financially to cope with the recession that struck in the early 1990s.

—The ability of the capital markets to respond—and overrespond—to changes in market conditions must not be underestimated. The high real interest rates in the 1980s drove up the return required from capital and altered the balance among competing claims for the proceeds of corporate enterprise. This alteration also created tremendous profit opportunities for the raiders and deal makers who could force companies to realign priorities. But as often happens, the market pushed a good idea too far and financed deals that probably should not have been considered.

—Policies often have unintended consequences. The decision at the federal level in the 1980s to cut taxes and run large budget deficits probably contributed to the jump in real interest rates. But the high rates in turn encouraged a broad change in the norms of corporate governance. Similarly, as Mark Roe contends, structures put in place in the 1930s and 1940s to limit financial institutions' concentration of power and exposure to risk may have led to the use of very blunt instruments in the 1980s—takeovers and financial restructuring—to impose the discipline of the capital market on public companies.

—The guy who owns the ball cannot be thrown out of the ballgame. In the years ahead, the suppliers of capital, especially the large institutional investors, will continue trying to influence management of corporations, and their baseball will be the broad range of financial securities they control.

—Issues of the control of corporations will not be settled in the financial arena alone. What corporations should do and who they should be accountable to are partly political and social questions. They should perhaps be addressed directly before we try to resolve the question of how corporations are to be governed.

Notes

1. This piece of the theory goes back to the 1960s when organizational economists first argued that the threat of takeovers provided the necessary discipline that prevented corporate managers from abusing their position and misusing corporate resources to their own benefit. In the 1980s, a similar argument was used to explain leveraged restructuring. See, for example, Robin Marris, *The Economic Theory of Managerial Captialism* (Free Press, 1964).

2. Michael Jensen, "Agency Cost of Free Cash Flow, Corporate Finance and Takeovers," *American Economic Review*, vol. 76 (May 1986, *Papers and Proceedings*), pp. 323–29, orginated this concept.

3. Both calculations are aggregated from firm-level data from Compustat. See Blair and Schary, "Industry-Level Indicators of Free Cash Flow" in this volume for details.

4. An earlier study by Margaret M. Blair and Robert E. Litan looked at aggregate returns to capital in just the manufacturing sector, and used the real return on AAA corporate bonds as a crude proxy for the cost of capital. Using those measures, the spread between the cost and returns to capital was enormous, though declining, for thirty years following World War II. Also, the crunch between the returns to capital in manufacturing and real interest rates first occurred earlier in the decade. See "Corporate Leverage and Leveraged Buyouts in the Eighties," in John B. Shoven and Joel Waldfogel, eds., *Debt, Taxes, and Corporate Restructuring* (Brookings, 1990).

5. For an example of an academic argument favoring takeovers as a way to mitigate or prevent managerial shirking, see David Scharfstein, "The Disciplinary Role of Takeovers," *Review of Economic Studies*, vol. 55 (April 1988), pp. 185–99. See Michael C. Jensen and Richard S. Ruback, "The Market for Corporate Control, The Scientific Evidence," *Journal of Financial Economics*, vol. 11 (April 1983), pp. 5–50, for a summary of early evidence on the effects of takeover activity on shareholders.

6. There are several other good reasons for focusing on excessive investment or empire building as a principal source of depressed returns for shareholders. First, many managerial abuses—excessive perquisites and bloated staffs, for example—can be thought of as a form of excessive investment. Second, Oliver Hart shows in his essay in this volume that incentive schemes that base managers' pay on the total value of the firm will encourage managers to eliminate true waste. But if the manager gets satisfaction from running a larger company, regular incentive compensation schemes may not be sufficient. Finally, what is excessive depends on the cost of capital or the discount rate used to evaluate future returns from investment. Investors could improve returns by eliminating ordinary wasteful practices at any time, but they would have an incentive to force cutbacks in investment only when high interest rates make such investment unprofitable.

7. Michael Porter has argued that the relationship between public corporations and the capital markets in the United States biases decisionmaking toward underinvestment, but the institutional structures in Germany and Japan may bias decisionmaking in the other direction. See "Capital Choices: Changing the Way America Invests in Industry," paper presented to the Council on Competitiveness, June 1992.

8. See, for example, Bronwyn H. Hall, "Corporate Restructuring and Investment Horizons," in Michael E. Porter, ed., *Investment Behavior and Time Horizon in American Industry* (Harvard Business School Press, forthcoming); and Margaret M. Blair and Martha A. Schary, "Industry-Level Pressures to Restructure," in this volume.

9. Two studies in this book lend credence to this assertion. Blair and Schary in "Industry-Level Pressures to Restructure," find that after 1985 restructuring activity appears to have been much less connected to fundamental characteristics of the industries in which the restructuring occurred. And Long and Ravenscraft find that although measures of cash flow performance improved significantly in the postbuyout period for leveraged buyouts before 1985, the measures failed to show improvement after the buyout for deals made in 1985 and later.

10. Senior debt is debt that has legal priority and must be paid off first (ahead of junior debt) in case of liquidation. Hart treats the relative seniority of various financial instruments as absolute—the last dime owed to holders of senior debt must be paid before any payments can be made to holders of junior debt, and holders of junior debt must be paid before equity holders. Most actual bankruptcy settlements, however, involve a less rigid distribution of payoffs, so the distinction between junior and senior debt is often blurred. Hart also notes that senior debt can help managers extract better terms in negotiations with suppliers or labor unions.

11. The simple model must be supplemented with assumptions about the information structure—that is, who knows what when—to yield unique predictions about the ways changes in capital structure affect shareholder value, for example, or changes in profit outlook affect optimal capital structure.

12. See, for example, Shoven and Waldfogel, eds., *Debt, Taxes, and Corporate Restructuring*.

Theories of Optimal Capital Structure: A Managerial Discretion Perspective

Oliver Hart

IN the thirty or so years since the Modigliani-Miller theorem, scholars have worked to relax the theorem's assumptions in order to obtain a better understanding of the capital structure of firms.[1] This work has produced some important insights but has not yet delivered a fully coherent theory of optimal capital structure. For example, at present we do not understand very well the distinguishing features of debt and equity or why these claims, as opposed to the many instruments that could be chosen, are most frequently issued by firms. Given this state of affairs, existing explanations of the debt-equity ratio must be seen as still preliminary, as must efforts to use these explanations to understand global trends such as the large increases in leverage in the United States and United Kingdom during the 1980s.

In the first part of this paper, I will argue that one reason progress on understanding capital structure has been limited is that relatively few analysts have adopted an explicit agency-theoretic or managerial discretion perspective. In particular, although the literature, starting with the work of Michael Jensen and William Meckling, frequently refers to conflicts of interest, most of it does not emphasize the conflict of interest between a firm's management and its security holders.[2] But I argue that this particular conflict of interest—that is, the idea that management is self-interested—is critical. In the absence of this conflict, optimal capital structure would look very different from what is observed in the world. In particular, firms would not issue senior or secured debt, whereas in fact a considerable amount of corporate debt has at least one of these

I thank Carliss Baldwin, Michael Brennan, Ian Cooper, Jim Poterba, Shan Li, Luigi Zingales, Jeff Zwiebel, and, especially, John Moore and Andrei Shleifer for helpful comments. I am also very grateful to John Moore for letting me include some of our unpublished joint work. Financial support from the National Science Foundation and the Center for Energy Policy Research at MIT is gratefully acknowledged.

features.[3] That is, standard departures from the Modigliani-Miller framework that focus on the role of taxes, asymmetric information, or incomplete markets but ignore managerial self-interest are not sufficient to explain observed capital structure.

In the second part of the analysis I will discuss what has been learned from the relatively few studies that have explicitly adopted an agency-theoretic perspective. This body of work, although itself quite preliminary, can explain the use of senior or secured debt or both, as well as shed light on some observed patterns of capital structure, including a number of findings from studies that measure the response of security prices to important events that affect optimal capital structure ("event studies").

Why an Agency Perspective Is Critical

To fix ideas, it will be useful throughout the paper to work with the following simple model, first laid out by Stewart Myers.[4]

Consider a firm consisting of assets in place and new investment opportunities, and suppose that it exists at three given dates (figure 2-1). At date 0 the firm's financial structure is chosen. At date 1 the assets in place yield a return of y_1 and a new investment opportunity costing i appears. At date 2 the assets in place yield a further return y_2 and the new investment opportunity—if it was taken at date 1—yields r. At this date the firm is liquidated, receipts are allocated to security holders, and the world ends.

Suppose that the firm is run by a single manager.[5] This manager decides whether to take the new investment opportunity. The variables y_1, y_2, i, and r are typically uncertain as of date 0 (however, with a probability distribution that is common knowledge). Assume for simplicity that the manager (and sometimes the market as well) learns the outcomes of y_1, y_2, i, and r at date 1: all uncertainty is resolved for the manager at this date. Finally, again for simplicity, assume an interest rate of zero.

I start with the case in which there are no taxes, the market is risk-neutral with regard to this firm's return (for example, because investors hold well-diversified portfolios), and the manager and the market have the same information at date 1 (as well as at date 0). Each of these assumptions will be relaxed in turn in what follows.

To consider what can be said about capital structure in the absence of a conflict of interest between the manager and security holders, I also make the following assumption:

Figure 2-1. Investment Decision

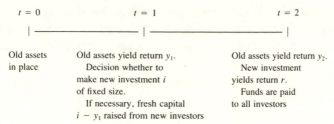

$t = 0$	$t = 1$	$t = 2$

| Old assets in place | Old assets yield return y_1. Decision whether to make new investment i of fixed size. If necessary, fresh capital $i - y_1$ raised from new investors | Old assets yield return y_2. New investment yields return r. Funds are paid to all investors |

—the manager is not self-interested, all decisions require the same amount of effort, and the manager is (in the absence of any incentive scheme) indifferent about whether the new investment opportunity is taken.

Finally, assume the manager's opportunity cost at date 0 is zero and that he has no initial wealth.

In this context the manager should invest if and only if the project has positive net present value ($r > i$). Moreover, it is very easy to implement this rule. Choose the firm's financial structure to be all equity at date 0, give the manager the authority to issue any new equity or any other claim needed to finance new investment, and provide the manager with a compensation package equal to a small fraction θ of the firm's date 2 liquidation receipts minus the amount received from any date 1 security issue plus any dividends paid at date 1. This makes the manager's payoff

$$(2.1) \quad \begin{cases} \theta\,(y_1 + y_2) & \text{if he does not invest} \\ \theta\,(y_1 + y_2 + r - i) & \text{if he invests} \end{cases}$$

It is easiest to understand this equation in three steps. First, if the manager does not invest, he may as well save the date 1 earnings y_1 (without interest), making the firm's date 2 liquidation receipts equal to $(y_1 + y_2)$; of these the manager obtains a fraction θ. Second, if the manager invests and $y_1 > i$, he will finance the investment out of retained earnings, save the amount $(y_1 - i)$ in a zero-interest-bearing account, and the firm's liquidation receipts will equal $(y_1 - i + y_2 + r)$. Third, if $y_1 < i$ and the manager invests, he issues new equity to the value of $(i - y_1)$, which implies that total date 2 profit net of the receipts from new equity at date 1 is $y_2 + r - (i - y_1) = y_1 + y_2 + r - i$.

Thus the equation represents the manager's payoff in all cases. Obviously a manager who maximizes his payoff will invest if and only if $r > i$, which is the efficient investment rule.[6]

Not only can the efficient outcome be achieved through an all-equity firm with a suitable compensation package for management, but any other initial capital structure may lead to inefficiency. Suppose, for example, that the firm's date 0 capital structure includes some senior debt that promises to pay an amount d at date 2, as well as equity; and suppose ownership of this debt is dispersed, so that renegotiation is hard to arrange. Then if the value of $y_1 + y_2$ (which, recall, is learned at date 1) turns out to be less than d, the manager may be unable to finance a new investment opportunity at date 1, even though it would be profitable. This is the consequence of a version of the well-known debt overhang problem, first pointed out by Stewart Myers. If the firm can only issue claims at date 1 that are junior to the existing debt, then the most that can be reserved for new date 1 claimants out of date 1 and date 2 receipts is $y_1 + y_2 + r - d$. However, if d is large, $y_1 + y_2 + r - d$ can be less than i, even though $r > i$. In this case, it will be impossible to find security holders at date 1 who are prepared to put up the needed investment funds $(i - y_1)$, and a profitable investment opportunity will be missed.[7]

We now see how the conclusion that an all-equity firm is optimal changes if one allows for taxes, incomplete markets, or asymmetric information.

Taxes

To begin with, suppose that there are no profits at date 1 $(y_1 = 0)$. Assume that any profit at date 2, net of investment costs, is subject to the corporation tax t_c but that interest payments are tax deductible. Also, for simplicity, ignore personal income taxes.[8]

It is clear that there is now a role for debt financing. Suppose no new investment at date 1 is ever warranted $(r < i)$. Then the efficient outcome for the firm can be achieved by having debt in the initial capital structure with a promised repayment d at date 2 that exceeds the highest possible value of y_2. (Of course, this debt will sell at a discount given that the firm will almost always default at date 2.) Then *all* the firm's date 2 receipts are paid out to creditors, no corporation taxes are incurred, and the firm's initial date 0 value of debt plus equity is Ey_2, where E stands for expected value.[9] In contrast, an all-equity firm would have a date 0 value equal to $Ey_2(1 - t_c)$, since it does have to pay corporation tax.

Now allow for profitable new investment projects $(r > i)$. Because high levels of debt can cause debt overhang, one might think there would be an interesting trade-off between debt and equity: a firm with low debt would pay high taxes and a firm with high debt might be unable to finance profitable projects. However, this is not so. The debt overhang problem arises only with respect to *senior* debt. One strategy open to a firm is to issue only junior (or subordinated) debt at date 0; this debt contains a covenant stating that the firm has the option to issue debt senior to it later. Under these conditions, the debt overhang problem disappears: new claimants at date 1 can be offered up to the full amount $y_2 + r$ of the firm's date 2 receipts (through dilution of the date 0 junior debt) and, of course, this exceeds i whenever $r > i$. Thus profitable projects can be financed. Moreover, *only* profitable projects will be financed, given the incentive scheme corresponding to equation 2.1. In addition, the firm still pays no corporation tax because all its receipts are paid out to creditors. Hence the efficient outcome is achieved, and the firm's date 0 value is $E \max (y_2 + r - i, y_2).$[10]

The theory therefore now predicts that there should be firms with 100 percent subordinated debt, something we do not observe (see note 3).

So far I have ignored the possibility of bankruptcy. But suppose the assumption that $y_1 = 0$ is dropped. If $y_1 > 0$, then if a firm wants to avoid paying corporation tax at date 1, it must have outstanding (short-term) debt that absorbs y_1 as interest. However, suppose a bad state of the world occurs, y_1 is low, and the promised interest payment $d_1 > y_1$. Under these conditions, a firm may have to default and may be forced into bankruptcy. Could the resulting bankruptcy costs limit the firm's desire to issue debt at date 0?

This is unlikely, given the working hypothesis that the manager is not self-interested. In view of this, why would the creditors not be prepared in advance to let the manager postpone any interest he cannot pay at date 1 until date 2 by letting him issue payment-in-kind (PIK) bonds?[11] Given the incentive scheme corresponding to equation 2.1, the manager has no incentive to postpone unless it is necessary. Thus if d_1 is chosen to be high, the manager will pay out any profit the firm makes at date 1 and avoid corporation taxes, but he will never need to default or go into bankruptcy if $y_1 < d_1$ because he can always postpone.

Of course, the Internal Revenue Service might view with suspicion a firm with huge levels of outstanding subordinated and postponable debt that mop up earnings in essentially the same way that equity is meant to.[12] In particular, the IRS might decide to treat the debt as if it were equity. The fear of this reaction may cause firms to issue less than

100 percent debt in the first place and to issue some senior debt. Although it would no doubt be possible to develop a theory of capital structure based on the fear of the reaction of the authorities, I do not know whether such a theory could explain the variations in capital structure observed across industries, countries, and over time. In any event, I am not aware of attempts to develop a theory along these lines.

Risk Aversion and Incomplete Markets

So far I have assumed that investors are risk-neutral. But what happens if they are not and if markets are incomplete?

Analysts often contend that firms issue debt because some investors are more risk averse than others and, by issuing debt as well as equity, the firms can cater to the risk averse. This argument implicitly supposes some market incompleteness, because, if a complete set of contingent security markets existed, investors could purchase the state-contingent securities they like without going through firms. However, even when markets are incomplete, firms should issue only junior or subordinated securities. That is, clientele effects cannot explain the existence of *senior* debt.

I develop the argument for a particular case of market incompleteness. Suppose that a firm is originally owned by N investors at date 0 with von Neumann-Morgenstern utility functions $U_1, \ldots U_N$ defined over date 2 wealth.[13] Assume that these investors invest only in this firm (an extreme form of market incompleteness) and cannot make any further capital contributions at date 1. The firm can, however, borrow and lend on the open market at date 1 at a riskless rate of interest of zero. The question I ask is: what kinds of securities should this firm issue?

Clearly it is Pareto optimal for the firm to invest at date 1 if and only if $r > i$ (recall that, as earlier, all the uncertainty is resolved at date 1).[14] This makes the firm's date 2 receipts (net of date 1 borrowing) equal to $R = \max (y_1 + y_2, y_1 + y_2 + r - i)$. These receipts should be allocated among the investors according to N sharing rules $s_1(\cdot), \ldots s_N(\cdot)$, so as to solve:

$$\text{Max } EU_1(s_1(R))$$
$$S.T. \ EU_i(s_i(R)) \geq \overline{U}_i \text{ for all } i = 2, \ldots, N,$$
$$\sum_{i=1}^{N} s_i (R) = R \text{ for all } R,$$

where the expectation is taken with respect to the distribution of R, and $\overline{U}_i$ denotes the reservation expected utility level for each investor, $i > 1$.

This is a classic risk-sharing problem and the details of the solution need not concern us here.[15] The important point is that there is a simple way to implement the optimum: give the manager the compensation package corresponding to equation 2.1. This ensures that he will invest if and only if $r > i$; issue N date 0 claims whose date 2 returns are defined by the functions $s_1, \ldots, s_N$; and give the manager the right to issue debt at date 1 that is senior to these claims. In other words, the N original claim holders have rights to the firm's date 2 receipts, but only after senior date 1 creditors have been paid off (this reduces the date 2 receipts $y_2 + r$ to $y_1 + y_2 + r - i$ in the event that $y_1 < i$ and the manager needs to borrow $(i - y_1)$ at date 1).

Such a scheme achieves the best of both worlds. On one hand it ensures that an efficient investment choice is made. On the other it ensures that, given investor attitudes to risk, total surplus is divided optimally. If the claims held by the original investors were not junior, the first goal would not generally be achieved. The reason is the debt overhang problem again: if y_1 and y_2 are small and initial investors have a senior claim to part of date 2 receipts, then it may be impossible to raise $i - y_1$ even if the investment is profitable.

Thus, even if investors are risk averse and markets are incomplete, the theory predicts that all claims issued by a firm should be subordinated.[16]

Asymmetric Information

Finally, what happens if the managers and the market do not have the same information at date 1? In particular, suppose that the manager learns the value of y_1, y_2, r, and i at date 1, but the market learns the value only of y_1 and i. Myers and Majluf have observed that under these conditions a manager of an initially all-equity firm who acts on behalf of initial shareholders may pass up some profitable investment projects if these can be financed only by issuing new equity at date 1.[17] The reason is that if y_2 is high but the market does not realize this, then the new equity issue will be sold at a discount relative to its true value, which may cause a large enough dilution of the initial equity that the wealth of initial equity-holders falls even though the new project is profitable. In contrast, profitable projects will always be undertaken if they can be financed out of retained earnings or by issuing debt because no dilution of initial equity occurs in these cases.

The Myers-Majluf analysis suggests why a firm might issue senior debt in addition to equity.[18] However, the effect disappears if the manager is paid according to equation 2.1.[19] This compensation package rewards the manager according to the *total* value of the firm at date 2, net of any cash inflows from date 1 security issues. Rather than just the value of initial equity. In particular, it is clear from the formula that whether or not the manager has private information about y_2 and r, he will wish to invest if and only if $r > i$. Hence the conclusion that all-equity firms (or, if taxes or market incompleteness are important, firms with junior debt claims) are optimal is robust to the introduction of asymmetric information as long as the manager is offered a compensation package like that in equation 2.1.[20]

In one part of their article Myers-Majluf appear to contend that a compensation package like that in equation 2.1 may be undesirable because it gives the manager no direct interest in the price at which new equity is offered, thus perhaps providing an incentive to favor friends with sweetheart deals. Unfortunately, such deals seem hard to avoid if the manager has private information: even if the firm issues no new shares, he can always tell friends to buy equity when it is undervalued and sell when it is overvalued. Also the formula in 2.1 at least makes the manager interested in the *value* of new equity because if, say, the manager sells new equity at too low a price, he may fail to raise $(i - y_1)$ and may have to forgo the new project. Moreover, the formula could presumably be modified to encourage the manager to be interested also in the price of new equity; in particular, he could be penalized if the firm's equity price were to rise significantly soon after the new issue (that is, if he underprices the new equity). Another possibility is to insist that the manager must always raise new capital through a rights issue, in which case the price of new equity does not matter to initial shareholders as long as the project is financed.[21]

Two other arguments against equation 2.1 and in favor of the idea that the manager acts on behalf of initial shareholders should be mentioned. First, because as a practical matter management holds significant equity in the firm, its interests are often said to be automatically aligned (at least partially) with those of initial shareholders. Apart from not explaining *why* management has a significant equity interest, this argument seems to ignore the fact that in public companies, management can vary its equity holding according to its information. In particular, even if management holds significant equity, this should not stop it from letting the firm issue new equity when the equity is undervalued: after all, there is nothing to prevent management from keeping its overall equity interest constant by buying part of the new issue itself if it is underpriced, thus avoiding wealth transfers from management to new shareholders.[22]

Second, the assumption that management acts on behalf of initial shareholders is sometimes justified because management has a fiduciary duty to this group and shareholders typically have votes. But it is difficult to know how important fiduciary duty is as an influence on management in practice. The sometimes extraordinary lengths to which managers go to defeat high-price hostile takeovers suggest that it is often not a dominant force.[23] And from a theoretical point of view, it is not very satisfactory to take as a given the existence of fiduciary duty and the fact that shareholders have votes: one would like to explain these things. Furthermore, it is far from obvious how one can explain them without dropping the maintained hypothesis that managers are selfless.

What an Agency Approach Can Deliver

We can summarize the argument so far as follows. If there were no significant conflicts of interest between insiders and outsiders, capital structure would look very different. All debt issued by firms would be unsecured and subordinated, and firms would easily avoid financial distress and bankruptcy costs by arranging in advance with creditors that debt could be forgiven or postponed at the manager's discretion.[24] In such a world there would be no reason to give shareholders (or any other outside group for that matter) votes. Why not give all the votes to informed management and rely on it to seek appropriate merger partners or to vote itself out of office if a better management team appears?[25]

The conclusion I draw from this is that conflicts of interest between insiders and outsiders are crucial for understanding even the most basic aspects of capital structure. In spite of this, surprisingly few scholars have adopted an agency perspective. For example, tax theories of financial structure, probably the largest part of the literature on capital structure, never mention agency problems. And the many scholars (starting with Jensen and Meckling) who argue that debt is costly because it causes management to favor shareholders at the expense of creditors typically do not model the more basic conflict of interest between management and security holders as a whole.

In the past few years, examinations of the conflict of interest between insiders and outsiders have begun to appear, but they are still in their infancy. Two strands have emerged. One analyzes entrepreneurial firms, that are essentially owned and controlled by managers, who may, however, be prepared to give up some control to persuade an outside investor to provide financing.[26] The conflict of interest arises because management receives some benefits from running the firm that cannot be transferred to outside investors. This part of the literature typically studies the optimal allocation of control between management and a single outside investor but does not analyze the choice between publicly traded securities such as debt and equity.

The second strand of the literature focuses on public corporations, in which management has a relatively small profit stake and rarely has voting control. Since Jensen and Meckling's work it has been recognized that an agency problem exists under these conditions because many of the costs and benefits of management's actions are borne by outside investors rather than by management itself. However, what is not clear in Jensen-Meckling or in other initial analyses is why it makes sense to use financial structure to solve this agency problem.[27] In particular, why not simply put management on an optimal incentive scheme such as that corresponding to equation 2.1?

Recently, scholars have tried to answer this question by being more specific about management's objectives. A traditional incentive scheme works well if agency problems arise only because management dislikes working hard. However, such a scheme is much less effective if the manager obtains large control rents from running the firm (control rents that cannot be charged for adequately ex ante, either because the manager has limited wealth or because he is risk averse and the rents are uncertain). These control rents may represent the utility the manager gets from the job or from presiding over a large and perhaps growing empire, or they may represent the monetary and nonmonetary perquisites the manager can get by virtue of his position of power. Incentive schemes may be less effective under these conditions because a *very* large incentive payment may be required to induce management to give up these control rents. It may be cheaper for investors to resort to mechanisms that force management to yield control or to curb its empire-building tendencies. Bankruptcy and takeover bids, both of which are intimately connected to a firm's financial structure, are examples of such mechanisms.

The idea that management likes to entrench itself and cares about the size of the empire under its control is, of course, not new. It was the basis of many early studies of management and is at the heart of Jensen's free cash flow hypothesis.[28] Moreover, the idea derives some empirical support from the fierce resistance of managers to many takeovers.[29] However, it is only very recently that the empire-building motive has been incorporated into theoretical models of capital structure. As we shall see, a number of basic aspects of capital structure can be explained in this way.

I will proceed by modifying my earlier model in two ways. In the first variation, I introduce the possibility that a firm's existing assets have an alternative use at date 1—in particular, that they can be liquidated.[30] However, for simplicity, I drop the assumption that there is a new investment opportunity at date 1. Under these conditions, debt may be useful to force the manager to liquidate the firm in a situation in which this is efficient but contrary to self-interest.

Variation 1

Suppose that $r = i = 0$, and that if a firm's assets are liquidated at date 1, they yield L in addition to the already realized date 1 return y_1. Assume that the manager and the market both learn y_1, L, and y_2 at date 1 (these may be uncertain ex ante, however). Efficiency dictates that liquidation should occur at date 1 if and only if $y_2 < L$. (I maintain the assumption of a zero interest rate.) However, suppose that the manager obtains large private benefits of control from running the firm between dates 1 and 2 and will therefore resist liquidation if at all possible. Moreover, for simplicity assume these private benefits are sufficiently large that no feasible incentive payment can persuade the manager to yield control voluntarily.[31]

The sequence of events is illustrated in figure 2-2. Given the large private benefits, the only way to get management to relinquish control at date 1 is through bankruptcy or takeover. I assume that no takeovers occur at date 1 because there are no potential acquirers and focus on bankruptcy.[32]

Assume that the firm's capital structure consists of equity and senior debt that is owed P_1 at date 1 and P_2 at date 2 (at the moment, I simply assume the debt to be senior; I consider why this might be desirable later). Suppose that the manager retains control if he does not default at date 1, but that default automatically triggers Chapter 7 bankruptcy, which in turn triggers complete liquidation of the firm. This sequence implicitly rules out renegotiation between creditors and the firm in or out of bankruptcy. Although the assumption of no renegotiation is strong, it is not unreasonable if creditors are dispersed: collective action problems can then make renegotiation difficult even under the supervision of a bankruptcy court. Given that default leads to bankruptcy and to the loss of control benefits, the manager never defaults voluntarily. Thus if

Figure 2-2. Liquidation Decision

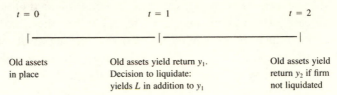

$t = 0$ $t = 1$ $t = 2$

Old assets in place / Old assets yield return y_1. Decision to liquidate: yields L in addition to y_1 / Old assets yield return y_2 if firm not liquidated

$y_1 \geq P_1$, he will pay P_1 to creditors at date 1 and save $y_1 - P_1$; $y_1 - P_1$ + y_2 will then be available for creditors and shareholders at date 2. Thus the date 1 value of the firm (the value of debt *and* equity, including interest and dividend payments) will be $y_1 + y_2$.

But what if $y_1 < P_1$? If $y_1 + y_2 \geq P_1 + P_2$, the manager can still avoid default at date 1 by issuing $P_1 - y_1$ dollars of new junior debt due at date 2 and repaying this together with the senior debt P_2 out of date 2 income y_2. Thus the date 1 value of the firm is again $y_1 + y_2$. However, if $y_1 < P_1$, and $y_1 + y_2 < P_1 + P_2$, then the manager cannot avoid default and liquidation will occur. In this case, the date 1 value of the firm is $y_1 + L$, of which the creditors receive Min $(P_1 + P_2, y_1 + L)$ and shareholders the rest.

Denoting the firm's date 1 market value by V_1, we can summarize the above discussion as follows:

$$V_1 = \begin{cases} y_1 + y_2 & \text{if } y_1 \geq P_1 \\ & \text{or } y_1 < P_1 \text{ and } y_1 + y_2 \geq P_1 + P_2 \\ y_1 + L & \text{otherwise.} \end{cases}$$

We are now in a position to discuss optimal capital structure. Suppose that capital structure is chosen at date 0 to maximize the total value of the firm.[33] If there is no ex ante uncertainty about y_2 and L, the first-best outcome can be achieved by setting $P_1 = 0$ if $y_2 > L$; and $P_1 > y_1$, $P_1 + P_2 > y_1 + y_2$ if $y_2 < L$.[34] The firm's date 0 market value is $V_0 = $ Max $(y_1 + y_2, y_1 + L)$.[35]

Matters become more interesting if y_2 and L are uncertain. To simplify, I will focus on the special case in which the vector (y_2, L) can take on just two values (y_2^A, L^A) and (y_2^B, L^B); see figure 2-3.

Obviously, if $y_2^A \geq L^A$, $y_2^B \geq L^B$, the first-best outcome can again be achieved with no date 1 debt; if $y_2^A \leq L^A$, $y_2^B \leq L^B$, the first-best can be achieved with high levels of date 1 and date 2 debt. The interesting case is $y_2^A > L^A$, $y_2^B < L^B$ (or vice versa). I divide this case into three subcases.

Figure 2-3. Liquidation Decision with Uncertainty

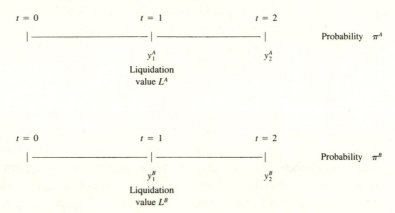

1. $y_1^A + y_2^A > y_1^B + y_2^B$. Here the first-best can again be achieved, for example, by setting $P_1 = y_1^A + y_2^A$, $P_2 = 0$. The reason is that the firm can avoid default in state A (by borrowing y_2^A) but not in state B. This is the efficient outcome.

2. $y_1^A + y_2^A \leq y_1^B + y_2^B$, $y_1^A > y_1^B$. Now the first-best can be achieved by setting $P_1 = y_1^A$, P_2 very large. The reason is that the firm can avoid default in state A (by paying y_1^A) but not in state B. Again this is efficient.

3. $y_1^A + y_2^A \leq y_1^B + y_2^B$, $y_1^A \leq y_1^B$. Now the first-best cannot be achieved. Given any value of P_1, P_2, default in state B occurs if and only if $y_1^B < P_1$ and $y_1^B + y_2^B < P_1 + P_2$. But these inequalities imply $y_1^A < P_1$ and $y_1^A + y_2^A < P_1 + P_2$, and hence default also occurs in state A. It is impossible to have liquidation in state B, where liquidation is efficient, without also having it in state A, where it is inefficient. Thus the choice is between having liquidation in both states or neither. The first, which can be achieved by setting P_1 and P_2 very large, is preferable to the second, which can be achieved by setting $P_1 = 0$, if and only if

(2.2) $$\pi^A L^A + \pi^B L^B > \pi^A y_2^A + \pi^B y_2^B$$

This completes the analysis of optimal capital structure in the two-state case. The main difference relative to the case of perfect certainty is that interior solutions occur: it may be optimal to choose debt levels to take intermediate values rather than zero or "very large." Also, high debt sometimes leads to inefficient liquidation and low debt sometimes prevents efficient liquidation (see the third subcase above).

Even this very simple model can explain why firms issue senior or secured debt. If P_2 were a junior claim, the firm would be able to issue debt senior to it at date 1 in the amount of y_2, and avoid bankruptcy whenever $y_1 + y_2 \geq P_1$. It is easy to check that in the second subcase above, the first-best outcome is no longer achievable under these conditions.[36]

To summarize variation 1, if management cannot be trusted on its own accord to liquidate the firm, debt *can* help put pressure on management. Moreover, in general, it is important that the firm's capital structure contain both short-term and senior, long-term debt: short-term debt to force management to pay out cash in the short run, leading in some circumstances to default and liquidation, and senior, long-term debt to prevent management from financing the payout by borrowing against long-run earnings.

Variation 2

The assumption in variation 1 that default and bankruptcy automatically lead to liquidation is strong. After all, Chapter 11 is specifically designed to avoid inefficient liquidation. The second variation of the earlier model avoids this assumption by considering firms that, although in financial distress, are not in danger of entering Chapter 7 bankruptcy or being liquidated.

In this variation the investment possibility i,r at date 1 is reintroduced.[37] However, I now suppose that L is so low that liquidation is no longer a viable alternative. So the firm must decide whether to expand at date 1 or to maintain the status quo. I also focus on long-term securities that pay out at date 2; in particular, I rule out short-term debt due at date 1. This assumption is restrictive but can be justified in the following way. Imagine that because liquidation is so unattractive, management can always default on short-term debt, declare Chapter 11 bankruptcy, keep creditors at bay, and run the firm as usual until date 2. Under these conditions, only long-term securities *can* have a role.[38]

And long-term securities do have a role. Suppose that management's empire-building tendencies mean that it always wants to make the new investment if at all possible (moreover, no incentive scheme can prevent this).[39] The only way to prevent management from expanding is to restrict access to capital. In other words, under the assumption that short-term debt is ineffective as a means of getting cash out of a firm, there is no way to stop management investing if $y_1 \geq i$. However, if $y_1 < i$, management needs to raise $i - y_1$ dollars from the date 1 capital market to invest. How easy or difficult this is depends on how much senior debt is already due at date 2.

To be specific, suppose that the firm's date 0 security structure consists of senior, long-term debt promising P_2 at date 2 plus equity.[40] Assume that management and the market observe y_2, r, and i at date 1. If $y_1 < i$, management will be able to raise the additional $i - y_1$ for investment if and only if

$$(2.3) \qquad\qquad i - y_1 \le y_2 + r - P_2.$$

This follows from the fact that, given that the manager will use the $i - y_1$ to invest, there will be $y_2 + r$ available at date 2 to be distributed to all security holders. Of this, P_2 has already been promised to date 0 creditors and the rest is available for new date 1 creditors. Thus the date 1 market value of the firm is

$$V_1 = \begin{cases} y_1 + y_2 + r - i & \text{if } y_1 \ge i \text{ or equation 2.3 holds} \\ y_1 + y_2 & \text{otherwise.} \end{cases}$$

It is again straightforward to analyze the firm's optimal capital structure in this second variation. Suppose management always needs to go to the capital market to invest ($y_1 < i$). If there is no ex ante uncertainty about y_2, i, and r, it is easy to achieve the first-best outcome. If $r > i$, set $P_2 = 0$; equation 2.3 is always satisfied and investment always takes place, which is efficient. In contrast, if $r < i$, set P_2 very large; equation 2.3 is never satisfied and investment never takes place, which is again efficient.

Matters become more interesting if y_2, r, and i are uncertain. To simplify, again suppose that (y_2, r, i) takes on just two values (y_2^A, r^A, i^A) and (y_2^B, r^B, i^B); see figure 2-4. It is again trivial to achieve the first-best outcome with no debt if $r^A \ge i^A$ and $r^B \ge i^B$, or with very large debt if $r^A \le i^A$ and $r^B \le i^B$. The interesting case is when $r^A > i^A$ and $r^B < i^B$. I divide this into two subcases.

1. $y_1^A + y_2^A + r^A - i^A > y_1^B + y_2^B + r^B - i^B$. Here the first-best can be achieved by setting P_2 somewhere between $y_1^B + y_2^B + r^B - i^B$ and $y_1^A + y_2^A + r^A - i^A$. Equation 2.3 is satisfied in state A but not in state B, and investment occurs only in state A, which is efficient.

In other words, the debt level is set somewhere between the maximized net value of the firm in state A and the maximized net value in state B.

Figure 2-4. Investment Decision with Uncertainty

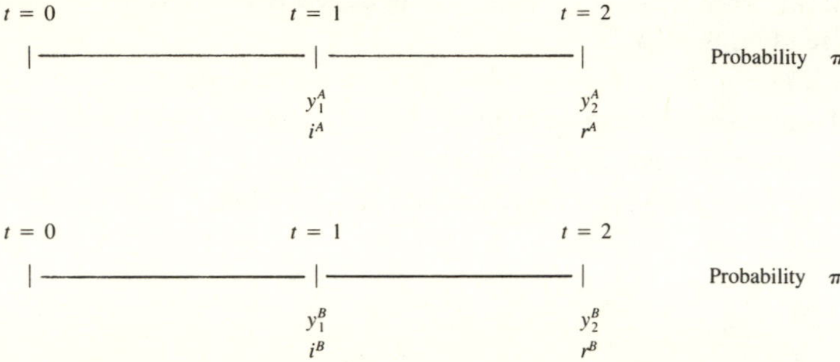

$t = 0$ $t = 1$ $t = 2$

| —————————————— | —————————————— | Probability π^A
                                y_1^A y_2^A
                                i^A r^A

$t = 0$ $t = 1$ $t = 2$

| —————————————— | —————————————— | Probability π^B
                                y_1^B y_2^B
                                i^B r^B

This gives management enough leeway to finance a profitable new investment in state A but prevents financing an unprofitable one in state B.

2. $y_1^A + y_2^A + r^A - i^A \leq y_1^B + y_2^B + r^B - i^B$. The first-best is no longer achievable for any choice of P_2. The reason is that

$$i^A - y_1^A \leq y_2^A + r^A - P_2 \text{ implies that}$$
$$i^B - y_1^B \leq y_2^B + r^B - P_2,$$

so it is impossible to have investment in state A without also having it in state B. Thus the choice is between having investment in neither state (set P_2 very large) or in both (set $P_2 = 0$). The first is preferable if and only if

$$\pi^A(r^A - i^A) + \pi^B(r^B - i^B) < 0.$$

Again this second variation can explain why not all debt is subordinated. If the date 2 debt were junior, then from the point of view of management trying to raise capital at date 1, the debt would be equivalent to equity because it can always be diluted. In other words, one might as well set $P_2 = 0$, which is not generally optimal.

The lesson from this second variation complements that from the first. If management is interested in empire building, the danger for security holders is that it will try to raise capital for unprofitable investment projects by issuing claims against earnings from existing assets. Senior, long-term debt can be useful in constraining management: this debt mortgages part of long-term earnings and reduces management's ability to dilute claims against earnings from existing assets.

The two variations are similar in economic terms. In fact, because liquidation can be thought of as negative investment, the reader may wonder whether they are identical. This is not the case, however, at least in modeling terms. In the liquidation variation, short-term debt is crucial, and a position has to be taken on what happens if management defaults at date 1 (I assumed that this triggered Chapter 7 bankruptcy and liquidation). The second variation ignores short-term debt and so date 1 default is not even an issue.

Observed Patterns of Capital Structure

A great deal of empirical work has lately been done on capital structure. Although not all the findings agree, some robust observations ("stylized facts") have emerged. I will take these facts as a given in what follows and consider what light the theory I have described can throw on them.

The stylized facts are that profitable firms have low levels of debt; firms with a large proportion of tangible assets have high levels of debt; firms with stable cash flows have high levels of debt; debt-for-equity swaps raise share prices; equity-for-debt swaps lower share prices; pure equity issues lower share prices.[41]

All of these facts *can* be explained by at least one of the variations of the basic theory described above. However, not all are inevitable consequences of the theory. In some cases the theory predicts that reversals should also be observed.

Consider the relationship between profitability and debt level. Variation 1 can certainly explain why profitable firms (in particular, those with high y_2's) can have low debt. Suppose L is fixed, but y_2 varies across firms, and this variation is observable. If y_2 is large ($y_2 > L$ for sure), it is optimal to set $P_1 = P_2 = 0$; whereas, if y_2 is small ($y_2 < L$ for sure), it is optimal to set P_1 and P_2 very large. Firms whose main asset is human capital might be examples of those whose going concern value substantially exceeds their liquidation value. In contrast, firms whose main assets consist of natural resources might have going concern values close to, or sometimes less than, their liquidation value.

However, a small change in variation 1 could generate a negative relation between profitability and the debt level. Suppose that, on average, profitable firms have liquidation values that are high relative to profitability. That is, the more profitable the firm, the more likely it is to satisfy the condition $y_2 < L$. In such cases large debt levels will be required in order to trigger liquidation of profitable firms.

Variation 2 also does not clearly predict the relationship between profitability and debt. If a firm's profitability refers to the value of new investment, it is optimal for profitable firms to have low debt (if $r > i$ for sure, the optimal $P_2 = 0$). However, if profitability refers to the value of old investments, then it is optimal for profitable firms to have high debt. In subcase 1 of the two-state case ($r^A > i^A$, $r^B < i^B$, $y_1^A + y_2^A + r^A - i^A > y_1^B + y_2^B + r^B - i^B$), the optimal P_2 lies between $y_1^B + y_2^B + r^B - i^B$ and $y_1^A + y_2^A + r^A - i^A$, and is thus increasing in $y_1^B + y_2^B$, $y_1^A + y_2^A$.[42]

Consider next the fact that firms with a large fraction of assets that are tangible have high debt. If tangibility is associated with high liquidation value, then variation 1 explains this fact rather clearly. Other things being equal, high L's make liquidation more attractive and so raise the optimal P_1, P_2 (it is more likely that $y_2 < L$ or that equation 2.2 will be satisfied). One possible offsetting effect is that firms with low L's (those whose main asset is human capital, for example) are arguably less likely to be sold off piecemeal in a Chapter 7 bankruptcy liquidation precisely because there would be such a great loss of value. If renegotiation can be relied on for such firms (in Chapter 11, say), it might make high debt *more* attractive when L is low. It is difficult to know how important this effect is in practice, however.

Variation 2 seems to have little to say about the relationship between debt and asset tangibility, because there is no obvious proxy for asset tangibility in this variation.

Consider now the relationship between debt and the stability of cash flows. The best way to understand this is to combine variations 1 and 2 in a very simple way. Suppose that liquidation and expansion are *both* options for the firm at date 1 but that expansion is never profitable ($r < i$ for sure). Suppose also that default at date 1 automatically triggers liquidation. Then the trade-off for initial security holders is between setting P_1, P_2 high to limit management's ability to expand, and setting P_1, P_2 low to avoid inefficient liquidation.

For example, assume y_1 and y_2 are perfectly certain and $y_2 > L$ for sure (so liquidation is always inefficient). Then the first-best outcome can be achieved by setting $P_1 = y_1$ and $P_2 = y_2$. The reason is that management never defaults, but because it has to pay out all its cash and its debt capacity is exhausted, it can never raise capital for unprofitable new projects. But if y_1 is uncertain, the first-best outcome is typically not achievable because it is impossible to prevent management from using current earnings for investment, and to exhaust the firm's debt capacity in all states of the world (this requires $P_1 \geq y_1$ and $P_1 + P_2 \geq y_1 + y_2$, for sure), without triggering inefficient liquidation in some states of the world (inefficient liquidation occurs whenever $P_1 > y_1$ and $P_1 + P_2 > y_1$

+ y_2). So there is now a trade-off for initial security holders. If inefficient liquidation poses a greater threat to the firm's total value than does carrying out unprofitable new investments, the optimal debt level will fall as y_1 becomes more uncertain (to reduce the chance that $P_1 > y_1$ and $P_1 + P_2 > y_1 + y_2$). But if unprofitable new investments pose the greater threat, the optimal debt level will rise as y_1 becomes more uncertain (to reduce the chance that $P_1 < y_1$ or $P_1 + P_2 < y_1 + y_2$).

So the theory can explain why firms with stable cash flows have more debt but can also explain the opposite.

I next explore the results of the various event studies on the effects of different kinds of recapitalizations on share prices. I will concentrate on variation 1, although similar results could undoubtedly be obtained from variation 2. In much of what follows, the driving force behind a recapitalization will be the threat of a hostile takeover.

DEBT-FOR-EQUITY SWAPS TYPICALLY RAISE SHARE PRICES.[43] To see that variation 1 can explain this, suppose that the management obtains private information just after date 0 that a hostile takeover is imminent (it will occur at date 1/2, say). Assume for simplicity that as far as the market is concerned this is a very unlikely event, so the anticipation of it has no effect on market value. However, if the management signals the event through a recapitalization, then the market of course reacts.

Assume also that for unspecified reasons (for example, historical reasons) the firm initially consists of 100 percent equity and that the hostile bid will succeed unless the management can convince the market that it will run the firm approximately efficiently (the idea is that management is safe if it is close to efficient, because there are some costs in making a bid).

Suppose it is known that for this firm $y_1 = 100$ and $L = 150$, as in figure 2-5. In the absence of any action by the management before a bid is made at date 1/2, market participants will reason that, if the bid fails, the management will *not* liquidate at date 1 because, given that the firm has no outstanding debt, it will be under no pressure to do so.[44] Anticipating this, shareholders tender to the bidder and the bid succeeds.

To prevent this outcome, the management must bond itself just after date 0 to take efficient action at date 1. An obvious way to do this is to make a debt-for-equity swap.[45] For example, suppose the management issues new short-term debt promising 250 (that is, sets $P_1 = 250$ and $P_2 = 0$) and uses the proceeds to buy back equity. Because $y_1 < P_1$ and $y_1 + y_2 < P_1 + P_2$, the new debt guarantees that the firm will default at

Figure 2-5. Recapitalization Decision in Face of Hostile Bid

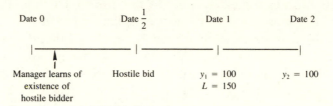

date 1 and be liquidated then, which is the efficient outcome. Thus the hostile takeover is thwarted, and the management retains control, if only until date 1.

What is the effect of the recapitalization on the value of equity? Before the recapitalization the equity was worth $y_1 + y_2 = 200$. Afterward the total value of the firm is $y_1 + L = 250$. Given that all the capital raised by the new debt is used to buy back shares, all of this 250 accrues to initial shareholders. Thus the effect of the recapitalization is to raise the value of equity by 50.

Variation 1 is thus consistent with the apparent fact that debt-for-equity swaps raise the value of equity. However, I now show that, under a different information structure, variation 1 predicts that such swaps can reduce the value of equity.

DEBT-FOR-EQUITY SWAPS CAN LOWER SHARE PRICES. Suppose that the vector (y_1, y_2, L) is known to take on two possible values. In figure 2-6 state A is the good state and state B the bad state. Assume that, ex ante, π^A is very close to 1 and π^B is very close to zero. However, imagine that the management receives private information just after date 0 that in fact state B is sure to occur (the receipt of this information is very unlikely ex ante). This information will very shortly become available to the market, at date 1/4, say. In addition everyone already knows that a hostile bid will be made at date 1/2. Again assume that the firm is initially all equity. The information structure is shown in figure 2-7.

Given that, in ex ante terms, state A is very likely, the management would have no incentive to deviate from the all equity structure in the absence of the information that state B is going to occur (in this case it would adjust its estimate of π^A even closer to 1). The point is that an all-equity firm is under no pressure to liquidate at date 1. But, since π^A is close to 1, this outcome is approximately efficient, so the management is safe from a takeover at date 1/2. The market's ex ante valuation of the initial equity is therefore approximately $y_1^A + y_2^A = 200$.

Figure 2-6. Liquidation versus Continuation in Good and Bad States

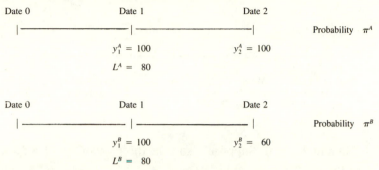

The management, however, knows that the market will soon learn to its surprise that the bad state *B* is the true state. Given this, the management's job will be in jeopardy unless it can bond itself to liquidate at date 1, since in state *B* liquidation is efficient.[46] One thing the management can do is to make a debt-for-equity swap. For example, it might set $P_1 = 180$. This commits it to liquidation at date 1 in state *B* and thus thwarts the hostile takeover at date 1/2.

Of course, given this information structure, the management's recapitalization signals that it has learned unfavorable information about the state, in particular that state *B* will occur. The new debt, however, is riskless (because $y_1^B + L^B = 180$) and so sells for 180. Since all of this accrues to initial shareholders, the value of equity when the recapitalization is announced is also 180. This represents a drop in equity value from 200 even though the recapitalization is in security holders' interests. The point is that the bad news about the state signaled by the recapitalization offsets the increase in bonding.[47]

Thus variation 1 can explain not only the apparent fact that debt-for-equity swaps raise the price of equity but also the reverse.

Let's turn now to equity-for-debt swaps. These are not simply the opposite of debt-for-equity swaps because the debt holders must be *persuaded* to sell their debt. Each small debt-holder always has the option to hold onto his debt and see it appreciate in value as others tender in the debt buyback.

EQUITY-FOR-DEBT SWAPS TYPICALLY REDUCE THE PRICE OF EQUITY. It is easy to see that variation 1 can explain how equity-for-debt swaps can reduce the price of equity. Suppose that there are two states of the world, as in figure 2-6, again with ex ante probabilities $\pi^A \simeq 1$, $\pi^B \simeq 0$. Now, however (for some historical reason), the initial capital structure consists of equity and senior debt promising P_1

Figure 2-7. Recapitalization Decision with Hostile Bid and Uncertainty

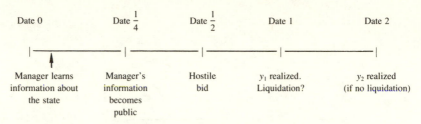

= 180 and $P_2 = 0$. Suppose also that the probability of a takeover at any time is zero.

If a recapitalization is at all costly for the management (for example, if it requires effort), then management will not bother to recapitalize given the ex ante probabilities $\pi^A \simeq 1$, $\pi^B \simeq 0$ (in state A it will be able to avoid default by issuing \$80 of date 2 debt, and state B is extremely unlikely). However, suppose the management obtains private information at date 1/4 that $\pi^A = \pi^B = 1/2$. It is now in its interest to buy back some of the debt to avoid default and liquidation in state B. For example, suppose that the management issues new equity worth \$20 and uses it to buy back \$20 of debt (so that P_1 falls to $P_1' = 160$). Such a swap is feasible even if the market deduces from the swap that the management has learned $\pi^A = \pi^B = 1/2$. The reason is that existing debt holders are indifferent between selling their debt back to the firm and not selling, since they are being offered one dollar for each dollar of debt, which is also what they get individually if they do not tender (with $P_1' = 160$, the firm's debt is riskless). Furthermore, after the swap, equity holders receive $y_1^A + y_2^A - P_1' = 40$ in state A and $y_1^B + y_2^B - P_1' = 0$ in state B, so the market value of equity is 20. By issuing a large (or infinite) amount of new equity (in effect, overwhelming initial equity holders), the management can indeed raise the \$20 necessary to buy back the debt.

Of course, this swap is very bad news for initial equity holders, both because it signals that the bad state is more likely and because the extent of management bonding falls. The value of their equity falls to zero on announcement of the swap (their ownership stake in the firm will be infinitely diluted by the new equity issue). In contrast, before the recapitalization, when the market assumed $\pi^A \simeq 1$, $\pi^B \simeq 0$, the value of initial equity was approximately $y_1^A + y_2^A - P_1 = 20$.

Thus equity-for-debt swaps can reduce the price of initial equity. However, again the opposite can occur under a different information structure.

EQUITY-FOR-DEBT SWAPS CAN INCREASE THE PRICE OF EQUITY. Suppose that the economy is again as in figure 2-6. Now, however, the market thinks that $\pi^A \simeq 0$ and $\pi^B \simeq 1$, whereas management learns privately just after date 0 that $\pi^A = 0.9$, $\pi^B = 0.1$ (information that will become available to the market at date 1/4). Also assume it is known that a bidder will appear at date 1/2. (So the information structure is as in figure 2-7.) Finally, suppose the initial capital structure of the firm is such that $P_1 = 180$ and $P_2 = 0$.

If state B were indeed very likely—as the market thinks—management would not wish to buy back a lot of debt at date 1/4, because this would commit it to an *inefficient* outcome at date 1 (the market knows that the management will never voluntarily liquidate then) and so a successful bid would occur at date 1/2. However, once the management learns that $\pi^A = 0.9$, $\pi^B = 0.1$, it may want to recapitalize, because if it buys back $20 of debt, it can avoid default in state B. Moreover, even though an inefficiency $L^B - y_2^B = 20$ is introduced in state B, the expected inefficiency as of date 1/2 is only $\pi^B \times 20 = 2$. So, as long as the bid costs exceed 2, the management will be safe from a date 1/2 bid even after the recapitalization.

The recapitalization works as before. The management issues new equity worth $20 and uses it to buy back $20 of debt. Creditors are indifferent between tendering and not tendering (they receive one dollar on the dollar either way because the firm is worth at least 160 in each state), whereas equity holders as a whole after the recapitalization receive $y_1^A + y_2^A - P_1' = 40$ in state A and $y_1^B + y_2^B - P_1' = 0$ in state B; that is, the value of all equity, using the newly signaled probabilities $\pi^A = 0.9$, $\pi^B = 0.1$, is $40 \times 0.9 = 36$. Because the value of new equity is 20, the value of initial equity is 16.

Before the recapitalization, the value of equity is $\pi^A(y_1^A + y_2^A - P_1)$ $+ \pi^B(y_1^B + L^B - P_1) \simeq 0$. Thus the recapitalization causes an *increase* in the value of equity even though it reduces the level of management bonding: the good news that state A occurs with probability 0.9 offsets the decrease in efficiency resulting from reduced bonding.

These last examples can throw light on one final kind of recapitalization: a pure increase in equity. Event studies find that this reduces the value of initial equity, and it is easy to see how. Simply take the first equity-for-debt example given earlier and note that, instead of using the $20 from the equity issue to buy back $20 of debt, the management could achieve exactly the same outcome by retaining the $20 in the firm and using it to repay some of the debt at date 1. The effect of this on the value of initial equity will be to reduce it (from $20 to zero), just as the event studies find.

On the other hand, the second equity-for-debt example also shows that new equity issues can sometimes *raise* the value of initial equity. Again let the management retain the $20 from the new equity issue and use it to repay some of the date 1 debt. Then the new equity issue causes the value of initial equity to rise from approximately zero to $16.

Conclusions

The many theories of capital structure—based on taxes, market incompleteness, asymmetric information, and so forth—are consistent with the apparent facts about capital structure that I have described in the previous section.[48] However, these theories do not explain an even more basic aspect of capital structure: the widespread use of senior or secured debt. Only the approach that focuses on the conflict of interest between insiders and outsiders seems capable of explaining both sets of observations.

Although this agency (or managerial discretion) approach is still in its infancy, I have described a version of it that is consistent with the findings of a number of recent event studies (as well as with various other stylized facts). At the same time, to explain these findings, it was necessary to make specific assumptions about the structure of information faced by the firm's managers and the market. With different assumptions the approach predicts that reversals of these findings should be observed. I suspect this is a feature of *any* theory of capital structure. That is, it is hard to imagine how a theory could explain the apparent facts independently of information structure.

The agency approach could be extended in many ways. The two variations described in the previous section could be combined, the model could be generalized to more periods to obtain a richer theory of the maturity structure of debt, and the sharp distinctions supposed between debt and equity could be relaxed.

This last extension deserves some elaboration. In the model I used earlier, the distinction between debt and equity is stark: equity holders are completely passive, and creditors automatically force a bankrupt firm into liquidation or prevent a financially distressed firm from raising new capital. In reality, of course, the picture is more complex. Equity holders have votes that can be used to replace management, particularly when tendered to a hostile bidder.[49] Creditors do sometimes renegotiate their debt to avoid a firm's liquidation or allow new investments to be financed (perhaps via Chapter 11 bankruptcy). In future work it would be desirable to consider these possibilities and to understand their implication for the firm's choice of debt-equity ratio.

A related issue concerns the role of bankruptcy procedure. In this paper, bankruptcy has, in effect, served as a punishment for managers of firms that have not paid their debts. This is questionable not only in positive terms but also from a normative point of view. Arguably, bankruptcy procedure should be designed more with the goal of maximizing the value of the firm than with punishing errant managers. Little work has been done on optimal bankruptcy procedures.[50] But it is to be hoped that the insights from the agency approach will be useful in guiding future work on this topic.

Finally, I should emphasize that, although I have advocated the agency approach over other approaches, such as those based on taxes or asymmetric information, I do not mean to suggest that these other approaches have nothing to offer. On the contrary, the agency approach could undoubtedly benefit greatly from being combined with them in future work.[51] One goal would be to explain observed variations in capital structure across industries and countries and over time. My point has simply been that trying to explain capital structure without being explicit about the conflict of interest between insiders and outsiders seems doomed to failure. The agency perspective is necessary for understanding capital structure, even if it may not by itself always be sufficient.

Comment by Paul R. Samuelson

Oliver Hart's provocative paper addresses an interesting question concerning optimal capital structure: "Why do firms issue senior debt?" I have two types of experience that may qualify me to discuss this. First, I once wrote a dissertation about investment and financing decisions with asymmetric information. Thus I can understand the mechanics of the paper, even if I can no longer place it in a proper academic context. Second, I have been involved with investments since 1977 and have purchased securities of companies with a variety of capital structures.

The paper presents several models and a variety of interesting results. My comments are highly selective. Managers of a firm acting in the interests of its shareholders (though not necessarily maximizing the total value of the firm) may prefer to issue senior rather than junior debt in the following circumstance: suppose at time zero, the firm requires outside financing and can obtain it either with senior or junior debt. Suppose for simplicity that the firm can issue senior debt that is risk-free in terms of default because it can always be repaid at time 2. Although the firm has no positive net present value investments to be made at time 1, it does have a risky negative net present value investment available.

If the firm could issue senior debt at time 1, it would be possible to finance such an investment and thereby increase the value of the firm's shares, even though the investment reduced the value of the firm's junior debt. But if investors could anticipate such an event, the junior debt could only be issued at time zero at a fair value, given the subsequent negative net present value investment. In this case, the firm's equity would be worth less with a time zero junior debt issue (by an amount equal to the negative net present value of the risky time 1 investment) than with an initial senior debt issue.

An example may illustrate my point. Suppose a firm requires at time zero an investment of 90. There is no payment at time 1 ($Y(1) = 0$) and a certain payment of 100 at time 2 ($Y(2) = 100$). Assume for the moment that the discount rate is zero, and the firm can issue risk-free senior debt with a certain payment of 90 to make the original investment. At time 1, there is an investment requiring 50 with payoffs at time 2 of zero or 90, with equal probability. Therefore, the negative net present value of the investment is -5: $(0.5 \times 0 + 0.5 \times 90) - 50 = -5$.

At time 1, with only senior debt outstanding, there will be no incentive to make the investment: the senior debt is worth 90 with or without the investment, and if the new junior debt is issued at a fair price (and a fair promised payment of 90), the equity will be worth only 5: $0.5 \times 0 + 0.5 \times 10 = 5$. Without the investment, equity will be worth 10, so the investment will not be made and the original value of the equity with senior debt will also be 10.

If, at time 1, however, there were junior debt outstanding with a face value of 130 (to be explained momentarily), there would be an incentive to make the investment. Without the investment, the equity would be worthless, and the junior debt would be worth 100 (the entire certain payoff of the original investment goes to pay junior debt). But new senior debt could be issued at a risk-free face value of 50 to make the investment. In this case the junior debt would be worth 90—$(0.5 \times 50) +$

$(0.5 \times 130) = 90$—and the equity would be worth 5: $(0.5 \times 0) + (0.5 \times 10) = 5$. The various scenarios are laid out below.

Without investment, with initial senior debt (face value = 90):

Firm   100
Debt   90
Equity 10

With investment, with initial senior debt (face value = 90) and junior debt (face value = 90):

Low firm value	100	High firm value	190	Expected value	145
Senior debt	90	Senior debt	90	Senior debt	90
Junior debt	10	Junior debt	90	Junior debt	50
Equity	0	Equity	10	Equity	5

Without investment, with junior debt (face value = 130):

Firm   100
Debt   100
Equity 0

With investment, with junior debt (face value = 130) and new senior debt (face value = 50):

Low firm value	100	High firm value	190	Expected value	145
Senior debt	50	Senior debt	50	Senior debt	50
Junior debt	50	Junior debt	130	Junior debt	90
Equity	0	Equity	10	Equity	5

In a firm financed initially with junior debt, managers acting in the interests of equity would have the incentive to make the negative net present value investment at time 1. Thus the original value of the equity will be less if junior debt is issued rather than senior debt originally. The difference in original value of the equity with junior rather than senior debt is equal to the negative net present value of the subsequent investment. In this case, then, senior debt serves as a bonding device to prevent managers from later acting in ways that benefit shareholders at the expense of other classes of investors such as holders of junior debt.

The first variation of Hart's agency model involving liquidation costs provoked a particular interpretation from me, which I hope is not entirely idiosyncratic. Liquidation might be thought of as the redeployment of assets catalyzed by financial disappointment. For this reason, debt may indeed serve as a trigger mechanism for scrutinizing how management is using the firm's assets. Perhaps the kindest explanation of leveraged buyouts would be that they discipline management with a sufficiently large amount of debt outstanding. However, debt is more likely to have the impact of a shotgun rather than a pistol, and must be seen in the context of other measures of management performance such as equity values.

The second variation of Hart's agency model was of less interest to me because the level of debt seems an awkward tool for enforcing capital budgeting. Investment decisions are difficult enough when managers have the right incentives. Can managers with the wrong incentives but facing the shotgun of a large amount of debt make better investment decisions?

I would also like to make four points regarding the "stylized facts" that the models seek to address. First, the optimal capital structure is typically characterized by the amount of debt and equity issued by a firm. However, the more important characterization involves how the risk of the firm is shared across the debt and equity securities. Companies differ enormously in the riskiness of their business. Therefore, the amount of debt and equity outstanding will not necessarily suggest how changes in the value of the firm are allocated between debt and equity. Because many explanations of capital structure depend on how changes in the value of the firm are absorbed, one needs to gather evidence not just about quantities of debt and equity but also about the riskiness of debt and equity.

Such a task would be difficult, however, because most medium to large U.S. companies, independent of their exact mix of debt and equity, place most of the burden of absorbing changes in the value of the firm on the equity outstanding and not on the debt. The value of most corporate debt, by contrast, is much more sensitive to interest rate changes than to changes in market values of firms. Moreover, corporate bond prices are sufficiently unreliable that estimating the sensitivity of bonds to firm risk would not be easy.

My second point concerns the restricted set of financing choices that a firm has at any given time. Although I spent some time looking at a variety of different securities in my dissertation, most companies can choose among only a small number. Companies must issue securities that are clearly understood (or those that investors believe are clearly understood) and that at least appear similar to other companies' offerings.

Third, capital structures are the result of both deliberate decisions and random events. A firm can become leveraged either deliberately or because of a decline in its market value. A model of optimal capital structure needs to incorporate both sequences of decisions and a range of future outcomes.

Fourth, financial transactions that provoke a significant change in the value of a firm's securities will be hard to explain without appealing to some sort of asymmetry argument—such as, different investors know different things. Particular price events are almost necessarily associated with a change in the information available to investors.

General Discussion

Barrie Wigmore observed that, even before the existence of a corporate profits tax that could have encouraged debt financing, a very subordinated security similar to the junior debt in Hart's model existed. Before 1930, he said, almost all corporations, with the exception of railroads, utilities, and oil companies, had preferred stock as their form of leverage. The stocks required no principal payment, they were outstanding to infinity, and they had a dividend that could be totally deferred at the discretion of management. The theoretical puzzle, then, Oliver Hart observed, is that once taxes were introduced, firms did not continue to use a subordinated debt instrument.

Dennis Mueller raised a question about who is supposed to be writing the contracts in Hart's models and in similar models. In this literature the discussion usually proceeds as if the principals write the contracts to give the agents the right incentives. But in fact the managers usually write the contracts, so whether to issue debt is also the manager's decision. If the problem in the model is one of a conflict of interest, why would managers issue senior debt as a way of providing themselves with a proper incentive?

Mueller noted that Hart shifts to the threat of takeover as the impetus that forces management to issue debt. In other words, it is ultimately the threat of takeover, not the debt contract, that has the effect of removing managerial discretion. But, he added, this is a very awkward and imperfect disciplining device.

Stuart Myers commented that Hart fails to prove some sort of conflict of interest between managers and the providers of capital is necessary to explain the use of ordinary looking senior debt. Since this theorem may be difficult or impossible to prove, Myers predicted an effort by scholars to come up with counterexamples to disprove it. Myers also questioned the technique of attributing arbitrary objective functions to managers as a modeling device because, he argued, it would always be possible to conceive of an objective function that will get any behavior the modeler is looking for.

Notes

1. For an excellent and comprehensive account of this literature, see Milton Harris and Artur Raviv, "The Theory of Capital Structure," *Journal of Finance*, vol. 46 (March 1991), pp. 297–355.

2. Michael C. Jensen and William H. Meckling, "Theory of the Firm: Managerial Behavior, Agency Costs and Ownership Structure," *Journal of Financial Economics*, vol. 4 (October 1976), pp. 305–60.

3. Clifford W. Smith, Jr., and Jerold B. Warner, "On Financial Contracting: An Analysis of Bond Covenants," *Journal of Financial Economics*, vol. 7 (June 1979), p. 122, found that in a random sample of eighty-seven public issues of debt registered with the Securities and Exchange Commission between January 1974 and December 1975, more than 90 percent of the bonds contained restrictions on the issuing of additional debt. Although the strength of such debt covenants declined during the 1980s, it is still very common for new public debt issues to contain some restrictions on new debt. See Richard Brook, "Debt Covenants and Event Risk: The Practitioner as Source of Evidence," working paper 51, Columbia University Law School, 1990.

Another factor worth noting is that for U.S. manufacturing companies traded on the New York and American stock exchanges (Compustat, Primary-Supplementary-Tertiary file) the average ratio of secured debt to total debt ranged from 22 percent to 33 percent between 1981 and 1989 (author's calculations).

4. See Stewart C. Myers, "Determinants of Corporate Borrowing," *Journal of Financial Economics*, vol. 5 (November 1977), pp. 147–75. Some of the ideas in this section parallel those found in Philip H. Dybvig and Jaime F. Zender, "Capital Structure and Dividend Irrevelance with Asymmetric Information," *Review of Financial Studies*, vol. 4 (1991), pp. 201–19.

5. In extensions, it would be important to allow for many managers, workers, and so forth.

6. Equation 2.1 also causes the manager to invest efficiently if r is uncertain at date 1, regardless of his attitude toward risk. This is because a risk-averse person is risk-neutral with respect to small bets and so, if θ is small, the manager will be interested in the expected net present value of investment. See Kenneth J. Arrow, *Essays in the Theory of Risk-Bearing* (Chicago: Markham Publishing, 1971).

7. When $y_1 + y_2 + r - d < i$ and $r > i$, it is in the collective interest of the initial creditors to forgive some of the initial debt d. However, if this debt is

dispersed, it will not be in any creditor's individual interest to forgive or rene-
gotiate debt and renegotiations are likely to break down. See, for example, Mark
J. Roe, "The Voting Prohibition in Bond Workouts," *Yale Law Journal*, vol. 97
(December 1987), pp. 232–79.

The debt overhang problem disappears if the new investment opportunity can
be spun off from the firm and financed as a separate corporate entity. However,
this may be difficult to arrange to the extent that the same management team
runs both firms and can use transfer pricing to reallocate profits between them.
Under these conditions, the market can keep track only of total profits ($y_1 + y_2$
or $y_1 + y_2 + r - i$) and project-specific financing is impossible.

8. This means that the issues raised in Merton H. Miller, "Debt and Taxes,"
Journal of Finance, vol. 32 (May 1977), pp. 261–75, do not arise.

9. I am ignoring the very small fraction of the firm's date 2 receipts used to
compensate the manager.

10. In a multiperiod model in which further investment may occur at dates 2,
3, . . . , it would presumably be efficient to ensure that the debt issued at date 1
is also subordinated, in the sense that it would contain a covenant allowing the
firm to issue debt senior to *it*.

11. PIK bonds, which give management the option of paying interest in cash
or in additional securities, have in fact been used extensively in LBOs during the
1980s. See Peter Tufano's paper in this volume; and Jeremy I. Bulow, Lawrence
H. Summers, and Victoria P. Summers, "Distinguishing Debt from Equity in the
Junk Bond Era," in John B. Shoven and Joel Waldfogel, eds., *Debt, Taxes, and
Corporate Restructuring* (Brookings, 1990), pp. 135–66.

12. In fact, before 1989 U.S. corporations apparently faced few restrictions
on their ability to use PIK bonds to wipe out taxable income. Since 1989 the
Revenue Reconciliation Act has constrained them. See Bulow, Summers, and
Summers, "Distinguishing Debt from Equity."

13. A person with a von Neumann-Morgenstern utility function evaluates a
gamble in terms of the expected utility of its return.

14. An outcome is Pareto optimal if it is impossible to make some people
better off without making others worse off.

15. See Robert Wilson, "The Theory of Syndicates," *Econometrica*, vol. 36
(January 1968), pp. 119–32.

16. Two points should be noted. First, there is an even simpler way to sustain
the optimum if financial intermediaries can be created without cost: the firm
issues 100 percent equity, the manager is given the right to issue new equity or
debt at date 1, and a financial intermediary repackages the net return R as the
N securities $s_1(\cdot), \ldots , s_N(\cdot)$. For a discussion of practical examples of this kind
of repackaging, see Robert C. Merton, "The Changing Nature of Debt and
Equity: Discussion," in Richard W. Kopcke and Eric S. Rosengren, eds., *Are the
Distinctions Between Debt and Equity Disappearing?* Federal Reserve Bank of
Boston Conference Series 33 (1989), pp. 44–48.

Second, the analysis of optimal security structure when markets are incomplete becomes considerably more complicated when the return from the investment, r, is stochastic. The reason is that the optimal investment rule is no longer
clear (it depends on attitudes toward risk) and must be derived endogenously

along with the optimal sharing rules. I conjecture, however, that the main result—that all claims issued by the firm will be subordinated—generalizes.

17. Stewart C. Myers and Nicholas S. Majluf, "Corporate Financing and Investment Decisions When Firms Have Information That Investors Do Not Have," *Journal of Financial Economics*, vol. 13 (June 1984), pp. 187–221.

18. Discussant Paul Samuelson presents an example of this case in his comments following this paper.

19. This observation is also made by Dybvig and Zender, "Capital Structure and Dividend Irrelevance with Asymmetric Information."

20. As far as I can see, this conclusion is also valid (at least approximately) in a multiperiod or infinite period context. The appropriate generalization of equation 2.1 is that the manager receives a small fraction θ of the total market value of the firm at date T (discounted to date 0), minus a fraction θ of any cash inflows to the firm at previous dates (discounted to date 0), plus a fraction θ of any dividends or interest paid at previous dates (discounted to date 0). Here T is the firm's last date in a finite horizon model and a far-off date if the horizon is infinite.

21. These arguments assume that it is always efficient for the manager to raise capital by issuing shares on the open market instead of borrowing or making private placements. Suppose, however, that borrowing or private placement is advantageous and it is difficult to measure objectively whether such deals are made on favorable terms. Shareholders may prefer to give the manager some equity in the firm rather than apply the formula in equation 2.1 to encourage him to make the effort to achieve a good deal. Under these conditions, the Myers-Majluf analysis may apply. However, this approach, by stressing the manager's effort, departs from the working hypothesis that the manager is selfless and his decisions are not costly to him.

22. This is a version of the Modigliani-Miller argument that investors can always undo a firm's financial structure by trading on their own account. If it is strapped for cash, management could always borrow to finance its purchases, using the acquired shares as collateral.

It is worth emphasizing that the assumption that management acts on behalf of shareholders is much less controversial in the case of a small private company in which management holds most or all of the equity and the equity cannot be easily traded.

23. See, for example, Macmillan's (unsuccessful) efforts to defeat Robert Maxwell, as described in Cynthia Crossen and Karen Blumenthal, "An Anti-Takeover Arsenal That Failed," *Wall Street Journal*, November 4, 1988, p. B1.

24. A qualification should be made here. Some scholars have argued that even if the management is selfless, senior or secured debt or both may be useful as a way of bonding the firm if it engages in strategic behavior in product markets or in bargaining with unions. See Carliss Y. Baldwin, "Productivity and Labor Unions: An Application of the Theory of Self-Enforcing Contracts," *Journal of Business*, vol. 56 (April 1983), pp. 155–85; James A. Brander and Tracy R. Lewis, "Oligopoly and Financial Structure: The Limited Liability Effect," *American Economic Review*, vol. 76 (December 1986), pp. 956–70; and Enrico C. Perotti and Kathryn E. Spier, "Capital Structure as a Bargaining Tool: The Role of

Leverage in Contract Renegotiation," Harvard University discussion paper 1548 (1991). Although strategic effects may well be important, however, it would be surprising if they alone could explain the widespread use of senior or secured debt or the variations in such debt across industries, countries, or over time.

25. Another qualification should be made. Giving votes to a dispersed group of security holders may increase management's bargaining power in negotiations with an acquirer. See Luigi Zingales, "Insiders' Ownership and the Decision to Go Public," Massachusetts Institute of Technology, 1991.

26. See, for example, Robert M. Townsend, "Optimal Contracts and Competitive Markets with Costly State Verification," *Journal of Economic Theory*, vol. 21 (October 1979), pp. 265–93; Douglas Gale and Martin Hellwig, "Incentive Compatible Debt Contracts: The One-Period Problem," *Review of Economic Studies*, vol. 52 (October 1985), pp. 647–63; Oliver Hart and John Moore, "Default and Renegotiation: A Dynamic Model of Debt," MIT Department of Economics working paper 520 (1989); Philippe Aghion and Patrick Bolton, "An Incomplete Contracts Approach to Financial Contracting," *Review of Economic Studies*, vol. 59 (July 1992), pp. 473–94; and Douglas W. Diamond, "Debt Maturity Structure and Liquidity Risk," *Quarterly Journal of Economics*, vol. 106 (August 1991), pp. 709–37.

Some of this literature is surveyed in Franklin Allen, "The Changing Nature of Debt and Equity: A Financial Perspective," in Kopcke and Rosengren, eds., *Are the Distinctions between Debt and Equity Disappearing?* pp. 12–38.

27. See, for example, Stephen A. Ross, "The Determination of Financial Structure: The Incentive-Signalling Approach," *Bell Journal of Economics*, vol. 8 (Spring 1977), pp. 23–40; and Sanford J. Grossman and Oliver D. Hart, "Corporate Financial Structure and Managerial Incentives," in John J. McCall, ed., *The Economics of Information and Uncertainty* (University of Chicago Press, 1982), pp. 107–37.

28. On the early managerial literature, see William J. Baumol, *Business Behavior, Value and Growth* (Macmillan 1959); Robin L. Marris, *The Economic Theory of Managerial Capitalism* (Glencoe, Ill.: Free Press, 1964); and Oliver E. Williamson, *The Economics of Discretionary Behavior: Managerial Objectives in a Theory of the Firm* (Prentice-Hall, 1964). On the free cash flow hypothesis, see Michael C. Jensen, "Agency Costs of Free Cash Flow, Corporate Finance, and Takeovers," *American Economic Review*, vol. 76 (May 1986), pp. 323–29.

29. See Michael J. Barclay and Clifford G. Holderness, "Private Benefits from Control of Public Corporations," *Journal of Financial Economics*, vol. 25 (December 1989), pp. 371–95, for additional empirical evidence that control rents are large.

30. This first variation is related to work by Rene Stulz, "Managerial Control of Voting Rights: Financing Policies and the Market for Corporate Control," *Journal of Financial Economics*, vol. 20, (January–March 1988), pp. 25–54; and Guozhong Xie, "Essays on the Theory of the Firm," Ph.D. dissertation, MIT, 1990. The present version is based on unpublished work that I have carried out with John Moore.

31. These private benefits are not modeled explicitly. One interpretation is that the manager obtains a great deal of utility from being in charge of an empire.

Of course, in reality, managers also care about their wealth. Thus future studies ought to relax the assumption that incentive schemes have no role to play.

32. In principle the firm's owners could remove the manager in other ways— by firing him, for example. But in the present model there is no real distinction between bankruptcy and a management firing (bankruptcy triggers liquidation, which can be thought of as representing the value of the firm if the manager is fired). One arrangement that I rule out is a *contingent* liquidation or firing contract, one in which the owners specify that the manager is fired if and only if $y_2 < L$. A contingent contract is enforceable only if y_2 and L are *verifiable*, as well as being observable to the manager and the market; arguably this is not the case. (A variable is verifiable if it can be litigated over. Many variables are observable to certain parties but not verifiable. For example, in the hearings before the Senate Judiciary Committee, Judge Clarence Thomas and Professor Anita Hill both presumably knew whether Thomas had sexually harassed Hill, but neither was able to establish the truth objectively. A variable that is not verifiable cannot be the basis of an enforceable, contingent contract.)

33. One interpretation is that the choice is made before an initial date 0 public offering by the original owner, who wishes to maximize his total receipts in this offering. Another interpretation is that the threat of a hostile takeover forces management to maximize market value at date 0.

34. In what follows, the possibility that $y_2 > L$ will be important. One point of view is that $y_2 \leq L$ always because there is nothing to stop outside bidders from competing in a Chapter 7 liquidation for the right to run the firm as a going concern. Two justifications for not adopting this point of view can be given. First, there may be insufficient time for outside bidders to raise the financing for their bids in a Chapter 7 liquidation. Second, if incumbent management has special skills, they may be the only party that can bid for the firm as a going concern, and although they may win the auction, they may end up paying the second highest value for the firm's assets, represented by the (piecemeal) liquidation value of L.

35. In discussing optimal capital structure, I always treat the manager's private benefit of control as a pure rent that does not enter into the firm's market value. Thus the manager's private benefits do not affect the initial choice of capital structure.

36. To see this, note that to obtain the first-best outcome one must have default in state B, that is, $y_1^B + y_2^B < P_1$. But this implies $y_1^A + y_2^A < P_1$, that is, there will also be default in state A.

37. This variation is based on Oliver Hart and John Moore, "A Theory of Corporate Financial Structure Based on the Seniority of Claims," NBER working paper 3431 (1990).

38. Another justification for ignoring short-term debt is that much of the analysis that follows applies when the firm needs to go to the capital market to finance new investment ($y_1 < i$); under these conditions short-term debt as a means for getting cash out of the company has little value.

39. This is again an extreme assumption, but the main ideas of the analysis should apply when management is interested in both empire building and financial compensation.

40. More general security structures, including debt of different seniorities, are considered in Hart and Moore, "Theory of Corporate Financial Structure."

41. For discussions of these, see Harris and Raviv, "Theory of Capital Structure"; Ronald W. Masulis, *The Debt/Equity Choice* (Ballinger, 1988); and Stewart C. Myers, "Still Searching for Optimal Capital Structure," in Kopcke and Rosengren, eds., *Are the Distinctions between Debt and Equity Disappearing?* For original sources, see Paul Asquith and David Mullins, Jr., "Equity Issues and Offering Dilution," *Journal of Financial Economics*, vol. 15 (January–February 1986), pp. 61–89; W. Carl Kester, "Capital and Ownership Structure: A Comparison of United States and Japanese Manufacturing Corporations," *Financial Management*, vol. 15 (Spring 1986), pp. 5–16; M. Long and I. Malitz, "Investment Patterns and Financial Leverage," in Benjamin M. Friedman, ed., *Corporate Capital Structures in the United States* (University of Chicago Press, 1985); Ronald W. Masulis, "The Effects of Capital Structure Change on Security Prices: A Study of Exchange Offers," *Journal of Financial Economics*, vol. 8 (June 1980), pp. 139–77; and Sheridan Titman and Roberto Wessels, "The Determinants of Capital Structure Choice," *Journal of Finance*, vol. 43 (March 1988), pp. 1–19.

42. For more on this, see Hart and Moore, "Theory of Corporate Financial Structure."

43. For a model close in spirit to this discussion see David A. Butz, "Bust-Up Takeover Bids and Asymmetric Information," University of California, Los Angeles, 1990.

44. Assume that the chances of another bidder appearing later are negligible.

45. I assume that it is too late to make such a swap after the takeover bid is announced.

46. I assume that bonding must occur before the market learns the true state at date 1/4 and a fortiori before a bid occurs at date 1/2 (dates 1/4 and 1/2 might be very close together).

47. The idea that a managerial action that serves shareholders can cause a decline in share price because the action reveals bad news about the company is far from new. See, for example, Andrei Shleifer and Robert W. Vishny, "Greenmail, White Knights, and Shareholders' Interest," *Rand Journal of Economics*, vol. 17 (Autumn 1986), pp. 293–309.

48. See Harris and Raviv, "Theory of Capital Structure."

49. Hostile takeovers played a background role in the analysis in the previous section.

50. An exception is Lucian A. Bebchuk, "A New Approach to Corporate Reorganizations," *Harvard Law Review*, vol. 101 (February 1988), pp. 775–804.

51. Asymmetric information played an important background role in the analysis of event studies in the previous section.

Routines, Cash Flows, and Unconventional Assets: Corporate Change in the 1980s

Sidney G. Winter

ANALYSTS of the wave of corporate takeovers and restructurings in the 1980s have agreed at least on some of the facts, but controversy flourishes regarding explanations and implications. Observers agree in particular on one key fact: the shareholders of acquired firms generally profited regardless of the means of acquisition. And although shareholders of acquiring firms sometimes suffered losses, they were able to finance activity that greatly enriched the shareholders of acquired firms, and they usually made modest gains themselves.[1] Substantial increases in efficiency, large transfers from third parties such as employees, or some combination of these would seem to be implied.

Interpretations of the facts cover a spectrum. At one end, assessments favor restructuring in general and hostile takeovers in particular as the market's answer to the difficulties shareholders face in curbing managerial power. A change of control or an increase in leverage that alters the context of control reins in the managers, possibly leaving them in charge but with very different constraints and incentives. Without this check from the market, managers might try to use the corporation's cash flow to enhance their compensation or on-the-job consumption, build corporate empires as monuments to their own egos, dispense perquisites and career advancement to protégés and flatterers, or sacrifice a portion of the shareholders' legitimate interests to satisfy the claims of diverse self-proclaimed stakeholders.

At the other extreme, critics see the mechanisms of direct and indirect restraint on managerial discretion in similar terms, but consider the consequences destructive. An accurate accounting, they claim, would typi-

I gratefully acknowledge support from the Brookings Institution and helpful comments from the participants in the Brookings conference. The views expressed here are my own and do not necessarily reflect those of the U.S. General Accounting Office.

cally show that the gains accruing to dealmakers and shareholders are offset by the losses imposed on employees, bondholders, customers of the acquired firm and its rivals (because of the company's greater market power in particular markets), and citizens in general (because of losses in tax revenues inflicted on the federal government). The identity of the principal losers may vary and there may be occasional efficiency gains from a change of management, but significant injuries to efficiency ramify much more broadly through the economy than the deals themselves. Takeover threats and high debt levels force management to focus on short-term results, on pain of dismissal or their firm's bankruptcy.[2]

The critics of restructuring give less credence to evidence of efficiency based on stock price behavior than do those favoring restructuring. Shareholders are not likely to be better informed than incumbent managers regarding the payoff for long-term corporate strategies: their vague sense of prospects makes them overly susceptible to the temptation of immediate returns blandished by the dealmakers. This distortion is made acute by institutional factors, such as a bias favoring short-term performance in the reward systems for institutional portfolio managers, that attenuate incentives to pay adequate attention to the long-term prospects. Led by managers forced to act as the passive servants of myopic shareholders, American corporations slide into economic decline.

My own perspective on corporate change is eclectic, evolutionary, and historical. It is eclectic because it acknowledges the diversity of restructuring activity and that the quests for a dominant explanation and normative verdict may prove futile. More significantly, it identifies an unexpected compatibility between the two polar interpretations. The key to this compatibility is high real interest rates. In the context of high real interest rates, the same anecdote can serve as a horror story for the viewers-with-alarm and as an exemplary case of capital market discipline for takeover advocates. High interest rates not only discourage investment, they encourage disinvestment. By a variety of channels they can destroy productive organizations. Such destruction may be viewed as economically efficient, provided that high market rates of return are believed to provide a socially appropriate rationale for the disinvestment.

The evolutionary perspective of this paper is, of course, the influence of evolutionary economics as propounded by Richard Nelson and me.[3] The evolutionary view of the business firm emphasizes imperfect information and calculation, routinized behavior, trial-and-error learning, and slow correction by environmental feedback.

The perspective is historical because it emphasizes that when the phenomenon examined is a dramatic episode that occurred at a particular time, the question "Why?" must be expanded to "Why *then*?" Explanations featuring considerations that have no chronological relation to the episode do not meet the challenge of the expanded question, whatever their appeal as responses to the short one.

This chapter first reviews some of the explanations for the wave of takeovers and restructuring in the 1980s, with particular attention to their historical relation to distinctive features of the period. It focuses on high real interest rates as a distinctive feature that has received little attention as a possible determinant of restructuring activity.[4] Next the chapter discusses the role of high real interest rates in relation to the problem of measuring the assets of a firm, and the numerous kinds of unconventional assets to which the economic logic of investment applies but that are not typically recognized as assets. What constitutes value-maximizing behavior can depend on the levels of unconventional assets present, and so can the incentives to seek control of a corporation. Finally, I address implicit contracts and breach of trust in relation both to the concept of unconventional assets and to whether shareholder gains are the results of rent transfers.

Corporate Restructuring in the 1980s: Why Then?

Corporate restructuring in the 1980s reduced managerial discretion in directing corporate development in general and using cash flow in particular. Dramatically increased leverage was only the most direct of several mechanisms that limited the choices of management in using cash flow. Therefore the fact that managers were so constrained strongly suggests that the divergence of interests between managers and shareholders was an important underlying issue.

Something more is required, however, to explain the timing, magnitude, and details of the developments. Merger and acquisition activity from 1980 to 1988 increased fivefold, with the main surge coming after 1983.[5] Leveraged buyouts, although always a modest fraction of the total activity, increased by a larger factor. Therefore the various hypotheses that feature conflicts between managers and shareholders as explanations for the events of the 1980s need to be supplemented with evidence that key conditions of these conflicts changed in ways that were either dramatic or unusually synchronized. The fact of conflict by itself does not pass the chronological test; Adolph Berle and Gardiner Means found that separation of corporate ownership and control was already widespread in the 1920s. If a starting date is to be assigned to this explanatory factor, it should presumably be no later than the late 1920s.[6]

Similarly, it may be that takeover premiums in the 1980s were partly paid for out of wage reductions forced on hourly labor or layoffs of redundant middle managers. These routes to increased profitability are hardly new, however. Why were they suddenly so important and why were they associated with takeovers and restructuring?

A plausible chronology is thus indispensable to an explanation of the restructuring wave, but the standards of plausible timing must not be emphasized too much. Undoubtedly, the phenomenon had a strong internal dynamic of its own; no isolated billiard ball produced runs of effects with attendant audible clicks. Rather, success bred success. The 1980s takeover activity had many of the attributes of good times in any industry or market. Successful innovations generated attention, imitation, and defensive maneuvering. Large quasi-rents accrued to the specialized resources involved in these activities, and more resources were attracted. All these resources, old and new, proceeded to look for more work. Whatever the original problem or stimulus may have been, the resulting major investment in "solutions" led to an intensive search for further profitable "problems," many of which might otherwise have escaped notice.

Numerous explanations for the restructuring are chronologically plausible. Indeed, the list is too lengthy to permit more than a brief presentation of some of the more prominent proposals.

The "technology" of corporate takeovers clearly advanced in the 1980s. The clearest and most widely cited example is the "invention" of original-issue high-yield bonds (junk bonds), first used in a takeover bid in 1984.[7] Although the timing of their appearance is about right for them to serve as an explanation, to ascribe a major role to them, one would have to think of them as a lever moving a lever moving the main phenomenon. They facilitated hostile acquisitions of large companies, extending the fear of attack into their boardrooms. Hostile tender offers, however, did not account for many mergers or acquisitions, and the dollar volume of merger and acquisition activity does not record all the defensive and quasi-voluntary restructuring moves that have displayed many of the same features and consequences as those that attend takeovers.[8] So, junk bonds facilitated some hostile takeovers, particularly large ones, which amplified managerial fears, which led to a greater receptivity to friendly takeovers and other restructuring measures.

Well before junk bonds appeared on the scene, other important developments had transformed the financial markets. In the inflationary environment of the late 1970s, borrowers competed for funds by offering higher yields. Financial innovations permitted this form of competition to escape from the restrictive box in which it had long been impounded, and the box itself was then largely dismantled by legislative action.[9] Borrowers courted investors from passbook savers to the managers of the largest pension funds with an ever-expanding array of new financial products. With their massive resources and activist strategies, institutional investors came into new prominence in the newly invigorated financial market. Playing to this clientele in particular, the deal makers found it easy to attract participation in schemes of a complexity and scale unthought of a few years earlier.

Along the way, attitudes toward acceptable levels of corporate debt changed dramatically. Why is a question virtually coextensive with the problem of explaining restructuring itself—in some cases the "restructuring" amounted essentially to more debt on the balance sheet. There were, however, some appropriately timed institutional changes that may have encouraged the use of debt: tax law changes in 1981 and 1986 and the new rules for chapter 11 bankruptcies established by the Bankruptcy Reform Act of 1978 (governing filings made after April 1, 1980).[10]

Intensified competition in output markets in the 1980s may also have energized restructuring activity. In some industries, tolerance for high wages and bloated corporate staffs eroded as profits came under pressure because of deregulation, the long-term trend toward internationalization of the economy, and the strong dollar early in the decade.[11] At the same time, the permissive antitrust policy of the Reagan years opened the way to restructurings that produced the functional equivalent of horizontal or market-extension mergers. According to a recent study of large hostile takeover contests, "Management buyout organizers and raiders thus serve as brokers working for the ultimate purpose of increased concentration. . . . The evidence is clear that the goal of divestitures is typically to realize gains from industry consolidation, not to improve performance through an incentive-intensive organizational form."[12]

Of all the circumstances that might account for the diverse phenomena of corporate restructuring, none is more plausibly linked to the results by chronology and logic than high real interest rates. As the inflation rate tumbled in the 1982 recession, nominal interest rates remained high, leading to unprecedented real rates of return on fixed income securities.[13] As the economy recovered, a rising federal deficit and weakening private saving held real rates high through the rest of the decade.

The evolution of real interest rates was dramatic. Margaret Blair and Martha Schary have presented various measures of the rates, including one computed as the nominal rate on Moody's Aaa-rated corporate bonds minus a three-year centered moving average of the percentage change in the GNP deflator.[14] This indicator of the cost of capital rose precipitously in 1980, relative to its previous twenty-five-year high in 1960. By 1984, as the takeover wave gained momentum, it was 3.34 times the 1960 peak. By 1988 it had declined to 2.24 times the 1960 peak. The stock market had to meet the rate-of-return challenge: in the early years of the 1980s, it did so mainly by keeping the numerators in price-earnings ratios low.

Most accounts of the takeover and restructuring wave give only passing attention to high interest rates.[15] In particular, accounts of the discipline that takeovers impose on managers often invoke the idea of "redeploying" assets and "moving resources to their highest-valued use." Such language, used without qualification, leaves the impression that cutbacks in investment and liquidations of assets were not a significant part of the story. The economic logic of adjustment to higher interest rates suggests, however, that such cutbacks and liquidations could be an important component of the response. The macroeconomic data of the 1980s seem to reveal this logic at work, showing domestic capital formation proceeding at a feeble pace that was sustained only with the aid of sharply increased capital inflows from abroad and an attendant sharp decline in net U.S. claims on foreigners. In the aggregate, the language of "redeployment" and "moving resources to the highest-valued use" misleads, unless it is plainly construed to include current consumption as the highest-valued use.

Without necessarily diagnosing "market failure," without denying the hostile takeover a constructive role in the corporate governance system, and certainly without any affront to economic theory, one can still assess some of the purported efficiency gains from takeovers as among the losses inflicted by a sharply reduced national saving rate.

Organizational Capital and Adjustment to Higher Interest Rates

Many criticisms of corporate restructuring allege damage to companies that is not captured by standard measures of financial health. These concerns can be linked to the observation that high interest rates promote investment cutbacks and liquidation, but the linkage depends on first expanding the concept of the assets and liquidation processes involved.

Unconventional Assets

The things a firm needs to carry on its business go well beyond anything that economic theory would call an input or that financial accounting would recognize as an asset or expense category.

Most fundamentally, for example, production requires coordination. Coordination is the result of organizational learning, which is mainly accomplished by "doing"—that is, by trial-and-error problem solving. Achieving coordination in a new firm or upon the introduction of a new process may be a good deal more expensive and time-consuming than maintaining coordination once effective organizational routines have been established. Maintaining coordination is certainly not cost free, however. In particular, employee turnover continually requires that new occupants of established organizational roles pick up the knowledge and skills required for the performance of those roles.

For accounting purposes, most costs of organizational learning are charged as costs of production at the time the learning occurs. In textbook economic theory, the standard approach is simply to assume firms are endowed with production functions and to ignore the costly processes by which they develop their routines. The idea that learning and technological change have investment aspects is, nevertheless, commonplace in the theoretical literature on these subjects.[16]

A similar situation exists with respect to other assets that are unconventional in the sense that they are ignored in financial accounting and in textbook economic theory. Like organizational routines, these assets are typically intangible and go unmeasured. The neglect of these assets in financial accounting and standard economic theory by no means implies that they have been left unanalyzed. There is at least one article on each, and a modest literature on many. In some cases, economists have gone beyond theorizing and developed estimates of their value.[17]

Reputational assets are built by behavior that forgoes current profit opportunities in the interest of affecting beliefs about future behavior, thus enhancing future profit opportunities. Ultimately, these assets correspond to beliefs of suppliers, consumers, and others in the system. A less tangible source of earning power would be hard to imagine, but that reputations do matter is equally hard to contest.

In a model developed by David Kreps, a firm's sole asset is its reputation for abstaining from exploiting its exchange partners.[18] Such a reputation is valuable because it opens the way to advantageous transactions that would otherwise be foreclosed by the transacting partner's rational wariness of being exploited. The firm may thus be conceived as a label to which a reputation and its value attach—and this reputation may survive repeated changes of transacting partners and firm owners. Each owner maintains the firm's reputation out of self-interested concern for sustaining the value of its reputational capital. Kreps's analysis provides, at least in an equilibrium context, a plausible explanation of how firms can induce employees to share some of the costs of firm-specific training in the face of the hazard that the employer might renege on a promise to let the investment be recouped later in higher pay.

Closely related logic is at work in some models where the private earning power associated with reputation is socially less desirable. A firm with market power may derive value from being known to deal harshly with new entrants to its market, even though, considering one entrant at a time, market-sharing accommodation might be more profitable.[19] Similarly, a firm may benefit from a willingness to endure a costly strike if its bargaining power in future negotiations is enhanced.

Unconventional assets in some ways akin to the reputational assets analyzed by Kreps were analyzed in some models of an earlier vintage. These treated the firm's transacting possibilities at a given time as founded on the effect of its past behavior rather than transacting partners' analysis of both the firm's behavior and motives. For example, E. S. Phelps and I considered the dynamics of price formation in an atomistic market that deviates from standard competitive theory in one key respect: firms have some short-run autonomy in pricing that derives from the (assumed) fact that it takes an actual price differential to move customers from one supplier to another.[20] In equilibrium, each firm charges the same price but winds up with its own stock of customers. The customer stock is an asset that could be cashed out, if the firm so wished, by raising prices and letting the customers slowly trickle away. A similar analysis of labor supply and the response to wage differentials was done by Dale Mortensen.[21]

Whatever the other merits of these models, each is plausible. Their principal affront to reality is not some flaw in their exposition of the influence of R&D, advertising, reputation for fair dealing, and so forth, but rather their exclusion of the matters that are focal in the other models. Although many real firms make all these sorts of investments, the models typically address a single departure from the conventional asset and input categories.

The idea that the ability of a firm to do business on any given day is strongly shaped by its holdings of unconventional assets is thus neither truly novel nor fully familiar. The various analyses of individual assets have introduced the idea that such assets are relevant to the functioning of real firms. But the idea remains somewhat unfamiliar because it is not part of the standard expositions of the firm in economics, accounting, finance, and law.[22] Further exploration of its implications may be useful.

Cash Flow and Valuation

As one reflects on the idea of a firm with diverse unconventional assets that do not appear on the balance sheet, a troubling question may arise: where are the returns to all these assets? More generally, shouldn't signs of their presence be detectable by examining indicators other than balance sheet entries?

The answer may be yes. The earning power of unconventional assets may be part of the explanation for a firm's market value exceeding its book value. Such discrepancies may, however, arise from other sources. Use of replacement cost rather than original cost valuations for conventional assets eliminates one major component of the discrepancy between market value and book value, leaving a residual factor (equal to Tobin's q minus one) that presumably reflects the market's appraisal of all the influences on future earnings that are not part of conventional accounting.[23] The existence of large takeover premiums suggests, however, that this appraisal must involve premises that are brought into question by a takeover attempt. Although the market is certainly not entirely blind to the earning power of unconventional assets, accounting conventions still may have an effect on firm valuation, especially when no alternative information is available. It is therefore useful to consider factors that influence the discrepancy between reports based on standard accounting and what a true economic accounting would reveal.

One important possibility regarding the missing earnings is that they are reinvested in unconventional assets. In a rapidly growing firm, accounting that recognized investments in unconventional assets would show lower current costs, higher earnings, higher retained earnings, and more rapidly rising total assets than standard accounting shows. When growth leveled off, the mix of errors would change: assets (unconventional ones included) would be greater than they appear on the standard accounts, as would equity and depreciation. Accounting earnings before interest would be correctly stated provided the new gross investment in unconventional assets hidden in current costs just matched the actual depreciation of those assets (at replacement value), and depreciation on conventional assets was accurately assessed. If earnings were computed net of interest on all the assets in an attempt at an approximate assessment of economic profit, the result would tend to be lower than that of a calculation based on standard accounting; the interest charge would be applied to the true, higher amount of assets.[24]

Interest Rates and Strategic Choices

How might the presence of unconventional assets affect the response of a firm to a substantial change in real interest rates, such as took place in the 1980s? Consider a firm in steady-state operation. Assume that it is operating in repetitive cycles, following established routines. It is not necessarily maximizing shareholder value, so there may be possibilities for increasing value through a policy change. The assessment of these possibilities is hindered, however, because publicly available information provides only an imperfect view of what is going on in the firm. The firm charges a price p per unit of output and incurs expenses m per unit for inputs that are being fully absorbed in current production—materials, energy, direct labor. The benefits from these expenditures derive entirely from their indispensability for current production. The net cash flow of the firm is also diminished by other costs, amounting to x per unit, the nature of which cannot be determined with any certainty by outside observers. Nevertheless, one can say what the firm is worth on the assumption that the prevailing pattern of steady-state operation continues indefinitely. If r is the appropriate rate of discount for the net cash flow received by shareholders, the *continuation value* of the firm is $V_c =$

$(1/r) (p - m - x)$ per unit output. (This continuation value corresponds to the market value of the firm only if the market agrees with the stated assumptions about the future of the firm.)

The unidentified costs x may be thought of as consisting of gross investment to maintain the stock of conventional and unconventional assets necessary to continue this routine performance, plus some expenses x_0 that have nothing to do with the ability of the firm to continue operating in this fashion (the subscript 0 stands for the value brought to the firm). The depreciation that needs to be covered can be represented as an (instantaneous) depreciation rate d times the replacement value of the stock of assets that supports production, k per unit output. Although the objects of the expenditure x_0 may be physically durable—for example, furniture for a continuing program to redecorate executive offices to an ever more luxurious standard—their durability is irrelevant to a forward-looking valuation. What matters is that the expenditure could be stopped without adverse consequences in either the short run or the long. The adverse consequences involved here are those that affect the residual income claimants of the firm, but it is also important to ask whether these expenditures not only detract from the value of the firm but are socially wasteful. They need not be, for they may consist in part of pure rent transfers. (Even overly luxurious offices presumably provide satisfaction for the executives that should be accounted as benefits in social cost-benefit analysis.)

Overall, $x = x_0 + dk$. The expenditure flow x is devoted to things that are clearly unnecessary and may or may not be durable plus things that are certainly durable and necessary but may or may not be conventionally accounted as assets. The important assumption is that outside observers cannot determine the individual values of x_0, d, and k. Ignorance regarding k may be partly attributable to imperfect knowledge of the amount and nature of unconventional assets present.

Does this ignorance matter? It does not matter to the value of the firm as long as the assumption is maintained of indefinitely continued steady-state operation. Various market participants might, of course, have different and changing opinions about the likely future values of p, m, r, x, and hence V—and thus have the basis for lively trading in the firm's stock. Indeed, given some assumptions about the correlations of the various parameters with other features of the economy—the return on the market portfolio, perhaps—more sophisticated financial analysis could be applied to valuing this firm without establishing any need to look inside x.

If, however, the firm contemplates a change of policy, perhaps occasioned by a change of managerial control, what is going on inside x may become highly relevant. If $x_0 > 0$, for example, an obvious move is to stop this cash drain (which is unnecessary by assumption) and increase the present value of the firm by x_0/r per unit of output. If $dk > 0$, the value of the firm might be further increased by getting it out of the steady state. For additional simplicity, assume that whatever conventional and unconventional assets are represented by k, they all depreciate at the same rate d, and none has any salvage value outside the firm. Assume also that x_0 is eliminated. The firm can be liquidated gradually by cutting gross investment to zero and letting the firm shrink by depreciation. For every unit of output produced before this *fadeaway* strategy is initiated, the present value returned is $V_F = (p - m)/(r + d)$.[25] For a given value of the product dk, V_F may be bigger than V_c if d is small and k is large. Note also that V_F does not depend on k at all, which is reasonable because under the fadeaway strategy the assets all represent sunk costs. On the other hand, V_c depends on both d and k, but only by way of their product.

Calculation reveals that (with $x_0 = 0$) V_c is larger than V_F when $(p - m)/k > r + d$. This makes familiar sense, because $r + d$ is the service price of the capital stock. The condition for making it worthwhile to keep replacing this capital as it wears out is that the return received per unit of capital at least suffice to cover the flow of interest and depreciation costs.

For a given value of the numerator in the continuation-value expression and a given interest rate, the incentives to change policies depend on the cost mix. (They also depend on the price of output, but it simplifies the discussion to assume that output units are chosen so that $p = 1$.) At least four dimensions of possible contrast are significant: the amount of outright waste x_0 relative to the amount of value-contributing expenses $m + dk$; the amount of necessary current expense m relative to the asset maintenance expenses dk; for given costs of asset maintenance, the extent to which the cost comes from high k and low d rather than the reverse; and the relative amounts of conventional and unconventional assets, to the extent that a high proportion of the latter leads to an underestimate of k and thus affects perceptions regarding the consequences of a policy change.

The various possibilities for enhancing value by a policy change are affected in different ways by interest rate changes. The simple waste elimination of cutting x_0 always increases value. In absolute dollar terms, however, it enhances value more when interest rates are low than when they are high. Recall also that the enhancement under discussion is the one assessed from the point of view of the recipients of the net cash flow. To the extent that x_0 consists of rent streams that are simply diverted from the managers formerly in control to those newly in control, it contributes to incentives to take control but is not a source of value enhancement for shareholders.

Although higher interest rates also reduce the value of the fadeaway strategy, they may make it more attractive relative to the continuation strategy. As r increases, the increment in value from abandoning continuation in favor of fadeaway increases, becoming positive at the point where $r + d = (p - m)/k$ (zero long-run *economic* profit from continuation). The gap increases sharply and subsequently narrows slowly as r rises further. Asymptotically, the values of the two strategies and of the difference between them all approach zero like $1/r$.

A mix of low m and high dk produces a higher value of the fadeaway strategy than the reverse mix because cash flow can initially be liberated at a higher rate without adversely affecting output. For a given value of dk, low d favors the fadeaway strategy because the adverse effects on output appear less quickly—or alternatively, high k is favorable because there is more wealth to liberate. Given the amount of conventional assets represented in k, the appeal of the fadeaway strategy increases with the level of unconventional assets.

Finally, the mix of conventional and unconventional assets makes no difference to the algebra, but it might make a difference to behavior. Assuming the intention is to continue to operate the business rather than sell or liquidate it outright, failure to maintain levels of conventional assets will be reflected by financial accounting and other management information systems. The pursuit of a fadeaway strategy with regard to conventional assets will be noticed and its implications assessed by market observers and firm participants. It could also speed the decline by encouraging the defection of the best talent.[26] Contemplation of these possibilities might induce reconsideration of the choice of strategy. By contrast, to the extent that slowly depreciating unconventional assets continue in the short term as an invisible source of current profitability, the cost savings from failing to maintain them presents a temptation not balanced by any adverse consequence that is made visible by standard accounting. Thus in addition to the effects that unconventional assets produce simply because they add to the capital intensity of production, there may be effects arising from a myopic failure to recognize that these assets must be maintained if their benefits are to continue.

Figure 3-1. Value of Hypothetical Firm at Various Interest Rates

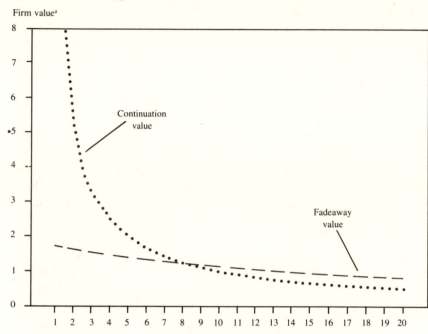

Source: Author's calculations.
a. Per dollar of initial output.

These relationships are illustrated in figures 3-1 and 3-2. Figure 3-1 shows the continuation and fadeaway values for the base case for various interest rates. In each of the three cases $p = 1.0$; values are shown per dollar of output at the time of the policy change. In the base case, $m = 0.7$, $k = 1.2$, and $d = 0.167$. Given these parameters, continuation has the higher value for real interest rates up to 8.3 percent. The top of figure 3-2 shows the difference between the fadeaway and continuation values for the base case and an alternative (low m, high k). Reducing m to 0.5 and raising k to 2.4, with d unchanged, leaves the continuation value unchanged, but increases the fadeaway value. As a result, fadeaway becomes superior at real interest rates above 4.17 percent. In the bottom panel of figure 3-2 (low d, high k), m is restored to 0.7 and k is held at 2.4 while d is decreased to 0.083. Again the continuation value is preserved and the fadeaway value is increased, lowering the crossover value of the interest rate to 4.17 percent.

If the firm is initially pursuing a continuation policy and the market values the firm accordingly, a rise in real interest rates will lower its value

Figure 3-2. Value of Hypothetical Firm, Difference between Fadeaway and Continuation Strategies

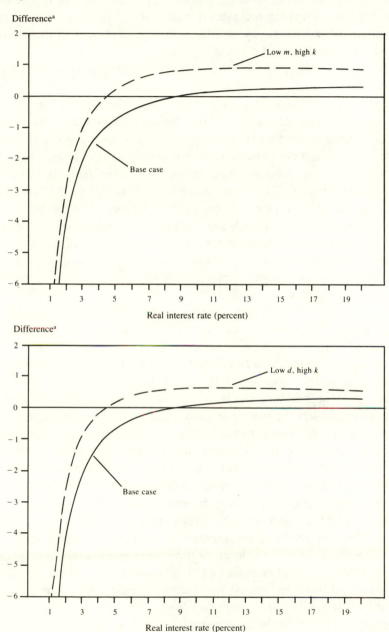

Difference[a]

Low m, high k

Base case

Real interest rate (percent)

Difference[a]

Low d, high k

Base case

Real interest rate (percent)

Source: Author's calculations.
a. Per dollar of initial output.

and may also make a switch to the fadeaway policy attractive. If such a switch requires a hostile takeover, a takeover premium may be registered. For example, as real interest rates increase from 4 percent to 6 percent, the premium explainable by such a scenario is 32.4 percent for low m, high k and 25.6 percent for low d, high k.

These same examples can serve to illustrate the consequences of misperceiving the firm's cost and asset mix. Imagine, for example, that the firm in the low m, high k variant is misperceived because half its capital consists of unconventional assets. Mistakenly identifying the depreciation on these unaccounted assets as true current expense, the market supposes that it is the base case firm. The interest rate rises from 4 percent to 6 percent, and acquirers who correctly perceive $m = 0.5$ offer a takeover premium of 30 percent, acquire the firm, adopt the fadeaway strategy, and make a profit. It does not matter whether the acquirers correctly perceive the expenditures that would be required to maintain unconventional assets because they have no intention of maintaining them. Observers, however, are puzzled: the identification of the firm as the base case would, if correct, make the acquirers' behavior unprofitable even at a 6 percent interest rate.

This account of the fadeaway strategy, which envisages the firm as continuing to operate but on an ever smaller scale, is of course much too simple. Because assets depreciate at different rates, the firm either has to adjust its routines to accommodate the use of the various assets in different proportions, or spend some cash to retard the decline of the more rapidly depreciating assets, or dispose of some of the more slowly depreciating assets, or use some combination of these approaches. In some cases the economics of the fadeaway strategy may be present even while the physical volume of production is temporarily maintained: the forgone investments may mean failure to build unconventional assets in ways that would permit the company to offer new products with competitive price and performance characteristics.

The same basic points could be developed in an optimal control framework. The firm would be represented as maximizing present value by continuously optimizing the levels of investment in a number of different assets, with investment rates limited by adjustment costs. Given an initial stationary position, an interest rate increase would set the firm moving toward a new equilibrium at generally lower levels of assets. Early in the adjustment the firm would disgorge cash as it held gross investment below maintenance levels for the assets. Such an adjustment pattern is no more than a special case, though perhaps an underemphasized one, of the familiar point that high interest rates depress investment. The image commonly evoked is cancelation of a project that represents net growth of the firm, perhaps in a new and adventurous direction. Gradual disinvestment in the firm's accustomed line of business is equally plausible so far as the economic logic is concerned.

A thoroughgoing optimization approach would also suggest, of course, that the shift from a continuation to a fadeaway strategy would take place smoothly, promptly, and without commotion. If firms are always maximizing present value (for residual claimants), an increase in the interest rate is no more an occasion for a hostile takeover or defensive restructuring than any other economic change. However, the managerial skills, character traits, and orientations appropriate to maintaining or growing a business may be very different from those appropriate to driving the business into the ground (even if in a way that maximizes present value). If that is true, the switch to a fadeaway strategy can reasonably be expected to be attended by changes in management, or threats to terminate the incumbent management that are severe enough to drive it in directions that are unfamiliar and not favored by its own standards.

Although cutbacks in investment provide a unifying theme, firms' responses to higher interest rates will be as diverse as their initial situations. Rapid sales growth might give way to slower growth, moderate growth to retrenchment, and gradual decline to immediate liquidation. The fadeaway strategy evoked above is most clearly relevant when the interest rate increase has the effect of switching the firm's policy into retrenchment from a previous position of stasis or moderate growth. One might say that fading away is most likely to be observed as the fate of a formerly healthy cash cow placed on a strict cost-control diet.

Patterns of slowed accumulation or actual dissipation of assets should also vary according to the assets' characteristics and their role in corporate earning power and growth. R&D spending is a prominent example of investment in an unconventional asset, and whether such spending is reduced by corporate restructuring has received particular attention.[27] According to the most careful empirical work, the answer seems to be an equivocal no so far as acquisition activity per se is concerned, but yes regarding the increased leverage that may either complement or substitute for (that is, defend against) acquisition. For my purposes, it is more relevant to note that neither acquisition activity nor leverage increases have been common among firms and industries that are R&D intensive. The reason may be that these firms and industries tend to have good underlying growth prospects, and the interest rates in the 1980s were not high enough to make them plausible fadeaway candidates. That R&D intensive firms and industries are rarely candidates for restructuring, however, does not contradict the logic of the fadeaway argument.[28]

How Free Is the Cash Flow?

In Michael Jensen's theory of takeover activity, the key variable, free cash flow, is defined as "cash flow in excess of that required to fund all of a firm's projects that have positive net present values when discounted at the relevant cost of capital."[29] His theory implies that takeovers are essentially shareholder rebellions against managers who use free cash flow for ends of their own rather than paying the cash to the shareholders. In the tradition of some earlier scholars, especially Robin Marris, Jensen sees managers as strongly disposed to actions that do not maximize values from the shareholders' point of view, and the market for corporate control is where clashes between managerial and shareholder interests are played out.[30]

Significant problems appear when one attempts to test the concept of free cash flow empirically. Most of the problems are associated with *free*, that is, with determining what portion of accounting cash flow (aftertax earnings plus depreciation) might be absorbed by projects that pass Jensen's test for net present value. The usual practice is to identify variables that are plausible proxies for investment opportunities and to employ these to estimate the separate influences of actual cash flow itself and of investment opportunity. The theory predicts that takeover activity or other activity related to corporate control should be higher when actual cash flow is higher (opportunity proxies constant) and lower when the proxies signal more favorable investment opportunity (cash flow constant).[31]

So far as I am aware, no study arrives at a free cash flow variable by subtracting from cash flow the estimated cost of profitable investment projects. I assume, however, that Jensen's intended interpretation of free cash flow is not so literal minded. Rather, the proposal is that one will find it fruitful to think about a corporation's governance and financial management "as if" free cash flow were a reasonably sharply defined amount. Quite likely there is no list of projects ranked by net present value. If there is, it is probably far from an exhaustive list of all the investment activities the company is undertaking because it will not include investments in the unconventional assets and probably in many conventional ones as well. For example, replacement investments may be excluded if they are modest or if they relate to market positions that the company is strategically committed to maintaining. If there are calculations of net present value, "at the relevant cost of capital" or otherwise, they are most likely included in individual project descriptions and regarded as *among* the significant indicators of the attractiveness of a project.[32] Further, project descriptions (including calculations of present value) are unreliable. The shakiness of the estimates and the differing perspectives of participants in decisionmaking may cause disputes. All these attributes of a real decision process are likely to be present, even assuming that the managers are pursuing increases in shareholder value in an exemplary fashion. They can be present simply because information is imperfect and costly to acquire, and different participants have different information; also, calculation is costly, time-consuming, and subject to error. Thus nobody knows how much free cash flow there is because nobody knows what the actual returns to various investments will be. In particular, observers disagree about the importance of maintaining or increasing investments in unconventional assets.

Compared with prospective investment returns that are always unpredictable, the amount of the check received for shares tendered is certain. When high current yields are available on safe investments and even higher yields on risky ones, rational calculation and irrational myopia pull in the same direction. The resulting force is all the stronger because the ultimate sources of business earnings power are incompletely identified and poorly understood. Although it is a convenient fiction to suppose that the level of free cash flow is a definite and knowable thing, in practice it may be difficult to distinguish the siren song of free cash flow from the appeal of a free lunch.

With no more boldness than is required to assume the existence of free cash flow in the first place, one can plausibly conjecture that a proper accounting might show that cash flow liberated through takeovers and thus restructurings arises from several sources. It might arise from cancelation of investments that are uneconomic from the company's standpoint but may not be so from a social standpoint (recognizing that the high interest rates may reflect flawed policy and thus pose the problem of "second best" policy choices in other areas). Cash flow could also be liberated by cancelation of investments that are sound from a private viewpoint but are forgone because of imperfect information, calculation errors, and irrationalities. These might include imperfect ability to measure returns, limited opportunities to convince shareholders and their portfolio-managing agents that the returns will be forthcoming, and disincentives to reveal information supporting the estimate of future returns because revelation will have adverse effects on the returns. The sources could also include failures of group decisionmaking in contexts where the short-run view has strong external validation and the long-run view does not, and participation in a general cultural disposition toward a short-run outlook that goes well beyond what prevailing interest rates rationally justify.[33] All these distortions are likely to be magnified in rough proportion to the importance of unconventional assets in the situation.

Expectations and Implicit Contracts as Unconventional Assets

Arithmetic and newspaper accounts combine to lend credibility to the interpretation of hostile takeovers offered by Andrei Shleifer and Lawrence Summers.[34] They contend that the premiums the shareholders of acquired firms receive in takeovers consist largely of transfers from employees of those firms. Under new control the firm reneges on the promises made by its former executives to its employees, and the proceeds of this breach of trust are largely captured by shareholders of the acquired firm as a result of the competition among potential acquirers.

The relevant arithmetic derives from the observation that labor costs are typically a large proportion of total costs (or sales revenue), but profits are relatively small. In the plausible example presented by Shleifer and Summers, a 5 percent overpayment to employees reduces the market value of the firm by 35 percent.[35] Small wonder, then, that a raider might succeed by offering shareholders a 30 percent gain in market value to be achieved by reducing wages by 5 percent, leaving 5 percent of the value of the firm as the gross return to the raider. In fact, the example understates the force of their point by neglecting preexisting leverage. It is the equity holders who have to be persuaded of the desirability of the takeover, and in the first approximation the gain in the market value of the firm accrues entirely to them. The percentage gain that can be offered the shareholders in this hypothetical deal is the 30 percent divided by the shareholders' initial share of the market value of the firm.

Newspaper accounts, corroborated by scholarly analyses, confirm that sacrifices by employees are important consequences of takeovers. Shleifer and Summers recount as their primary example the takeover of TWA by Carl Icahn. A conservative estimate of the value of wage concessions extracted from the pilots, flight attendants, and machinists amounted to one and one-half times the takeover premium, $600 million in wage concessions against a takeover premium of at most $400 million.[36] And because agreements between Icahn and the unions largely precluded any cutback in operations, the estimate of gains from the concessions was not qualified in any direct way by the possibility that significant output was forgone. Although Sanjai Bhagat, Shleifer, and Robert Vishny emphasize gains from horizontal mergers as the primary sources of takeover premiums, they too include numerous cases in which layoffs may have contributed substantially.[37] Finally, many journalistic accounts of takeovers and restructurings, such as the Safeway leveraged buyout, provide vivid examples of the pecuniary and nonpecuniary costs that a change in control can impose on employees.[38] These examples offer support to those who present the most negative assessments of the motivating forces and consequences of battles for corporate control.

As noted earlier, the gains achievable by expropriating employees' interests can provide an adequate incentive-based explanation of corporate restructuring in the 1980s only if a good answer can be provided for "why *then*?" Whether the analysis emphasizes pay cuts or layoffs, the obvious question is why excess labor cost was allowed to accumulate in the first place.[39] The same answers to the timing question that have been discussed for conflicts between managers and shareholders can be applied to the specific managerial sin of permitting bloated payrolls. Perhaps the invention of junk bonds facilitated the takeovers that permitted the shareholders to discipline the managers who had let the payrolls get out of control. Here, however, I focus on the tendency of high real interest rates to promote disinvestment in unconventional assets related to long-term relationships between firms and employees. Similar considerations would apply to relationships with suppliers and other transacting partners.

The treatment of these issues by Shleifer and Summers is a convenient jumping-off point for the discussion. They discuss the possible increases in efficiency resulting from long-term relationships with employees, the prohibitive costs of fully organizing these relationships through explicit contracting, and the resulting economic role of implicit contracts sustained largely by trust. (They refer both to Kreps's reputation model and to the point that people who are trustworthy may tend to wind up in positions where trustworthiness is valuable.) Not only is it possible that hostile takeovers enrich shareholders primarily through rent transfers that involve a breach of trust, but the breach of trust may itself have detrimental long-term consequences for the efficiency of the economy as a whole. Each such event diminishes the prospects for establishing efficient long-term relationships in the future. "The larger the fear of takeovers spreading through the economy, the more severe are the limitations on contracting, and the larger is the welfare loss."[40]

This is an important line of argument, but it has some loose ends. First, the concept of an implicit contract requires more critical scrutiny when the supposed contract is being breached than when it is being observed. When the contract is being observed, it does not greatly matter whether the arrangement has genuine kinship to an explicit contract (involving an exchange of promises but suffering from the legal defect of vagueness) or whether the situation could be better described in terms of individual expectations that are borne out over an extended period. When the relationship breaks down, however, the appropriateness of the language of "breach" (with its presumed behavioral implications) depends critically on what the original basis of the relationship was. An objective assessment of that may be hard to come by, considering that the agreement was vague in the first place and much may have occurred since it was entered into.

Assume A recruits B to work for her, giving the recruiter's usual biased account of the advantages of the position and noting that it is permanent in the sense that if B does a good job he can expect to be kept on. Does B have an implicit long-term employment contract? Fifteen years later, B is still working for A and has in fact done a good job, but there has been no further discussion about the permanence of the job. If he did not have an implicit long-term contract a week after he was hired, does he have one after fifteen years? A machine is invented that offers a low-cost replacement for most of the workers B supervises, and B is let go along with those workers. Is that a breach of trust? Will B become less trusting, or will he philosophically accept A's version of the original understanding: although she had no specific reason to think at the time that her need for B's services would not continue and has proved her good faith in that regard for fifteen years, she certainly did not and could not rule out the possibility that something might come up. She has to earn a living; B has to earn a living. And B no longer makes a contribution working for A. What does economics or morality suggest as a reply to A?

A second loose end in Shleifer's and Summers's analysis is whether the firm that breaches its implicit contracts in the aftermath of a takeover is itself likely someday to need the reputation it forfeits. If the answer is yes, the action might be a mistake. If the answer is no, something must have changed to make the reputation less valuable. In that case, the same issues arise that surfaced in the case of A and B. Trust is a valuable thing, but so is the capacity for adjustment to changed economic circumstances. The appropriate trade-offs are not at all clear in principle. When real interests are at stake, contention, anger, and disappointment are to be expected. "Implicit contract" and "breach of trust" tend to act as a thumb on the rhetorical scale, tipping the balance in favor of trust and against adjustment.

These strands can be brought together and connected to interest rates as a determinant of the economic context of transacting relationships. An easy case is the suggestion that a firm might be making a mistake by expropriating its current workers and forfeiting a reputation that would be useful in the future. Such behavior is indeed likely to be a mistake if the interest rate is low enough, but it is sure not to be a mistake if the interest rate is high enough: at a high enough interest rate there is no economic future. An increase in real interest rates is therefore a theoretically straightforward explanation for an epidemic of reneging on implicit contracts. Such behavior is just a facet of the general enhancement of the value of the fadeaway strategy; cashing out reputational assets is more profitable than maintaining them.

There is a related but more subtle theoretical point. Suppose two firms have had an advantageous long-term relationship in a context where uncertainty and the need for continuing adjustment limits the effectiveness of formal contracting as a governance mode. The relationship is supported by safeguards, but fundamentally it is held together by its future: last year's deal is successfully consummated today only because failure to do so sacrifices the possibility of the next deal. Then the interest rate goes up. Soon thereafter a difficulty arises in the relationship that is novel in detail but no more consequential than many that have been successfully overcome in the past. In the new context, one party might review the situation somewhat as follows. Accepting this proposal for adjustment of the existing contract looks expensive to our side, considering the growth of past-due accounts receivable and the dour look on our banker's face. By comparison, the prospective gains from maintaining the relationship through the next deal seem noticeably smaller. Perhaps our old friend is in the same fix as we are, or worse, and his proposal reflects this. Maybe he will not be around to deal with next year anyway. It may be a question of survival for him, but is for us too. Tell him we cannot agree and will litigate if we have to.

Pushed by this compelling thought, two parties who would actually

benefit from continuing to deal with each other, high interest rates not-
withstanding, may fail to do so. This illustrates the role of the interest
rate as a determinant of cooperative behavior in iterated games.[41]

In short, the fact that reputation will be valuable in the future does
not make it immune to sacrifice in the cause of bolstering cash flow when
interest rates have increased. Such a sacrifice may be inefficient from a
systemwide viewpoint or even from the viewpoint of the joint interest of
just two transacting partners, but that does not make the sacrifice irrational from the individual actor's viewpoint.

The other fork of the interpretive choice discussed earlier was the
possibility that something has changed, something that makes the firm's
reputation with its employees less valuable than it was before. The something may, again, be related to the interest rate. Consider two firms, one
of which has been growing at 4 percent a year, the other at 1 percent.
The interest rate increases, and optimal growth rates fall by 3 percent in
both cases. The firm that was growing at 4 percent a year is still growing
and needs new employees. If new employees need firm-specific training
before their full value can be realized, the growing firm needs to persuade
them that, one way or another, it will pay for the training. They will not
be asked to share in the training costs and then confront a wage no higher
than what they could have been earning elsewhere. The shrinking firm,
however, has overcapacity in an unconventional asset: there are more
trained employees available for hire than it needs. It is in a position to
exert monopsony power to ensure that it, and not the workers, receives
all the quasi-rents from firm-specific knowledge. Paying a bit more than
the opportunity wage of the workers suffices for the declining firm with
more than enough trained employees to draw on. It does not suffice for
the growing firm, which must either accept the full cost of the training
directly or behave in a way that persuades prospective new hires that any
contribution they make can be recouped.

In this contrast, the point of zero growth has a special significance. A
change of character is most to be expected from firms that are pushed
from growth into decline. Those that continue to grow even in an environment of high interest rates will need to maintain their reputations as
good employers.

Conclusion

Takeovers and restructurings can reasonably be viewed with considerable ambivalence. They may force managers to conform to what the

market says is right: many of the changes imposed may improve efficiency when evaluated at prevailing prices and interest rates. To the extent that rent transfers are involved, the hardships and sacrifices entailed may be little different from those that a progressive economy usually requires. If prevailing interest rates are not accurate measures of social time preference, however, much of the performance may be destructive and the sacrifices may be occurring in the cause of regress rather than progress.

In principle, the best thing to do to correct the situation would be to bring down real interest rates. The recession of the early 1990s provided a temporary fix. In the longer term, reducing real interest rates requires raising the national saving rate, preferably back to the levels typical of 1950–79. As a first and indispensable policy step, the federal deficit should be reduced. But since that problem seems so intractable, what should be done if real interest rates cannot be reduced? One might then prefer to protect, somehow, the "inefficient" investment programs that the raiders attack. (That would mean suffering the self-indulgence of empire builders in preference to that of raiders, traders, and empire dismantlers.) At a minimum, it would be desirable to try to shape an institutional context that does not encourage a short-term outlook to a degree even greater than high real interest rates imply.[42]

If the role of high interest rates is acknowledged, the verdict on the corporate control struggles of the 1980s turns out to be mixed even when the enthusiasts of capital market discipline are conceded most of their argument. Several other qualifications ought to be included, however. In particular, the activism of the dealmakers and the furious pace at which control struggles proceed make it unlikely that forgone future earnings are being assessed with reasonable objectivity and sophistication. Indeed, real sophistication may be a utopian goal for the time being, given the problems of assessing the earning power of unconventional assets.

Returning to the basic empirical issue, shareholder gains may be coming at the expense of the future of the companies and the national economy to an even greater degree than prevailing interest rates can justify and to a greater degree than we now know how to calculate.

Comment by Gordon Donaldson

Sidney Winter's paper presents a point of view I find congenial. In explaining the events of the 1980s with regard to corporate restructuring ("why *then*?"), the list of factors that influenced the course of business history must be expanded well beyond phenomena purely of the capital market. I, too, have a perspective that is "eclectic, evolutionary, and historical." My views are primarily driven by my own research into the causes and consequences of restructuring by U.S. corporations in the 1980s, beginning with the "why then" question concerning the structure in the 1960s and 1970s.

The 1980s were marked by substantial "efficiency gains" to the benefit of equity holders. These gains were attributed to the energetic intervention of various corporate and individual activists. As Winter suggests, these were in part aggregate efficiency gains, resulting from a newly invigorated and sharply refocused management (new or old) and from substantial transfers from the other constituent interests that lost power in a changed economic and competitive environment. In some cases the "efficiency gains" also included wealth consumption, to the extent that in servicing the excessive debt that funded purchase or defense, managers did not maintain organizational capital and therefore placed their firms' future competitive advantage at risk.

A number of evolutionary changes at work in the 1970s challenged the established corporate and financial strategy and structure and set the stage for the restructuring of the 1980s. Winter enumerates many of these, including bankruptcy law and regulatory enforcement. To this list I would add two that seem particularly important to me.

One factor was a generational change in attitudes toward the capital markets and risk taking. The executives of the 1960s and 1970s had come to adulthood in the 1930s against a background of collapsed confidence in equity markets and lending institutions. The capital market was anything but perfect. Debt was a four-letter word. The key to personal and corporate survival was self-sufficiency and independence from the capital markets.

A second, and related, factor was the concept of the individual corporation as an investment vehicle. In the 1960s there were still many investors whose portfolios consisted of a few companies and who were motivated by a long-term, buy-and-hold investment strategy. Management could conceive of an identity of interest among loyal shareholders, employees, and career managers for whom the individual enterprise was *the* portfolio and within which growth, superior return, and diversification of risk could be realized. But the 1970s accelerated the transformation of the typical shareholder into a diversified investor for whom the market was the portfolio and the individual firm an incidental data point. The 1980s brought this transformation dramatically to the attention of management. As a result there was a growing recognition among people working in corporate investment of the need to maximize return per dollar invested and to focus on "pure plays" in which the firm had a unique and sustainable competitive advantage. In the 1980s it was the professional investor, not the corporation, who assembled the portfolio to suit the objectives of particular investment funds.

Winter's principal thesis is that in explaining the restructuring of the 1980s, insufficient attention has been given to the influence of the rising cost of capital in slowing and redirecting corporate investment. The basic argument makes sense: persistently low rates of saving and rising interest rates would at some point have a harmful effect on new investment. However, long-term capital budgeting decisions are not highly sensitive to modest or short-term swings in the interest rate. Broadly speaking, companies fund strategies, not projects, and product market strategies are built around imprecise expectations of future rates of return conditioned by the presumed state of the economy, the industry, and the response of competitors. When the imprecise expectations of interest rates are factored in, the rates rarely become the focus of the investment decision unless a dramatic and persistent shift in rates is clearly under way. In my own view, although interest rates may have had some influence on the restructuring of the 1980s, they were overshadowed by forces in the product market and capital market that had transferred power from investors of human capital to investors of financial capital—with dramatic results.

Winter's cost-of-capital argument is linked to the significance of "reputational" or organizational capital for which the funding is conventionally expensed rather than capitalized. Rising cost of capital is said to induce a fadeaway strategy under which such expenditures are not maintained and long-term competitive strength is eroded. Although I accept the importance of these invisible assets, which may be critical to long-term profitability, I would argue that it is not the cost of capital alone but the total servicing of highly leveraged capital structures that drives out all expenditures not critical to short-term profit. Thus while I agree with Winter's conclusion, I consider the causal forces more complex and the causal relationships hard to define.

Winter properly calls attention to the overgeneralizations sometimes associated with the free cash flow theory of leveraged buyout efficiencies. At worst, the theory can be a convenient rationalization for economies that place the corporate future at risk. In particular, Andrei Shleifer's and Lawrence Summers's argument, cited by Winter, is persuasive that substantial economies may come from transfers of wealth from other constituencies whose bargaining power has weakened.[43] Though it is impossible to document, the loss of trust by career employees that is essential to the effectiveness of the product market must at some point affect the collective commitment and competitive strength of the firm.

In this regard, Winter cites the "vivid" example of the LBO of Safeway, rightly pointing to costs imposed on employees. Safeway management conceded that while the LBO was very good for managers and shareholders, it had a mixed record for employees. Some good employees lost their jobs through no fault of their own, and others held on only by accepting major wage reductions. Like Winter, I do not make judgments as to whether these transfers of wealth were economically justified, but I make the point to underline a major source of LBO efficiency and the practical significance of breach of trust.

In conclusion, though I disagree on the relative importance of higher interest rates in explaining the financial restructuring of corporate enterprise in the 1980s, I am very much in sympathy with Winter's cautionary comments on how to interpret the results and with his general policy recommendations. I would echo his concluding sentence: "Returning to the basic empirical issue, shareholder gains may be coming [to some extent] at the expense of the future of the companies, [their employees] and the national economy . . . and to a greater degree than we now know how to calculate."

Comment by John C. Coffee, Jr.

Sidney Winter's provocative paper turns on two ideas: the premise that takeover targets have significant "unconventional assets" that are intangible, unmeasured, and probably unmeasurable, and the claim that high interest rates in the 1980s made it rational for takeover entrepreneurs to neglect these unconventional assets and adopt a "fadeaway" strategy. Obviously, such a theory suggests that takeovers do not increase social wealth, even if they maximize private wealth. In particular, it supplies a rival interpretation to Michael Jensen's well-known theory that corporate managers hoard free cash flow within the firm even when they lack net present value investment opportunities.[44]

Although Winter's analysis is creative, I doubt that it explains the data. Few will question his claim that high interest rates can produce disinvestment and underdepreciation; however, his attempt to place "un-conventional assets" at center stage of the takeover debate will produce greater controversy. It will offend purists' preference for parsimony in model building because it invents and relies on a new and largely unver-ifiable category: unconventional assets. For efficient-market theorists it fails to explain why the market cannot detect such underfunding of the implicit depreciation reserves on these unconventional assets. Neither of these objections gives me much trouble, because I accept his claim that there are unconventional assets. Still, I have trouble with the mechanics of his theory. For high interest rates to supply a motive for takeovers, it is necessary to assume that Winter's fadeaway scenario works essentially as follows: the bust-up takeover entrepreneur pays a premium for the target, intending to run its businesses for only a few years. Accordingly, the acquirer does not replace or restore these unconventional assets be-cause it believes it can sell the firm at an inflated value that does not reflect the deterioration and depreciation done over the interim to these assets. In short, from such a perspective, this is a fool's market in which damaged goods are being dumped on unsuspecting buyers because of their inability to monitor the adequacy of the implicit depreciation and amortization reserves for unconventional assets that do not appear on the company's balance sheet.

Although such transactions may have occurred, the informational asymmetry does not seem sufficiently great to work as a generalized explanation for takeovers in the 1980s. There are at least three problems with such a theory. First, it does not fit well with the data now available about takeovers—in particular, acquirers' tendency to focus on highly diversified conglomerate firms.[45] I know of no reason to suppose that conglomerates have a higher level of unconventional assets than less diversified firms, and thus I am puzzled as to how Winter's theory of unconventional assets can explain the tendency of takeover entrepreneurs to focus on diversified firms.

A second problem is that Winter's theory seems to presuppose that at some point the deteriorated, posttakeover firm will be sold by the take-over entrepreneur at an inflated price to an underinformed buyer. But the ultimate buyers of the target's assets during the 1980s were either other firms in the same industry[46] or the management of the division in a leveraged buyout. These are precisely the buyers that would know the most about the assets they are acquiring. Thus any inflation in the price they paid seems better explained by the market power they were acquir-ing (and by the relaxation of antitrust enforcement in the 1980s). Put differently, the takeover entrepreneurs who engaged in bust-up takeovers in the 1980s seem best viewed as business brokers.[47] Essentially, they arbitraged the difference between the firm's stock price and the asset value of its various divisions (as going concerns). At least to the extent that these entrepreneurs sold the assets they purchased to other firms in the same industry, it is difficult to accept Winter's contention that under-informed buyers were systematically overreached by the fadeaway strat-egy. Indeed, when one is selling to well-informed buyers, a fadeaway strategy of not replacing critical assets sounds disastrous.

A third problem with the unconventional asset theory is that it over-looks the mirror-image possibility of unconventional liabilities. This may sound facetious, but it is not so intended. Firms could have intangible liabilities as well as intangible assets. These liabilities could also explain why the ratio of a firm's market value to the replacement cost of its assets (Tobin's q) could be low. For example, the large conglomerate bureauc-racy might be inefficiently slow or indecisive about reaching decisions that nondiversified firms reached more quickly. Its multiple hierarchical layers of executives, each redundantly reviewing the last's decision, there-fore would represent not only an excessive investment in monitoring but also a barrier to efficient and timely decisionmaking. Obviously, this suggestion challenges the Williamsonian model of the "M-form" firm; less obviously, it provides an alternative interpretation to Jensen's free cash flow hypothesis because it posits not simply a bias toward earnings retention within the conglomerate but a dysfunctional organizational structure that creates negative synergy. If one accepts this premise that the organizational form of the large conglomerate could have become inefficient by the 1980s, then it is more likely that takeovers would be viewed as efficiency-promoting. Of course, unconventional assets and unconventional liabilities could coexist, even in the same firm. Also, high interest rates could increase the incentive to let some assets deteriorate. But to the extent that the claim of hidden unconventional assets can be countered by the parallel claim that there are also hidden liabilities, it loses much of its explanatory power. What Winter views as a socially inefficient fadeaway can alternatively be viewed as efficient liquidation, depending on whether one emphasizes unconventional assets or unconventional liabilities.

These objections do not deny, however, that there could be an incentive for the takeover bidder to let some unconventional assets deteriorate. Specifically, the acquirer's rational incentive would be to let those intangible assets deteriorate over its period of interim ownership that could not be effectively conveyed to others. Which are these assets? In particular, the acquirer firm's reputational capital cannot easily be liquidated or transferred (if the firm as a whole is being sold off piecemeal to other firms in related industries).[48] Thus, there could be an incentive to behave opportunistically to bondholders, employees, and other constituencies because such conduct would not taint the firm's assets in the hands of their eventual, long-term owner (which has its own reputational capital).

Before unconventional assets can supply a broader explanation for takeovers, however, one needs to identify some proxy for unconventional assets that can be measured. All proxies are imperfect, but the closest that I can think of is research and development expenditures. Many have feared R&D cuts as a result of takeovers. Yet, the evidence seems to show to the contrary that the targets of takeovers are not R&D–intensive companies. In the fullest study to date, Bronwyn Hall reports that neither target nor bidder appears to have reduced R&D expenditures significantly in the wake of a takeover (although some linkage was observed between increased leverage and reduced R&D investment).[49] Andrei Shleifer and Robert Vishny conclude more generally that, aside from LBOs, "there is not much evidence that takeovers result in large capital spending cuts."[50]

Of course, R&D could be a poor proxy or one limited to a small subset of the general population. Thus it may be useful to consider some specific takeovers. Possibly the most dramatic takeover of the 1980s (and at the time the largest) was the battle over Revlon, which was ultimately won by Ronald Perelman.[51] Perelman was a known takeover raider and thus fits Winter's description of the sort of person who would buy a firm to resell it after first running down its unconventional assets. What did Perelman do once in control of Revlon? The record is fairly clear: he halted the trend toward diversification started by the previous management, sold off the health care division, and refocused the company on its core business: cosmetics. In fact, the previous management had reduced the investment and advertising budget of the cosmetics division to support expansion into health care, but under Perelman this was reversed. Following the acquisition, Revlon substantially increased its investment in cosmetics and in fact tripled its advertising budget.[52] This is only one anecdote, but it certainly suggests that even classic takeover raiders do not necessarily reduce funding for those businesses they deem to have profitable opportunities for growth. Rather, they focus on selling off the fringe businesses that surround the core business.

In 1991 Revlon sold some of its core cosmetics lines to Procter & Gamble.[53] Does this potentially confirm Winter's fadeaway thesis? I think not. Rather, it underscores the importance of the identity of the buyer in a selloff after a takeover. The new data reveal very clearly that the typical buyer is either a company in the same line of business as the divested division or the management of the divested division. A head-to-head competitor such as Procter & Gamble has considerable strategic intelligence about its principal rivals, such as Revlon, and usually knows if the latter's business is declining. If it pays a premium, this is most likely for market power. In the other typical case—the LBO—the incumbent operating management that buys the division knows even more than the senior management selling it and has even less reason to overpay (since it is not acquiring market power). If instead the buyers in selloffs had been public shareholders in initial public offerings or in other diversified conglomerates inclined to hoard free cash flow, then such a market failure story would be more credible. The evidence suggests, however, that underinformed buyers are not a factor in the market for divested assets. If they are not, the fadeaway strategy cannot supply a motive for takeovers.

At times, the Winter thesis uses arguments that may render it nonfalsifiable. At the conference at which he delivered his paper, I and others voiced the concern that his focus on the target's balance sheet ignored the target's income statement. Even if the assets are unconventional and thus hidden, their presence should show up through generating additional cash flows. Yet this seems not to be the case, as the available evidence shows "that acquired firms are less profitable than those buying them."[54] In his revised paper, Winter advances a different argument for the fate of the missing earnings attributable to unconventional assets. At this point, nothing becomes verifiable. Both the unconventional assets and their missing earnings elude measurement. Perhaps, such assets and earnings are better described not as unconventional, but as phantom.

The now documented pattern of selloffs and refocusing on the target's core business following the target's acquisition can be better explained in other ways. First, the pattern may simply reflect the increasing oligopolization of some markets in the wake of weak antitrust enforcement (a trend that began in the 1980s). Second, it strongly suggests the inefficiency of the large multidivisional corporation as an organizational form. Third, a significant portion of the takeover premium (probably 25 percent or slightly more)[55] may be attributable to the staff reductions and layoffs that the acquirer intends to make through consolidating its business with that of the target. This could be either opportunistic or efficient, depending on additional factors not here relevant.

This brings me to the "why then" part of Winter's account of takeovers. He focuses on the role of high interest rates, but the more striking phenomenon in my judgment is the stock market's sudden distaste for the large conglomerate firm, which had formerly traded at a premium. Of course, the market could have simply watched the performance of most conglomerate acquisitions and come to the conclusion that they generally did not work. However, an alternative possibility is that, quite apart from the efficiency of the conglomerate form, institutional investors, who began to dominate the securities markets in the 1980s, had a special distaste for them. Institutional investors tend to hold a diversified portfolio of securities. Are they then interested in investing in the securities of diversified corporations that themselves hold a portfolio of companies, as the Williamsonian M-form firm largely does? This seems redundant. As a result, a market penalty may be placed on the use of the conglomerate form. From this perspective, the Icahns, Perelmans, Edelmans, and other individual takeover entrepreneurs can be viewed as arbitrageurs seeking to liberate the negative synergy in busting up the large firm.[56] Such an arbitrageur recognizes that the bust-up or liquidation value of a target is considerably higher than the firm's stock market trading value because of the impact of the market penalty for use of the conglomerate form. Acting entirely rationally, the takeover entrepreneur effectively splits the difference between these two values with the target's shareholders by offering a premium for their shares.

This claim that the market acquired a special distaste for the conglomerate (which may have exceeded the distaste justified on pure efficiency grounds) is also difficult to verify, but the idea of nonrational market discounts is gaining favor.[57] As with Winter's account, this view does not necessarily find the takeover movement to generate observable efficiencies: implicit contracts may be disrupted, wealth transfers from stakeholders to stockholders may be encouraged, and so forth. But it is rooted in a historical development—the rise of the institutional investor—that responds to Winter's entirely appropriate demand that a theory explain not only "why" but "why then."

For Winter, the question of "why then?" is answered by the high interest rates of the 1980s. For me, it is better answered by the apparent failure of the conglomerate firm and market discounts associated with the rise of the institutional investor.

General Discussion

Bronwyn Hall suggested that R&D expenditures would not be a good example of unconventional assets for Winter's theory for two reasons. First, the magnitude of spending on R&D is clearly observable, and the market appears to account for that spending in the value of the firms in sensible ways. Second, Hall's own work has shown that R&D–intensive industries and companies have not been significant takeover targets.

Winter responded that the validity of his argument is sensitive to where the firm is in relation to a zero growth rate. If a firm is growing very rapidly, the long-term costs of breaching contracts or cutting back on investments in unconventional assets may be high. But these costs may be negligible for a firm that is growing very slowly or declining. Winter suggested that if R&D–intensive firms are typically also growing very rapidly, they would not be candidates for restructuring under his theory, and Hall's evidence would not be damaging to the theory.

Hall also urged Winter to distinguish between observable and unobservable assets, adding that the unobservable ones may in fact be subject to being run down without being seen by the marketplace.

Frank Lichtenberg said there is a lot of evidence that targets of mergers or acquisitions are declining in the sense that their employment, output, and market share have been going down for as much as five years preceding the takeovers. He views takeovers as an intervention by a remedial management team attempting to stop the decline. Even if there is evidence, for example, that employment in a firm declines 10 percent after a takeover, it is important to think about what the alternative would have been. Since the firm was already declining, the alternative might have been even more severe.

Winter noted that the possibility that the firms were already in decline before the takeover would not be damaging to his theory at all. In fact, he said, firms in decline are the most vulnerable to being pushed into a faster fadeaway than they would have suffered otherwise.

Lichtenberg cited work by David J. Ravenscraft and F. M. Scherer showing that acquisitions made during the conglomerate era of the late 1960s had the kind of pattern Winter was talking about—that is, the target firms were relatively profitable, but they were run into the ground by empire-building acquirers.[58] He argued that a lot of what was happening in the 1970s and 1980s was an effort to reverse that.

Martin Lipton took the opposite position. Many companies in the early to mid-1980s, he said, did extensive restructuring studies on themselves. The company would look at itself just the way a takeover entrepreneur or leveraged buyout entrepreneur would look at it to try to understand what expenses could be eliminated, what changes could be made. The idea was to come up with a restructuring value so that the company was better prepared to deal with a takeover bid if it should come. In those studies, he said, it became clear that there was substantial unconventional asset value in most companies.

Lipton suggested that there are two types of takeover targets. There have long been what he called "scavenger bait," companies that are running down. The scavenger sees the opportunity to take over the company at a favorable price, liquidate it or change it, and make a profit. But most companies in the mid- to late 1980s were not like that, he claimed. In fact, "they were very successful companies with very significant unconventional assets. They were targets of takeovers because the market had mispriced those companies." It was possible, he said, to adjust R&D or advertising or other expenditures in these companies and thereby justify the premium.

Lipton argued that other takeovers occurred because "they were sold" by salespeople who were part of a "tremendous infrastructure built up to do these transactions." They were "the product of the ability to do junk bond financing and, with little or no equity, gamble on appreciation of assets within a short period of time."

Dennis Mueller said that if he were going to build a theory of takeovers around the idea of unconventional assets, he would argue that their presence increases the likelihood that the market would have trouble evaluating the assets. This would lead to significant differences among investors in valuations, opening the way for more active takeover trading in such firms.

Mueller also argued that the takeover wave of the 1980s should not necessarily be viewed as unique. If there had been no merger wave in the 1980s, it would have been the first time in a century, in a nonwartime period, that the United States experienced a rapid rise in the stock market and did not have a merger wave. In this sense the 1980s were not different from the 1960s, the 1920s, or even the 1890s. "What happens in periods of rapid stock market values is that people suddenly become risk takers, and a variety of debt instruments appear that would not appear under more stable times." Other patterns, too, are similar to previous takeover waves. "The acquiring firms generally outperform the market up to the merger, and not much happens with their shares at the time the merger is announced, and then their share prices fall afterwards," Mueller claimed.

Nonetheless, he argued ironically, there is always a different story about what is going on. "In the merger wave of the 1960s, we put together the conglomerates and M-form companies, and everybody at that time was saying this is efficiency-creating. In the 1980s we take them all apart and everybody is saying now we are creating even more efficiency by taking them all apart."

Winter took seriously the argument that the takeover wave of the 1980s was driven by the need to dismantle conglomerates, but claimed that it would not be inconsistent with his story to observe that a lot of the activity was bust-up activity. Corporate staff, he noted, may often be "an expenditure that can be cut without having anything disastrous happen soon." But, he noted, saying that nothing terrible happens soon is not quite the same thing as saying that these expenditures were wasted. Rather, it may mean that these expenditures do not pay at high interest rates. "But that is the key point," Winter said.

Stewart Myers and Oliver Hart both observed that high interest rates alone would increase the value of a fadeaway strategy, and questioned what role unconventional assets play and whether they were really a necessary part of Winter's story. If the key part of the theory were the high interest rates, Myers argued, this should affect long-lived assets the most. And yet, he said, Winter does not seem to be suggesting that unconventional assets are more long-lived than conventional assets. Beyond that, he could not see any reason why the market would be less likely to evaluate unconventional assets in a reasonable way, or why raiders would be more likely to want to run them down than they would be to run down conventional assets.

The key role that unconventional assets play, Winter answered, is that the outside investors may misunderstand what proportion of expenditures are really current expense and what proportion are really investment or maintenance of depreciating assets. They may also underestimate the value of a company's capital stock by not recognizing the unconventional assets. The takeover raiders, however, understand that a firm with a large proportion of unconventional assets is really one with high capital stock and low marginal cost. For these firms, Winter argued, a rise in real interest rates drives the largest wedge between the value of a continuation strategy and the value of a fadeaway strategy. The takeover raiders tried to capture that difference in value by shifting such a firm into a fadeaway strategy.

Myers noted that the role of unconventional assets becomes more clear when it is connected to breach of contract. To the extent that unconventional assets are embodied in firm-specific human capital, it may be better to keep them for a while without paying for them by breaching the implicit contracts management had with workers, for example. Hart asked whether the need to breach the old contracts was the reason why a takeover and a new management team are needed to accomplish the changes.

Mark Warshawsky noted that the timing was not quite right to support the argument that real interest rates drove restructuring, since real interest rates peaked in the early 1980s but restructuring activity peaked in the late 1980s.

A number of participants questioned whether the rate of spending on investment had actually slowed in the 1980s as Winter's theory suggests. This is an empirical question whose answer seems to depend on the measurement used. Warren Farb argued that, while both the gross and the net investment rates were low in the U.S. relative to major competitor countries, they were high by this country's own historical standards. Charles Schultze asserted, however, that the gross investment numbers are high in constant dollars but these numbers are distorted by the large share of spending on computers, which depreciate rapidly and have decreased dramatically in price. In current dollars, he said, net domestic investment from 1951 to 1980 averaged 7.5 percent of net national product but averaged only 4 percent in the 1980s.

Mueller pointed out that research he has done with Elizabeth Reardon supports Winter's arguments by showing that the marginal return to investment was less than the cost of capital for much of the 1970s and

1980s.[59] "This suggests that we are investing too much, even though we are not investing very much," he said. "One explanation might be that the cost of capital is so high that the capital markets are not placing a high value on the investments that are being made."

Notes

1. See Gregg A. Jarrell, James A. Brickley, and Jeffry M. Netter, "The Market for Corporate Control: The Empirical Evidence since 1980," *Journal of Economic Perspectives*, vol. 2 (Winter 1988), pp. 49–68.

2. Other factors may also dispose American managers toward a short-term view, including market interest rates that lead to high hurdle rates for investment projects, cultural tendencies, corporate governance institutions, and business procedures. See Jay W. Lorsch and Elizabeth A. MacIver, "Corporate Governance and Investment Time Horizons," and Carliss Y. Baldwin and Kim B. Clark, "Capabilities and Capital Investment: New Perspectives on Capital Budgeting," in Michael Porter, ed., *Investment Behavior and Time Horizon in American Industry* (Harvard Business School Press, forthcoming). See also Martin Lipton and Steven A. Rosenblum, "A New System of Corporate Governance: The Quinquennial Election of Directors," *University of Chicago Law Review*, vol. 58 (Winter 1991), pp. 187–253, esp. section 2.

3. For a full exposition of these arguments, see Richard R. Nelson and Sidney G. Winter, *An Evolutionary Theory of Economic Change* (Harvard University Press, 1982).

4. Margaret M. Blair and Robert E. Litan first called attention to the role of high real interest rates in "Explaining Corporate Leverage and Leveraged Buyouts in the Eighties," in John B. Shoven and Joel Waldfogel, eds., *Debt, Taxes, and Corporate Restructuring* (Brookings, 1990).

5. Blair and Litan, "Explaining Corporate Leverage," pp. 47–48.

6. See F. M. Scherer, "Corporate Takeovers: The Efficiency Arguments," *Journal of Economic Perspectives*, vol. 2 (Winter 1988), pp. 69–82, citing Adolph A. Berle, Jr., and Gardiner C. Means, *The Modern Corporation and Private Property* (Commerce Clearing House, 1932).

7. Michael C. Jensen, "Takeovers: Their Causes and Consequences," *Journal of Economic Perspectives*, vol. 2 (Winter 1988), p. 38.

8. Because many of the "friendly" takeovers are motivated by short- or long-run defensive considerations, the measured merger and acquisition activity does include a part of the defensive or quasi-voluntary response to the takeover environment. A company that simply finances a stock buyback by issuing debt will show up in measures of leverage but not in the merger figures. A company that slakes shareholder cash thirst by reducing earnings retention to pay higher dividends will escape detection in all these measures but may nevertheless be responding to the same environment.

9. Important events include the appearance of interest-bearing checking accounts in some states in the early 1970s and their full legitimation by federal legislation in 1980, the appearance of money market mutual funds in the 1970s and their spectacular growth as interest rates rose after 1977, the phaseout of the regulation Q ceilings on interest paid by banks and thrifts (except commercial checking accounts) in the early 1980s, the subsequent appearance of deposit brokers who gathered together large sums for placement in federally insured accounts, and the expansion of thrift asset powers in the early 1980s. Many of these events were directly related to the collapse of the savings and loan industry, either as cause or as part of policy initiatives to cure the industry's ailments. See Lawrence J. White, *The S&L Debacle: Public Policy Lessons for Bank and Thrift Regulation* (Oxford University Press, 1991).

10. For example, the Economic Recovery Act of 1981 may have encouraged mergers and acquisitions because it allowed for more rapid depreciation of acquired assets, and also because its reduction of capital gains tax rates increased the after-tax gains to the acquired firm's shareholders. The Tax Reform Act of 1986 largely reversed these changes. However, its elimination of favored tax treatment for capital gains may have reduced the appeal of equity relative to debt in corporate capital structures at a time when high interest rates had made the deductibility of interest costs considerably more salient. The Bankruptcy Reform Act of 1978 increased the autonomy of managers in firms undergoing reorganizations and also reduced the procedural obstacles to reorganizations. The result may have been increased managerial tolerance for the bankruptcy risks associated with high leverage. On this last point see Mark J. Roe, "Antitrust, Corporate Bankruptcy, and the 1980s Takeover Wave," working paper, April 1991.

11. See the comment by Oliver E. Williamson on the paper by Andrei Shleifer and Lawrence H. Summers in Alan J. Auerbach, ed., *Corporate Takeovers: Causes and Consequences* (University of Chicago Press, 1988) pp. 61–67.

12. Sanjai Bhagat, Andrei Shleifer, and Robert W. Vishny, "Hostile Takeovers in the 1980s: The Return to Corporate Specialization," *Brookings Papers on Economic Activity, Microeconomics 1990*, p. 44.

13. For long-term rates, there is the question of whether investors believe that they will receive a real return computed by subtracting current inflation from the nominal yield or whether they expect a resurgence of inflation to eat away at that return. Considering the real beating suffered by holders of long-term fixed income securities in 1979–81, it is hardly surprising that wariness persisted and nominal rates remained high.

14. See "Industry-Level Pressures to Restructure" in this volume.

15. For example, Jensen, "Takeovers," p. 33, mentions higher real interest rates as one of several developments that made cutbacks in oil exploration economically appropriate in the late 1970s and early 1980s and that led to hostile takeovers when managements failed to respond to the signals. The role of interest rates is highlighted by Blair and Litan in "Explaining Corporate Leverage."

16. For a recent example, see Saman Majd and Robert S. Pindyck, "The Learning Curve and Optimal Production under Uncertainty," *RAND Journal of Economics*, vol. 20 (Autumn 1989), pp. 331–43, where the asset is the firm's cumulative production and the associated cost reduction achieved through learning.

17. See, for example, Bronwyn H. Hall, "The Value of Intangible Corporate Assets: An Empirical Study of the Components of Tobin's Q," National Bureau of Economic Research and University of California at Berkeley, 1990.

18. David M. Kreps, "Corporate Culture and Economic Theory," in James E. Alt and Kenneth A. Shepsle, eds., *Perspectives on Positive Political Economy* (Cambridge University Press, 1990).

19. This is the problem faced by the incumbent firm in Reinhard Selten, "The Chain Store Paradox," *Theory and Decision*, vol. 9 (1978), pp. 127–59. A satisfying resolution of the paradox involving a "small" amount of incomplete information was provided by David M. Kreps and Robert Wilson, "Reputation and Imperfect Information," and a related problem is addressed in Paul Milgrom and John Roberts, "Predation, Reputation, and Entry Deterrence," both in *Journal of Economic Theory*, vol. 27 (August 1982), pp. 253–79, 280–312.

20. Edmund S. Phelps and Sidney G. Winter, "Optimal Price Policy under Atomistic Competition," in Edmund S. Phelps and others, *Microeconomic Foundations of Employment and Inflation Theory* (Norton, 1970), pp. 309–37.

21. "A Theory of Wage and Employment Dynamics," in Phelps and others, eds., *Microeconomic Foundations of Employment and Inflation Theory*, pp. 167–211. Related examples of theoretical models featuring unconventional assets include Steven C. Salop, "Wage Differentials in a Dynamic Theory of the Firm," *Journal of Economic Theory*, vol. 6 (August 1973), pp. 321–44, where the asset is employees for whom turnover costs are already sunk, and Edward C. Prescott and Michael Visscher, "Organization Capital," *Journal of Political Economy*, vol. 88 (June 1980), pp. 446–61, where the asset is information about, or possessed by, a firm's employees.

22. The idea is, however, akin to the broad interpretation of a "state description" of a firm in evolutionary economics. See Nelson and Winter, *Evolutionary Theory of Economic Change*, especially pp. 14–21. A more closely related discussion is my account, "Knowledge and Competence as Strategic Assets," in David J. Teece, ed., *The Competitive Challenge: Strategies for Industrial Innovation and Renewal* (Cambridge, Mass.: Ballinger, 1987). Some recent work on business strategy is also related; see David J. Teece, Gary Pisano, and Amy Shuen, "Dynamic Capabilities and Strategic Management," working paper EAP-38, Center for Research in Management, University of California, Berkeley, June 1992, and references there to the "resource-based" and "dynamic capabilities" perspectives on strategy. However, all these contributions have their particular objects of devotion among the unconventional assets, whereas the present account is fully ecumenical.

23. Tobin's *q* is the ratio of the market value of a firm to the replacement cost of its assets.

24. I refrain from discussing the tax implications of these issues, not being qualified to do so with any completeness. One obvious point is that the neglect of the unconventional assets can confer the benefits of tax deferral while the firm accumulates such assets, assuming each year's returns are reinvested in more unconventional assets and the investment is treated as current expense. Tax considerations lie behind some recent efforts to give unconventional assets explicit recognition because there are tax incentives to distinguish such assets from non-

amortizable good will. See General Accounting Office, *Tax Policy: Issues and Policy Proposals Regarding Tax Treatment of Intangible Assets*, GAO/GGD-91-88 (August 1991).

25. The term *liquidation* ordinarily denotes prompt liquidation; *gradual liquidation* places the emphasis on the result rather than the process of continuing to do business. Thus far, I have not come up with a term superior to *fadeaway strategy*.

26. As observed by David J. Ravenscraft and F. M. Scherer, *Mergers, Selloffs, and Economic Efficiency* (Brookings, 1987), labeling a business a cash cow may have incentive effects that directly injure performance. It presents managers and employees with prospects of diminished opportunities for promotion and pay increases and a reduced quality of worklife relative to what they might have believed in the absence of the labeling.

27. Bronwyn H. Hall, "The Effect of Takeover Activity on Corporate Research and Development," in Auerbach, ed., *Corporate Takeovers*, pp. 69–96; and Hall, "The Impact of Corporate Restructuring on Industrial Research and Development," *Brookings Papers on Economic Activity, Microeconomics 1990*, pp. 85–135.

28. It may be helpful to state what the relationship between R&D activity and restructuring would be if in fact R&D capital were known to be the only, or by far the most consequential, type of unconventional asset. A firm that has high R&D capital relative to output, operating in an industry environment of technological maturity and dwindling opportunity, becomes a candidate for restructuring as interest rates rise. This is an example of the case of low m, high dk, low d, and high k.

29. Jensen, "Takeovers," p. 28.

30. Robin Marris, *The Economic Theory of Managerial Capitalism* (Macmillan, 1964), p.

31. For example, Margaret M. Blair, "Theory and Evidence on the Causes of Merger Waves," Ph.D. dissertation, Yale University, 1989, explained variations in takeover activity across industries and time with a regression model that proxied industry investment opportunities by capacity utilization, industry growth rate variables, and the ratio of investment to value of shipments. The last was assumed to indicate investment opportunity at the industry level in spite of its possible contamination by misuses of cash flow in particular firms. Blair and Schary in this volume use a similar model to explain financial restructuring activity.

32. In a report on twelve case studies of financial management in major corporations in the 1970s, Gordon Donaldson observed that while the companies were well staffed to perform discounted cash flow analysis, such analysis did not dominate decisionmaking and was sometimes ignored entirely, in part because managers considered long-term organizational survival more important than shareholder wealth. There were, however, emerging signs of tightening capital constraints that were associated with the rising importance of institutional investors as a constituency. See Gordon Donaldson, *Managing Corporate Wealth: The Operation of a Comprehensive Financial Goals System* (Praeger, 1984), esp. pp. 83–85, 120–26.

33. For evidence that Americans may be afflicted with such a cultural disposition, see John Immerwahr, *Saving: Good or Bad? A Pilot Study on Public Attitudes Towards Saving, Investment, and Competitiveness* (Public Agenda Foundation, 1989), and international comparisons of saving rates—for example, *Economic Report of the President, February 1990*, pp. 126–28.

34. Andrei Shleifer and Lawrence H. Summers, "Breach of Trust in Hostile Takeovers," in Alan J. Auerbach, ed., *Corporate Takeovers: Causes and Consequences* (University of Chicago Press, 1988), pp. 33–56.

35. Shleifer and Summers, "Breach of Trust in Hostile Takeovers," p. 36.

36. Shleifer and Summers, "Breach of Trust in Hostile Takeovers," p. 50.

37. Bhagat, Shleifer, and Vishny, "Hostile Takeovers in the 1980s."

38. See, for example, the major article on the Safeway LBO by Susan C. Faludi, "Safeway LBO Yields Vast Profits But Exacts a Heavy Human Toll," *Wall Street Journal*, May 16, 1990, p. A1, and the letters in response from Safeway CEO Peter A. Magowan and others, *Wall Street Journal*, June 15, 1990, p. A11.

39. In the case of layoffs, only an upper-bound estimate is typically provided of the slack that might have been involved, an estimate assuming that the laid-off labor was contributing no value.

40. Shleifer and Summers, "Breach of Trust in Hostile Takeovers," p. 46.

41. For a formal treatment, see Dilip Abreu, "On the Theory of Infinitely Repeated Games with Discounting," *Econometrica*, vol. 56 (March 1988), pp. 383–96.

42. For example, governance reform along the lines proposed by Lipton and Rosenblum, "A New System of Corporate Governance," might be helpful.

43. Shleifer and Summers, "Breach of Trust in Hostile Takeovers."

44. See Michael Jensen, "Agency Costs of Free Cash Flow, Corporate Finance, and Takeovers," *American Economic Review*, vol. 76 (May 1985), pp. 323–29.

45. I have discussed this tendency at length elsewhere as an explanation for the bust-up takeover in the 1980s. See John C. Coffee, Jr., "Shareholders Versus Managers: The Strain in the Corporate Web," *Michigan Law Review*, vol. 85 (October 1986), pp. 1–109. According to one estimate, 60 percent of the unrelated acquisitions taking place between 1970 and 1982 had been divested by 1989. See S. Kaplan and M. Weisbach, "Acquisitions and Divestitures: What Is Divested and How Much Does the Market Anticipate?" University of Chicago, School of Business, 1990.

46. See Sanjai Bhagat, Andrei Shleifer, and Robert Vishny, "Hostile Takeovers in the 1980s," p. 44.

47. Bhagat, Shleifer, and Vishny, "Hostile Takeovers."

48. Such a piecemeal liquidation to buyers in related industries is, of course, what the evidence shows. See Bhagat, Shleifer, and Vishny, "Hostile Takeovers." Even if the old firm had an enviable reputation for fairness to bondholders and employees that reduced its costs of contracting with these groups, acquirers who purchase its divisions would have no way of purchasing that reputation. Such an asset is not only unconventional, it is unsellable as well.

49. See Bronwyn Hall, "Impact of Corporate Restructuring," p. 85.

50. Andrei Shleifer and Robert Vishny, "The Takeover Wave of the 1980s," *Science*, vol. 249 (August 17, 1990), pp. 745–49.

51. See *Revlon* v. *MacAndrews & Forbes Holdings, Inc.*, 506 A.2d 173 (Del. 1986).

52. Shleifer and Vishny, "Takeover Wave," pp. 746–47.

53. Revlon sold its crown jewel, Max Factor cosmetic division, to Procter & Gamble in April 1991 for $1.14 billion. See Anthony Ramirez, "P&G Gets Revlon's Max Factor," *New York Times*, April 11, 1991, p. D1.

54. See Shleifer and Vishny, "Takeover Wave," p. 747.

55. See Bhagat, Shleifer, and Vishny, "Hostile Takeovers," p. 44 (attempting to capitalize value of savings from layoffs and employment attrition).

56. I have discussed this arbitrage theory of bust-up takeovers in Coffee, "Shareholders versus Managers."

57. See R. Kraakman, "Taking Discounts Seriously: The Implications of 'Discounted' Share Prices as an Acquisition Motive," *Columbia Law Review*, vol. 88 (June 1988), pp. 891–941. See also Andrei Shleifer and Lawrence Summers, "The Noise Trader Approach to Finance," *Journal of Economic Perspectives*, vol. 4 (Spring 1990), pp. 19–33.

58. Ravenscraft and Scherer, *Mergers, Sell-Offs, and Economic Efficiency*.

59. Dennis C. Mueller and Elizabeth Reardon, "Rates of Return on Corporate Investment," Department of Economics, University of Maryland, College Park, 1992.

Industry-Level Indicators of Free Cash Flow

Margaret M. Blair
and Martha A. Schary

THE 1980s witnessed the innovation and highly visible use of leveraged buyouts; the introduction, rise, and demise of junk bond issues; a large number of mergers; and an increase in corporate leverage. Why the 1980s? How can these phenomena be explained? How were they related, and were they driven by the same forces?

Michael Jensen has argued that free cash flow is the force behind these phenomena.[1] A firm has free cash flow when it retains cash after all desirable investment opportunities have been taken. Jensen argues that restructuring accompanied by payouts of cash can rein in managers who may otherwise make bad investments with these excess corporate resources or misuse them by awarding themselves too many perquisites.

This paper develops an empirical specification of free cash flow to more fully test Jensen's hypothesis. We construct indicators of free cash flow at the industry level for 1971 through 1989. In the companion paper that follows, we test whether our measures of the components of free cash flow help explain the distribution of restructuring activity across industries and over time.

Our indicators of free cash flow at the industry level include two components: the quality of investment opportunities and the rate of cash generation. Free cash flow is present at the industry level when current and future investment opportunities are poor but the industry continues to generate a high rate of cash from past investments. More specifically, the quality of investment opportunities is defined as the difference be-

We would like to thank Yosi Amram, Sarah Lane, Michael Salinger, Don Smith, Robert Taggart, Jr., and Barry Bosworth for helpful comments on earlier drafts. We have been assisted by research assistants Mel Campbell, Igor Dukovich, Faye Mazo, Adam Metter, Angela Silva, and especially Murat Iyigun and Girish Uppal. Financial support has been provided by the Boston University Manufacturing Roundtable and the Brookings Institution.

tween the expected return on investment and the return required to cover taxes, economic depreciation, and the cost of funds. The latter has been called the "cost of capital," and many have argued that an increased cost of capital or a higher cost of capital relative to the cost in competitor nations is the cause of the slowdown in investment and decline in competitiveness in U.S. industry in the past decade.[2] We argue that high cost of capital alone is not sufficient to ensure that firms and industries face poor investment opportunities. They must also face low or declining expected returns. But as an empirical matter, the rise in the cost of capital in the 1980s was the most significant event affecting the investment climate for most firms in most industries.

By examining the changes over time in the two components of free cash flow, the rate of cash generation and the quality of investment opportunities, we document how the 1980s differed from previous decades. The theory of free cash flow as promulgated by Jensen focuses on the agency problem of the modern corporation (the potential conflict of interest on the part of managers who control but may not own the firm) and does not address the issue of what changed in the 1980s. However, we argue that the agency problem is exacerbated when the investment climate deteriorates. Managers' desire to retain and invest their firm's cash flow may clash with shareholders' desire for the highest possible return. When free cash flow is high, the agency problem becomes particularly acute.

Our indicators of free cash flow are innovative in several respects. First, they capture both parts of the definition of free cash flow. We measure cash flow directly and develop a measure of how rich or poor the investment climate is. Determining the latter measure is the difficult part. To do so, we use a direct measure of the key factor that corporate managers or outside investors would consider in deciding whether to invest in a given company or project: the relationship between the cost of capital and the expected returns to investment.[3]

Second, our free cash flow indicators are estimated at the industry level. As our companion paper demonstrates, there was a dramatic rise in financial restructuring activity in the 1980s very shortly after an economywide rise in the cost of capital. There were also large differences in the distribution of financial restructuring activity over time and across industries. To test for a causal link between restructuring and investment opportunities, we need to know how the difference between the returns and the costs of capital varied over time and across industries.

Third, our industry-level estimates are built up from firm-level data. Thus they avoid the aggregation error identified by Carl W. Kester and

Timothy Luerhman that is present in previous work. Previous estimates of the cost of capital have relied on an estimate of the cost of funds that was constructed using a "typical" capital structure for the national economy. Kester and Luerhman argued that this approach is misleading and that the cost of funds should be calculated at the firm level and then aggregated.[4]

Finally, our indicators of the quality of investment opportunities were checked for robustness by comparing them with alternative estimates. The basic time-series and cross-sectional pattern we find is robust to these other estimates.

Our key findings can be summarized as follows:

—Differences in the quality of investment opportunities were fairly large, both over time and across industries.

—The expected return on investment displayed wide and consistent differences across industries. In the aggregate, this measure did not change dramatically, although it did drop from 17 or 18 per cent in the late 1970s to 14 or 15 percent in the last three years of the 1980s.

—The effects of changes in tax policy were small, but in the aggregate they tended to reduce the cost of capital during the last few years of the 1980s relative to the previous ten years.

—The most significant factor driving the trend in the opportunity cost of capital was the rise in real interest rates in the early part of the decade and their decline in the later part. Nominal interest rates peaked in 1981, whether measured by rates on U.S. government bonds or corporate bonds. Real interest rates peaked three years later, driving the cost of capital to its highest point.

The implications of our work must be put into context. Our model takes expected returns as exogenous and does not explore the macroeconomic sources of these changes. But the model does enable us to identify which industries in which years were likely to be under the most pressure to cut back on investment. If the free cash flow explanation of financial restructuring has any merit, we should find that restructuring transactions were disproportionately concentrated in these industries.

An Empirical Definition of
Free Cash Flow

Free cash flow has proven to be an empirically elusive concept. First, measuring excess cash alone is not sufficient; a measure of the quality of investment opportunities is needed. Second, the quality of investment opportunities is based on the expected rate of return on all opportunities, including those not taken. Accurate measurement of the quality of investment opportunities can only be made at the level of the firm and requires detailed project information. At the industry level, proxies must be used for both expected returns and the minimum required return on the marginal project, which is the cost of capital.

The framework introduced in this section addresses these issues, primarily by example. First, we present our model. Next, we present the data and results for the industrial chemicals industry to illustrate many of the empirical issues we have wrestled with.[5] Then we show how this approach can be used to analyze free cash flow and the cost of capital for the United States as a whole. Finally, calculations of the cost of capital from this study are compared with those from earlier studies to illustrate important methodological differences.

The Model

There are three primary components to our definition of free cash flow: the rate of cash generation, the expected return on future investment opportunities, and the minimum required return on those opportunities. The minimum required return, or the cost of capital, is by far the most complicated, so we begin with a description of its derivation.

In the common definition the cost of capital is the pretax return that a firm must earn, gross of economic depreciation, to satisfy the demands of holders of debt and equity. New projects are expected to earn at least this rate of return, or they will represent an economic loss. Formally, the cost of capital is derived from a model of investment demand first developed by Robert Hall and Dale Jorgenson.[6] In their model, the steady-state cost of capital services for new investment is defined as

(1) $$c = (WACC + \delta) * (1 - A)/(1 - t).$$

The $WACC + \delta$ is the real cost of funds plus the rate of economic depreciation. The second term $(1 - A)/(1 - t)$ reflects the tax incentives to invest. The A in the numerator is the fraction of the cost of new investment paid for by the government through tax deductions and investment tax credits. It is the sum of the present value of the expected depreciation tax shields and the investment tax credit. The t in the denominator is the tax rate on corporate profits, so division by the expression $(1 - t)$ increases the required return to a pretax level.

Our measure of the quality of investment opportunities is the expected return on new investment less the cost of capital.[7] Because we argue that the measure of expected return we use should be regarded as net of economic depreciation, we created a comparable measure of the cost of capital by subtracting the rate of economic depreciation from the expression in equation 1.[8] In other words, we actually computed the cost of capital as

$$(1') \qquad c = [(WACC + \delta) * (1 - A)/(1 - t)] - \delta.[9]$$

In this study as in much previous work, the cost of funds is the weighted average cost of capital (WACC). The WACC is easy to use—it is simply the returns demanded by each type of securityholder after corporate taxes, weighted by the fraction of that type of security in the capital structure of the firm. The WACC must be in real terms, so the estimated value is also adjusted for inflation.[10] This measure of the cost of funds is useful because it allows us to capture the impact of capital structure on the attractiveness of investment opportunities through its impact on the discount rate used to evaluate projects.[11] Thus the empirical use of the WACC is consistent with the theoretical model of investment demand laid out by Hall and Jorgenson.

The other component of the quality of investment opportunities is the expected return on new investment. Capturing expectations is the thorny issue with this component. As a first approximation we use each industry's historical return on assets, under the assumption that the past is a good predictor for the future. Our definition of the expected return is

$$(2) \qquad\qquad r = \text{operating profits} / \text{assets}.$$

Operating profits are revenues minus operating costs.

Assuming that most of an industry's new investments are similar to those made in the past and that the past returns on these investments are good predictors of future returns, the average historical return in an industry is a good proxy for the marginal expected return for most firms.

In sum, using equations 2 and 1', the quality of investment opportunities is measured as $r - c$. We call this the squeeze on capital because it measures the pressures an industry faces to cut back on investment spending or to disinvest: $SQZ = r - c$.[12] When SQZ is small or less than zero, the industry has few investment opportunities that will generate a positive net return.

Table 4-1. Cash Generation Rate and Net Returns to Capital (SQZ), by Industry State

Industry state	Cash generation rate	Net returns to capital (SQZ)
Free cash flow	> 0	< 0 or small
Declining industry	< 0	< 0 or small
Growing industry, internal funds used for investment	> 0	> 0 and large
Growing industry, external funds used for investment	< 0	> 0 and large

The final component of free cash flow is the rate of cash generation. In this case historical data are clearly appropriate because the presence of excess cash from past investments (combined with a paucity of good investment opportunities) is what creates the agency problem. The amount of excess cash generated is defined as operating profits less required payments, and the rate of cash generation is

(3) $C = $ (operating profits $-$ taxes $-$ interest $-$ dividends) / assets.

Dividends are subtracted from operating profits because the omission or reduction of a dividend payment is usually of great concern to shareholders.[13] Industries with C less than zero face cash flow shortages; industries with C greater than zero are candidates for free cash flow.

SQZ and C can be used to determine which industries are most likely to have free cash flow. When excess cash is being generated ($C > 0$) and there is a dearth of investment opportunities (SQZ very small or negative), the industry has a high probability of having free cash flow. Table 4-1 categorizes the other possible outcomes, under the assumption that internally generated funds, when available, are used before external funds.[14]

Free Cash Flow Calculations: Industrial Chemicals Industry

The calculation of SQZ is lengthy and can be confusing because of the large number of inputs required. To illustrate how we performed these calculations, we walk through our data and intermediate results for the chemicals industry. Most of the calculations are for the cost of capital, so these are done first. Table 4-2 summarizes the data used as inputs and table 4-3 shows the results.[15]

The two left columns in table 4-2 show the relative shares of two of the three assets included in the property, plant, and equipment account

Table 4-2. Industrial Chemicals Industry Data for Cost-of-Capital Calculation, 1971–89[a]
Percent unless otherwise specified

Year	Equipment/ PPE[c]	Structures/ PPE[c]	Capital structure[b]				Beta[d]	Nominal expected return on market[e]		Nominal required return on equity[e]	
			Common equity	Preferred equity	Short-term debt	Long-term debt		RP	AF	RP	AF
1971	60	18	68	1	15	16	1.08	14	11	14	11
1972	66	18	70	1	15	14	1.08	14	10	14	10
1973	65	18	65	1	19	15	1.08	14	11	15	11
1974	61	16	54	1	26	19	1.08	15	14	16	14
1975	59	15	62	1	21	17	1.08	15	13	16	13
1976	60	13	60	1	21	18	1.09	15	13	16	14
1977	62	16	50	1	26	23	1.09	15	14	15	15
1978	68	15	47	1	30	23	1.05	16	15	16	15
1979	66	12	48	1	31	20	1.09	17	14	18	15
1980	69	12	49	1	30	21	1.08	19	13	19	14
1981	68	12	42	1	31	26	0.99	21	13	21	13
1982	65	15	44	1	31	25	1.03	20	14	21	14
1983	65	16	52	0	29	19	1.02	19	12	19	12
1984	65	17	48	0	33	19	1.02	20	12	20	12
1985	66	19	53	0	31	16	1.06	18	11	18	11
1986	66	18	57	0	27	16	1.07	15	10	16	10
1987	64	20	58	0	27	15	1.07	16	10	16	10
1988	60	18	57	0	30	13	1.10	16	11	17	11
1989	59	18	56	0	30	13	1.09	16	10	17	10

Sources: Expected return on the market, analysts' forecast method, is from Burton Malkiel, "The Capital Formation Problem in the United States," *Journal of Finance*, vol. 34 (May 1979), pp. 291–306, and Malkiel, "The Influence of Conditions in Financial Markets on the Time Horizons of Business Managers: An International Comparison," in Michael E. Porter, *Investment Behavior and Time Horizon in American Industry* (Harvard Business School Press, forthcoming). Beta is from Merrill Lynch, *Security Evaluation*, various issues. All other data are from Compustat. Calculations from DATA1.
a. Includes SIC 2800–2829 and 2860–2869.
b. Representative only. Firm-level data used to calculate WACC. All other data series are asset-weighted averages of firm-level data.
c. PPE is property, plant, and equipment.
d. Risk factor measured by ratio of covariance of return on a firm's stock with market return to variance of market return, asset-weighted average for industry.
e. RP is constant risk premium method. AF is analysts' forecast method.

(PPE). The two included are equipment and structures; the missing asset is land.[16] Thus the two ratios included are not expected to add to 100 percent, and a decrease over time in their sum implies an increase in the relative value of land. Only equipment and structures have allowable depreciation deductions in the U.S. tax code.

The four columns under the heading "capital structure" show the composition of financing for the industry. These aggregate data were not actually used in the calculation of the WACC (our measure of the cost of funds), which was done at the firm level. They are reported to give the reader a sense of the approximate composition of the WACC.

Kester and Luehrman have argued that aggregate measures of capital structure should not be matched with aggregate measures of returns on equity and debt to compute an aggregate WACC. This is because the required return on equity for any given firm is a function partly of how much debt the firm has. Thus unless the calculation of the WACC is done at the firm level, the measured required return on equity will not be appropriate for the actual proportion of equity in the capital structure.[17] All the estimates of the WACC in this and our companion paper are therefore made at the level of the firm and then aggregated up to the industry or economywide level.

The final five columns in table 4-2 illustrate how the required return to equity holders was calculated. The approach we used captures the true opportunity cost to investors because it measures the return shareholders would get if they put their funds in an alternative investment of comparable risk. This risk factor is measured at the firm level by "beta," which is the covariance of the return on that firm's stock with the market return divided by the variance of the market return. Column 7 shows the asset-weighted average beta for the industry. Again, this data series is representative only: the actual calculation of the required return on equity was done at the firm level.

Two estimates of the cost of equity were made using the capital asset pricing model (CAPM).[18] The return on ten-year Treasury bonds was used to measure the risk-free rate. We measured the expected return on the market in two ways throughout this paper. The first assumed that the expected return on the market is a constant 7 percent above the Treasury bond rate. This is called the constant risk premium (RP) approach. The second method used forecasts of the return on the stock market. These forecasts are the aggregation of firm-level forecasts of return made by *Value Line* analysts and developed by Burton Malkiel.[19] We call this the analysts' forecast (AF) approach. The RP method generated a higher level and a steeper rise in the expected return on the market in the early 1980s than the AF method because the risk-premium part of the calculation in the AF method declined when real interest rates rose during that period. In fact, from 1981 to 1985, when real interest rates were highest, analysts' forecast estimates of the risk premium were near zero.

We use two measures of the expected return on the market in this paper because scholars have not reached a consensus on a simple predictive model. Historically, the return on the market has averaged 12 percent (in nominal terms) but has varied by more than 20 percent, making predictions using historic returns very imprecise.[20] The RP approach uses historical information in the form of a long-run average to predict the future. Seven percent is the difference between the historical average return on the market and the historical average return on Treasury bonds. The RP method uses this difference in returns as an estimate of the premium required by investors for the risk of investing in stocks rather than in safe government securities.[21]

Recent research has demonstrated that the risk premium changes over time, but unfortunately it has not produced a clear measure of the expected risk premium.[22] The expected return on the market from analysts' forecasts incorporates a changing risk premium, but it is not the only possible choice. Most of the results we present, however, are qualitatively robust to both our choices for measuring the expected return on the market.

To jump ahead a bit, it is important to understand the link between the choice of the measure of the expected return and the degree of industry variation in the cost of capital. Our hypothesis requires that the cost of capital be sufficiently high to generate a low squeeze on capital and also that the cost of capital increase (or the expected return on new investment decrease) during the period of or just preceding restructuring. Because we use the CAPM to measure the expected return on the market, industries with high betas will have higher expected returns, and as the risk premium increases, high-beta industries will experience a faster increase in the required return on equity. Moreover high or rising levels of the risk premium produce wider industry spreads in the cost of equity and consequently in the cost of capital.

Thus the method of measuring the expected return on the market has an important effect on the time-series and cross-sectional pattern of the cost of capital. If the true risk premium is negatively correlated with the level of the risk-free rate, then the constant risk premium approach overestimates the expected return on the market in periods of high in-

Table 4-3. Calculation of Free Cash Flow, Industrial Chemicals Industry, 1971–89

Percent unless otherwise specified

Year	Real cost of funds[a] RP	AF	Economic depreciation rate	A^b	$(1-A)/(1-t)^c$	Cost of capital[a] RP	AF	Operating profit rate	Squeeze on capital[a] RP	AF	Cash generation rate
1971	5	3	9	0.33	1.28	9	6	17	8	11	8
1972	6	3	9	0.35	1.24	10	6	18	9	12	9
1973	4	2	9	0.30	1.34	9	6	21	12	15	10
1974	2	1	9	0.29	1.36	5	4	22	16	17	11
1975	2	0	8	0.28	1.38	5	3	19	13	15	9
1976	5	3	8	0.21	1.52	11	10	19	8	9	9
1977	3	3	9	0.22	1.49	9	8	19	10	10	9
1978	3	2	10	0.24	1.47	8	8	19	11	11	9
1979	3	2	9	0.21	1.46	8	6	19	11	12	9
1980	4	2	10	0.21	1.46	11	7	17	6	10	8
1981	5	1	9	0.23	1.42	11	6	15	4	9	6
1982	7	4	9	0.22	1.45	15	10	15	0	4	5
1983	9	5	9	0.22	1.45	17	12	16	−1	4	6
1984	10	6	9	0.21	1.45	18	13	18	0	6	8
1985	9	6	9	0.22	1.44	18	12	16	−2	4	8
1986	8	5	9	0.23	1.43	16	11	17	1	5	6
1987	9	5	9	0.28	1.19	12	8	18	6	11	8
1988	9	6	9	0.22	1.18	12	8	21	9	13	11
1989	8	5	8	0.23	1.17	11	7	20	9	13	10

Source: Authors' calculations from DATA1.

a. RP is constant risk premium method. AF is analysts' forecast method.

b. Present value of depreciation tax shields and investment tax credits per unit of investment. See text.

c. Influence of tax code on cost of capital. See text.

terest rates. The industry variation in the cost of capital will also be too wide under this measure. On the other hand, the *Value Line* estimates of firm-level expected return used by Malkiel as the basis for his aggregate estimates of the return on the market appear to be more conservative than forecasts made by analysts at other firms.[23] So estimates of the cost of capital based on *Value Line* data may be low relative to others generated by analysts' forecasts and the cross-sectional variation also too narrow. In our sample period the cross-sectional variation is smallest during periods of high interest rates. Returning to table 4-2, the swings in the chemical industry's required return on equity are amplified because its beta is greater than one.

Table 4-3 uses the data from table 4-2 to calculate free cash flow variables. The first two columns show the real cost of funds as measured by the real WACC under the two alternative assumptions about return on the market. This component is calculated two ways at the firm level. Each uses the AAA bond rate for the preferred stock return, the prime rate for the short-term debt, and the Baa rate for the long-term debt.[24] The two measures differ by using the two measures of the cost of equity discussed above for the equity portion of the capital structure. The measures of industry-level real cost of funds reported here are asset-weighted averages of firm-level real WACCs.

The rate of economic depreciation is also shown in table 4-3. Mervyn King and Don Fullerton have calculated the rate on equipment and structures for three sectors of the economy.[25] We constructed a weighted average of these rates using the asset-composition data from the first two columns of table 4-2 as weights. Fluctuations in the economic depreciation series arise from changes in the weights.

Construction of the present value of depreciation tax shields and investment tax credits, A in table 4-3, took several steps. First, we created a stylized history of the tax code that included the depreciation schedules for equipment and structures. Next, we calculated the present value of depreciation tax shields for each year, using the after-tax AAA bond rate as the discount rate. These steps are discussed in more detail in the appendix. Third, we calculated a weighted average of the present values for equipment and structures, again using the data in the first two columns of table 4-2 as weights. This calculation was done at the industry level.

The tax code influences the cost of capital through the term $(1 - A)/(1 - t)$, the annual values of which are shown in table 4-3. This term was calculated directly from A and the corporate tax rate series given in the appendix. On average taxes raised the required return on a project by 20 to 50 percent. Changes in the tax policy and changes in the AAA bond rate caused $(1 - A)/(1 - t)$ to fluctuate. The effects of the 1986 Tax Reform Act are visible in the final three years, while the high real interest rates of the 1980s offset the tax reduction from the 1981 tax reform.[26]

The two cost-of-capital series in table 4-3 were calculated directly from the data series in columns 1 through 5. The cost of capital contains the same pattern of fluctuations as the real cost of funds. For example, the cost of funds reached a low point in 1974, as did the cost of capital (1975 for the analysts' forecast series). This was the result of unexpected inflation. The rate of change in the GNP deflator averaged 5.6 percent between 1971 and 1973 and then shot up to 9 percent in 1974 and 1975. By 1975 capital markets were beginning to incorporate expectations of higher inflation, so 1974 and 1975 were the years with the lowest real cost of funds. On the other hand, the high positive values for the cost of funds and the cost of capital after 1983 coincided with a period of low inflation. These findings suggest that the measure of inflation used to adjust nominal returns is very important. We used the average of the last three years' actual inflation experience, based on the GNP deflator.[27]

Table 4-3 shows the expected operating profit rate calculated as the current return on assets. Surprisingly, given the major restructuring this industry has undergone, the series is relatively stable, declining from 19–20 percent in the 1970s to a low of 15 percent in the early 1980s before returning to 20 percent in the late 1980s.

The squeeze on capital declined dramatically during the 1980s, primarily because the cost of capital rose so sharply. The chemicals industry fits the pattern suggested by those who have argued that the deterioration in the U.S. competitive position is linked to a rise in the cost of capital. For many industries in our sample, the cost of capital rose sharply in the 1980s and the return was flat or slightly declining. Although the results for the chemicals industry suggest that the cost of capital alone would be a good proxy for the quality of investment opportunities, the results reported below show that the squeeze on capital more completely captures variations in industry experience.

The final column in table 4-3 shows the rate of cash generation. After starting at 8-9 percent, the rate declined to a low of 5 percent in 1982 before returning to its former level. The final three columns together suggest that the chemicals industry experienced free cash flow during the mid-1980s, when cash generation rates had largely recovered but investment opportunities were still weakening.

In her case study in this book, Sarah Lane has found that merger and takeover activity in the industrial chemicals industry was strongest from 1985 through 1988. Financial restructuring, including divestitures, leveraged buyouts, and leveraged recapitalizations, began in 1984 and continued through the end of the decade, contributing significantly to the rise in book value debt-to-asset ratios. Capacity shutdowns were heaviest in 1982–84, the three years following the recession. The value of the squeeze for this industry was at its lowest in 1982–86 and was recovering somewhat by 1987–88.

The Cost of Capital in the United States

We argue that the quality of investment opportunities should be measured by the squeeze on capital, not just the cost of capital. But it is useful to compare our measures of the cost of capital in the United States with previous calculations. This section reports the results of aggregating our industry estimates of the cost of capital to the national level and comparing them to estimates from previous studies.

Tables 4-4 and 4-5 give the basic data and calculations for the cost of capital, the rate of operating profit, and the rate of cash generation.[28] The data in table 4-4 are similar to aggregate measures reported by other researchers, with the exception of the beta. This series is the asset-weighted average of firm-level betas and in theory should equal 1.0. However, the larger industries in our sample had betas well below 1.0, while the smaller industries typically had betas above 1.0. For example, in 1979 the weighted average beta for the largest five industries, accounting for 46 percent of all assets, was 0.80.

The U.S. aggregate numbers have a pattern similar to that of the chemicals industry. The cost of capital rose sharply in the 1980s (table 4-5). The rate of operating profits fell slightly during the period. As with the chemicals industry, the U.S. economy as a whole experienced a negative squeeze on capital in 1983-85. The overall rate of cash generation was fairly stable at 5 to 7 percent throughout the period and lower than the rate for the chemicals industry alone. The U.S. aggregate free cash flow series is useful as a benchmark for our industry numbers; we are not suggesting that the entire U.S. corporate sector was experiencing free cash flow.

Table 4-4. U.S. Aggregate Data for Cost-of-Capital Calculation, 1977–89[a]
Percent unless otherwise specified

Year	Equipment/ PPE[c]	Structures/ PPE[c]	Capital structure[b]					Beta	Required return on market[d]		Required return to equity[d]	
			Common equity	Preferred equity	Short-term debt	Long-term debt	Total debt/ assets		RP	AF	RP	AF
1977	62	22	51	1	30	18	54	0.95	15	14	15	14
1978	62	21	48	1	33	18	56	0.95	16	15	16	15
1979	62	20	47	1	34	18	57	0.95	17	14	17	14
1980	63	20	51	1	32	16	57	0.95	19	13	19	13
1981	66	18	47	1	35	18	57	0.94	21	13	21	13
1982	66	20	48	1	34	18	57	0.94	20	14	20	13
1983	67	20	53	1	31	15	57	0.93	19	12	18	12
1984	65	20	49	1	34	16	59	0.93	20	12	19	12
1985	62	23	51	1	33	15	61	0.94	18	11	17	11
1986	61	23	54	1	31	15	61	0.94	15	10	14	9
1987	61	23	54	1	31	15	62	0.94	16	10	15	9
1988	59	23	52	1	31	16	63	0.95	16	11	15	10
1989	58	23	54	1	30	15	65	0.95	16	10	15	10

Source: Authors' calculations.
a. Asset-weighted averages of firm-level data. Excludes public utilities and financial services.
b. Representative only. Firm-level data used to calculate WACC.
c. PPE is property, plant, and equipment.
d. RP is constant risk premium method. AF is analysts' forecast method.

Table 4-5. U.S. Aggregate Data, Free Cash Flow Variables, 1977–89[a]
Percent unless otherwise specified

Year	Real cost of funds[b]		Economic depreciation rate	A^c	$(1-A)/(1-t)^d$	Cost of capital[b]		Operating profit rate	Squeeze on capital[b]		Cash generation rate
	RP	AF				RP	AF		RP	AF	
1977	2	1	10	0.24	1.45	7	6	17	10	11	7
1978	1	1	10	0.24	1.46	7	6	17	10	11	7
1979	4	1	10	0.23	1.43	9	5	18	9	13	7
1980	3	1	10	0.21	1.46	9	6	17	8	11	6
1981	4	1	10	0.24	1.41	10	5	16	6	11	6
1982	6	4	10	0.23	1.43	13	10	15	2	5	5
1983	7	5	10	0.23	1.43	15	11	15	-0.1	4	6
1984	8	5	10	0.22	1.44	16	12	16	-0.5	4	7
1985	8	5	10	0.22	1.44	15	11	15	-0.5	4	6
1986	7	4	10	0.23	1.43	13	10	14	1	4	6
1987	7	4	9	0.28	1.20	10	7	14	4	7	6
1988	7	5	9	0.23	1.17	10	7	14	4	7	6
1989	6	4	9	0.23	1.16	9	6	14	5	8	6

Source: Authors' calculations from DATA1.
a. Asset-weighted averages of firm-level data. Excludes public utilities and financial services.
b. RP is constant risk premium method. AF is analysts' forecast method.
c. Present value of depreciation tax shields and investment tax credits per unit of investment. See text.
d. Influence of tax code on cost of capital. See text.

As we discussed earlier, these series differ from those in previous studies because ours are based on firm-level calculations of the WACC. Thus they avoid the problem identified by Kester and Luerhman. To illustrate the magnitude of this issue, we calculated a cost-of-capital series from the aggregate data reported in tables 4-4 and 4-5.[29] The resulting aggregate series, which uses aggregated inputs, a methodology similar to that used in previous studies, was 2 to 9 percentage points higher than the two series shown in Table 4-5 (which are based on firm-level data). The series constructed from aggregate inputs reached a peak difference of 9 points in 1980 and 1981 for measures using the constant risk premium and 8 points for the analysts' forecast measures of the cost of capital. These were the years with the decade's highest inflation. Further examination revealed that there is an important interaction between the level of aggregation and the measure of the real after-tax cost of debt. As inflation increases, the difference widens between calculating this term of the WACC with aggregated inputs and calculating it at the firm level and then aggregating. This suggests that as inflation rises, the method that uses aggregate capital structures to calculate the aggregate nominal cost of funds, and then subtracts the inflation rate, is an increasingly poor proxy for the aggregation of firm-level measures of the real cost of funds. As inflation fell during the 1980s, the series based on aggregate capital structures and those based on firm-level capital structures converged. Thus it seems that Kester and Luerhman have made an empirically important point.

Our results differ from those of three other studies in levels and trends (figure 4-1).[30] Only one of the other series shows a similar rise in the cost of capital in the early 1980s.

The study by Eiji Tajika and Yuji Yui used essentially the same model for the cost of capital, but used the Baa rate for the cost of equity (as well as the return on long-term debt).[31] The authors explain the sharp drop in their series in 1975 as the result of unexpectedly high inflation and the increase in mid-1980s as the result of unexpectedly low inflation.

Robert N. McCauley and Steven A. Zimmer used price-earnings ratios for cost of equity.[32] The measure of earnings they used in the ratios was adjusted in several ways. Depreciation was added back to net earnings because it is a noncash expense; inventory valuation adjustments were standardized across firms; liability values were adjusted for the decline in real value resulting from inflation; and growth prospects were taken into account. The resulting cost-of-equity series drives much of the pattern of their cost-of-capital numbers (figure 4-1). McCauley and Zim-

Figure 4-1. U.S. Cost of Capital, Five Estimates, Selected Years, 1970–89

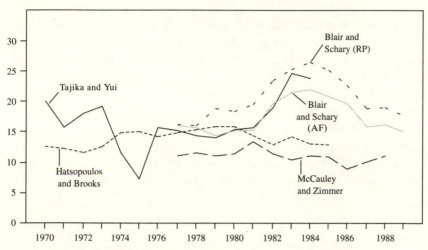

Sources: Results of constant risk premium method (RP) and analysts' forecast method (AF) as reported by the authors (economic depreciation added); Eiji Tajika and Yuji Yui, "Cost of Capital and Effective Tax Rate: A Comparison of U.S. and Japanese Manufacturing Industries," *Hitotsubashi Journal of Economics*, vol. 29 (December 1988), p. 199; Robert N. McCauley and Steven A. Zimmer, "Explaining International Differences in the Cost of Capital," *Federal Reserve Board of New York Quarterly Review*, vol. 13 (Summer 1989), table 2; and George N. Hatsopoulos and Stephen H. Brooks, "The Gap in the Cost of Capital: Causes and Remedies," in Ralph Landau and Dale W. Jorgenson, eds., *Technology and Economic Policy* (Cambridge, Mass.: Ballinger, 1986), figure 12-1.

mer's cost-of-equity series is lower than those of the other studies, and this difference flows through to their cost-of-capital numbers. A second difference between our methodology and theirs accounts for the difference in volatility in the cost of capital. We used a perpetual profit rate, while the profit rate they used was tied to the life of the asset. We used the present value of depreciation tax shields, which can fluctuate with the tax code and the Aaa bond rate used for discounting. They solved a multiperiod equation using the actual depreciation schedule. Their methodology is a form of intertemporal smoothing that created very stable cost-of-capital numbers.

Finally, George N. Hatsopoulos and Stephen H. Brooks used a "steady-state growth model" for the cost of equity.[33] They considered it a reasonable approximation when applied to a large group of companies. The key component of the model is the expected growth in dividends. Hatsopoulos and Brooks solved their simultaneous equation model for the expected growth in dividends; this yielded a single number for the entire period of their model, 1961–84. Thus they too employ a form of intertemporal smoothing. Between 1975 and 1985 their cost of equity was stable, ranging from 13 to 15 percent, resulting in a smooth cost-of-capital series.

Empirical Analysis

This section presents the results of a detailed analysis of our indicators of free cash flow for eighteen industries. These industries were selected because we knew from previous work that they had either very high levels or very low levels of merger activity (appendix table 4-A1).[34] First we analyze the time series properties of the free cash flow measures and identify the sources of variation. Then we examine the data cross-sectionally to understand the extent to which there are common or industry-specific patterns of variation. Finally, we compare our results with data constructed for the companion paper, which uses a data set with many more industries and many more firms per industry.[35]

The Time-Series Pattern

Table 4-6 shows the mean values across the eighteen industries for our measures of the components of free cash flow.[36] The first six columns show that the nominal return on equity closely followed the pattern of the required return on the market. The pattern of the real cost of funds is somewhat different, however, because it was also influenced by interest rates and inflation.

The rate of economic depreciation was virtually constant. The tax factor, $(1 - t)/(1 - A)$, ranged from 1.25 to 1.33 in the early part of the 1970s, then rose to 1.5 in 1976 and stayed at this level until 1987, when it returned to its previous range. Changes in the discount rate appear to have had a larger effect on the tax factor than most of the changes in the tax code. The large changes of the Tax Reform Act of 1986, however, reduced the value of depreciation tax shields between 1987 and 1989.

The mean industry value for the cost of capital was low during the 1970s (especially in 1974–75) and relatively high in the mid-1980s. The operating profit rate declined from a high of 18 percent between 1977 and 1979 to 13 or 14 percent between 1982 and 1987. Under the combined pressure of the rising cost of capital and declining operating profit rate, the squeeze on capital fell to its lowest levels (below zero for the RP version; 1 to 3 percent for the AF version) from 1982 through 1986. Finally, the mean industry rate of cash generation declined slightly from 7–8 percent in the 1970s to 4–6 percent in the late 1980s. Not surprisingly, these industry mean series closely reflect the economywide series reported in tables 4-4 and 4-5.

Table 4-6. Mean Industry Values for Indicators of Free Cash Flow and Components, Eighteen Industries, 1971–89
Percent unless otherwise specified

Year	Required return on market[a]		Nominal required return on equity[a]		Real cost of funds[a]		Economic depreciation[b]	$(1 - A)/(1 - T)$[b]	Cost of capital[a]		Operating profit rate	Squeeze on capital[a]		Cash generation rate
	RP	AF	RP	AF	RP	AF			RP	AF		RP	AF	
1971	14	11	15	11	5	3	8	1.25	8	5	15	7	10	6
1972	14	10	14	10	5	3	8	1.26	9	6	16	7	10	7
1973	14	11	15	11	4	2	8	1.33	7	5	18	10	13	8
1974	15	14	15	14	1	0	8	1.29	3	2	18	15	16	8
1975	15	13	16	13	1	−1	8	1.28	3	1	17	14	16	7
1976	15	13	16	14	4	3	8	1.49	10	8	17	7	9	8
1977	15	14	15	15	3	3	8	1.48	8	8	18	9	10	8
1978	16	15	16	15	3	3	8	1.50	8	7	18	10	11	8
1979	17	14	17	15	3	2	8	1.46	8	6	18	10	12	8
1980	19	13	19	14	4	2	7	1.52	10	6	17	6	10	7
1981	21	13	22	14	6	2	8	1.48	12	6	16	4	9	6
1982	20	14	21	14	8	5	8	1.52	16	11	13	−3	3	4
1983	19	12	19	12	9	6	8	1.52	18	12	14	−4	1	5
1984	20	12	20	12	10	6	8	1.53	19	13	15	−4	2	6
1985	18	11	18	11	9	6	8	1.52	18	12	14	−4	2	6
1986	15	10	16	10	8	5	8	1.51	16	11	14	−2	2	5
1987	16	10	16	10	8	5	8	1.32	13	8	14	1	6	4
1988	16	11	16	10	8	5	8	1.26	12	8	15	3	6	3
1989	16	10	16	10	7	5	8	1.24	11	7	15	4	8	6

Sources: Authors' calculations from DATA1. AF version of required return on market from Malkiel, "Capital Formation Problem," and "Influence of Conditions in Financial Markets."
a. RP is constant risk premium method. AF is analysts' forecast method.
b. Excludes oil and gas exploration, SIC 1300–1329, because industry does not report fixed assets in same manner as other industries.

From a policy perspective, the sources of the variation in the squeeze on capital are of great interest. Did rising real interest rates in the 1980s drive up the required return on capital? Did the large changes in the tax code in the 1980s improve the quality of investment opportunities? To answer these questions, we developed an explicit expression for the variance of the squeeze on capital.[37] This allowed us to isolate the relative contribution of the variance of each component to the total variance. The results for the mean industry values are that 68 percent of the variance in the mean industry squeeze on capital (58 percent for the analysts' forecast version) arose from the variance in the cost of capital, leaving 32 percent (42 percent for the analysts' forecast version) to be explained by the variance of operating profits and the covariance between the cost of capital and operating profits. Of the variance in the mean industry cost of capital, 41 percent is explained by the variance in the return on the stock market (50 percent in analysts' forecast version), and another large share is explained by the covariances among the stock market returns and returns on other securities. Less than 1 percent of the variance of the mean industry cost of capital arose from the variance of the tax factor $(1 - t)/(1 - A)$.[38]

This implies that virtually all of the fluctuation in the squeeze on capital in the 1970s and 1980s was from the cost side and that the risk premium and interest rates were by far the largest contributors to changes in the cost of capital. The direct impact of interest rates was muted because only the after-tax cost of debt enters into the WACC. But, especially in the RP version, interest rates had a powerful indirect effect because changes in the Treasury bond rate were the main force behind the movements in our measure of the required return on equity. In the AF method of measuring the cost of capital, the fact that the risk premium declined when interest rates rose offset both the direct and indirect impact of higher interest rates, but the role of interest rates was still strong.

Cross-Sectional Variation

Although the time pattern of the industry means reveals a falling squeeze on capital through 1986 and a rising one thereafter, these results may not reflect the experience of all industries. This section takes a closer look at the cross-sectional variation in our measures of the components of free cash flow.

Figure 4-2. Frequency Distribution of Cost of Capital, 1971–89[a]

Cost of capital (percent)

	1971	1972	1973	1974	1975	1976	1977	1978	1979	1980	1981	1982	1983	1984	1985	1986	1987	1988	1989
-4	0	0	0	0	0	0	0	0	0	0	0	0	0	0	0	0	0	0	0
-3	0	0	0	0	1	0	0	0	0	0	0	0	0	0	0	0	0	0	0
-2	0	0	0	0	0	0	0	0	0	0	0	0	0	0	0	0	0	0	0
-1	0	0	0	0	0	0	0	0	0	0	0	0	0	0	0	0	0	0	0
0	0	0	0	2	4	0	0	0	0	0	0	0	0	0	0	0	0	0	0
1	0	0	0	2	3	0	0	0	0	0	0	0	0	0	0	0	0	0	0
2	0	0	0	6	5	0	0	0	0	0	0	0	0	0	0	0	0	0	0
3	1	0	3	3	2	0	0	0	1	0	1	0	0	0	0	0	0	0	0
4	3	1	4	2	1	1	1	1	0	1	1	0	0	0	0	0	0	0	0
5	7	5	4	1	1	0	1	0	5	1	0	0	0	0	0	0	0	0	1
6	3	5	4	0	1	0	4	5	6	7	4	0	0	0	1	0	0	0	0
7	2	4	1	2	0	5	2	3	1	5	8	0	0	0	0	0	2	0	5
8	1	2	1	0	0	4	4	4	1	2	3	1	0	0	0	1	5	7	7
9	1	1	1	0	0	2	1	1	2	1	1	2	0	0	1	0	6	7	5
10	0	0	0	0	0	2	1	0	1	1	0	0	1	1	0	1	5	4	0
11	0	0	0	0	0	1	1	2	0	0	0	10	1	0	0	3	0	0	0
12	0	0	0	0	0	2	2	2	1	0	0	2	6	2	4	6	0	0	0
13	0	0	0	0	0	0	1	0	0	0	0	2	4	4	3	6	0	0	0
14	0	0	0	0	0	1	0	0	0	0	0	0	5	6	7	1	0	0	0
15	0	0	0	0	0	0	0	0	0	0	0	1	0	4	2	0	0	0	0
16	0	0	0	0	0	0	0	0	0	0	0	0	1	0	0	0	0	0	0
17	0	0	0	0	0	0	0	0	0	0	0	0	0	1	0	0	0	0	0
18	0	0	0	0	0	0	0	0	0	0	0	0	0	0	0	0	0	0	0

Source: Authors' calculations from DATA1.
a. Number of industries in each year with cost of capital at each level. Mean values in boxes.

Figure 4-2 presents a frequency distribution of the cost of capital across the eighteen-industry sample. The analysts' forecast measure of the cost of capital was used for this analysis because, of the two measures of cost of capital we consider, it generates a narrower spread of values across industries.[39] But even this measure produces a surprisingly wide spread, 7 percentage points on average. Industries consistently appearing at the lower end of the distribution are crude petroleum and natural gas extraction, household appliances, and paper and allied products. Industries consistently at the high end are drugs, lumber and wood products, and agricultural chemicals.

The frequency distribution for operating profits (figure 4-3) shows a wide variation across industries, with an average spread between the minimum and maximum values of 17 percentage points. Petroleum and coal products (refining) and drugs are consistently at the low end, while cement and stone products (including structural clay, plaster, and gypsum) is at the high end.

Figure 4-3. Frequency Distribution of Operating Profits, 1971–89[a]

Operating profit rate (percent)

	1971	1972	1973	1974	1975	1976	1977	1978	1979	1980	1981	1982	1983	1984	1985	1986	1987	1988	1989
0	0	0	0	0	0	0	0	0	0	0	0	0	0	0	0	0	0	0	0
1	0	0	0	0	0	0	0	0	0	0	0	0	1	0	0	0	0	0	0
2	0	0	0	0	0	0	0	0	0	0	0	1	0	0	0	0	0	0	0
3	0	0	0	0	0	0	0	0	0	0	0	0	1	0	0	0	0	0	0
4	0	0	0	0	0	0	0	0	0	0	0	0	0	0	0	0	0	1	1
5	0	0	0	0	0	0	0	0	0	0	0	1	1	0	0	0	0	1	0
6	0	0	0	0	0	0	0	0	0	0	0	0	0	0	0	0	0	0	0
7	0	0	0	0	0	0	0	0	0	0	0	1	0	2	0	2	1	0	1
8	0	0	0	0	0	0	1	0	0	0	0	1	0	1	2	0	1	0	1
9	2	0	0	0	0	0	0	0	0	1	2	1	1	0	0	1	0	0	0
10	0	0	0	0	1	1	0	0	1	0	0	1	2	1	2	1	1	0	0
11	1	1	0	0	0	0	0	0	0	2	1	1	0	0	0	0	3	1	1
12	1	2	1	1	1	1	1	0	1	1	1	0	0	0	3	1	0	0	1
13	1	3	1	1	2	1	2	2	0	1	2	0	0	0	1	2	1	2	1
14	1	1	3	3	0	0	0	0	1	1	1	1	1	1	0	2	3	3	0
15	2	1	1	2	1	1	0	1	0	1	2	1	1	1	1	3	0	1	3
16	5	2	2	1	3	3	3	2	3	2	2	2	3	2	0	1	1	0	
17	1	2	2	1	3	1	0	4	2	1	0	1	2	0	1	2	2	3	2
18	1	0	0	1	1	1	2	1	2	2	0	1	2	3	2	2	1	2	2
19	1	2	1	1	2	1	1	2	2	1	2	2	0	4	1	0	3	0	0
20	1	1	1	1	1	3	2	0	0	1	1	2	2	0	2	1	0	0	3
21	0	1	1	0	0	1	0	2	0	0	2	0	1	0	1	0	0	1	1
22	0	1	2	3	1	3	2	0	2	0	1	0	0	1	0	1	0	1	0
23	0	0	0	0	1	1	2	1	0	0	1	1	0	0	0	0	1	0	0
24	0	0	0	1	0	0	2	3	2	2	0	0	1	1	0	0	0	1	0
25	1	1	1	0	1	0	0	0	1	1	0	0	0	0	0	0	0	0	1
26	0	0	1	1	0	0	0	0	1	1	0	0	0	0	0	0	0	0	0
27	0	0	1	0	0	0	0	0	0	0	0	0	0	0	0	0	0	0	0
28	0	0	0	0	0	0	0	0	0	0	0	0	0	0	0	0	0	0	0
29	0	0	0	0	0	0	0	0	0	0	0	0	0	0	0	0	0	0	0
30	0	0	0	0	0	0	0	0	0	0	0	0	0	0	0	0	0	0	0
31	0	0	0	0	0	0	0	0	0	0	0	0	0	0	0	0	0	0	0
32	0	0	0	0	0	0	0	0	0	0	0	0	0	0	0	0	0	0	0
33	0	0	0	1	0	0	0	0	0	0	0	0	0	0	0	0	0	0	0
34	0	0	0	0	0	0	0	0	0	0	0	0	0	0	0	0	0	0	0

Source: Authors' calculations from DATA1.

a. Number of industries in each year with operating profits at each level. Mean values in boxes.

Not surprisingly, the squeeze on capital also shows a wide distribution of values in every year of the sample period (figure 4-4). The average annual difference between the minimum and the maximum was 16 percentage points; it was 22 points in 1974 and 21 points in 1983. Industries frequently at the high end are agricultural chemicals, petroleum and coal products (refining), and petroleum and natural gas extraction. Industries at the low end are primary nonferrous metals, metalworking machinery, and cement and stone products.

Thus there is a wide range of values for the squeeze on capital in any year, even using the measure for the cost of capital that produces the narrowest industry distribution. But there is also a strong common time trend. The eighteen industries generally show a decline in the value of the squeeze from 1971 to the mid-1980s and a rise thereafter. Most of this trend comes from the cost side. The levels and trends in the returns to capital are not nearly as uniform. Thus there are substantial differences across industries in the impact of changes in the cost of capital that analyses of aggregate data miss.

Figure 4-5 shows the components of the squeeze on capital—the operating profit rate and the cost of capital calculated using both the RP and AF forecast approaches—for three industries. In all three the analysts' forecast measure of the cost of capital is lower than the constant risk premium approach, with the difference between the two widening from 1983 to 1987, when the risk premium as measured by the AF method fell significantly below its previous level. The radio and television broadcasting industry had operating profit rates and cost of capital close to the U.S. average, with no strong trend. By either measure of the cost of capital, the industry experienced a tremendous deterioration in the quality of investment opportunities during the mid-1980s. The drug industry, by contrast, had profit rates well above the U.S. average. The industry also experienced a tighter squeeze on capital as the cost of capital rose in the mid-1980s; but because its returns were so high, the pressures generated by this squeeze may not have been terribly strong. The book industry had rising profit rates from 1974 through 1984, but was still caught by the rise in the cost of capital. The three cases show that the rise in the cost of capital hit all industries, but that its impact on the squeeze differed depending on industry-specific patterns in the returns to capital.

These simple analyses raise questions about the source of industry and firm-level variation in the quality of investment opportunities. A few

Figure 4-4. Frequency Distribution of Squeeze on Capital, 1971–89[a]

Squeeze on capital (percent)

Squeeze	1971	1972	1973	1974	1975	1976	1977	1978	1979	1980	1981	1982	1983	1984	1985	1986	1987	1988	1989
-12	0	0	0	0	0	0	0	0	0	0	0	0	0	0	0	0	0	0	0
-11	0	0	0	0	0	0	0	0	0	0	0	0	1	0	0	0	0	0	0
-10	0	0	0	0	0	0	0	0	0	0	0	0	0	0	0	0	0	0	0
-9	0	0	0	0	0	0	0	0	0	0	0	1	1	0	0	0	0	0	0
-8	0	0	0	0	0	0	0	0	0	0	0	1	0	0	0	0	0	0	0
-7	0	0	0	0	0	0	0	0	0	0	0	1	0	0	0	0	0	0	0
-6	0	0	0	0	0	0	0	0	0	0	0	0	2	0	0	0	0	0	0
-5	0	0	0	0	0	0	0	0	0	0	1	0	0	1	1	0	0	0	0
-4	0	0	0	0	0	0	0	0	0	0	1	0	1	1	0	0	0	0	0
-3	0	0	0	0	0	0	0	0	0	0	2	0	1	1	0	0	2	0	0
-2	0	0	0	0	0	0	0	0	0	0	2	1	0	1	1	0	0	0	0
-1	0	0	0	0	0	0	0	0	0	0	0	1	0	3	1	1	0	0	0
0	0	0	0	0	0	0	1	0	0	0	0	0	1	0	0	0	0	0	3
1	0	0	0	0	0	0	0	0	0	0	1	0	1	1	2	2	1	0	0
2	0	0	0	0	0	0	0	0	0	0	0	0	2	1	1	1	2	0	1
3	0	0	0	0	0	0	0	0	0	1	1	0	2	2	2	2	1	0	0
4	0	0	0	0	0	2	0	0	0	0	1	1	2	1	2	2	0	0	0
5	0	1	0	0	0	0	0	0	0	0	1	0	3	2	3	1	1	2	3
6	0	1	0	0	0	3	0	0	1	2	1	2	1	1	1	3	0	1	2
7	4	3	0	0	0	1	2	1	1	1	3	1	0	0	0	2	0	1	1
8	3	3	1	0	0	2	3	3	0	1	2	0	1	2	1	0	5	1	1
9	0	0	1	0	0	1	1	1	1	0	2	0	2	1	0	0	1	5	1
10	3	1	2	0	0	3	1	3	1	4	1	3	0	1	1	1	1	1	3
11	2	2	3	2	1	1	3	2	2	0	0	1	1	0	0	0	0	1	1
12	1	2	1	2	2	2	2	3	4	3	1	0	0	0	0	0	0	0	3
13	3	2	2	0	2	1	2	2	3	1	1	0	0	0	0	0	0	1	1
14	0	0	2	3	2	0	1	1	2	0	2	0	0	0	1	0	1	0	0
15	0	0	0	2	3	0	0	1	1	0	0	0	0	0	0	0	0	1	0
16	1	1	1	1	1	1	1	0	0	1	2	0	0	0	0	0	0	0	0
17	0	1	0	3	3	0	0	1	0	1	0	0	0	0	0	0	0	0	1
18	0	1	3	3	1	1	1	0	0	1	1	0	0	0	0	0	0	0	0
19	1	0	1	0	1	0	0	0	0	0	0	0	0	0	0	0	0	0	0
20	0	0	0	0	0	0	0	0	0	0	0	0	0	0	0	0	0	0	0
21	0	0	0	0	0	0	0	0	0	1	0	0	0	0	0	0	0	0	0
22	0	0	1	0	0	0	0	0	2	0	0	0	0	0	0	0	0	0	0
23	0	0	0	0	0	0	0	0	0	0	0	0	0	0	0	0	0	0	0
24	0	0	0	0	0	0	0	0	0	0	0	0	0	0	0	0	0	0	0
25	0	0	0	0	1	0	0	0	0	0	0	0	0	0	0	0	0	0	0
26	0	0	0	0	0	0	0	0	0	0	0	0	0	0	0	0	0	0	0
27	0	0	0	1	0	0	0	0	0	0	0	0	0	0	0	0	0	0	0
28	0	0	0	0	0	0	0	0	0	0	0	0	0	0	0	0	0	0	0
29	0	0	0	0	0	0	0	0	0	0	0	0	0	0	0	0	0	0	0
30	0	0	0	0	0	0	0	0	0	0	0	0	0	0	0	0	0	0	0
31	0	0	0	0	0	0	0	0	0	0	0	0	0	0	0	0	0	0	0
32	0	0	0	1	0	0	0	0	0	0	0	0	0	0	0	0	0	0	0
33	0	0	0	0	0	0	0	0	0	0	0	0	0	0	0	0	0	0	0

Source: Authors' calculations from DATA1.

a. Number of industries in each year with squeeze on capital at each level. Mean values in boxes.

Figure 4-5. Operating Profit Rates and Cost of Capital, Three Industries, 1971–89

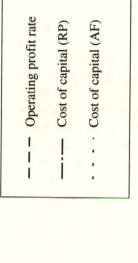

Percent

Industry with rising operating profit rate:
books

- - - Operating profit rate

-·-·- Cost of capital (RP)

········ Cost of capital (AF)

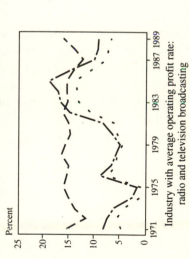

Percent

Industry with average operating profit rate:
radio and television broadcasting

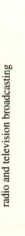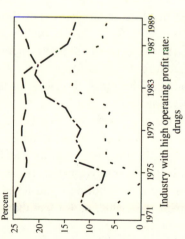

Percent

Industry with high operating profit rate:
drugs

Source: Authors' calculations.

simple calculations illustrate the relative size of the contributions of each component to the industry variation. In theory, the cost of funds should differ across firms as the risk of existing assets (business risk) and financial structures differs. The cost of capital will differ across firms because of the differences in the cost of funds and in the allocation of assets between equipment and structures. Analysis at the industry level is meaningful if the variation in the mix of assets, financial structures, and degrees of asset risk within industries is less than the variation across industries. We proceed under the assumption that the cross-industry variation is the larger of the two, deferring a complete analysis to a later time.

Industry differences in the cost of funds could lead to potentially large differences in the industry-level cost of capital because the cost of funds must be increased to cover taxes, magnifying its relative impact. At the sample mean value of the tax factor (1.43), a difference of 2 percentage points in the cost of funds will lead to a 2.86 point difference across industries in the cost of capital.

Because economic depreciation enters the equation for the cost of capital in two places and with opposite signs, the net effect of industry differences in economic depreciation is smaller than the effect of the cost of funds. At the tax factor's mean value, a 2 point increase in economic depreciation will lead to a 0.86 point increase in the cost of capital.

The third component that differs across industries is the tax factor $(1 - A)/(1 - t)$. If the real cost of funds plus economic depreciation equals 10 percent, then an increase in the tax factor from 1.4 to 1.5 increases the required return on capital by 1 percentage point. In any one year the range in values for the tax factor is fairly large. Over time this range averages 0.5. But the years with the largest industry differences are the years with the lowest cost of funds, so the net observed effect on the cost of capital is fairly small.

Finally, figure 4-6 shows the frequency distribution for the second indicator of free cash flow, the cash generation rate. With a few exceptions, the distribution is clustered around the mean, although it spreads out in the 1980s, and a few industries fall below zero for the first time late in the 1980s.

In sum, there is enormous variation among industries in the components of free cash flow. Industry trends for the squeeze on capital follow the aggregate trends, but the level of the squeeze on capital is strikingly different across industries. Industry differences in the cost of funds account for most of the industry variation in the cost of capital.

Figure 4-6. Frequency Distribution of Cash Generation Rate, 1971–89[a]

Cash generation rate (percent)

	1971	1972	1973	1974	1975	1976	1977	1978	1979	1980	1981	1982	1983	1984	1985	1986	1987	1988	1989
-15	0	0	0	0	0	0	0	0	0	0	0	0	0	0	0	0	1	1	0
-14	0	0	0	0	0	0	0	0	0	0	0	0	0	0	0	0	0	0	0
-13	0	0	0	0	0	0	0	0	0	0	0	0	0	0	0	0	0	0	0
-12	0	0	0	0	0	0	0	0	0	0	0	0	0	0	0	0	0	0	0
-11	0	0	0	0	0	0	0	0	0	0	0	0	0	0	0	0	0	0	0
-10	0	0	0	0	0	0	0	0	0	0	0	0	0	0	0	0	0	0	0
-9	0	0	0	0	0	0	0	0	0	0	0	0	0	0	0	0	1	0	0
-8	0	0	0	0	0	0	0	0	0	0	0	0	0	0	0	0	0	0	0
-7	0	0	0	0	0	0	0	0	0	0	0	0	0	0	0	0	0	0	0
-6	0	0	0	0	0	0	0	0	0	0	0	0	0	0	0	0	0	0	0
-5	0	0	0	0	0	0	0	0	0	0	0	0	0	0	0	0	0	0	0
-4	0	0	0	0	0	0	0	0	0	0	0	0	0	0	0	0	0	1	0
-3	0	0	0	0	0	0	0	0	0	0	0	1	0	0	0	0	0	0	0
-2	0	0	0	0	0	0	0	0	0	0	0	2	0	0	0	0	0	0	0
-1	0	0	0	0	0	0	0	0	0	0	0	0	1	0	0	1	2	0	0
0	0	0	0	0	0	0	0	0	0	0	0	0	1	0	0	0	0	1	1
1	0	0	0	0	0	0	0	0	0	0	0	1	0	1	0	0	0	0	1
2	0	0	0	0	0	0	0	0	0	0	1	1	0	1	0	2	0	0	1
3	0	0	0	0	0	0	0	0	0	0	1	3	0	1	1	0	1	2	1
4	2	0	0	2	0	0	0	0	0	2	1	1	1	0	2	0	1	0	0
5	1	2	1	0	0	2	0	1	1	3	3	0	2	1	2	0	3	1	4
6	4	5	2	2	5	0	2	0	1	0	1	1	2	0	3	4	1	2	1
7	5	2	2	3	3	4	2	6	4	5	4	3	5	5	3	9	3	3	0
8	4	3	5	3	6	4	6	3	3	4	6	4	3	6	6	1	2	2	3
9	2	5	3	2	6	5	2	2	2	2	1	2	2	3	1	0	3	0	2
10	0	1	3	2	0	2	4	3	5	1	0	0	0	0	0	1	1	1	2
11	0	0	1	4	0	1	2	2	2	1	0	0	0	0	0	0	0	2	1
12	0	0	0	0	0	0	0	1	0	0	0	0	0	0	0	0	0	0	1
13	0	0	0	0	0	0	0	0	0	0	0	0	0	0	0	0	0	0	0
14	0	0	0	0	0	0	0	0	0	0	0	0	0	0	0	0	1	0	0
15	0	0	1	0	0	0	0	0	0	0	0	0	0	0	0	0	0	0	0
16	0	0	0	0	0	0	0	0	0	0	0	0	0	0	0	0	0	0	0

Source: Authors' calculations from DATA1.
a. Number of industries in each year with cash generation rate at each level. Mean values in boxes.

Alternative Estimate of Expected Return

An alternative data source for the returns to capital is that generated by the Bureau of Economic Analysis. Although our measure of the operating profit rate is aggregated from the firm level, BEA aggregates historical plant-level data to the industry level. Because the bureau is not working with accounting statements but with actual reported expenditures, there is some possibility that their series may be less noisy than the aggregates we constructed. This benefit must be balanced against the fact that the BEA's industry definitions do not correspond exactly to those used in this study (BEA's industry groups are somewhat more aggregated).

The BEA returns fall monotonically from 1971 to 1986 and rise in 1987 and 1988. (BEA data for 1989 were not available when this paper was written.) The use of the BEA series lowered the squeeze on capital by 3 to 4 points on average at the mean industry values, making the picture of the decline in investment opportunities even more gloomy. But the basic time profile did not change. Thus our indicators of investment opportunities appear robust to alternative data sources in the aggregate.

Comparison with the Seventy-One-Industry Data Set

The data used in this paper came primarily from DATA1, which is limited to eighteen industries and consists of larger and more stable firms, that have consistent investor following and do not tend to come and go from the sample. This is because we limited the sample to firms followed by Compustat, Merrill Lynch, and *Value Line.* By contrast, the data set used for our companion paper (DATA2) was taken entirely from Compustat. Its coverage is much broader, including many more industries and many more firms per industry. It also includes smaller firms and has a fairly large number of entries and exits from the sample. Although we believe the larger data set is more representative of the whole U.S. economy, we needed to know whether key findings of this paper about the cost and returns to capital at the industry level hold for it as well.

In this section we present the frequency distributions of the year-to-year changes in each component of the squeeze on capital for the larger data set. We consider the distribution of changes because of the strong common time trend in these variables. By examining the changes in the cost and returns to capital we can better understand how the economy-wide shock of increasing real interest rates hit each industry.

There is a spread of 6 to 12 percentage points across industries in the change in operating profit rate in any given year (table 4-7). This distributional pattern is similar to the results for DATA1, presented in figure 4-2 (although that figure showed the distribution of operating profit levels, not the year-to-year changes as we show here). Most industries also had a similar change in the cost of capital in each year. The observations are clustered around the mean change. This illustrates the strength of the common time trend in the industry estimates of the cost of capital.

Table 4-7. Frequency Distribution for Year-to-Year Changes in Operating Profit Rate, Cost of Capital, and Capital Squeeze, Seventy-One Industries, 1979–89[a]

Percent

Year	Mean change in return	Number of industries in each range							
		Less than −6.0	−5.9 to −3.0	−2.9 to −1.0	−0.9 to 0	0.1 to 1.0	1.1 to 3.0	3.1 to 6.0	More than 6.1
		Operating profit rate							
1979	0.55	0	2	15	24	19	7	4	0
1980	−1.14	1	1	21	26	11	10	1	0
1981	0.71	0	5	13	21	23	7	1	1
1982	−1.14	4	11	25	13	15	3	0	0
1983	−0.02	2	6	9	11	17	22	3	1
1984	1.30	0	0	12	12	21	16	9	1
1985	−0.94	2	9	26	21	11	2	0	0
1986	−1.46	1	7	23	17	14	7	2	0
1987	0.37	0	1	11	10	24	19	6	0
1988	0.54	1	4	10	12	16	20	7	1
1989	−0.64	1	5	12	15	25	9	3	1
		Cost of capital (RP)[b]							
1979	0.12	1	0	12	45	10	3	0	0
1980	2.69	0	0	0	1	0	31	38	1
1981	0.99	0	0	2	9	27	32	1	0
1982	2.53	0	0	1	0	0	10	52	8
1983	0.84	0	0	0	1	6	57	7	0
1984	1.27	0	0	1	2	24	42	2	0
1985	−1.20	0	1	28	39	3	0	0	0
1986	−2.34	0	28	42	1	0	0	0	0
1987	−3.68	3	54	13	1	0	0	0	0
1988	0.07	0	1	7	21	37	5	0	0
1989	−0.46	0	1	44	24	1	1	0	0
		Capital squeeze (RP)[b]							
1979	1.56	1	2	8	15	28	14	3	0
1980	−1.84	3	46	18	3	1	0	0	0
1981	0.52	0	8	33	16	7	5	2	0
1982	−4.34	32	35	4	0	0	0	0	0
1983	−0.58	4	17	21	12	11	4	2	0
1984	−0.56	0	4	29	15	5	12	5	1
1985	−0.05	2	3	15	23	9	9	0	0
1986	0.33	0	2	3	5	10	31	19	1
1987	4.01	0	0	0	0	1	12	45	13
1988	0.23	0	4	8	14	16	21	6	2
1989	0.21	0	2	6	9	15	29	9	1

Sources: Authors' calculation from DATA2.
a. Number of industries in each year with year-to-year changes in given range.
b. RP is constant risk premium method.

Table 4-7 shows that a common factor influenced movement in the squeeze variable, but the effects differed from industry to industry. For example, in 1986 the mean change in the squeeze was positive, but 37 percent of the industries had negative changes. Thus while there was a strong economywide factor affecting investment opportunities in the 1980s, there were also strong industry-specific effects that can be exploited in testing the hypothesis that financial restructuring was a response to the presence of free cash flow.

Conclusions

In the debates about the causes of takeovers and financial restructuring activity that reshaped the corporate sector in the 1980s, the charge was often made that the firms taken over were underperforming. Poor performance was generally attributed to bad management and specifically to overretention of free cash flow.[40] Our findings are important from a policy perspective because they suggest that, indeed, many firms may have had free cash flow, but there was a significant macroeconomic factor that led to its sudden presence in so many companies.

Our industry-level measures indicate the cost of capital, which is the minimum return investors require to finance future investment, rose dramatically in the first half of the 1980s. The increase was worse in some industries than in others, but it affected all industries to some degree. The decade was also different from its predecessors in that the realized returns to capital in many industries fell. In the aggregate the decline was not as large as the increase in required returns, but, if our measure of realized returns is an accurate barometer of expected returns on future investments, then clearly the climate for new investment in many industries was hit with a double whammy. The expected profitability of future investments fell just as the profitability required by the capital markets climbed to unprecedented highs.

The rate of cash generation by industry also fell somewhat in many industries in the 1980s, but not nearly as much as our measure of the investment climate. Taken together, then, the squeeze on capital and the cash generation rate suggest that from 1982 through 1989 the U.S. corporate sector was caught up in an epidemic of free cash flow.

Appendix

Our measure of the quality of investment opportunities is the difference between the expected return and the required return. In their classic article on valuation, Merton H. Miller and Franco Modigliani used an equation for the value of the firm that is also based on this difference.[41] The equation has two components: the value of the firm under current earnings and the value of the firm with growth opportunities:

(1) $$V = CF/c + [I * (r - c)/c],$$

where V is the value of the firm, CF the current cash flows, c the cost of capital, r the expected return on capital, and I the amount to be invested. The familiar difference $r - c$ (our "squeeze on capital" variable) enters the second term to capture the net profit rate of new investment. If $r - c$ equals zero, the value of the firm is determined by its current cash flows. As Miller and Modigliani demonstrated, this valuation model is equivalent to the other commonly used valuation models. Thus there is a strong intellectual foundation for the measure of the quality of investment opportunities used in this paper.

To construct the cost of capital, we refer to the literature on public finance, where the "cost of capital services" is the minimum required profit rate to undertake investment. All empirical formulations are derived from a model of investment demand first introduced by Robert Hall and Dale Jorgenson.[42] This model can be briefly summarized.

First, the present value of the profits from the purchase of a new asset is established:

(2) $$PV(profits) = \int_0^\infty (1 - t)pe^{-(WACC + \delta)u}du$$

where p is a profit rate of the firm. It is assumed that the initial payment on the asset is 1. In this model after-tax profits are discounted at the WACC and fall each year by the amount of economic depreciation δ. Equation 2 can be integrated to a more simple expression:

(3) $$PV(profits) = \frac{(1 - t)p}{WACC + \delta}$$

The after-tax cost of the project is found by subtracting the present value of depreciation tax shields and the investment tax credit A from the initial payment: Cost $= 1 - A$.

Equating the cost of the project to its value and solving for p gives

(4) $$p = (WACC + \delta) * [(1 - A) / (1 - t)].$$

This gives the minimum rate of return required for the present value of the investment to be equal to its cost. As mentioned in the text, we do not use p as the cost of capital. Instead, we subtract economic depreciation, and use $c = p - \delta$. Thus p is a rate of profit gross of economic depreciation, and c is a rate of profit net of depreciation. We subtract δ to make the cost of capital comparable to our measure of the return on capital.

In the literature on public finance the cost of funds is commonly measured by WACC because of its ease of use and power in exposition. It is part of a capital budgeting technique (the adjusted discount rate method) in which the effects of the financing mix are captured in the discount rate, not the cash flows.[43] Thus use of the WACC is consistent with Hall's and Jorgenson's model of new investment. The WACC is forward looking because it incorporates investors' current opportunity cost.

Two data sets were constructed for use in this paper and in its companion in this volume. The first, DATA1, consists of data on 245 firms in 18 industries. The main data gathered at the firm level for DATA1 were financial statements from Compustat, betas from Merrill Lynch, and analysts' forecasts from *Value Line*. DATA1 covers the period 1971–89.

The first step in construction of DATA1 was the selection of industries for detailed study. In previous work, we had analyzed the patterns of merger activity at the industry level for 1960-87.[44] We expected a link between the financial restructuring activity studied in our companion paper and merger activity, so we chose industries with unusually high or low rates of merger activity in the 1980s in the hopes of ending up with a large variation in free cash flow. Initially, 21 industries were selected, and after we required that each have a minimum of 7 firms a year, 18 industries remained in DATA1. These and the number of firms they contain are listed in table 4-A1.[45]

The second data set, DATA2, covers only 1977–89, but is much broader in its coverage. All data were taken from Compustat. DATA2 covers 4,049 firms in 71 industries (financial services and public utilities are excluded).

All firms in DATA1 are in DATA2. For the industries it includes, DATA1 covers 40 to 50 percent of the assets of DATA2, with a range from 20 percent for petroleum extraction to almost 100 percent for lumber and wood products and metalworking machinery.

Table 4-A1. Selected Industries in DATA1, by Level of Merger Activity

Industry	SIC	Number of firms
High-merger		
Crude petroleum, natural gas, liquefied natural gas extraction	1300–1329	24
Food products, except grain mill products and beverages	2000–2039 2050–2079 2090–2099	19
Paper and allied products	2600–2699	14
Industrial chemicals	2800–2829 2860–2869	15
Drugs	2830–2839	17
Agricultural and other chemical products	2870–2899	12
Petroleum and coal products	2900–2999	23
Engines, turbines, and general industrial machinery	3500–3519 3560–3569	9
Lighting and other electrical equipment	3600–3629 3640–3649 3690–3699	15
Household appliances	3630–3639	10
Radio and television broadcasting	4830–4899	8
Low-merger		
Lumber and wood products	2400–2499	8
Books, greeting cards, and miscellaneous publishing	2730–2749 2770–2779	10
Primary nonferrous metals	3330–3399	11
Cement, structural clay, plaster, gypsum, and stone	3240–3259 3270–3289	11
Metalworking machinery	3540–3549	7
Transportation by air	4500–4599	10
Food stores	5400–5499	20

Source: DATA1.

Betas

The betas in DATA1 are from Merrill Lynch and have been updated every year since 1977. The 1977 beta is used for 1971–77. DATA2 uses the beta for the most recent reporting year (usually 1990) on Compustat for all years. Theoretically, betas are supposed to be stable, changing only with changes in the firm's capital structure. Empirically, betas are measured on monthly data over five years and do move quite a bit from year to year. This difference between the two data sets could potentially produce a difference in the cost of funds calculated from them. Empirically, however, the difference in the beta series does not seem to lead to substantive differences in the calculated cost of funds.

Balance Sheet and Income Statement Data

Most of our firm-level data came from Compustat (PC-PLUS version of August 1991). The basic variables were constructed as follows, using Compustat names: cash generation rate $(C) = (OIBDP - TXT - XINT - DIVC - DIVP) / AT$; operating profits rate $(r) = (OIBDP / AT)$; market value of equity $(MKVALF)$; value of preferred stock $(PFSTK)$; long-term debt $= (DLTT)$; short-term debt $(LT - DLTT)$.

We found that many firms had perverse data in which reported total debt was less than the reported components. Thus we took the total and subtracted out a summary of the short-term components.

Yield on Long-Term Debt

We made two attempts to construct a better proxy for the yield on long-term debt than the Baa rate. First, we tried to collect data on the quality of outstanding bonds at the firm level so that we could construct the weighted average yield to maturity by industry, with the amount of bonds at each quality level as the weights. Too few rated bonds were issued in each industry to make this a reliable measure.

Second, we constructed an index of the yield to maturity on new bond issues from *Moody's Bond Survey* and data on junk bonds supplied to us by Barrie Wigmore.[46] Because the *Bond Survey* reports the yield on new issues by bond quality, the constructed index incorporates the changing quality of new issues during the sample period. We found, however, that there were many suspect yields or missing yields in Wigmore's data. When we substituted the Baa rate for these yields (Baa is the lowest quality yield consistently reported by Moody's) our constructed index was extremely close to the Baa rate in value. Because debt is a relatively small part of the capital structure, the substitution of the Baa rate for the constructed index did not change the WACC significantly, so for comparability with other studies we used the Baa rate.

Required Return for Preferred Stock

We used the Aaa rate for preferred stock because the widely reported index of yields on preferred stock is based largely on public utility stocks (public utilities are excluded from our analysis) and comprises a relatively small number of issues. We believed the Aaa bond rate better captured the broad industry mix in our data.

Property, Plant, and Equipment

A consistent series on equipment and structures gross of depreciation was not available, so we used the following variables, which are net of depreciation, from Compustat: total property plant and equipment (*PPENT*), buildings (*PPENB*), and equipment (*PPENME*). Thus we are implicitly assuming that the relative proportions of equipment are the same net or gross of depreciation.

Compustat data for these variables are noisy and are often missing. (Few firms have a consistent, smooth time series.) Consequently, we eliminated all firms with ratios of equipment to total property or structures to total property that were more than two standard deviations from the industry mean, and then aggregated to industry levels by taking asset-weighted averages of firm-level ratios. This produced smoother and more reliable series for these ratios.

Economic Depreciation

The industry-level economic depreciation rates were calculated from the share of assets by type in each industry and the economic depreciation rates by asset type and general industry group as given in King and Fullerton.[47] These rates are constant over time, so the ensuing economic depreciation rate varies over time from the changing mix of asset types.

Industry	Equipment	Structures	Inventories
Manufacturing	0.1331	0.0343	0
Commerce	0.1710	0.0247	0
Other Industry	0.1302	0.0304	0

Depreciation Tax Shields

The first step in constructing the depreciation tax shields was to identify the depreciation-allowable method, the allowable life of equipment and structures, the corporate tax rate, and the availability of an investment tax credit (ITC) for each year. These data, summarized in table 4-A2, are based on a stylized history of the U.S. tax code developed from various sources (see the source note to table 4-A2).

Once the tax history was developed, the present value of depreciation tax shields (*A*) was calculated. The after-tax AAA bond rate from the

Table 4-A2. Depreciation Tax Shield Components, 1970–89

Years	Life of assets (years) Equipment	Structures	Depreciation method, equipment[a]	ITC (percent)	Marginal corporate tax rate (t)
1970–72	7	28	DDB	0	0.48
1973–75	7	28	DDB	5	0.48
1976–78	7	28	DDB	10	0.48
1979–80	7	28	DDB	10	0.46
1981–82	5	15	ACRS	10	0.46
1983–86	5	15	ACRS	10	0.46
1987	7	31.5	MACRS	0	0.40
1988–89	7	31.5	MACRS	0	0.34

Sources: King and Fullerton, *Taxation of Income from Capital*, pp. 202–08; Alan Auerbach, "Corporate Taxation in the United States," *Brookings Papers on Economic Activity, 2: 1983*, table 2 and appendix A; and Richard Brealey and Stewart Myers, *Principles of Corporate Finance*, 2d ed. p. 94, and 4th ed., p. 105.

a. DDB: double-declining balances; ACRS: accelerated cost recovery system; MACRS: modified accelerated cost recovery system. Straight-line depreciation used for structures in all years.

Economic Report of the President was used to discount the depreciation expenses, and the ITC was subtracted. This method results in a separate value for *A* for equipment and structures. Using the relative magnitude of these two asset types by industry, an industry average *A* is found. These data are summarized in table 4-A3.

Alternative Measure of Operating Profits

The numerator of the alternative measure of operating profits was taken from the "Gross Product by Industry, 1977–88," BEA NIWD (BE-54) tape from the Bureau of Economic Analysis, released in February 1991. For earlier years we used the "GNP by Industry, 1945–87" tape released by BEA in early 1989. We added the inventory valuation adjustment, capital consumption allowance, and interest to profits at the industry level. Thus our payments to capital is net of economic depreciation.

The denominator in the alternative measure of operating profits was taken from the "Wealth Data Tape" released by BEA in July 1990. Our measure is the sum of equipment and structures at the industry level, adjusted by a capital stock factor intended to gross up the measure of buildings and equipment to account for other kinds of assets. BEA reports only buildings and equipment. So we used Compustat data to construct an industry-level ratio of the capital stock not reported by BEA to reported capital stock. This was the ratio of the sum of land, natural resources inventories, and non-interest-bearing assets to the sum of build-

Table 4-A3. Depreciation Tax Shield Value, 1971–89

Year	After-tax AAA rate (percent)	Present value of ITC and depreciation tax shields[a]	
		Equipment	Structures
1971	0.9	0.43	0.43
1972	1.3	0.42	0.41
1973	0.5	0.36	0.38
1974	−0.3	0.36	0.42
1975	−0.5	0.37	0.44
1976	1.1	0.28	0.28
1977	0.7	0.29	0.29
1978	0.8	0.29	0.29
1979	0.4	0.27	0.29
1980	1.6	0.26	0.24
1981	2.4	0.29	0.26
1982	4.0	0.28	0.22
1983	4.4	0.28	0.22
1984	4.9	0.28	0.21
1985	4.5	0.28	0.22
1986	3.5	0.29	0.23
1987	3.7	0.37	0.24
1988	4.2	0.31	0.19
1989	3.4	0.32	0.21

a. The present value of ITC and depreciation tax shields = depreciable basis times PV [(depreciation schedule, AAA rate $*(1 - t)]*t - ITC$. Depreciable basis = $1 - ITC$.

ings and equipment. (Compustat variables $(PPENNR + PPENLI + INVT + CH + XPP)/(PPENB + PPENME)$.) The BEA capital stock measures were then multiplied by 1 plus this ratio. For consistency, we constructed the industry aggregates using data only from firms that reported positive values for buildings and equipment. This eliminated many small firms that reported only inventories. This ratio ranged from 0.23 to 4.0.

As we mentioned in the text, the BEA industry definitions are more aggregated than our own. We based the capital stock adjustment factor on industry definitions comparable to BEA's industry definitions. The estimated BEA operating profit rates are at BEA's industry level. Where the BEA industry data were more aggregated than our own, we assumed that the same rate of return applied to all parts of the more aggregated industry.

Comment by George N. Hatsopoulos

Margaret Blair's and Martha Schary's paper makes at least four provocative and useful contributions to the literature on capital costs and corporate restructuring. It clearly points out that returns on capital may differ substantially from the marginal cost of capital. It shows that there was, indeed, a squeeze on the net return to capital in the late 1970s to mid-1980s. It provides evidence that the cost of capital may differ from industry to industry, something that has been discussed in the past but never specifically shown. And finally, it advances an explanation for the inordinate rise in leverage and restructuring in U.S. industry during the 1980s.

Let me address each of these points separately. By separating out industries, the authors are forced to work with very small samples of firms, which tends to result in high volatility and numbers that are not always credible. I have worked with smaller samples, and the only thing I have found reasonably satisfying in looking at the relation between the cost of equity and the cost of risk-free debt is big aggregates. For example, I have used data for the nonfinancial corporate sector from the Federal Reserve, with adjustments done at the aggregate level. I have found anything less than that to be troublesome.

Blair and Schary identify a clear squeeze in the mid-1980s, but in my own work going back to 1983, that squeeze showed up earlier in the aggregates, coming mainly from the returns side.[48] That squeeze was most severe in 1982 because of the recession that year, and then went away.

Is this squeeze a reasonable, plausible explanation for the high leverage experienced in the 1980s? I am concerned about giving this factor too much weight as a cause of leveraged restructuring. First, there is a timing problem. According to my calculations, the aggregate squeeze started in the mid-1970s, after the first energy crisis, and persisted through 1982, yet high leverage began showing up in 1984. That was when net new equity issues suddenly became huge negative numbers—$80 billion to $100 billion a year. By 1986–88, in the aggregate, the returns were again higher than the cost of capital. Yet the leverage continues.

The second problem I have with the theory is that a squeeze should be reflected in investment rates. If there is a squeeze, investments fall. I

Table 4-A4. Maximum Taxation of Returns from Investments Totally Financed by Debt and Totally Financed by Equity, 1980, 1982, 1987[a]

| | 1980 | | | 1982 | | | 1987 | | |
| | All | All | | All | All | | All | All | |
Item	debt	equity	Difference	debt	equity	Difference	debt	equity	Difference
Operating return	100.0	100.0	. . .	100.0	100.0	. . .	100.0	100.0	. . .
Total taxes	70.0	72.0	2.0	50.0	65.0	15.0	28.0	52.0	24.0
Corporate	0	46.0	. . .	0	46.0	. . .	0	34.0	. . .
Investor taxes, interest, and dividends	70.0	18.0	. . .	50.0	13.5	. . .	28.0	9.0	. . .
Capital gains	0	8.0	. . .	0	5.5	. . .	0	9.0	. . .

a. Assumed payout ratio for all-equity investments is 50 percent.

would expect the squeeze to affect the investment rate much more than it affects leverage: leverage is a second-order change. Yet there was not much reduction. There was reduction in net capital formation, but on gross capital formation, there was no reduction in the nonfinancial corporate sector, at least in the aggregate. Therefore, I do not see the relationship very clearly.

In my opinion there were two causes of leveraged buyouts—a tax cause and the use of new financial instruments. The tax changes were significant. Given the extreme case of a project financed totally by equity versus one financed only by debt and financed by an individual at the highest bracket, the total taxation in 1980 of debt and equity was about the same. By 1982 the difference was 15 percentage points, and by 1987 it became 24 percentage points (table 4-A4). The second cause of buyouts in the 1980s was the relaxation by the IRS of strict regulations segregating debt holders from equity holders. Because of that relaxation, people invented innovative financial instruments. These two conditions go further than the squeeze on capital to explain the leverage and restructuring in the 1980s.

Comment by Stewart C. Myers

Margaret Blair's and Martha Schary's paper proposes an interesting specification of Michael Jensen's free cash flow theory of the market for corporate control, otherwise known as the "management is an off-balance-sheet liability" theory of corporate finance. According to that theory, managers of mature, profitable companies tend to hold on to cash that should be paid out to investors and tend to waste the cash in organizational slack, investments with negative net present value, or ill-advised acquisitions. These companies then become targets for reform in "diet deals," that is, in takeovers, LBOs, and restructurings.

The free cash flow theory has many clear supporting examples, but it is not fully worked out. Sometimes it sounds like good guys versus bad guys: the good guys force out the bad guys, the managers who retain and waste cash. But the theory does not fully explain where the bad guys come from or why the good guys do not lose their virtue once they have taken charge.

Blair and Schary propose a partial answer: good guys became bad guys when the real cost of capital increased drastically without a corresponding increase in the profitability of new investment. The investment programs of targets for diet deals were not always bad; they were made so by the rise in real interest rates and costs of capital in the early and mid-1980s. Cash cow companies became targets only because they did not cut back their operating, investment, and acquisition plans quickly enough. Organizational momentum, the tendency to keep plowing free cash flow back into the business, created waste and was disciplined.

This interpretation rings true when one remembers the unprecedented rise in real interest rates in the early 1980s. That rise naturally led investors to favor quicker payoffs and probably accounted for the short-termism that critics of managers and the stock market so often complain about. Blair and Schary argue that takeovers, LBOs, and restructurings occurred because some managers of mature companies took too *long* a view of their businesses: they did not cut back investment in response to the squeeze of operating profitability versus the cost of capital. In other words, they did not embrace short-termism quickly enough.

The real cost of capital for most corporations did rise sharply in the early 1980s. I recently completed a study of costs of capital for major oil companies from 1965 to 1985 using methods different from Blair and Schary's. There was a dramatic increase in 1980 immediately after the Federal Reserve shifted from control of interest rates to control of monetary growth.

Thus, I agree completely with the Blair-Schary premise. However, I also appreciate how difficult it is to give the premise a correct numerical expression. The hardest step of all is measuring possible changes in the expected risk premium embedded in the cost of capital.

Blair and Schary use the capital asset pricing model (CAPM), assuming a market risk premium equal to a long-run historical average. This follows standard practice and gives reasonable numbers. Using this average forecloses any possibility of tracking changes in expected risk premiums, but there is no simple, practical alternative. Shorter averages simply pick up noise, that is, the unanticipated ups and downs of the stock market. (The annual standard deviation of returns on Standard and Poor's Composite Index is roughly 20 percent.)

There are a few forward-looking estimates of the expected market return or risk premium. Examples include the *Value Line* series used by Blair and Schary and the estimates developed by Robert Harris and Felicia Marston.[49] These estimates are extracted from the discounted cash flow (DCF) model of stock valuation, which says that stock price equals the present value of expected future dividends. The discount rate is the expected rate of return. This can be calculated given stock prices and forecasts for dividends.

These DCF estimates might seem better than CAPM estimates based on historical data, but I am skeptical. I think DCF returns for the stock market as a whole are biased downward. They cannot be calculated for stocks that do not pay dividends, which are riskier and should offer higher expected returns. Also, dividend forecasts tend to miss some of the upside potential of growth stocks.

I also think that analysts' forecasts of earnings and dividends are sticky and that the DCF returns therefore do not respond fast enough when conditions in capital markets change. This would generate spurious movements in implied risk premiums when interest rates fluctuate.   ·

Let me now turn from Blair's and Schary's estimates of costs of capital to their interpretation of the free cash flow theory. They propose that companies with a squeeze on returns will be targets for takeovers, LBOs, or restructurings that drastically increase leverage. The squeeze is measured by the difference between the average book rate of return on assets and the cost of capital. If the squeeze becomes smaller, or more negative, the probability of a takeover, LBO, or restructuring increases.

There are dangers here. First, the book rate of return on assets is liable to well-known biases. Second, the squeeze variable may confuse average and marginal returns.

Remember the basic theory: when corporate momentum leads to continued large outlays or acquisitions despite increases in the real cost of capital that make some of these investments uneconomical, discipline is provided by increased leverage or some change in corporate control. That story does not require negative net returns on average, only at the margin.

Imagine a company that has become accustomed to earning an average 10 percentage points over the cost of capital and is expanding aggressively. Now imagine the company's cost of capital increases by 5 percentage points. This drives the net present value of many investment projects negative: all those projects earning from zero to 5 percentage points above the previous cost of capital. The rate of expansion should therefore be cut back. If the cutback does not come, the company becomes the natural target for good guys that would put its investment program on a diet. Yet the company would not show up as strongly squeezed under Blair's and Schary's definition because its average return would still exceed the cost of capital by roughly 5 percentage points.

In other words, "squeeze" might be better defined as the *change* in the spread between the rate of return on capital and the cost of capital. This might also sidestep the accounting biases, since the level of the book rate of return would not be so important.

Let me balance these criticisms by pointing out how difficult it is to estimate changes in expected profitability and the cost of capital. Blair's and Schary's line of attack makes sense, and they have assembled a large amount of the right kind of data. The payoff will come in their companion paper and in their future work in this area.

General Discussion

Dennis Mueller called attention to the social costs behind the free cash flow theory. He noted that in any industry and year in which the marginal return to capital was less than the cost of capital, cash flow was clearly being wasted by managers who continued their investment programs. This is also true in any industry or year in which managers perceive that they have a negative cost of capital. Mueller observed that if managers actually perceive the cost of capital to be negative at any time, they would be encouraged to waste assets on poor investments even if they did not have any cash flow. They could just issue equity, he said, and invest the cash in things that would make their shareholders worse off.

"Clearly society would be much better off," he said, if capital were transferred from these industries to industries in which the cost was realistically viewed as positive, and the marginal return exceeded the cost. For this reason, the appropriate way to measure the cost of capital is to use measures that effectively capture the opportunity cost, which is what investors could earn with an alternative investment of comparable risk. Martha Schary responded that using the capital asset pricing model to measure the cost of equity was intended to achieve exactly that.

Frank Lichtenberg questioned whether restructuring should be viewed as something imposed on managers from the outside or something they undertake themselves. Ron Daniels said he would have expected more managers to undertake restructuring themselves if the squeeze on capital resulted from rising cost of capital rather than from a fall in returns. This is because the squeeze should then be viewed by managers as an exogenous shock and not a reflection of their own malfeasance. If the squeeze resulted from decreasing returns, however, that may reflect poorly on management's competence, and the restructuring would be more likely to require third-party intervention, he suggested.

Paul Francis and Darius Gaskins argued that leveraged restructurings were more supply driven than demand driven in the sense that they were done because the financial markets were willing to supply unusually cheap capital in the form of junk bonds. Steve Zimmer suggested that there was something of a self-fulfilling prophecy at work. During the late 1980s the yield on highly rated bonds included an additional risk factor to compensate bondholders for the risk that the issuer might restructure and become more highly leveraged. But this meant that the spread between the yield on highly rated bonds and the yield on low-rated bonds was reduced to unusually low levels, which meant that the penalty for leveraging up was reduced.

Because these supply-side effects were so important, Francis argued that the cross-industry distribution of leveraged restructuring activity should be explained by factors that influence the willingness of financial markets to supply debt capital to an industry. For example, he said, the few industries in which leverage capital was restricted were those with uncertain cash flows or those that were heavily regulated.

Oliver Hart expressed concern about the inability of researchers to distinguish empirically between marginal and average returns to capital. It is possible, he noted, for average returns to be high and marginal returns to be low, or vice versa. In the former case, the optimal capital structure would include a lot of leverage, but in the latter, low leverage would be preferred. Hart also commented that it is important to know the initial debt levels. If marginal returns fall, he said, there would be much less need for restructuring in firms that are already highly leveraged than in firms that are not.

Mark Warshawsky questioned whether industries are the right unit of analysis for looking at the free cash flow theory. Because this theory is about managerial incentives, he argued, and because managers operate in firms, the appropriate unit of analysis is the individual company. Schary responded that using a firm-level analysis would introduce even more noise into estimates of the components of free cash flow than the authors found at the industry level. But aggregating all the way up to the level of the whole economy, as George Hatsopoulos suggested, would make it impossible to identify industry differences. These are important, she argued, because leverage and merger activity seems to happen at different rates in different industries.

Notes

1. Michael C. Jensen, "Agency Costs of Free Cash Flow, Corporate Finance, and Takeovers," *American Economic Review,* vol. 76 (May 1986, *Papers and Proceedings,* 1985), pp. 323–29.

2. See, for example, Louis S. Richman, "How Capital Costs Cripple America," *Fortune,* August 14, 1989, pp. 50–54; and "Capital Punishment," *Economist,* May 23, 1992, p. 71. The argument was first made in George N. Hatsopoulos, *High Cost of Capital: Handicap of American Industry* (Washington: American Business Conference, 1983).

3. Examples of other work using indicators of free cash flow include Brent Ambrose and Drew Winters, "Does an Industry Effect Exist for Leveraged Buyouts?" *Financial Management,* vol. 21 (Spring 1992), pp. 89–101; and Kenneth Lehn and Annette Poulsen, "Free Cash Flow and Stockholder Gains in Going Private Transactions," *Journal of Finance,* vol. 44 (July 1989), pp. 771–87. Both studies look at actual cash flow. Lehn and Poulsen also use the growth rate of sales, while Ambrose and Winters use the growth rate of assets as proxies for investment opportunities. In our companion paper in this volume, we use the growth rate of assets in addition to indicators developed in this paper to help explain restructuring activity.

4. Carl W. Kester and Timothy Leurhman, "Cross-Country Differences in the Cost of Capital: A Survey and Evaluation of Recent Empirical Studies," Harvard Business School, 1991. This point is discussed more fully later.

5. The selection of the industrial chemicals industry allows the results of the

model to be linked with the evidence on restructuring in the industrial chemicals industry developed in Sarah Lane, "Corporate Restructuring in the Chemicals Industry," later in this volume.

6. Robert E. Hall and Dale W. Jorgenson, "Tax Policy and Investment Behavior," *American Economic Review*, vol. 57 (June 1967), pp. 391–414. See also James M. Poterba, "Comparing the Cost of Capital in the United States and Japan: A Survey of Methods," *Federal Reserve Bank of New York, Quarterly Review*, vol. 15 (Winter 1991), pp. 20–32, for an introduction to this model and a survey of empirical issues associated with its implementation.

7. Often Tobin's q is used to measure the quality of investment opportunities. However, Eric B. Lindenberg and Stephen A. Ross have shown that empirical estimates of q are noisy results of lengthy calculations from accounting data. See "Tobin's q Ratio and Industrial Organization," *Journal of Business*, vol. 54 (January 1981), pp. 1–32. Our measure of investment opportunity is based on slightly different elements of the financial statement and perhaps has a stronger signal-to-noise ratio. We will be exploring this matter in future research.

8. Economic depreciation is commonly thought of as the decline in the value of an asset that results from the fall in productivity as it ages. We argue that ordinary maintenance costs have already been deducted from the measure of returns we use, even though that measure is gross of accounting depreciation. Thus we interpret our measure of expected returns as including an expectation that the firm will maintain the underlying assets to create a perpetual stream of returns and that the measure should therefore be regarded as net of economic depreciation. See Jack E. Triplett, "Measuring the Capital Stock: A Review of Data Needs for Productivity, Production Analysis, and the NIPA," Washington, Bureau of Economic Analysis, April 22, 1991, for a complete and helpful discussion of economic depreciation and related concepts.

9. The definition of the cost of capital in equation 1' is also used by Mervyn A. King and Don Fullerton, but in few other studies. See *The Taxation of Income from Capital: A Comparative Study of the United States, the United Kingdom, Sweden, and West Germany* (University of Chicago Press, 1984), p. 344. When we compare the results of our study with previous empirical work, we add back the rate of economic depreciation to our measure of the cost of capital.

10. We used a rolling average of the rate of change of the GNP deflator as our measure of inflation.

11. Stewart C. Myers calls the WACC the classic textbook formula in his comparative analysis of capital budgeting methods. See "Interactions of Corporate Financing and Investment Decisions—Implications for Capital Budgeting," *Journal of Finance*, vol. 29 (March 1974), pp. 1–25. See also D. R. Chambers, R. S. Harris, and J. J. Pringle, "Treatment of Financing Mix in Analyzing Investment Opportunities," *Financial Management*, vol. 11 (Summer 1982), pp. 24–41; and Robert A. Taggart, Jr., "Capital Budgeting and the Financing Decision: An Exposition," *Financial Management*, vol. 6 (Summer 1977), pp. 59–64, and Taggart, "Consistent Valuation and Cost of Capital Expressions with Corporate and Personal Taxes," *Financial Management*, vol. 20 (Autumn 1991), pp. 8–21.

12. In our companion paper, we call this the "net returns to capital," but here, because of its repeated role, we use the shorter expression "squeeze," or the variable name SQZ.

13. The numerator to equation 3 is a definition of free cash flow used by several authors, beginning with Lehn and Poulsen, "Free Cash Flow and Stockholder Gains."

14. See Stewart Myers, "The Capital Structure Puzzle," *Journal of Finance,* vol. 39 (July 1984), pp. 575–92.

15. Two data sets were constructed for the cost of capital and SQZ calculations used in this study and the companion paper. DATA1 includes firm-level data for 245 selected firms in 18 industries, and covers 1971–89; DATA2 includes firm-level data for 4,049 firms in 71 industries, and covers 1977–89. Differences between the two data sets are discussed in detail in the appendix. DATA1 is used for the chemicals industry calculations shown in tables 4-2 and 4-3.

16. Inventory is a tangible asset that could potentially experience economic depreciation, but King and Fullerton, *Taxation of Income from Capital,* show a zero rate of economic depreciation for this asset. Inventories receive no depreciation allowances in the tax code.

17. See Kester and Leurhman, "Cross-Country Differences in the Cost of Capital."

18. In the CAPM, the cost of equity is computed as $k_c = r_f + \beta(r_m - r_f)$, where r_f is the risk-free rate, r_m is the rate of return on the market, and β is the firm-level beta.

All returns calculated in this paper are rounded to the left of the decimal place. As many have noted, numbers for calculated cost of capital are noisy; including digits to the right of the decimal place would suggest greater precision than we believe our data permit.

19. See Burton G. Malkiel, "The Capital Formation Problem in the United States," *Journal of Finance,* vol. 34 (May 1979), pp. 291–306, and Malkiel, "The Influence of Conditions in Financial Markets on the Time Horizons of Business Managers: An International Comparison," in Michael E. Porter, ed., *Investment Behavior and Time Horizon in American Industry* (Harvard Business School Press, forthcoming).

20. See Roger Ibbottson and Rex A. Singefeld, *Stocks, Bonds, Bills, and Inflation: The Past and the Future* (Richard D. Irwin, 1992), pp. 14, 73.

21. Poterba, "Comparing the Cost of Capital," pp. 20–32, summarizes the difficulties in measuring the cost of equity. He finds that historical data, such as we use here, provide noisy results and seems to prefer an alternative, price-earning ratios, to calculate the cost of equity. However, P/E ratios also have their problems: a large number of adjustments must be made to reported earnings, and the ratio can change in value relatively quickly. In a previous version of this paper, we used a three-year average P/E ratio to calculate the cost of equity. Conference participants found the ensuing cost of capital series far too volatile to be credible as an estimate of managerial expectations. Thus we now base our main calculations on the capital asset pricing model.

22. See, for example, Eugene F. Fama and Kenneth R. French, "Business Conditions and Expected Returns on Stocks and Bonds," *Journal of Financial*

Economics, vol. 25 (November 1989), pp. 23–49, for a clear exposition of this issue, and Wayne E. Ferson and Campbell R. Harvey, "The Variation of Economic Risk Premiums," *Journal of Political Economy,* vol. 99 (April 1991), pp. 385–415, and the references cited in both papers.

23. Robert S. Harris and Felicia C. Marston calculate an expected return on the market using the broader coverage of analysts' forecasts in the IBES tape. Their series begins as 20.08 percent in 1982 and declines almost monotonically to 15.06 percent in 1989. See "Estimating Shareholder Risk Premia Using Analysts' Growth Forecasts," *Financial Management,* vol. 21 (Summer 1992), pp. 63–70. On the other hand, Eugene F. Brigham, Dilip K. Shome, and Steve R. Vinson compare the IBES and *Value Line* forecasts for the electric utility industry in 1983 and 1984. They find no statistical difference between the forecasts. See "The Risk Premium Approach to Measuring a Utility's Cost of Equity," *Financial Management,* vol. 14 (Spring 1985), pp. 33–45.

24. See the appendix for a discussion of alternative ways to construct the required return on long-term debt and the problems these approaches present.

25. King and Fullerton, *Taxation of Income from Capital.*

26. Barry Bosworth and Gary Burtless report that other researchers have found the same offsetting effects. See "Effects of Tax Reform on Labor Supply, Investment, and Saving," *Journal of Economic Perspectives,* vol. 6 (Winter 1992), pp. 3–25.

27. In an informative survey, A. Steven Englander and Gary Stone compare two predictors of inflation: surveys of expectations and historical inflation. See "Inflation Expectations Surveys as Predictors of Inflation and Behavior in Financial and Labor Markets," *Federal Reserve Bank of New York, Quarterly Review,* vol. 14 (Autumn 1989), pp. 20–32. The three surveys they evaluated focus on the consumer price index, not the GNP deflator, but the authors found that none provided very good inflation forecasts. Of the three, the one Englander and Stone found most reflective of financial markets' expectations did not outperform lagged inflation during the sample period.

28. These data are from DATA2, a second data base used primarily in the companion paper. The capital mix numbers, the shares of equipment and structures, the real cost of funds, and beta were aggregated from firm-level data; the remaining series were asset-weighted averages of industry-level calculations. Utilities and financial services were excluded.

29. Two measures of the weighted average cost of capital (WACC) were constructed from the aggregate capital structure weights shown in table 4-4 and the alternative measures of the return on equity, the Aaa bond rate for preferred stock, the prime rate for short-term debt, and the Baa rate for long-term debt. These aggregate values were then adjusted by values of economic depreciation, A, and $(1 - A)/(1 - t)$, which are the asset-weighted averages of industry-level data, as reported in table 4-5.

30. As noted earlier, to make our numbers comparable, economic depreciation was added back to the results we report in table 4-5.

31. Eiji Tajika and Yuji Yui, "Cost of Capital and Effective Tax Rate: A Comparison of U.S. and Japanese Manufacturing Industries," *Hitotsubashi Journal of Economics,* vol. 29 (December 1988), pp. 181–200.

32. See "Explaining International Differences in the Cost of Capital," *Federal Reserve Board of New York, Quarterly Review,* vol. 13 (Summer 1989), pp. 7–28.

33. See "The Gap in the Cost of Capital: Causes and Remedies," in Ralph Landau and Dale W. Jorgenson, eds., *Technology and Economic Policy* (Ballinger, 1986), pp. 221–80. See also Poterba, "Comparing the Cost of Capital in the United States and Japan," for an overview. Finally, Hatsopoulos, "High Cost of Capital," contains a detailed description of this method of calculating the cost of equity.

34. DATA1, which was used for the detailed industry-level analysis, contains the firm-level data for these eighteen industries. The individual firms were selected because we could get data on them from Compustat, Merrill Lynch, and *Value Line.* See the appendix for more details.

35. The larger data set (DATA2) includes more firms because we imposed only one restriction: that the firm appear in Compustat for at least three years and have the data necessary for a given calculation. We also restricted the sample in DATA1 to 1977–89. See the appendix for details.

36. For all constructed series, the median industry value was almost always equal to the mean, with occasional differences of at most two points. Each industry aggregate is an asset-weighted average of firm-level data.

37. The squeeze on capital is a linear function of two components, r and c, so the formula for its variance is straightforward. However, c is a nonlinear function of its components, which leads to complicated expressions for its variance. We used Taylor series approximation for the variance of a nonlinear function suggested by Alexander A. Mood, Franklin A. Graybill, and Duane C. Boes, *Introduction to the Theory of Statistics,* 3d ed. (McGraw-Hill, 1984), p. 181.

38. Other authors have found that changes in the tax code during the 1980s did not affect investment and the effective tax rate. See Bosworth and Burtless, "Effects of Tax Reform on Labor Supply, Investment, and Saving"; and James M. Poterba, "Why Didn't the Tax Reform Act of 1986 Raise Corporate Taxes?" in *Tax Policy and the Economy,* no. 6 (MIT Press, 1982), pp. 43–58.

39. One important factor leading to industry differences in the cost of capital is the industry beta. High-risk premiums accentuate these differences, and low-risk premiums dampen them. In the analysts' forecast measure, the risk premium declines during the sample period, thereby narrowing the differences among industries in the measured cost of capital.

40. See Michael C. Jensen, "Eclipse of the Public Corporation," *Harvard Business Review,* vol. 89 (September–October 1989), pp. 63–74, for a particularly interesting and provocative argument of this type.

41. Merton H. Miller and Franco Modigliani, "Dividend Policy, Growth, and the Valuation of Shares," *Journal of Business,* vol. 34 (October 1961), pp. 411–33. Our equation is a simplification of their equation 12, p. 417.

42. See Hall and Jorgenson, "Tax Policy and Investment Behavior."

43. See Donald Chambers, Robert Harris, and John Pringle, "Treatment of Financing Mix in Analysis of Investment Opportunities," *Financial Management,* vol. 11 (Summer 1982), pp. 24–41, for a discussion of this capital budgeting method and two others, the adjusted present value (APV) and the flows to equity

methods. Readers familiar with capital budgeting will note that the valuation model outlined above is equivalent to an APV setup. The base net present value (NPV) includes the effects of the financing mix, while the adjustment shows the side effects of the tax laws on investment.

44. See Margaret M. Blair, Sarah J. Lane, and Martha A. Schary, "Patterns of Corporate Restructuring, 1955–87," Brookings discussion papers in economics 91-1 (January 1991).

45. We also limited our sample to twenty-five firms a year. This affected the number of firms in two industries: crude petroleum, natural gas, and NGL extraction; and petroleum and coal products.

46. See Blair and Schary, "Industry-Level Pressures to Restructure," in this volume for more details on Wigmore's data.

47. See King and Fullerton, *Taxation of Income from Capital*.

48. Hatsopoulos, *High Cost of Capital*.

49. Harris and Marston, "Estimating Shareholder Risk Premia," pp. 63–70.

Industry-Level Pressures to Restructure

Margaret M. Blair and
Martha A. Schary

DURING the 1980s, many corporations in the United States undertook financial transactions that dramatically altered their capital structure, their ownership structure, their relationship to the financial markets, or sometimes all three. Although no two companies restructured in exactly the same way, numerous transactions were characterized by the removal of equity from publicly traded status (sometimes accompanied by a change in managerial or shareholder control); large increases in leverage, with new debt often substituting for equity in the capital structure; and increased reliance on high-risk, high-yield debt instruments (junk bonds and other so-called tailored securities) for financing major deals. Financial transactions with these features were rare before the 1980s, but by the end of the decade nearly every corporation had been affected by pressure to restructure. Hundreds of companies were restructured; many others altered their investment strategies or financing choices or even their corporate bylaws to protect themselves from an unwanted takeover or forced restructuring.

An important question, both for policymakers and theorists interested in understanding corporate performance and financial market behavior, is why that pressure emerged when and where it did. This question, of course, has two parts: When and where did restructuring take place, and why did it occur there? In this paper we address the first question in

We would like to thank Brookings and the Boston University Manufacturing Roundtable for financial support for this project. We also thank Girish Uppal, who provided months of dedicated research assistance, and research and staff assistants Igor Dukovich, Paul Rathuoz, Irene Coray, Adam Metter, Murat Iyigun, Marc Rysman, and Rajashree Paralkar. Finally, this paper has benefited from helpful comments by Darius Gaskins, Dennis Mueller, Michael Salinger, Barry Bosworth, Clifford Winston, Robert Vishny, and participants in the NBER Summer Institute, Corporate Finance Session. We especially thank Steve Sharpe for alerting us to some peculiarities in one of our data sources that we were then able to account for properly.

detail, showing how the 1980s were unique in the kinds of financial restructurings that occurred, as well as in their pace and intensity. Using new data that provide broader coverage than has been possible in previous studies, we measure the incidence of restructuring activity over the decade and across industries. Finally, we try to shed light on *why* by examining whether these measured patterns are consistent with various theories about the causes of restructuring activity.

To answer the *when* and *where*, we identified three categories of restructuring events—private buyouts, large increases in leverage, and junk bond issues—and then screened more than 10,800 publicly traded firms listed in the Compustat PCPlus data base for 1971 to 1990 to find which firms, in which years, engaged in any of these activities. Because Compustat identifies each firm's major lines of business, we have been able to track the incidence of restructuring events by industry as well as by firm and year. Our approach stemmed from the idea that economy-wide pressures encouraged or forced firms to restructure. Firm and industry characteristics, however, probably resulted in more pressure on some firms and industries than on others. The types of restructuring activity we have focused on represent some of the most aggressive responses to these pressures. We have also explored the links among these three kinds of events, the rise in corporate takeovers of all types, and the general rise in corporate debt in the 1980s.

We have found that firms engaging in one or more financial restructurings were disproportionately responsible for the increase in debt in the corporate sector as well as for acquisition and divestiture activity. Companies that had large increases in debt were typically underleveraged relative to their industry average before the restructuring.[1] But those that were targets of private buyouts had debt-to-total asset ratios similar to others in their industry, and junk bond issuers were already highly leveraged before the event. The firms involved in any of these restructuring events typically experienced a marked slowdown in the growth rate of their assets after the event.

Answering the question of why all this occurred is more complicated. Several theories have been put forth to explain the restructuring phenomenon, each with its own implications for the characteristics of firms and industries where financial restructuring would most likely take place. We will discuss them in detail later, but a theory we have been especially interested in testing is that corporations in many industries restructured financially in the 1980s because they had relatively poor investment opportunities, made worse by unusually high costs of capital. With real interest rates higher in the 1980s than in any other postwar decade, the cost of capital for many industries may have exceeded the returns that could be earned from new investments.[2]

Although the link between a company's financial structure and its investment opportunities is still poorly understood, many restructuring transactions of the 1980s committed firms to pay out a larger proportion of their cash flow than they had previously. It seems unlikely that this kind of restructuring would be attractive for companies that were growing rapidly and badly needed new investment capital.[3] It might, however, have been attractive for those with strong cash flow from past investments but limited opportunity for further investment. Thus this free cash flow hypothesis suggests that firms in industries with strong cash flows but weak investment opportunities and high capital costs would be under the strongest pressure to restructure financially.[4]

Other theories have suggested that the federal tax reform acts of 1981 and 1986 stimulated much of the restructuring, or that firms were simply responding to the improved capacity for debt that resulted from higher stock prices and smooth predictable cash flows, or that innovations in financial markets and bankruptcy law reforms may have made it more attractive for the suppliers of capital to hold debt instruments and less worrisome to corporate managers to rely on debt. Finally, some have argued that financial markets engaged in a frenzy of excesses and that greedy investment bankers led equally greedy raiders to engage in speculative takeover behavior. This behavior may have been facilitated by deregulation in the financial market and new kinds of financial instruments but had very little underlying economic rationale.

Our investigation found that firms that underwent financial restructuring were concentrated in industries that were generating cash but had poor investment opportunities, as measured by the difference between the gross return to capital and the opportunity cost of capital. This finding is stronger in the early part of the decade for private buyouts and junk bond issues. While it is very consistent across alternative versions of the model used to explain all three types of restructuring activity, it is not always statistically significant.

We also found that private buyouts and junk bond issuances were more likely to occur in industries that were not technologically intensive, while leveraged restructurings were more concentrated in high-technology industries. The debt capacity theory got very little support, however, except possibly to help explain private buyouts in the early part of the decade. For financial restructuring activity after 1985, none of the theories we examine seems to provide much explanation.

Financial Restructuring Events

Restructuring is a broad term, encompassing many kinds of transactions. Previous studies have focused on narrowly defined types of restructuring transactions, such as leveraged buyouts, or hostile takeovers, and have generally worked with very small samples that make it meaningless to talk about time or industry distribution of restructuring activity.[5] Or they have worked with highly aggregated data in which heterogeneous events are lumped together.[6] Our analysis is based on firm-level and industry-level data for well-defined transactions. Our coverage is broad enough, however, that we can effectively address questions relating to the incidence over time and across industries of certain kinds of activity.

Data Description

We have identified three types of change in the financial or ownership structures of firms that are of a character or magnitude to suggest that the companies involved were undergoing dramatic changes in their operating philosophies or financial styles. For each category of restructuring we have identified all the events experienced by firms in the broad population of publicly traded companies tracked by Compustat.

The events we have studied are private buyouts, including leveraged buyouts, of whole, publicly traded companies; new issues of below-investment-grade debt; and very large year-to-year increases in debt-to-assets ratios, which we call leveraged restructuring events. This section briefly describes the data on each kind of event and how the events are related to each other, to merger and takeover activity, and to broad changes in corporate sector debt levels. Because we wanted to link data on the restructurings to characteristics of the firms undergoing them and of their industries, we looked only at events involving firms in the population tracked by Compustat. The data appendix gives full details of our sample and of the variables we have constructed.

PRIVATE BUYOUTS. Private buyouts are transactions in which whole, publicly traded companies are sold to groups of individual investors, or to closely held companies that were created to do the deal, or to companies without significant operating experience before the deal. Al-

Table 5-1. Financial Restructuring Events, by Type, 1979–89
Millions of 1982 dollars

Year	Private buyouts[a]		Junk bond events[a]		Leveraged restructurings[a]	
	Number	Value[b]	Number	Value[c]	Number	Value[d]
1979	0	0	0	0	15	6,246
1980	1	0	22	851	10	568
1981	16	2,442	15	1,190	15	1,351
1982	27	4,564	16	1,255	25	7,027
1983	30	1,829	31	2,679	17	898
1984	68	13,769	42	4,112	34	6,384
1985	46	9,448	59	5,051	32	12,935
1986	39	25,653	96	13,835	53	24,777
1987	29	16,606	69	17,335	49	24,950
1988	67	25,919	64	11,937	59	28,683
1989	49	50,301	54	10.289	48	17,540
Total	372	150,531	468	68,534	357	131,359

Source: Authors' calculations. See appendix.
a. See appendix for definition and details of construction.
b. Book value of assets of firms undergoing private buyouts. If that was unavailable, the consideration paid for the firm as reported by Automatic Data Processing was used. If that was unavailable, book value of assets as reported by ADP was used. Value was missing for fourteen deals.
c. Total face value of junk bonds issued.
d. Book value of incremental debt taken on by restructuring firms.

though our data sources begin in 1979, we found no private buyouts in the Compustat population before 1980, and then only one. For 1980 through 1989, we identified 372 private buyouts involving firms with a total real value of assets (in 1982 dollars) of more than $150 billion. Of these, 285 were classified as leveraged buyouts by our original sources.[7]

The number and dollar value of private buyouts in each year is shown in table 5-1. Measured by the number of transactions, the two most active years were 1984 (sixty-eight events) and 1988 (sixty-seven events). Measured by total dollar volume, 1989 was by far the most active year, with more than a third of the total activity. The leveraged buyout of RJR Nabisco greatly skews this measure, however, because it accounted for 57 percent of the dollar volume in 1989 and a little more than one-sixth of the dollar volume of all private buyouts during the decade.[8] Without this deal, 1988 would have been the year of highest dollar volume.

JUNK BOND ISSUES. Junk bond issues were compiled from comprehensive lists of all underwritten, original-issue junk bonds issued by companies in industries other than the financial and electric utility industries. We combined all issues by an individual firm in the same year into a single "junk" event. This procedure yielded a total of 468 junk events from 1980 through 1989 involving 387 Compustat firms. As table

5-1 shows, the peak year for junk activity was 1986 when measured by the number of events (ninety-six), but 1987 when measured by value.

LEVERAGED RESTRUCTURINGS.   A list of leveraged restructurings was constructed from Compustat files by identifying firms that underwent an especially large year-to-year change in the ratio of total debt to total assets. Because both debt and assets are measured at book value, such changes cannot be driven by changes in stock market valuations. They must result from actions by the company to issue new debt, sell off assets, or make other financial choices that radically alter its capital structure.

We defined a large increase in leverage ratio as a year-to-year change that was in the 95th percentile or higher among all year-to-year changes in the ratios between 1971 and 1989 for nonfinancial, nonutility firms listed in Compustat. For the most part, large, publicly traded firms do not tend to change their leverage ratios dramatically from year to year, so the distribution of one-year changes is clustered around zero but with a large right-hand tail. Only 8.1 percentage points separate the bottom quartile from the top quartile of such changes during the two decades covered by the data. An increase in debt-to-assets ratio of 22.9 percentage points (for example, a change from a ratio of, say, 40 percent to 62.9 percent) marks the 95th percentile point.[9]

We also required that the increase in debt move the firm from a relatively modest debt-to-assets ratio to a high ratio and that this high level persist for at least one year. This requirement was designed to eliminate big increases in leverage by firms that were already highly leveraged, or increases that were reversed the following year. In practice, this meant that a company could not undertake more than one leveraged restructuring in any four-year period.

These steps yielded a list of more than 1,200 leveraged restructurings. About two-thirds involved very small firms with only a few years of data in Compustat. Because these had a low asset base, a single debt issue could cause a large change in their ratios. They were also often subject to fluctuations in the amounts of their assets that were large relative to their starting size. The combination gave them unstable capital structures. So we decided to focus on larger firms—firms that at some point during the time we tracked them had total assets (book value) worth $50 million or more in 1982 dollars.

We were left with 431 leveraged restructurings from 1971 through 1989 involving 419 firms. Large one-year increases in leverage were very rare among large firms in the 1970s. For this reason, and for consistency with

Table 5-2. Asset Size of Restructuring Firms, by Type of Restructuring, Selected Periods, 1979–89
Millions of 1982 dollars

	Event year			
Type of restructuring	1979–82	1983–85	1986–89	1979–89
PBO firms[a]				
Mean	175	187	644	420
Median	42	40	105	61
Number of observations[b]	40	134	184	358
JUNK firms[a]				
Mean	599	596	875	765
Median	222	315	432	373
Number of observations	53	132	283	468
LRS firms[a]				
Mean	493	630	776	690
Median	83	131	246	182
Number of observations	65	83	209	357

Source: Authors' calculations. See appendix.
a. Book value of assets in year of event. For private buyouts, if book value was unavailable in Compustat for event year, deal value (or alternatively book value of assets) from Automatic Data Processing was used.
b. Value is missing for fourteen PBO events.

the analysis of private buyouts and junk bond issues, we focus in the sections that follow on the 357 events involving 350 firms from 1979 through 1989. As table 5-1 shows, the peak year for leveraged restructuring activity, by number of events and value, was 1988.

Characterizing the Restructuring Firms

Although the three types of restructuring events were different, they were related in some ways. All three either directly increased the debt of the firms involved or were associated with increased leverage, and all three were virtually confined to the 1980s. The pace of each began slowly in the early 1980s, at first affecting only a few, typically small, firms. Activity picked up speed during the decade, with more and larger companies involved almost every year until activity peaked in 1986–88. And, as we show later, the firms that undertook these restructurings were disproportionately responsible for takeovers and divestitures, as well as for the overall increase in corporate sector leverage.

Table 5-2 shows the asset size of firms undergoing restructuring in 1979–82, in 1983–85, and in 1986–89. The mean and median asset size of firms involved in these activities increased significantly during the decade. Firms undergoing leveraged restructuring (LRS) were larger than firms undergoing private buyouts (PBOs). Firms issuing junk bonds

Figure 5-1. Aggregate Debt-to-Assets Ratios, Restructuring and Nonrestructuring Firms, 1979–90ª

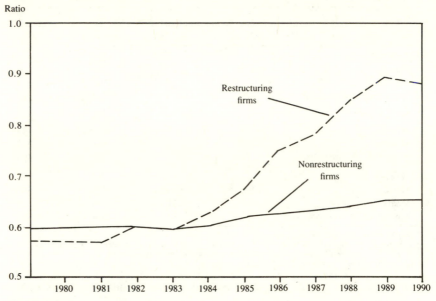

Source: See appendix.
a. Ratios are the sum of all debt across firms in group divided by the sum of all assets across these firms.

(JUNK) were typically somewhat larger than LRS companies in all three subperiods.[10]

Although the entire corporate sector increased its debt-to-assets ratio during the 1980s, restructuring firms as a group increased theirs at a far faster rate. Figure 5-1 shows the aggregate debt-to-assets ratios (book value) in each year of the 1980s for 967 companies that undertook at least one of the types of financial restructurings we tracked and the same measure for all other nonfinancial, nonutility firms.[11] The ratio is essentially flat—0.57 to 0.60—through 1983 for both firms undertaking restructuring and for those not doing so. It then rises modestly to 0.66 by the end of the decade for nonevent firms. But it soars for restructuring firms.[12] By the end of the 1980s, restructuring firms as a group had total debt outstanding equal to nearly 90 percent of the book value of their assets. From 1979 through 1989 restructuring firms accounted for a declining share of the assets of all nonfinancial, nonutility firms (from 6.5 percent in 1979 to 5.0 percent in 1989), but they accounted for a rising share of the incremental debt taken on by nonfinancial, nonutility firms during this period (from 6.1 percent in 1979 to 9.9 percent in 1989).

For more detail on the sources of the increases in average leverage, table 5-3 shows the mean and median debt-to-assets ratios before and after events for firms undertaking the three kinds of restructurings in each of the three subperiods. The ratios reported have been normalized by subtracting the average debt-to-assets ratios for nonevent firms in each firm's industry in the relevant year.[13] Thus the numbers reported are the means and medians of each firm's deviation from its industry average. The LRS firms in all three periods were typically underleveraged relative to their industry in the year before the restructuring. But PBO firms had leverage ratios similar to others in their industry, and firms issuing junk bonds were already more highly leveraged than others in their industry in the year before the event.[14] After the restructuring, these firms were more highly leveraged than average for their industry.[15] For all three kinds of events, the mean increase in debt-to-assets ratios from one year before the event to one year after is positive and statistically significant, except for JUNK events in the early part of the decade and PBOs in the early and middle parts. For PBOs there are very small samples with postevent information.

When we examined the overlap between events, we found that firms involved in one restructuring event were more likely to engage in other kinds of restructuring activity than were nonevent firms. One out of six of the event firms was involved in more than one kind of financial restructuring, and eighteen were involved in all three kinds.

Although these numbers may not seem high, for comparison we calculated that companies undergoing leveraged restructuring were six times more likely to be junk bond issuers and five times more likely to be PBO targets at some time during the 1980s than non-LRS firms listed in Compustat.[16] Junk bond issuers were also about six times more likely to be LRS firms and four times more likely to be PBO targets than nonissuers, and buyout targets were about four times more likely to be junk bond issuers and five times more likely to have undertaken leveraged restructurings than nontargets.

In part these observations pertain because some events we identify separately were really part of the same broadly defined restructuring effort. For example, Beatrice, Safeway, and R. H. Macy were all targets of private buyouts in 1986. Not surprisingly, all had large enough increases in leverage to satisfy our test for having undergone a leveraged restruc-

Table 5-3. Debt-to-Assets Ratios of Restructuring Firms Relative to Their Industry, by Type of Restructuring, Selected Periods, 1979–89[a]

	Event year			
Type of restructuring	1979–82	1983–85	1986–89	1979–89
PBO firms				
Year $t - 1$				
Mean	−.011	.041[b]	−.001	.001
Standard error	(.014)	(.016)	(.009)	(.007)
Median	−.026	−.040	−.010	−.021
Number of observations	38	114	154	306
Year $t + 1$				
Mean	.006	.276	.249[b]	.246
Standard error	(.095)	(.202)	(.052)	(.050)
Median	−.038	.235	.271	.234
Number of observations	9	25	56	90
$(t + 1) - (t - 1)$				
Mean	−.027	.234	.263[b]	.254[b]
Standard error	(.088)	(.191)	(.059)	(.054)
Median	.048	.262	.278	.268
Number of observations	9	25	54	88
JUNK firms				
Year $t - 1$				
Mean	.079[b]	.093[b]	.158[b]	.135[b]
Standard error	(.015)	(.012)	(.015)	(.010)
Median	.080	.112	.124	.110
Number of observations	51	119	225	395
Year $t + 1$				
Mean	.100[b]	.166[b]	.208[b]	.187[b]
Standard error	(.012)	(.012)	(.018)	(.011)
Median	.112	.142	.175	.150
Number of observations	53	125	226	404
$(t + 1) - (t - 1)$				
Mean	.019	.060[b]	.069[b]	.062[b]
Standard error	(.014)	(.013)	(.020)	(.012)
Median	.017	.012	.030	.022
Number of observations	51	115	193	359

Table 5-3. *(continued)*

Type of restructuring	Event year			
	1979–82	*1983–85*	*1986–89*	*1979–89*
LRS firms				
Year $t - 1$				
Mean	− .098[b]	− .054[b]	− .071[b]	− .070[b]
Standard error	(.012)	(.013)	(.008)	(.006)
Median	− .076	− .092	− .120	− .098
Number of observations	60	80	196	336
Year $(t + 1)$				
Mean	.269[b]	.278[b]	.258[b]	.264[b]
Standard error	(.050)	(.022)	(.017)	(.014)
Median	.271	.284	.204	.251
Number of observations	60	80	199	339
$(t + 1) - (t - 1)$				
Mean	.367[b]	.332[b]	.331[b]	.335[b]
Standard error	(.048)	(.024)	(.018)	(.014)
Median	.324	.424	.323	.345
Number of observations	60	80	196	336

Source: Authors' calculations. See appendix.

a. Average debt-to-assets ratios for each firm's industry (constructed from data on all nonevent firms in the industry) are subtracted from each firm's debt-to-assets ratio before computing summary statistics. Means and (in parentheses) standard erros of the means are asset-weighted.

b. Significant at 90 percent level in a two-tailed test.

turing during that same year. Similarly, Southland Corporation and Burlington Holdings issued junk bonds in 1987, and both were also identified as undergoing leveraged restructurings that year. If events that involve a single firm in the same year are treated as a single (albeit multifaceted) restructuring, the 1,197 separately identified events collapse to 1,128 more broadly defined financial restructurings.

The restructuring firms were also responsible for more than their share of merger and takeover activity. Junk bond issuers and LRS companies were two and one-half times as likely to acquire another company and three times more likely to sell off part of themselves in a divestiture than companies that did not undertake financial restructuring. Companies that were bought out in a PBO were more than one and one-half times as likely to have made an acquisition and more than twice as likely to have divested part of themselves than firms that were never buyout targets. About four out of ten leveraged restructurings and more than half the JUNK events had acquisitions associated with them.[17] These accounted for 8.3 percent of all acquisitions made by nonfinancial firms from 1979 through 1989.[18] Only 16 percent of LRS and JUNK events had associated divestitures, but these accounted for 11 percent of all divestitures by nonfinancial firms.

Restructuring and Slower Growth

A key hypothesis about restructurings is that the firms engaging in them often did so to increase the rate at which they were paying out cash to investors, even though the payouts were often achieved at the cost of a slower or negative growth. For buyouts this hypothesis seems indisputable: a substantial payout was made to the shareholders at the time of the buyout, and for PBOs that were financed by large increases in debt (76 percent of the PBO events were identified as leveraged buyouts, according to the original data sources), a large part of future cash flow was, of necessity, committed to repaying the debt. Other studies have confirmed that companies undergoing leveraged buyouts reduced their rate of investment for at least a few years after the buyout.[19]

It was not so obvious whether the additional debt taken on in LRS and JUNK restructurings would be associated with higher payouts and reduced growth or the opposite. The debt could be used to buy back stock or increase payouts to shareholders, or for the more traditional purpose of financing investment. Or the money could be used to finance acquisitions, an activity that might be part of a growth and investment strategy, or part of a redeployment or consolidation strategy in an industry that is retrenching.[20] In other words, debt-based financial restructurings could be associated with slow growth, slow rates of investment, and retrenchment by a company (or its industry) or they could be associated with rapid growth and high rates of investment.

One important piece of evidence points strongly to the slow-growth hypothesis: all three types of events seemed to mark turning points for the companies involved, after which the growth rates of their assets slowed significantly. Of 429 firms for which pre- and postevent rates could be calculated, more than two-thirds experienced a slowdown in the real growth rate of assets after restructuring.[21] This suggests that the increased leverage associated with each kind of event was not typically used to finance further growth—whether by acquisition or by internal growth.

Table 5-4 shows growth rates of assets before and after restructuring for companies involved in the three kinds of events for the three subperiods.[22] LRS and PBO firms had similar patterns of real asset growth rates before restructuring—the average rate for both was positive (and close to the average asset growth rate for Compustat firms as a whole during the corresponding periods). And the growth rate before the event was higher for restructurings that took place late in the decade than for those that occurred early. The average was also higher than the median growth rate for buyouts and leveraged restructurings in all three periods, suggesting that the larger firms were also growing more rapidly.

JUNK firms were typically growing much faster before issuing the junk bonds than either LRS or PBO firms were before their restructurings, with both the average and the median growth rates exceeding the average for the other kinds of restructurings in all three periods.

Finally, for all three kinds of events in all three periods, the mean and median growth rates of assets slowed markedly after restructuring. And, with two exceptions, the postevent growth rates for the three kinds of restructuring in all periods were considerably below average asset growth rates for Compustat firms as a whole. The exceptions were early and mid-decade junk bond issues. While growth rates following junk bond issues in these subperiods fell relative to growth rates before the issues, both the average and the median remained high relative to the average asset growth rate for Compustat firms as a whole.

Table 5-4 also shows the mean and median difference between firms' growth rates before and after the restructuring. The mean and median differences are always negative (except the median in the case of early-period PBOs, where there is a sample size of only four) and nearly always statistically significant. (The exceptions are middle-period JUNK events and early and middle-period PBOs. In the latter two cases, again, sample sizes are very small.) This suggests that restructured firms typically grew much more slowly after the event than before it.

For leveraged restructurings and junk bond issuers we also looked for evidence that large payouts were made to shareholders in the years surrounding the events, either by paying out a significant share of assets as dividends, or by firms' large net repurchases of their own stock, or both. For about 25 percent of the LRS events and 17 percent of the JUNK events for which they could be calculated, associated payouts to shareholders exceeded 5 percent of the assets of the firms during the year of restructuring.[23] The asset-weighted average payout was about 45 percent of assets for LRS firms and 29 percent for JUNK firms.

For comparison, we took a random sample of 482 observations on nonrestructuring firms with a time distribution that mirrored the distribution of restructuring events.[24] We found, to our surprise, that 26 per-

Table 5-4. Real Growth Rate of Assets before and after Restructuring, by Type of Restructuring, Selected Periods, 1979–89

Type of restructuring	Event year			
	1979–82	1983–85	1986–89	1979–89
PBO firms				
Years $t - 4$ to $t - 1$[a]				
Mean	.035[b]	.024	.132[b]	.113[b]
Standard error	(.020)	(.015)	(.032)	(.020)
Median	−.036	−.021	.054	.003
Number of observations	36	108	143	287
Years $t + 1$ to $t + 4$[c]				
Mean	−.051	−.007	−.070[b]	−.061[b]
Median	(.051)	(.059)	(.031)	(.026)
Standard error	−.070	−.056	−.061	−.061
Number of observations	5	17	30	52
$(t + 1$ to $t + 4) - (t - 4$ to $t - 1)$				
Mean	−.147	−.082	−.158[b]	−.152[b]
Standard error	(.115)	(.096)	(.077)	(.060)
Median	.044	−.047	−.169	−.149
Number of observations	4	14	25	43
JUNK firms				
Years $t - 4$ to $t - 1$[a]				
Mean	.222[b]	.230	.272[b]	.256[b]
Standard error	(.030)	(.159)	(.040)	(.051)
Median	.186	.084	.163	.160
Number of observations	48	100	156	304
Years $t + 1$ to $t + 4$[c]				
Mean	.043	.040[b]	.001	.015
Standard error	(.033)	(.024)	(.023)	(.015)
Median	.064	.046	−.024	.004
Number of observations	47	99	135	281
$(t + 1$ to $t + 4) - (t - 4$ to $t - 1)$				
Mean	−.186[b]	−.225	−.294[b]	−.259[b]
Standard error	(.050)	(.199)	(.049)	(.072)
Median	−.172	−.062	−.252	−.155
Number of observations	43	80	83	206

Table 5-4. (*continued*)

Type of restructuring	Event year			
	1979–82	*1983–85*	*1986–89*	*1979–89*
LRS firms				
Years $t - 4$ to $t - 1$ [a]				
Mean	.052[b]	.065[b]	.155[b]	.120[b]
Standard error	(.025)	(.016)	(.031)	(.020)
Median	−.011	.031	.087	.045
Number of observations	54	69	163	286
Years $t + 1$ to $t + 4$ [c]				
Mean	−.133[b]	−.001	−.079[b]	−.069[b]
Standard error	(.043)	(.237)	(.012)	(.012)
Median	−.046	.014	−.059	−.043
Number of observations	47	59	122	228
$(t + 1$ to $t + 4) - (t - 4$ to $t - 1)$				
Mean	−.194[b]	−.057[b]	−.165[b]	−.141[b]
Standard error	(.044)	(.030)	(.028)	(.019)
Median	−.120	−.034	−.129	−.114
Number of observations	41	50	89	180

Source: Authors' calculations. See apppendix.

a. Growth rates for each firm are computed as the three-year average of the one-year rates of change in real (1982 dollars) total assets (book value) from four years before the event through one year before the event. Standard errors of the means are in parentheses.

b. Statistically significant at the 90 percent level in two-tailed test.

c. Computed for each firm as above from the year after each event through the fourth year after each event. For events that occurred in 1987, a two-year growth rate was used (1988–90), and for events that occurred in 1988, a one-year growth rate was used (1989–90). For 1989 events, no postevent growth rate was computed.

cent of these randomly chosen firm-years also had associated payouts (calculated the same way as above) greater than 5 percent of observation-year assets: the average size of the payouts was 27 percent of observation-year assets. In other words, companies that underwent financial restructuring in the 1980s were no more likely to have made large payouts to shareholders than nonrestructuring firms. But the payouts made by LRS firms were larger relative to firm size than those made by nonrestructuring firms.

In sum, it appears that firms issuing junk bonds were growing rapidly before the issues and used the funds from them to finance acquisitions. But these companies did not continue to grow as fast after the transaction. Leveraged restructurings firms increased their debt for a variety of reasons, but their growth also slowed after the restructuring. When the LRS firms used the increased debt to pay dividends and buy back shares—as one-fourth of them did—the payouts were very substantial relative to the size of the firms.

Industry Patterns of
Financial Restructuring

Table 5-1 showed that financial restructuring activity was not randomly distributed throughout the 1980s but was heavily concentrated in 1986–89. Figures 5-2, 5-3, and 5-4 show the distribution of the three kinds of restructurings during the decade and across broad industrial sectors. The allocation of vertical space is proportional to each sector's contribution to GNP in 1985; the size of the dots is indicative of the size of the transaction. These diagrams make it clear that durable and nondurable goods manufacturing were major targets of restructuring, in absolute terms and especially relative to their size in the economy. The natural resources sector seems to have had few buyouts. Transportation, communications, and utilities had relatively little LRS or PBO activity but high numbers of junk bond issues.[25]

The variation in intensity of restructuring at the industry level shown in these figures prompted us to investigate the incidence of 1980s financial restructuring activity across more narrowly defined industries.

Research Strategy

Only a few studies have attempted to use information about the industry distribution of restructuring activity to help explain its causes or implications.[26] We believe this is useful for several reasons. First, we suspect that both economywide and industry-specific factors pressured firms to restructure. For example, the quality of investment opportunities facing individual firms is likely to be highly correlated across firms in the same industry. If investment opportunities were an important driving force in restructuring, we would expect this factor to produce different rates of restructuring in different industries, potentially allowing us to identify one of the causes of restructuring.

Second, although some firms might respond very aggressively to external pressures, others might respond more modestly and might not undergo a restructuring event as we defined it. Thus we might not be able to distinguish the pressures facing the restructured firms from those facing other firms in the same industry. Finally, our measures of restructuring, and of the factors pressuring firms to restructure, are rather noisy at the industry level. But because they are aggregated from firm-level data, they are far less noisy than the firm-level data they came from. Our approach was to divide the economy into seventy-one industry categories

Figure 5-2. Incidence of Private Buyouts, by Value (1982 Dollars) and Industry Sector, 1979–89[a]

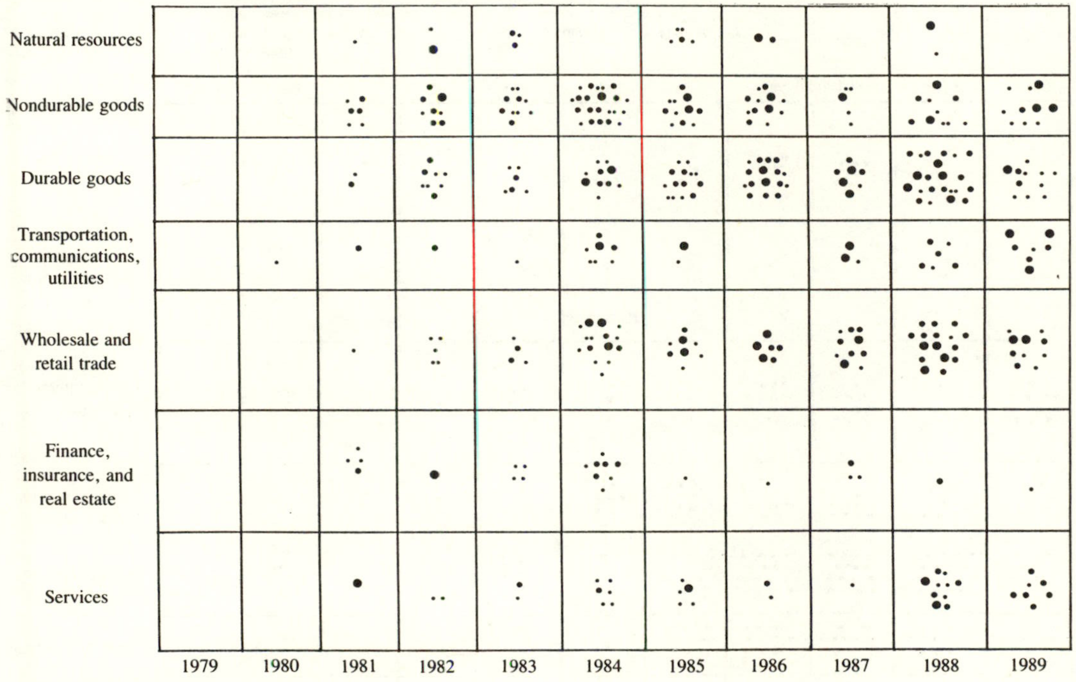

Source: Authors' calculations. See appendix.
a. The allocation of the vertical space is proportional to the size of each sector's contribution to GNP in 1985.
● Buyout of firm with total assets greater than $500 million.
● Buyout of firm with total assets greater than $50 million and less than $500 million.
· Buyout of firm with total assets less than $50 million.

Figure 5-3. Incidence of Junk Bond Events, by Value (1982 Dollars) and Industry Sector, 1979–89[a]

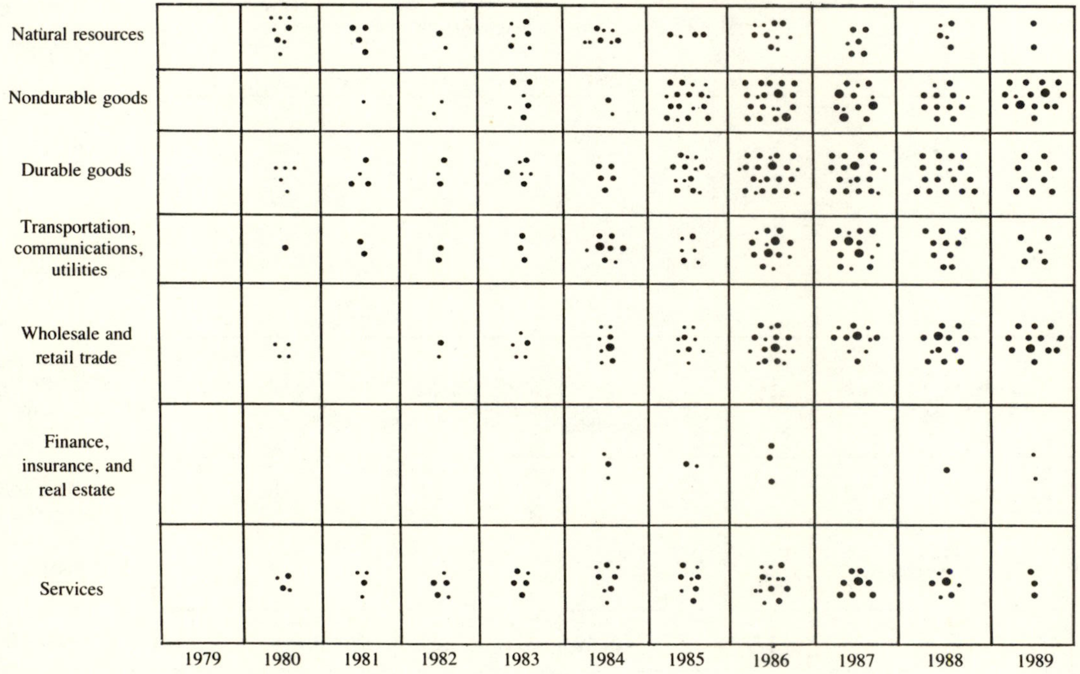

Source: Authors' calculations. See appendix.
a. The allocation of the vertical space is proportional to the size of each sector's contribution to GNP in 1985.
● Junk bond issues with total value greater than $500 million.
● Junk bond issues with total value greater than $50 million and less than $500 million.
· Junk bond issues with total value less than $50 million.

Figure 5-4. Incidence of Leveraged Restructuring Events, by Value (1982 Dollars) and Industry Sector, 1979–89[a]

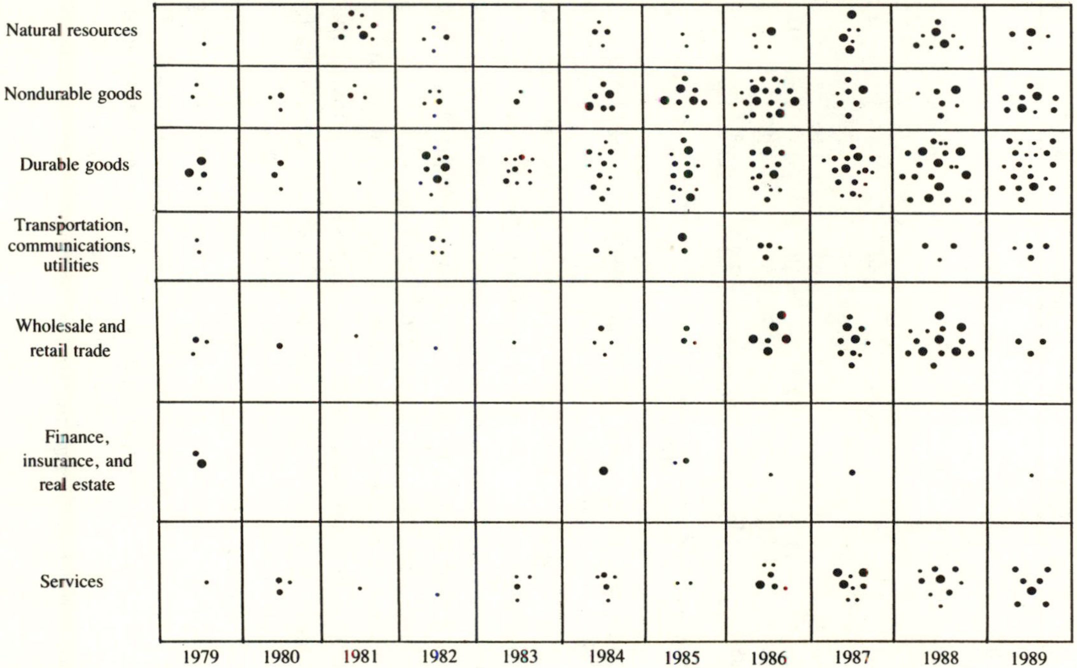

Source: Authors' calculations. See appendix.
a. The allocation of the vertical space is proportional to the size of each sector's contribution to GNP in 1985.
● LRS event involving firm with increase in debt greater than $500 million.
● LRS event involving firm with increase in debt greater than $50 million but less than $500 million.
· LRS event involving firm with increase in debt less than $50 million.

Table 5-5. Mean and 90th Percentile of Industry Restructuring Rates, by Type of Event, 1979–89
Value of restructuring events as percent of value of assets

	Private buyouts		JUNK events		LRS events	
	Mean[a]	90th percentile[b]	Mean[a]	90th percentile[b]	Mean[a]	90th percentile[b]
1979	0	0	0	0	0.55	1.68
1980	0	0	0.23	0.60	0.45	1.86
1981	1.07	5.12	0.33	0.71	0.23	1.36
1982	1.29	5.64	0.36	0.78	0.63	2.46
1983	0.07	3.54	0.83	2.71	0.44	2.54
1984	3.92	6.70	0.89	2.44	1.15	4.21
1985	3.91	6.43	1.03	2.94	1.32	4.41
1986	2.56	6.93	1.43	5.05	2.06	7.49
1987	3.14	13.68	2.32	6.28	3.97	11.82
1988	3.10	8.12	1.49	4.55	3.07	9.88
1989	4.23	9.11	0.89	2.38	2.41	4.77

Source: Authors' calculations.
a. Mean value of all nonzero industry-level restructuring rates.
b. 90th percentile of all nonzero industry-level restructuring rates.

at the two- to three-digit standard industrial classification (SIC) code level.[27] This level of disaggregation provides reasonably homogeneous groupings but is fine enough to distinguish between high-growth, technology-intensive industries, such as pharmaceuticals, and more mature businesses, such as commodity chemicals. It also ensures that the sample of publicly traded firms in each industry is large enough to minimize small-sample problems when industry aggregates are constructed from firm-level data.

For each industry, we measured the rate of each kind of activity as the value of restructuring transactions involving firms in the industry divided by total assets in the industry in that year.[28] Table 5-5 reports the mean and 90th percentile rate of restructuring at the industry level for industries that had some restructuring in the relevant year. Many industries had no restructuring in some years. These statistics reflect the changing intensity of activity over time and indicate significant variation across industries in intensity. We then asked how these measures of restructuring were related to industry-level factors that, according to various restructuring theories, might influence the pace of activity.

Theories with Industry-Level Implications

FREE CASH FLOW THEORY. The argument with the strongest predictions about the distribution of financial restructuring activity across industries is that restructuring was undertaken to force companies to reduce the amount of cash retained for investment or other purposes and instead to redirect this cash to the financial markets for redeployment into more attractive investments. This argument has implications for both the timing and the distribution of restructuring activity across industries.

The emergence of high real interest rates in the 1980s from the low rates that had generally obtained since World War II raised the hurdle rate for new investment and increased the number of firms with cash flow in excess of attractive investment opportunities (free cash flow). Table 5-6 shows three measures of the real interest rate from 1955 through 1989: the three-month Treasury bill rate, Moody's Aaa bond rate, and the six-month commercial paper rate, all adjusted for inflation. The latter two are representative of rates that top-rated corporations pay to borrow. All three indicate that the real borrowing costs facing even highly rated corporations were higher in every year from 1981 through 1989 than in any year in the previous twenty-five.

As our companion paper in this volume shows, the increase in real interest rates affected the cost of capital by different degrees in different industries. Moreover, even increases of similar magnitude had a much greater impact in some industries than in others. Mature industries with a broad base of revenues from past investment but little room for profitable growth or expansion (radio and television, tobacco, food processing, and certain retail franchises come to mind) and industries with very long lead times and a slow pace of technological change (oil, forest products, and other natural resources) would be under the most pressure to cut back on investment. Equity prices in these industries would benefit most from implementing the discipline and tax advantages of higher leverage. Rapidly growing, technology-intensive industries such as scientific instruments, telecommunications equipment, computers, and biotechnology would be less likely to feel pressure to restructure and pay out more cash because firms in these industries often need more cash for investments than they generate.

We tested this theory by asking whether the pace of restructuring was related to variables intended to measure the attractiveness of investment opportunities and the cash-generating capabilities in each industry. The first variable was the ratio of expenditures on R&D to sales, by industry, as an indicator of how technology-intensive each industry is. The free cash flow theory predicts that restructuring activity should be more intense in industries with low ratios of R&D to sales.[29]

The second factor is the growth rate of assets in the industry. Firms that underwent restructuring experienced a slowdown in their growth

Table 5-6. Real Interest Rates, 1955–89[a]

Year	Three-month Treasury bill	Moody's Aaa bonds	Six-month paper
1955	−1.01	0.30	−0.58
1956	−0.77	−0.07	−0.12
1957	0.29	0.91	0.83
1958	−0.82	1.13	−0.20
1959	1.38	2.36	1.95
1960	1.27	2.75	2.19
1961	0.76	2.73	1.35
1962	1.18	2.74	1.67
1963	1.37	2.48	1.77
1964	1.60	2.45	2.02
1965	1.34	1.88	1.77
1966	1.93	2.18	2.60
1967	0.61	1.80	1.39
1968	0.95	1.79	1.51
1969	1.31	1.66	2.46
1970	0.85	2.44	2.11
1971	−0.98	2.07	−0.21
1972	−1.56	1.58	−0.90
1973	0.28	0.68	1.39
1974	−0.57	0.12	1.39
1975	2.60	0.39	−2.12
1976	−2.64	0.80	−2.29
1977	−1.52	1.24	−1.17
1978	−0.38	1.13	0.39
1979	1.65	1.24	2.52
1980	2.31	2.75	3.10
1981	5.66	5.80	6.39
1982	4.03	7.13	5.23
1983	3.98	7.39	4.24
1984	6.07	9.20	6.65
1985	4.40	8.29	4.93
1986	3.06	6.10	3.47
1987	2.79	6.35	3.82
1988	3.15	6.17	4.14
1989	4.27	5.41	4.95

Sources: Authors' calculations from *Economic Report of the President*, various years.
a. Inflation adjustment for all three measures is a three-year centered moving average of the percentage change in the GNP deflator.

rates. But was the slowdown a feature only of the company that had undergone restructuring, or of the entire industry of which it was a part? We test this question using a three-year centered moving average of the annual growth rate of assets of nonrestructuring firms in each industry as an indicator of how the investment opportunities in that industry might have been viewed by participants other than the restructuring firms themselves. If growth in the industry reflects true investment opportunities, the free cash flow theory predicts that restructuring will be most intense in industries with low growth rates. But if the industry's growth rate is excessive—reflecting empire building or speculative behavior, for example—then restructuring might be a mechanism for the financial markets to rein in growth and could be positively related to the growth rate of assets.

The third factor that could affect the pace of restructuring is the cash generation rate: gross cash flows of an industry, minus interest, dividends, and taxes paid, divided by the assets of the industry. Because restructuring activity in a given year influences the value of this variable in that year, we measured the variable in the year preceding the event. Industries generating very little (or negative) surplus cash would not be likely candidates for restructuring motivated by free cash flow. Thus the theory of free cash flow predicts a positive relationship between restructuring and cash generation.

Finally, we considered a direct measure of the quality of investment opportunities, net returns to capital, which is the difference between the gross rate of returns to capital and the opportunity cost of capital in each industry. The gross rate of returns is constructed very simply as gross operating profits in each industry divided by the value of assets in that industry. The opportunity cost of capital is a more complex and potentially controversial calculation, discussed in detail in our companion paper in this volume. The cost of capital is intended to measure the gross rate of return required to cover taxes, depreciation, and obsolescence, and still provide a return to suppliers of capital that compensates adequately for risk and for the cost of investments foregone.[30] The net returns to capital is a key variable in our test of the free cash flow hypothesis. By measuring this variable at the industry level, we hope to capture the impact of both economywide factors (such as the rise in real interest rates, which is one factor in measuring the cost of capital) and industry-specific factors (such as a decline in gross returns due to import competition, changing relative prices, or other factors) that affect the returns expected from investment in a given industry. To the extent that our measure of the net returns to capital is indicative of the quality of investment opportunities, the free cash flow theory predicts that restructuring activity should be negatively related to this measure (the lower the value, the worse the quality of investment opportunities and the more restructuring we would expect).

In a simple preliminary test of this relationship, we estimated a measure of the correlation over time and across industries between all three measures of the rate of restructuring and the two measures of net returns developed in the companion paper. This correlation was negative and statistically significant (or very nearly so) at the 95 percent level in a two-tailed test for all three kinds of restructuring and both measures of net returns.[31]

DEBT CAPACITY THEORY. The debt capacity theory has two parts. The first is that rising stock prices during the 1980s enabled firms to issue more debt, or even substitute debt for equity, without increasing their debt-to-assets ratios on a market-value basis. In fact, by this argument, companies had to increase debt just to maintain the same financial structure that existed at the beginning of the decade. The second part of the theory is that debt was increased the most by firms that had high debt capacity in the form of steady, predictable, recession-proof cash flows, and whose risk of bankruptcy remained low even at higher debt-to-assets ratios.[32] The higher stock prices part of the theory could explain the timing of financial restructuring, but it is not clear that rising stock prices by themselves would lead to greater use of debt. Higher stock prices might be expected to encourage firms to seek outside financing for expansion. But coming at a time when borrowing costs were unusually high in real terms, one might have expected that firms would take advantage of the higher securities prices by issuing additional equity instead of issuing debt and buying back equity.

The predictable cash flow part of the argument has clear, testable implications for the distribution of restructuring activity across industries (although by itself it does not explain the timing of the surge in financial restructuring). Those industries with little variance in cash flow should have experienced the most restructuring; those with high variance should have experienced the least.[33]

Thus the debt capacity theory predicts that restructuring will be most intense in industries in which the ratio of debt to market value before restructuring is low in relation to that industry's riskiness, and there is little variance in cash flows.

"GREED AND FINANCIAL EXCESSES" THEORY. Although appealing in many respects, the theory that restructuring was driven by greed and financial excesses suggests behavior that has little or no underlying economic motivation and is random and opportunistic. Thus it does not make informative predictions about patterns of restructuring that can be tested against empirical evidence. Almost any cross-sectional or time series pattern—or none at all—could emerge. But as a first pass, we would argue that evidence that restructuring activity is not randomly distributed over time and across industries, but instead is concentrated in certain sectors of the economy or in certain time periods, would be inconsistent with the greed and financial excesses story.

CHANGES IN THE TAX CODE. The argument that changes in the tax code in the 1980s made debt more attractive and thus led to restructuring comes from the simple idea that for any given level of bankruptcy risk, businesses should try to make maximum use of the tax savings available to firms financed with debt. Corporations pay interest with pretax dollars and dividends with aftertax dollars. Thus because debt is taxed at a lower rate than other sources of financing, firms should balance the lower cost of this financing source against the additional bankruptcy risk they might be incurring. For the 1980s the argument is that changes in the tax code made debt more attractive.[34]

But two strong counterarguments can be made. First, tax shields favoring debt have existed for years, yet corporate debt ratios were relatively constant from World War II until the 1980s. The limited use of debt financing (given its tax subsidy) has been a longstanding puzzle in corporate finance theory. Second, during the 1980s the corporate tax rate fell, which decreased the value of the shield and made debt a less attractive financing source on the margin. Thus the simple tax code theories are not very convincing.

However, firms should minimize the burden of all taxes, corporate and personal, paid on corporate income. Although simple comparisons of the tax treatment of debt and equity can be made, the full effect of changes in the tax code also depends on additional details of the tax code and investor behavior.[35] We did not attempt to construct a detailed measure of effective personal and corporate tax rates, but used two crude proxies.

The first indicator of the effect changes in the tax code might have had on restructuring activity is the ratio of the maximum personal tax rate on ordinary income to the maximum corporate tax rate. All else being equal (a heroic assumption), as this ratio decreases, firms should favor

Table 5-7. Indicators of Tax Policy Effects, 1970–89

Year	Ratio of maximum personal tax rate to maximum corporate tax rate	Ratio of maximum capital gains rate to maximum personal tax rate
1970	1.46	0.42
1971	1.46	0.47
1972	1.46	0.50
1973	1.46	0.50
1974	1.46	0.50
1975	1.46	0.50
1976	1.46	0.50
1977	1.46	0.50
1978	1.46	0.48
1979	1.56	0.40
1980	1.52	0.40
1981	1.50	0.34
1982	1.09	0.40
1983	1.09	0.40
1984	1.09	0.40
1985	1.09	0.40
1986	1.09	0.40
1987	0.96	0.73
1988	0.82	1.00
1989	0.82	1.00

Source: For maximum corporate tax rate, Jane Gravelle of Congressional Research Service. For maximum capital gains rate, Congressional Budget Office, *How Capital Gains Tax Rates Affect Revenues: The Historical Evidence* (March 1988). For maximum personal tax rate (1979–87), Joseph A. Pechman, *Federal Tax Policy* (Brookings, 1987); and (1988–89) Jane Gravelle, Congressional Research Service.

more debt because the tax advantage of debt increases. (Of course equity continues to be taxed twice—at the corporate level and at the personal level—and is thus never desirable from a tax standpoint alone. We are arguing that on the margin, given whatever the firm's reasons are for issuing equity, debt becomes relatively more attractive.) The ratio was flat at 1.46 during the 1970s, then after increasing modestly in 1979 to 1.56, it decreased steadily to a low of 0.82 in 1989 (table 5-7). The second ratio we used is the ratio of the top capital gains rate to the maximum personal tax rate on ordinary income. As this ratio increases, capital gains are taxed relatively more than other forms of income, reducing whatever advantages equity has over debt so that corporations should favor more debt. This ratio was constant at 0.50 throughout most of the 1970s, then (after some adjustment) dropped to 0.4 in 1982 and stayed there until 1987, and rose to 1.0 in 1988 and 1989 (table 5-7). These two crude measures of the effect of taxes change in a stepwise fashion every few years and do not vary by industry. Thus they may help explain the pattern of financial restructuring over time but not across industries.

The first of the measures points toward an increase in the optimal amount of debt by corporations during the 1980s, while the second suggests a decline and then after 1986 an increase. Thus the tax-change variables work against each other before 1986 but then combine forces to favor more debt and, presumably, more restructuring to achieve higher debt levels.

Industry-Level Determinants of Restructuring Activity

The previous discussion suggests a formal model of restructuring activity as a function of a set of macroeconomic and industry-specific conditions that determine the choice of capital structure. Restructuring is triggered when those conditions reach some threshold point. Because the variables we are trying to explain (the rates of leveraged restructuring, junk bond issues, and private buyout activity) can be zero but cannot be negative, there is a censored sample structure in which

$$Y_{is} = f(X), \text{ if } f(X) > Y_{is}^*$$
$$Y_{is} = 0, \text{ if } f(X) \leq Y_{is}^*,$$

where Y_{is} is the observed rate of restructuring activity in industry i in year s, $f(X)$ is a measure of the intensity of pressures to restructure, X is the set of explanatory variables, and Y_{is}^* is some unobservable threshold value, beyond which firms make major adjustments in their capital structure and restructuring activity is observed.

Because the functional form of f is unknown, we let $f(X) = a + \beta'X$. This gives a Tobit model that can be easily estimated with standard statistical packages. The variables included in X are those discussed in the previous section. First there are four variables related to the free cash flow hypothesis (the ratio of R&D to sales in the current year, a three-year centered moving average of the growth rate of assets of non-restructuring firms, the lagged value of the industry cash generation rate, and the current value of the rate of net returns to capital for the industry). Then there are variables for debt capacity (the lagged ratio of industry debt to market value adjusted for risk and the variance of cash flow for the industry from 1971 through 1989), and two tax variables (the maximum personal tax rate on ordinary income divided by the maximum corporate tax rate, and the maximum capital gains rate divided by the maximum personal tax rate on ordinary income). The tax variables change over time but are constant across industries; the cash flow variance is constant over time for each industry. All other explanatory variables vary both over time and across industries. (Details of the construction of these variables are given in the data appendix.)

Regression Results

The basic model was estimated separately for each kind of restructuring for 1979–89 and the results are shown in table 5-8. We also tried a second permutation on our basic model that captured more precisely the definition of free cash flow. Free cash flow exists in industries with positive rates of cash generation and poor investment opportunities. In the basic regression, variables measuring these characteristics enter independently. In the alternative version they interact. In place of the variables for net return on capital and cash generation rate, we substituted a single variable equal to the net return on capital if the cash generation rate was positive; the variable was zero otherwise.

These variables—the net returns to capital variable, or in its alternative form, the net returns interacted with the cash dummy—are key ones for the free cash flow theory. During our research, we tried a number of variations on our measures of net returns and on the model itself. We consistently found that the estimated coefficients on the net returns variable were negative, but the significance level varied from version to version, sometimes indicating a strong effect, sometimes a statistically insignificant effect. The results we report here and in the subsequent tables follow that pattern. For this version, we used the measure of net returns computed with a constant risk adjustment in the measure of cost of equity.[36]

As predicted by the free cash flow theory, we find negative coefficients on the net return variables for all three kinds of restructuring activity, but these coefficients are statistically significant only for the regressions explaining PBO and LRS activity. In an alternative version that was identical except that it used the measure of net returns computed with a varying risk premium, we found qualitatively similar results.

Consistent with the free cash flow theory, the degree of technological intensity (as indicated by the ratio of R&D to sales) is a negative and statistically significant explainer of PBO activity and JUNK activity, but it is positive in the model explaining LRS activity (and statistically sig-

Table 5-8. Determinants of Financial Restructuring Activity, 1979–89

Explanatory variable	Expected sign on coefficient	PBO activity (1)	PBO activity (2)	JUNK activity (1)	JUNK activity (2)	LRS activity (1)	LRS activity (2)
Ratio of R&D to sales	−	−.710[a] (−3.290)	−.684[a] (−3.202)	−.219[a] (−3.370)	−.231[a] (−3.584)	.153 (1.341)	.193[a] (1.716)
Three-year moving average growth rate, nonrestructured assets	−/+	−.029 (−.730)	−.028 (−.702)	.017 (1.477)	.017 (1.447)	.060[a] (2.652)	.062[a] (2.756)
Lagged cash generation rate	+	.170 (1.132)	...	−.042 (−.969)	...	.188[a] (2.113)	...
Net returns to capital	−	−.244[a] (−1.975)	...	−.018 (−.516)	...	−.133[a] (−1.980)	...
Net return times cash generation dummy	−	...	−.247[a] (−2.168)	...	−.040 (−1.280)	...	−.084 (−1.394)
Lagged ratio of debt to market value	−	−.053 (−1.448)	−.063[a] (−1.730)	.007 (.704)	.009 (.839)	.027 (1.283)	.020 (.938)
Variance of cash flow	−	.053 (.865)	.053 (.879)	−.002 (−.125)	.002 (.132)	−.044 (−1.192)	−.049 (−1.338)
Ratio of maximum personal tax rate to maximum corporate tax rate	−	−.187[a] (−4.389)	−.184[a] (−4.409)	−.047[a] (−4.318)	−.044[a] (−4.145)	−.038[a] (−1.843)	−.043[a] (−2.142)
Ratio of maximum capital gains rate to maximum personal tax rate	+	−.027 (−.766)	−.028 (−.865)	−.009 (−.973)	−.005 (−.605)	.038[a] (2.016)	.028 (1.585)
Number of observations	...	781	781	781	781	781	781
R^{2b}	...	.121	.122	.113	.112	.098	.093

Source: See appendix for details on construction. Numbers in parentheses are t-statistics.
a. Significant at 90 percent level in two-tailed test.
b. Based on pseudo R^2 statistic computed for each regression from the value of the likelihood functions according to G. S. Maddala, *Limited-Dependent and Qualitative Variables in Econometrics* (Cambridge University Press, 1983), p. 39

nificant at the 90 percent level, or very nearly so). The growth rate of assets is a statistically significant determinant of restructuring only for LRS activity, and here it is positive. As discussed earlier, the expected impact of this variable is ambiguous because it can be interpreted either as an indicator of real investment opportunities or as a measure of empire-building behavior. The cash generation variable is statistically significant only for LRS activity, but it has the expected positive sign.

These variables provide a mixed verdict on the free cash flow theory, with the theory working best to explain private buyout activity. The cash generation and net returns variables also help to explain leveraged restructuring activity and have the expected signs under the free cash flow theory, but the signs on the growth rate of assets and R&D to sales variables in the LRS model run counter to those expected by the free cash flow theory.

The debt capacity theory fares worse. The risk-adjusted, lagged debt-to-market-value ratio gets a negative and statistcally significant coefficient, as predicted by the debt capacity theory, in one version of the model explaining PBO activity, but it is statistically insignificant in the other version, and comes in positive—counter to the theory—in the models explaining JUNK and LRS activity. The variance of cash flow is never significant in any model.

The tax theory does a little better. The ratio of the maximum personal tax rate to the maximum corporate tax rate has the predicted negative sign and is highly statistically significant in all the models. In the models explaining LRS activity, the ratio of the maximum capital gains rate to the maximum personal tax rate also has the predicted positive sign and is statistically significant, but this variable is negative and insignificant as an explainer of the other two kinds of restructuring activity.

Our measures of the tax effects are fairly crude and tend to move in a stepwise fashion over time. We suspected that the tax variables were acting like time-trend variables in the regressions. When the model was reestimated without the tax variables, but including a time trend, the results were qualitatively similar. The finding of a significant coefficient on the time trend variable suggests that some macroeconomic factors (other than those embodied in the free cash flow and debt capacity variables) may influence restructuring activity. But we suspect that we are not capturing the true tax effect very well. More sophisticated measures of the effect of changes in the tax code are needed.

The models explain only 9 to 12 percent of the variance in the rates of all three types of restructuring activity (according to the value of R^2).

Models used to explain investment or financing behavior of firms, which our models resemble, typically have very low explanatory power, but even so, this is disappointing.[37]

Was There a Change in the Model?

Several recent studies have suggested that the restructuring activity of the late 1980s may have been different in motivation and character from that of the early 1980s. Barrie Wigmore, for example, reports a marked decline in the credit quality of junk bonds issued after 1985 and two studies of LBO performance find a decline in postevent performance for deals later in the decade.[38] To explore this possibility, we split the data into two time periods, 1979–85 and 1986–89, and estimated the Tobit model separately on data for each period.

The difference in the results across the two subperiods is striking.[39] Moreover, sharper differences emerge among the different types of activity. Consider first the results for both time periods for PBO activity, reported in table 5-9. For the early period, our model explains nearly 18 percent of the variance of activity. Both the free cash flow theory and the debt capacity theory get modest support. The signs on all of the free cash flow variables are as predicted, but only the R&D-to-sales ratio is statistically significant at the 90 percent level.[40] The risk-adjusted lagged debt-to-market-value ratio comes in with a negative sign, as predicted by the debt-capacity theory, and is statistically significant. But the other key variable for the debt capacity theory, the variance of cash flow, comes in with a positive and statistically significant sign, counter to the theory. Neither of the tax variables were important determinants of PBO activity in this period, however.

For 1986–89 the explanatory power of the model falls by almost 75 percent, and only the tax variables are statistically significant explainers of private buyout activity. But the second tax variable, the ratio of the maximum capital gains tax rate to the maximum personal tax rate, has a sign opposite that predicted by the tax theory. Again, we suspect these variables are simply acting like a time trend in the regressions.

The results for JUNK activity are reported in table 5-10. In the early period, the free cash flow variables now work rather well to explain junk bond issuances. As predicted by the free cash flow theory, the ratio of R&D to sales has a negative and statistically significant coefficient, as do the net returns variables. The cash generation rate is positive, although

Table 5-9. Determinants of Private Buyout Activity, 1979–89

Explanatory variable	Expected sign on coefficient	1979–85		1986–89	
		(1)	(2)	(1)	(2)
Ratio of R&D to sales	−	−1.164[a]	−1.108[a]	−.264	−.231
		(−3.393)	(−3.303)	(−.910)	(−.797)
Three-year moving average growth rate, nonrestructured assets	−/+	−.073	−.065	.095	.095
		(−1.319)	(−1.189)	(1.400)	(1.394)
Lagged cash generation rate	+	.302	. . .	.205	. . .
		(1.126)		(1.079)	
Net returns to capital	−	−.222	. . .	−.255	. . .
		(−1.329)		(−1.282)	
Net return times cash generation dummy	−	. . .	−.227	. . .	−.222
			(−1.502)		(−1.224)
Lagged ratio of debt to market value	−	−.085[a]	−.103[a]	.044	.033
		(−1.746)	(−2.150)	(.735)	(.549)
Variance of cash flow (t-statistic)	−	.169[a]	.152[a]	−.117	−.114
		(2.030)	(1.925)	(−1.216)	(−1.198)
Ratio of maximum personal tax rate to maximum corporate tax rate	−	−.984	−.984	−1.454[a]	−1.513[a]
		(−.016)	(−.016)	(−1.841)	(−1.925)
Ratio of maximum capital gains tax rate to maximum personal tax rate	+	−6.467	−6.502	−.576[a]	−.606[a]
		(−.014)	(−.014)	(−1.628)	(−1.728)
Number of observations		497	497	284	284
R^{2b}		.179	.179	.046	.045

Source: See appendix for details on construction. Numbers in parentheses are t-statistics.
a. Significant at 90 percent level in two-tailed test.
b. Based on pseudo R^2 statistic. See table 5-8.

it is not quite statistically significant at the 90 percent level. The growth rate of assets is positive, but not statistically significant. The debt capacity variables get no support. The ratio of debt to market value does not help explain JUNK activity, while the variance of cash flow is positive and statistically significant or nearly so, which is counter to the debt capacity theory. Only one of the tax variables is significant and has the predicted sign.

The explanatory power of the model falls by more than a third in the later period (from a level that is already low). None of the coefficients are statistically significant except the ratio of R&D to sales, which has the predicted negative sign.

The results for LRS activity are different again (table 5-11). Here the free cash flow variables do not fare at all well in the early period. The

Table 5-10. Determinants of Junk Bond Activity, 1979–89

Explanatory variable	Expected sign on coefficient	1979–85		1986–89	
		(1)	(2)	(1)	(2)
Ratio of R&D to sales	−	−.176[a]	−.154[a]	−.320[a]	−.327[a]
		(−2.933)	(−2.682)	(−3.099)	(−3.177)
Three-year moving average growth rate, nonrestructered assets	−/+	.010	.012	−.032	−.032
		(1.152)	(1.427)	(−1.354)	(−1.354)
Lagged cash generation rate	+	.066	. . .	−.058	. . .
		(1.576)		(−.858)	
Net returns to capital	−	−.056[a]	. . .	−.040	. . .
		(−2.136)		(−.604)	
Net return times cash generation dummy	−	. . .	−.040[a]	. . .	−.082
			(−1.686)		(−1.395)
Lagged ratio of debt to market value	−	.006	.003	.005	.006
		(.822)	(.427)	(.257)	(.302)
Variance of cash flow	−	.022[a]	.020	−.035	−.031
		(1.694)	(1.549)	(−1.129)	(−.995)
Ratio of maximum personal tax rate to maximum corporate tax rate	−	−.019[a]	−.021[a]	.311	.356
		(−2.431)	(−2.678)	(1.261)	(1.464)
Ratio of maximum capital gains rate to maximum personal tax rate	+	−.048	−.046	.119	.142
		(−.803)	(−.768)	(1.074)	(1.313)
Number of observations		497	497	284	284
R^{2b}		.111	.107	.073	.072

Source: See appendix for details on construction. Numbers in parentheses are t-statistics.
a. Significant at 90 percent level in two-tailed test.
b. Based on pesudo R^2 statistic. See table 5-8.

R&D-to-sales ratio and the growth rate of nonrestructured assets have statistically significant positive signs (counter to the theory) in both versions of the model, and the lagged cash generation rate and net returns variables are not significant at all. Likewise, neither of the debt capacity variables is statistically significant, and only one of the tax variables has statistically significant coefficients. In 1986–89 the explanatory power of the model as a whole again falls, this time by about half. Only the cash generation and net returns variables come in with the predicted signs and high t-statistics. But no other variables are statistically significant explainers of LRS activity in the later period.[41]

Taken together, these results are difficult to interpret. Clearly we have not designed a single model that consistently explains all three kinds of restructuring activity. To the extent that they are captured by the variables

Table 5-11. Determinants of Leveraged Restructuring Activity, 1979–89

Explanatory variable	Expected sign on coefficient	1979–85		1986–89	
		(1)	(2)	(1)	(2)
Ratio of R&D to sales	−	.154[a]	.173[a]	− .047	.012
		(2.191)	(2.525)	(−.231)	(.059)
Three-year moving average growth rate, nonrestructured assets	−/+	.028[a]	.030[a]	.032	.037
		(2.296)	(2.524)	(.644)	(.747)
Lagged cash generation rate	+	.069	. . .	.403[a]	. . .
		(1.139)		(2.516)	
Net returns to capital	−	− .023	. . .	− .434[a]	. . .
		(−.630)		(−2.970)	
Net return times cash generation dummy	−	. . .	− .011	. . .	− .268[a]
			(−.329)		(−2.121)
Lagged ratio of debt to market value	−	.009	.006	.034	.017
		(.768)	(.543)	(.784)	(.390)
Variance of cash flow	−	− .020	− .023	− .052	− .054
		(−.910)	(−1.114)	(−.768)	(−.791)
Ratio of maximum personal tax rate to maximum corporate tax rate	−	− .018[a]	− .018[a]	.491	.257
		(−1.650)	(−1.703)	(.933)	(.492)
Ratio of maximum capital gains rate to maximum personal tax rate	+	.088	.092	.269	.148
		(.977)	(1.021)	(1.139)	(.638)
Number of observations		497	497	284	284
R^{2b}		.080	.078	.042	.022

Source: See appendix for details on construction. Numbers in parentheses are *t*-statistics.
a. Significant at 90 percent level in two-tailed test.
b. Based on pseudo R^2 statistic. See table 5-8.

in our model, the free cash flow theory helps explain part of the industry and time distribution of private buyouts and junk bond issuances early in the decade; but in general the explanatory power of the variables is weak and gets weaker later in the decade. These variables have no explanatory power for leveraged restructuring activity early in the decade but do seem to help explain leveraged restructuring later in the decade.

The variables intended to capture the debt capacity theory only help explain private buyout activity early in the decade. While one of the tax variables, the ratio of the maximum personal tax rate to the maximum corporate tax rate, is a significant explanatory variable in most versions of the model, we believe it is merely acting like a time trend.

These results suggest several modest conclusions. First, the three kinds of restructuring activity, while apparently similar in their pace and in their impact on leverage and growth, were probably driven by somewhat different factors. The free cash flow theory works best to explain private buyout activity and junk bond issuances before 1986, while the two most important free cash flow variables—cash generation and net returns to capital—may have been part of the explanation for leveraged restructuring activity in 1986–89. It also appears that private buyouts were concentrated in industries that had low levels of debt relative to their market value and riskiness, at least before 1986. But except for that, the debt capacity theory gets no support as an explanation for financial restructuring activity.

By late in the decade, the already weak explanatory power of our models breaks down even further, and none of the theories explored in this analysis seems able to explain the pace distribution of restructuring activity over time and across industries.

Conclusions

On the whole our findings support a multicause theory of financial restructuring in the 1980s. The rise in capital costs and associated free cash flow, which put pressure on firms with weak investment opportunities to reduce investments and increase payouts, probably played some part. Two findings support this conclusion. First, firms that restructured usually experienced a sharp slowdown in the growth rate of assets after the restructuring event. Second, the consistent finding of negative coefficients on the net returns variable in the regression models explaining restructuring activity suggests that restructuring was concentrated in industries and years where the net returns to capital were low. The latter finding was weak and not always statistically significant, but it was robust to many alternative specifications.[42]

We have found very little evidence to support the debt capacity theory of restructuring, except possibly for private buyouts early in the decade. We suspect that tax changes may have had something to do with fueling restructuring activity. Certainly changes in the tax code in 1981 and especially in 1986 would have, if taken by themselves, encouraged firms to take on higher proportions of debt in their capital structures. But because the complete effect of these changes was also influenced by inflation, the tax status of asset holders, the periods different assets were held, and each firm's choice of capital structure, we were unable to test this hypothesis in our model with any confidence.

Even giving all our stories the full benefit of the doubt, we can explain only a small proportion of restructuring activity. At best we explain about 18 percent of the variance of private buyout activity in 1979–85. For all three kinds of activity, the explanatory power of our model collapses in 1986–89. Thus we must conclude that a great many firm-specific, highly idiosyncratic factors were at work in addition to the industry-level and macroeconomic pressures we have identified.

Moreover, by the late 1980s, the explanatory power of all our theories of financial restructuring breaks down so completely that we must entertain the possibility this activity took on a life of its own, going forward indiscriminately in industry after industry without regard to the underlying forces that may have made it rational in the early years.

Appendix

This appendix defines the leverage-increasing events analyzed in the paper and discusses the details of the other variables used in the regression analysis.

Compustat

The universe of firms for this study is the Compustat PCPlus data base (Standard & Poor's Compustat Services, Inc.), August 1991 version. The file has data on 13,431 publicly traded firms from 1971 through 1990. A full twenty years' worth of data is not available for most firms.

Private Buyouts (PBOs)

The initial list of private buyouts came from a subset of "the M&A Database," supplied to Brookings for use in this and related projects by IDD Information Services of New York (formerly ADP). The raw file was cleaned at Brookings and three selection criteria were applied. First, all transactions must have closed from 1979 through 1989 and resulted in a change in control of a company. Second, at least one piece of value information had to be available, in the following preferred order: the value of the deal, or the book value of assets of the target firm, or the annual revenues of the firm. Third, at least one of these value measures had to be greater than or equal to $5 million in 1982 dollars. The application of these criteria yielded a data base with more than 13,500 transactions.[43] Next we extracted all transactions in which the acquiring entity was either a group of private investors or a closely held firm with no known operating line of business before the deal. We further narrowed this group to include only whole-company transactions (no divestitures) and only companies that were listed in Compustat the year preceding the year in which the deal was closed.[44] We also eliminated a few deals involving firms whose industry could not be identified, and one deal involving a firm in the iron ore mining industry (we had to exclude iron ore mining from our analysis for lack of supporting data from other sources).

These steps yielded 372 private buyouts involving 371 Compustat companies during the 1980s.[45] The definition of value of a private buyout used here is the total book value of assets in 1982 dollars of the target firm in the year of the event, if that information is available from Compustat. If not, it is the value of the deal in 1982 dollars or the book value of assets as reported by IDD if the value of the deal is unavailable.[46] Value is missing for 14 PBOs.

In the regression analysis, the PBO dependent variable is the rate of PBO activity by industry and year. For each industry-year this is measured as the sum of the asset value of firms undergoing PBOs divided by the sum of the value of assets in the industry-year. Asset data are from Compustat.

Junk Bond Issues (JUNK)

Data on original-issue junk bonds were supplied by Barrie A. Wigmore of Goldman Sachs (for 1980 through 1988) and by Martin Fridson of Merrill Lynch (for 1989).[47] These data are comprehensive lists of all underwritten junk bonds issued by nonfinancial companies except electric utilities—832 bond issues. Excluded are debt issued in exchange offers and privately placed issues, previously issued junk bonds, and bonds downgraded to junk status. We cut the sample to issuing firms that were tracked by Compustat, which yielded 571 issues.[48] The terms of the individual issues are not of interest for this study, so all junk bonds issued by a single firm in a given year were combined into "junk bond events" whose value is the total face value of all the bonds issued that year by that firm.[49] This yielded 364 junk bond events.

In the regression analysis, the JUNK dependent variable is the rate of junk bond activity by industry and year. For each industry-year this is measured as the sum of the face value of junk bonds issued divided by the sum of the value of assets in the industry-year. Asset data are from Compustat.

Leveraged Restructuring (LRS) Events

LRS events are defined as large year-to-year changes in a firm's debt-to-asset ratio. To operationalize this definition, we first identified a group of firms for which the debt-to-asset ratios could be compared and then established a definition of "large." We began with all firm-years in the combined Compustat file, 1971–90. Firms in banking, financial services, and public utilities were eliminated from the sample because their leverage patterns are so different from those of other industries. In addition, we eliminated any firm-years with debt-to-asset ratios greater than 4.0 because we believed these data to be unreliable. Finally, we eliminated any firm with fewer than three consecutive years of data.

To define a large change in leverage, we constructed a list of all year-to-year changes in the debt-to-asset ratio for all the remaining firm-years. From this list we eliminated firms with changes in the debt-to-asset ratio greater than 4.0. Then we constructed an overall distribution of year-to-year changes in the debt-to-assets ratio and industry-level distributions of levels of debt-to-assets ratios.[50]

The definition is intended to capture a fundamental change in leverage policy that persists for some time. Consequently, we defined LRS events as year-to-year changes that met three tests: they were above the 90th percentile of the overall distribution of changes; the firm had a level of debt-to-assets ratio below the 75th percentile for its industry in the year preceding the event; the firm had a debt-to-assets ratio above the 75th percentile for its industry in the year of the event and the year following the event. This definition implies that a firm can undergo only one LRS event in any four-year period.

Compustat sometimes reports debt and asset numbers on a consolidated basis for companies that have financial subsidiaries. Compustat provides clear coding that enabled us to identify a group of about 35 large firms that began reporting balance sheet numbers on a consolidated basis in 1987. For these firms Compustat also provides the unconsolidated numbers, which we used. Unfortunately, there are also cases in which there is no clear coding to signal that reported numbers are consolidated and no alternative unconsolidated numbers. Thus we have reason to believe that some LRS events in our list may result from the consolidation of balance sheets with financial subsidiaries. Moreover, our aggregate leverage numbers (for both event and nonevent firms) may be biased upward. We had no effective way to screen out this problem. Although it clearly introduces noise into our results, we have no reason to believe it introduces any bias in the time pattern or industry distribution of LRS events. In particular, we have no reason to believe that our approach to defining and identifying LRS events should have biased us toward finding that leveraged restructuring activity was more predominant in the the 1980s than in the 1970s, other than the fact that the Compustat population grew during the period.[51] But in fact more than 80 percent of the 438 events we identified occurred after 1978, swamping what could be accounted for by the growth of the Compustat population. For this reason, and for consistency with the analysis of private buyouts and junk bond issues, we further narrowed our focus to the 364 events (involving 357 firms) from 1979 through 1989.

The value of LRS events used in this study is the dollar value of incremental debt incurred by the firm undergoing the event in the year of the event.

In the regression analysis, the LRS dependent variable is the rate of LRS activity by industry and year. For each industry-year this is measured as the sum of the incremental debt from LRS events divided by the sum of value of assets in the industry-year. Four industry-years (out of 781) had a decline in debt in the year in which an LRS event occurred. This could happen in a small industry if assets declined sufficiently that debt could fall and the debt-to-assets ratio still rise. In these cases we set the rate of LRS activity to zero for purposes of regression analysis. Asset data are from Compustat.

Other Variables

All data are from Compustat unless otherwise noted. Industry aggregates are the sum of firm values unless otherwise noted.

R&D/SALES. Research and development spending divided by sales (XRD/SALE in Compustat). The ratio is taken for the year corresponding to the observation year of the restructuring activity variable.

GROWTH RATE OF NONRESTRUCTURED ASSETS. Three-year centered moving average of annual percentage changes in assets of firms that never underwent restructuring in each industry. The Compustat asset variable AT was used.

VARIANCE OF CASH FLOW. The variance of the annual percentage change in operating income before depreciation (OIBDP in Compustat) by industry, 1972–90. This variable differs by industry, not over time.

DEBT/MARKET VALUE. Total liabilities divided by the sum of market value of equity (MKVALF), book value of preferred stock (PREFSTK), and book value of debt (LT), adjusted for risk. The unadjusted measures of debt to market value were regressed on an estimate of the value of the asset beta for each industry-year, and the residuals from this regression were used as the measure of adjusted debt/market value. The asset beta was calculated as

$$\text{equity beta}/(1 + \text{debt} * (1 - t)/\text{market value}).$$

The equity betas were asset-weighted averages of firm-level equity betas provided by Compustat (variable BETA); debt and market value were as defined above, and t is the statutory corporate tax rate. See the appendix to the companion paper for our measures of the statutory corporate tax rate.

In equilibrium, industries with high betas (risky cash flows) would in general be able to support less debt than industries with low betas. The estimated regression equation was:

$$\text{Debt-to-market} = 0.676 - 0.260 * \text{Asset beta}.$$

The residuals from this equation measure how far the debt-to-market value of each industry-year deviates from the value that would be predicted based on that industry's measure of risk. But this ratio is directly affected by the restructuring events we are trying to explain. Thus to avoid confusing cause and effect, we used the measure for the year preceding the observation year for the restructuring activity variable.

CASH GENERATION RATE. Cash flow by industry and year is defined as operating income before depreciation, less interest expense, dividends, and taxes. The cash generation rate is cash flow divided by total assets: (OIBDP − XINT − DV − TXT)/AT in Compustat. This variable is also directly affected by restructuring, so again we measured it for the year preceding the observation year for the restructuring activity variable.

NET RETURNS TO CAPITAL. The difference between the gross returns to capital and the cost of capital.

GROSS RETURNS TO CAPITAL. The ratio of operating income before depreciation divided by assets (OIBDP/AT in Compustat).

COST OF CAPITAL. The companion paper provides a full discussion of the construction of alternative measures of this variable.[52]

Table 5-A1. Industry Definitions

Industry code	4-digit SIC	Industry definition
1.0	0100-0999	Agriculture, forestry, and fishing
13.1	1300-1329	Crude petroleum, natural gas, liquid natural gas extraction
13.8	1380-1389	Oil and gas field services
15.0	1500-1599	General building contractors and real estate developers
16.0	1600-1699	Heavy construction contractors
20.1	2000-2039 2050-2079 2090-2099	Food products, except grain mill products and beverages
20.4	2040-2049	Grain mill products
20.8	2080-2089	Beverages
21.0	2100-2199	Tobacco manufacturers
22.1	2200-2249 2260-2279	Weaving mills and textile finishing and other textile mill products
22.5	2250-2259 2280-2299	Knitting, yarn, and thread mills
23.0	2300-2399	Apparel and other finished products made from similar materials
24.0	2400-2499	Lumber and wood products
25.0	2500-2599	Furniture and fixtures
26.0	2600-2699	Paper and allied products
27.1	2700-2729	Newspapers and periodicals
27.3	2730-2749 2770-2779	Books, greeting cards, and miscellaneous publishing
27.5	2750-2769 2780-2799	Commercial and other printing and printing trade services
28.1	2800-2829 2860-2869	Industrial chemicals (organic and inorganic), plastics, and synthetics
28.3	2830-2839	Drugs
28.4	2840-2849	Soaps, detergents, and toilet goods
28.5	2850-2859	Paints and allied products
28.7	2870-2899	Agricultural and other chemical products
29.0	2900-2999	Petroleum and coal products
30.0	3000-3099	Rubber and miscellaneous plastic products
32.0	3200-3299	Stone, clay, glass, and concrete products
33.1	3300-3329	Primary iron and steel industries
33.3	3330-3399	Primary nonferrous metal industries
34.2	3420-3429 3450-3459	Cutlery, hand tools, and hardware; screw machine products, bolts, similar products

Table 5-A1. *(continued)*

Industry code	*4-digit SIC*	*Industry definition*
34.4	3400-3419 3430-3449	Metal cans, shipping containers, plumbing and heating and fabricated structural metal products
34.6	3460-3489	Metal forgings and stampings, coating and engraving services, and ordnance and accessories
34.9	3490-3499	Miscellaneous fabricated metal products
35.1	3500-3519 3560-3569	Engines and turbines and general industrial machinery
35.2	3520-3539	Farm machinery and construction and related machinery
35.4	3540-3549	Metalworking machinery
35.5	3550-3559	Special industrial machinery
35.7	3570-3579	Office, computing, and accounting machines
35.8	3580-3599	Refrigeration, service machinery, other machinery
36.1	3600-3649 3690-3699	Household appliances, lighting, and other electrical equipment
36.5	3650-3669	Radio, television, and communication equipment
36.7	3670-3679	Electronic components and accessories (includes TV tubes and semiconductors)
37.1	3700-3719	Motor vehicles and equipment
37.2	3720-3729 3760-3769	Aircraft, guided missiles, and parts
37.4	3730-3759 3770-3799	Shipbuilding, repairs, and other transportation equipment
38.1	3800-3829 3870-3879	Scientific instruments and measuring devices, watches and clocks
38.3	3830-3859	Optical, medical, and ophthalmic goods
38.6	3860-3869	Photographic equipment and supplies
39.0	3900-3999	Miscellaneous manufacturing
42.0	4200-4299	Trucking and warehousing
44.0	4400-4499 4600-4699	Water transportation and pipelines (except natural gas)
45.0	4500-4599	Transportation by air
47.0	4700-4799	Transportation services
48.1	4800-4829	Telephone, telegraph (the communications services)
48.3	4830-4899	Radio and television broadcasting
50.1	5000-5079 5090-5139 5150-5199	Miscellaneous wholesale trade
51.4	5140-5149	Wholesale trade, groceries, and related products
52.0	5200-5299	Building materials, garden supplies, and mobile home dealers

Table 5-A1. (*continued*)

Industry code	4-digit SIC	Industry definition
53.0	5300-5399	General merchandise stores
54.0	5400-5499	Food stores
56.0	5600-5699	Apparel and accessory stores
57.0	5700-5799	Furniture, home furnishing, equipment stores
58.0	5800-5899	Eating and drinking places
59.0	5900-5999	Miscellaneous retail stores
65.0	6500-6999	Real estate
67.0	6700-6799	Holding companies and investment trusts
70.0	7000-7099	Hotels and other lodging places
72.0	7200-7299	Personal services
73.0	7300-7399	Business services
75.0	7500-7699	Automotive and miscellaneous repair service
78.0	7800-7999	Motion pictures, amusement, and recreation services
85.0	8000-8099	Health services
	8100-8199	Legal services
	8200-8999	Educational, social, and other services

Comment by Darius Gaskins

This paper is a careful study of the determinants of the wave of financial restructuring during the 1980s. The most valuable information is Blair's and Schary's statistical portrayal of restructuring events in figures 5-2, 5-3, and 5-4, which show that in the early 1980s there was considerable interindustry variation in the types of restructuring. Moreover, in five of the seven industrial sectors there appears to have been a rise in the number of events each year. What is not shown is that by 1990 the number of restructurings across all industries fell dramatically as the financial resources available for such activity dried up.

The econometric results of this study were unfortunately rather inconclusive in terms of testing the authors' hypotheses. But there is a plausible story compatible with the data and the regression results. The story begins with the premise that at any point in time there is a confluence of actors and motivations that would drive a firm to restructure by increasing its debt level. Not the least of these actors are rent-seeking investment bankers who profit primarily through restructuring activity. In addition, many restructurings enriched the management of the affected firms. The necessary but missing ingredients are a willing lender and the acceptance by the board of directors of the proposed transaction. In this story, significant factors that permit restructurings are an increase in the willingness to lend or a decrease in the price of debt or both. A new instrument such as junk bonds obviously permits a new kind and level of restructuring. Similarly the deregulation of the savings and loan industry permits additional restructuring activity if less oversight and the financial pressure of higher-cost funds drove the lenders to take on more risky investments. Not surprisingly, the decline of restructuring activity in 1990 occurred simultaneously with the crash of the junk bond market and the crisis in the banking and savings and loan industries.

This story is compatible with the increase in restructuring events noted above. As one or more firms in an industry "successfully" restructure, it becomes acceptable for other similar firms to follow. Moreover, as activity increases there is greater peer pressure on boards of directors to allow restructuring, just as potential lenders play follow the leader. A significant part of this story is that after the trend is well established the economic rationale for restructuring becomes much less relevant. It is only at the beginning of such a period that one would expect the economic circumstances of the potential restructurers to be important. This story is consistent with the econometric results of the paper, which found some statistically significant economic causes of restructuring during the first half of the 1980s. The largely random pattern of events in the later 1980s is compatible with the idea that restructuring became a thoroughly acceptable fad.

This story also suggests a research strategy for evaluating the evidence more fully. The strategy would be to focus exclusively on the financial transactions that took place at the beginning of the decade and to explore more fully both the ex ante rationale (at least as expressed by management and financial analysts) and the ex post conduct of the restructured firms. The authors of this study did attempt this kind of evaluation when they compared the ex post payout practices of restructured firms with a random sample of nonevent firms. Their comparison is startling because firms that underwent financial restructuring events were no more likely to have made large payouts to shareholders than nonrestructuring firms. This may have been the result of different financial starting points, but the result certainly deserves more scrutiny.

This study represents an important step in the attempt to understand the restructuring of the 1980s. Further research should pay attention to the supply side of these transactions as well as the changes in company behavior that followed the restructurings.

Comment by Dennis C. Mueller

Margaret Blair's and Martha Schary's paper and its companion piece represent an ambitious attempt to describe and analyze LBOs and other restructuring activity in the 1980s. My comments are offered in the spirit of trying to glean even more information from the data than the authors. The reader will recognize a symbiosis between the two papers. Some of the comments made on the other paper are applicable to this one, and some of my remarks are relevant for the other paper as well. But I shall focus on this paper.

Empirical research on industrial organization is characterized by two *Weltanschauungen*: one group of observers sees the world as divided into industries and analyzes events in terms of their consequences for industry behavior and performance; the other sees the world as populated by firms, and analysis focuses on the behavior of firms. In this paper the authors adopt the perspective of the first group; I have always had the second perspective. My comments reflect this difference.

Let us assume that all companies can be placed in one of four categories: neoclassical firms in mature industries with limited investment opportunities, neoclassical firms with good investment and growth opportunities, managerial firms in mature industries, and managerial firms with good investment and growth opportunities. By a neoclassical firm I mean one that chooses its investment, dividend, and debt policies to maximize the wealth of its shareholders. A managerial firm is one in which managers have sufficient discretion to pursue their own objectives at the expense of shareholder wealth. Now if one assumes that all four types can exist in the economy, and perhaps even within a single industry, then the relationship between a given variable and restructuring activity will vary among them. This variability may account for the poor explanatory power of Blair's and Schary's equations, for they assume both that all firms in an industry are driven by the same motivation and that a common relationship holds across industries.

The main observation to be made about neoclassical firms is that they have no need to restructure to avoid takeover. Because by definition they are doing what needs to be done to maximize shareholder wealth, a takeover raider would not be able to improve on the choices the present management is making. In the context of the evidence Blair and Schary present, one expects the ratios of debt to equity for neoclassical firms to have increased as the tax advantages of debt increased. Neoclassical firms might also have issued debt or even junk bonds to undertake a wealth-generating acquisition, so that debt issuance need not always have signaled efforts by management to avoid takeover.

Many hypotheses have been put forward regarding the conflicts between managers' and shareholders' interests. Two that seem particularly relevant to takeovers and LBOs are managers' direct pursuit of high incomes and perquisites and their pursuit of growth (empire building), which might also lead to higher incomes and perquisites in the long run. One of the first things an LBO-sponsoring firm such as Kohlberg, Kravis, and Roberts often does when it takes over a company is to sell the company plane and close the executive dining room, suggesting that managerial perquisites are the target of the takeover. But perquisites such as these are recorded as business expenses. Reported profits are net of these and will thus not be a good measure of free cash flow. Profits will be a good measure, however, if managers are pursuing excessive growth, because this will result in overretention and reinvestment of reported profits. A decision as to which of these two uses of managerial discretion exists or dominates should be made before undertaking empirical work.

If managerial pursuit of growth is the cause of takeovers, a key explanatory variable should be the investment opportunities of the firms. The interests of managers and shareholders need not be in conflict in industries with attractive investment and growth prospects, because the rate of growth that is optimal from the point of view of shareholders is likely to be large enough to satisfy managerial desires for growth. The conflict between managers and shareholders over dividends and retentions will exist only for firms with limited investment and growth opportunities. Blair and Schary seek to capture these differences with industry-level variables, but important differences among firms will exist at the level of industry aggregation the authors adopt. For example, pharmaceutical firms have very large cash flows. Many also have attractive investment opportunities. Note in this context that a broad definition of overinvestment should be used—one that includes acquisitions of other firms, R&D, and advertising, as well as capital equipment—since there is no reason to expect that a management pursuing excessive growth will preclude any particular form of growth and investment. Free cash flow should accordingly be measured by adding R&D and advertising expenditures back into reported profits.

A good measure of the extent of overinvestment is a firm's ratio of marginal return on investment to the cost of capital. Elizabeth Reardon and I have developed a methodology for measuring these ratios, and we cite earlier studies that make similar measurements.[53] The ratios, calculated at the level of the firm, would be ideal candidates for explanatory variables in a firm-level cross-sectional model, but once again only if managerial discretion manifests itself as excessive growth. If managers merely overconsume perquisites, the threat of takeover and investment opportunities or returns on investment may be uncorrelated.

A leveraged buyout or the issuance of more debt is one response to the danger of a hostile takeover. But there are others—for example, the introduction of a poison pill. John Burgess has found that debt and poison pills are strong substitutes.[54] After firms introduce a poison pill, they significantly reduce the amount of debt they have outstanding. The existence of a poison pill should be both a right-hand and ideally a co-determined variable in a firm-level model of LBO activity.

Before summarizing my arguments, I shall make two additional but unrelated points. First, the motivation for issuing debt to avoid being taken over seems different from that for issuing junk bonds to finance a takeover. I question using the same specification for both decisions. Second, I am uncomfortable with measuring debt changes for a single year. A management could launch a program to increase its leverage over three to five years, and thus a longer interval for the accumulation of debt would be optimal.

To summarize the main points, I would like to see a truly firm-level analysis to complement Blair's and Schary's industry-level model. Under the assumption that excessive growth and investment ensues from managerial discretion—what I take to be the free cash flow hypothesis tested by Blair and Schary—the key explanatory variable would be the ratio of the marginal return on investment relative to the cost of capital for the firm, or some proxy thereof. If this ratio is not less than 1.0, there is no free cash and there is nothing that a change in management can accomplish. When this ratio is low, a firm becomes a potential target for a hostile takeover. This variable should be a key one in explaining the probability of a hostile takeover, the probability of an LBO, and the probability (or amount) of debt increase. But in addition to increasing its leverage, a management can reduce the threat of takeover in two other ways: it can introduce a poison pill, or more simply, it can increase its dividends and eliminate overinvestment. Thus hostile takeovers, LBOs, debt increases, the introduction of poison pills, and dividend increases are all potential candidates for codetermined variables in a full-blown free cash flow model. In addition to marginal return on investment relative to the cost of capital, an important potential explanatory variable is the fraction of shares outstanding held by management.

If it is salaries and perquisites that managerial discretion enhances, then it is these, relative to some optimum of shareholder-wealth maximizing, that must be explanatory variables rather than the marginal returns on investment relative to the cost of capital.

General Discussion

Bronwyn Hall was intrigued by the finding that industries with high R&D intensity were more likely than others to undergo leveraged restructurings. Her own research has suggested that when firms increase their leverage significantly, spending on R&D is reduced. But she has not found that high-R&D industries were especially targeted for this kind of restructuring.

Several participants were concerned that the various kinds of financial restructuring events considered in the paper were not really distinct events. Carl Ferenbach noted, for example, that the mechanism typically used for private buyouts was to create a new company to be the acquirer, and that this new firm would issue high-yield (junk) debt. It is usually very difficult to make a trading market in a junk bond issue of less than $100 million, he noted, so that tended to put a floor under the size of the issues, at least under issues that were publicly traded. But, as Peter Tufano found, much of the debt used to finance acquisitions, especially debt issued in amounts smaller than $100 million, was privately placed.

Hall noted that if the free cash flow theory is really about the difference between neoclassical firms (in which managers always maximize the value of the firm) and managerial firms (in which managers pursue their own interests), the appropriate unit of analysis is the firm level, as Dennis Mueller argued. But the characteristics of a firm should be measured relative to other firms in the same industry. If the cause of free cash flow is declining investment opportunities, as Blair and Schary suggest, industry-level analysis might be appropriate.

William Long observed that firm-level data are very noisy and can lead to strange results unless researchers carefully account for extreme values in the data. Aggregating to the industry level helps reduce the noise in the data, which, he said, is mostly messing up the results. But he was concerned that the regression analysis at the industry level, in which the variable being explained is the number or value of transactions, does not follow any standard modeling approaches. He suggested that it would be useful to start with a more explicit model of the probability that a firm in a given industry will undertake some financial restructuring.

Hall was also concerned about possible simultaneity in the regression analysis. Does a low rate of growth of assets or low net return on assets cause restructuring, or could the causality be running the other way? The direction of causality cannot be determined for sure with the modeling approach used, she noted.

Darius Gaskins suggested that the motives of managements in each transaction must be considered because some transactions might have been undertaken by managements at their own initiative, while others might have been imposed from outside. Margaret Blair responded that the theories being tested were about exogenous factors that would have affected firms across the board. Whether the change was imposed from without or undertaken from within should not be important for these theories.

David Ravenscraft observed that firms increase their debt levels for many reasons, including share repurchase, financial distress, and financing of acquisitions. Carliss Baldwin agreed, noting that there is a vast difference between using bonds as a cheap source of capital to finance growth and using them as an instrument of control to rein in growth. There is likely to be some of both activities in the data used in this paper, she said, suggesting that it would be worthwhile to look separately at the firms that had large payouts.

Blair responded that one lesson from the paper was that financial restructuring was a heterogeneous process. Although it is important to know what the universe of transactions looked like, it is also important to do further research on smaller samples in which there is more similarity among transactions.

Notes

1. Our method of defining leveraged restructuring events somewhat biased the results in this direction.

2. See Margaret M. Blair and Martha A. Schary, "Industry-Level Indicators of Free Cash Flow," in this volume for a detailed empirical analysis of the relationship between costs and returns to capital at the industry level in the 1980s. See also the chapter by Sidney Winter for a discussion of the impact of higher capital costs on corporate resource allocation and investment behavior.

3. Such firms might have been forced to go to the debt markets to fund further investment and growth if the equity markets were closed to them for any reason. This could explain why rapidly growing firms sometimes issued junk bonds or undertook other large increases in debt, but it cannot explain why some firms would buy back their equity or issue debt and use the proceeds to pay special dividends, or why firms in mature industries would suddenly leverage themselves very highly. Virtually all Compustat firms have equity that trades publicly and have some following in the financial markets. This suggests that the companies we consider in this study all have relatively good access to the equity markets.

4. This hypothesis is laid out in detail in Margaret M. Blair and Robert E. Litan, "Corporate Leverage and Leveraged Buyouts in the Eighties," in John B. Shoven and Joel Waldfogel, eds., *Debt, Taxes, and Corporate Restructuring* (Brookings, 1990), pp. 43–80. The argument that an increase in the cost of capital could encourage the use of debt contracts builds on the free cash flow arguments of Michael C. Jensen, "Agency Costs of Free Cash Flow, Corporate Finance, and Takeovers," *American Economic Review*, vol. 76 (May 1986, *Papers and Proceedings*, 1985), pp. 323–29.

5. Examples include Steven N. Kaplan, "The Effects of Management Buyouts on Operating Performance and Value," *Journal of Financial Economics*, vol. 24 (October 1989), pp. 217–54, which examines thirty-three management buyouts; Kaplan and Jeremy C. Stein, "How Risky Is the Debt in Highly Leveraged Transactions? Evidence from Public Recapitalizations," working paper 3390, (Cambridge, Mass: National Bureau of Economic Research, June 1990), which studies twelve recapitalizations; Frank Lichtenberg and Donald Seigel, "The Effects of Leveraged Buyouts on Productivity and Related Aspects of Firm Behavior," *Journal of Financial Economics*, vol. 27 (September 1990), pp. 165–94, which examines 131 LBO's; and Sanjai Bhagat, Andrei Shleifer, and Robert W. Vishny, "Hostile Takeovers in the 1980s: The Return to Corporate Specialization," *Brookings Papers on Economic Activity, Microeconomics, 1990*, pp. 1–72, which analyzes seventy-two hostile takeovers.

6. Examples include Devra L. Golbe and Lawrence J. White, "A Time Series Analysis of Mergers and Acquisitions in the U.S. Economy," in Alan J. Auerbach, ed., *Corporate Takeovers: Causes and Consequences* (University of Chicago Press, 1988), pp. 265–310; Ben S. Bernanke and John Y. Campbell, "Is There a Corporate Debt Crisis?" *Brookings Papers on Economic Activity, 1:1988*, pp.

83–125; and Blair and Litan, "Corporate Leverage and Leveraged Buyouts in the Eighties."

7. The raw files used as the primary source for private buyouts included an indicator for whether each transaction was an LBO. Many—but not all—acquisitions by private investors or other similar entities were also identified as LBOs. Likewise, most transactions called LBOs had acquirers that met our criteria for private buyer; but some did not and were not considered to be private buyouts. See the data appendix for more details.

8. The real (1982 dollars) total value of assets of this firm in 1989 was $28.83 billion.

9. Bronwyn Hall used a similar technique to determine a population of firms that had undergone significant increases in leverage. She defined "large increase" arbitrarily, requiring that the change be 75 percentage points or more. See "The Impact of Corporate Restructuring on Industrial Research and Development," *Brookings Papers on Economic Activity, Microeconomics, 1990*, pp. 85–124. In our sample, a change of that magnitude would have been well into the upper 1 percentile.

10. That LRS firms were larger than PBOs was partly a result of the size screen applied in identifying LRS events (which eliminated the smallest firms), but it is also true that PBOs were relatively rare among very large firms. Only seven private buyouts involved firms with assets greater than $3 billion in real (1982) dollars, but thirty-two leveraged restructurings involved firms with assets of this magnitude or greater.

11. Although we identified 977 firms that were restructured, 10 (2 LRS firms and 8 JUNK firms) did not have sufficient data available in Compustat for this and all subsequent analyses.

12. In some respects, this is not surprising, since our definition of LRS events required a large increase in leverage. But if the increases were quickly paid down by growing cash flows or by asset sales, this would mitigate the impact on the aggregate debt-to-asset ratio of the restructuring firms over time. Moreover, our measure of the ratio for restructuring firms is biased downward by the fact that PBO firms typically drop out of the Compustat population just as their leverage is significantly increased. While Compustat sometimes tracks firms that have been bought out (in the sense that a controlling interest changes hands) but that continue to have some publicly traded securities, about 78 percent of our PBO target firms were dropped from the Compustat listings within a year after the event.

13. Each event firm is assigned to an industry at the two- to three-digit standard industrial classification (SIC) level, and the average debt-to-asset ratio for that industry is computed using all the other firms in Compustat that are in the same industry. Industry assignments are discussed in greater detail in the next section. See the data appendix for a list of industry definitions.

14. This fact may simply explain why the debt issued by these firms was rated below investment grade.

15. Because PBO firms typically drop out of Compustat in the year of the buyout or shortly after, postevent measurements for them must be interpreted carefully. Nonetheless, although the samples are smaller, the postevent data we

do have on PBOs generally fits the pattern described. See the chapter by William Long and David Ravenscraft in this volume for an analysis of leveraged buyout transactions that includes data on firms that do not continue to trade publicly after the buyout.

16. For example, 17.4 percent of LRS firms were also junk bond issuers, but only 2.9 percent of non-LRS firms were. Similarly, 12.3 percent of LRS firms, but only 3.0 percent of non-LRS firms, were targets of private buyouts. These numbers probably understate the relatedness among restructuring events. Companies that underwent more than one kind of restructuring activity were identified by matching routines based on Center for Uniform Securities Information and Pricing identification numbers. In some cases, events that radically alter a firm's identification also result in a change in the CUSIP number. Thus our matching routines might not always be able to identify a linkage between transactions involving a company before and after the transforming event. This same caveat applies to the estimates reported below of the relationships between financial restructuring events and acquisitions and divestitures.

17. Acquisitions, or divestitures, done in the year before, the year of, or the year after the financial restructuring were regarded as associated with that restructuring.

18. The acquisitions were not trivial relative to the size of the companies. For leveraged restructurings, they averaged 12 percent of the event-year assets of the firm; for JUNK events, they averaged 26 percent.

19. See Steven Kaplan, "Effects of Management Buyouts on Operating Performance and Value"; Abbie J. Smith, "Corporate Ownership Structure and Performance: The Case of Management Buyouts," *Journal of Financial Economics*, vol. 27 (September 1990), pp. 143–64; and Lichtenberg and Siegel, "The Effect of Leveraged Buyouts."

20. In an acquisition, shareholders of the target company receive a substantial payout even if the shareholders of the acquiring company do not.

21. We reiterate that one must be especially cautious in statements about postevent behavior of PBO firms. But the subset of buyouts for which we have postevent data fit the pattern of slow growth relative to growth before the restructuring.

22. These are absolute growth rates computed in real dollar terms but not adjusted for growth rates of the firm's industry. In the regression analysis of the next section, we test whether restructuring was related to industry growth rates.

23. In particular, we measured total dividends paid (on common and preferred stock) over a five-year period (two years before, year of, and two years after the event), plus total stock purchases (common and preferred) over the same period, minus total stock sold. If data were missing for any years within the five-year period, we treated the missing values as zeroes.

24. We started with a sample of 500 firms, but only 482 had the necessary data to compute associated payouts.

25. By construction, leveraged restructuring and junk bond issues could not occur in the utilities (electric, gas, and sanitary services) or financial industries (banks; credit agencies; securities, real estate and insurance dealers and brokers; and insurance companies). Real estate developers and management companies,

as well as holding companies and investment trusts, were not excluded, however. Nor were airlines, telephone or telegraph services, and radio and television broadcasting—all industries that had a large number of junk bond issuers.

26. Stephen S. Roach looked at changes in leverage by very broadly defined industrial sectors, classifying each sector as "cyclical" or "stable." He concluded that most of the increase in debt in the 1980s was caused by increases at firms in the stable sectors. See "Defusing the Debt Bomb," Special Economic Study, Morgan Stanley, New York, October 15, 1990. John D. Paulus and Stephen R. Waite looked at high-yield bond issues and LBO activity in about a dozen industries. They found that industries with high measures of LBO intensity were generally growing more slowly than other manufacturing industries or than the U.S. economy as a whole. Within these industries, the segments that accounted for most of the high-yield bond use related to LBOs were underperformers in sales growth within their industries. See "High-Yield Bonds, Corporate Control, and Innovation," in Frank J. Fabozzi, ed., *The New High-Yield Debt Market: A Handbook for Portfolio Managers and Analysts* (New York: HarperBusiness, 1990), pp. 3–28. Bronwyn H. Hall examined corporate takeovers and large year-to-year changes in corporate leverage ratios. She found that leveraged and other private buyouts were overwhelmingly concentrated in low-technology or stable-technology industries, with little spending on research and development relative to sales. See "Corporate Restructuring and Investment Horizons," paper in Michael E. Porter, ed., *Investment Behavior and Time Horizon in American Industry* (Harvard Business School Press, forthcoming). Finally, Blair and Litan, "Corporate Leverage and Leveraged Buyouts," looked at increases in leverage in fourteen industries and concluded that the industries that increased their ratios of interest to cash flow the most during the 1980s were those with slow rates of asset growth. The findings of the last three studies are consistent with the free cash flow hypothesis.

27. See Appendix table 5A-1 for a list of the seventy-one industries.

28. The value of restructuring transactions is measured the same as in table 5-1 and figures 5-2, 5-3, and 5-4.

29. Bronwyn Hall has studied the relationship between this variable and several kinds of restructuring, including takeovers, leveraged buyouts, and large leverage increases. See, for example, "Corporate Restructuring and Investment Horizons." She has concluded that leveraged buyouts and other private buyouts were much more prevalent in low-R&D industries, in industries with steady cash flows, and in industries that have been downsizing under pressure from foreign competition.

30. The paper discusses alternative methodologies for measuring the cost of capital, its components, and the net return to capital (which is called "the squeeze" in the other paper). In particular, it examines the impact on measures of the cost of capital, and then on net returns, when two different measures of the cost of equity are used. In the regression results that follow, we report results using only one of these measures, but we discuss how using the alternative measure would affect the results.

31. Our measures of correlation were the coefficients on the net returns variables in Tobit regressions of the rate of restructuring activity on net returns

and a constant over 1979-89. This measure adjusts for the fact that there are many observations in the restructuring-rate series that have a value of zero. The two measures of net returns are those discussed in the companion paper, one using a constant risk premium (SQZCON below) and the other using a changing risk premium in the measure of the cost of equity (SQZCHG). The coefficients and t-statistics are: PBO rate (on SQZCON): -0.043 (-1.713); PBO rate (on SQZCHG): -0.046 (-1.616); JUNK rate (on SQZCON): -0.096 (-4.277); JUNK rate (on SQZCHG): -0.112 (-4.502); LRS rate (on SQZCON): -0.109 (-2.621); LRS rate (on SQZCHG): -0.152 (-3.231).

32. See Stephen S. Roach, "Defusing the Debt Bomb," for an exposition of this argument.

33. Roach "Defusing the Debt Bomb," argues that, at least at broad sectoral levels, this was in fact true. But Blair and Litan, "Corporate Leverage and Leveraged Buyouts," found evidence that increases in leverage at the level of more narrowly defined industries were uncorrelated with the stability of cash flow.

34. Another argument is that bankruptcy risk fell for many firms, thus increasing their debt capacity. However, Ben S. Bernanke, John Y. Campbell, and Toni M. Whited have suggested that bankruptcy risk may actually have increased during the 1980s. See "U.S. Corporate Leverage: Developments in 1987 and 1988," *Brookings Papers on Economic Activity, 1:1990*, pp. 255–78.

35. Richard A. Brealey and Stewart C. Meyers, *Principles of Corporate Finance*, 4th ed. (McGraw-Hill, 1991), chap. 18, provide a very accessible analysis of personal and corporate taxes. The analysis in Jane G. Gravelle, *Corporate Tax Integration: Issues and Options*, Congressional Research Service report 91-482 (June 14, 1991), shows that real effective rates vary significantly with inflation, how long assets are held, and a number of other variables.

36. See the companion paper for a full discussion of how the use of a time-varying risk premium changes the measure of the cost of capital and consequently the measure of net returns.

37. Randall Morck, Andrei Shleiffer, and Robert W. Vishny, for example, get R^2 values ranging from .16 to .26 in their model attempting to explain the growth rate of investment with variables proxying for financing activity and fundamentals such as cash flow and sales growth. See "The Stock Market and Investment: Is the Market a Sideshow?" *Brookings Papers on Economic Activity, 2*:1990, p. 178.

38. See Barrie A. Wigmore, "The Decline in Credit Quality of New-Issue Junk Bonds," *Financial Analysts Journal*, vol. 46 (September–October 1990), pp. 53–62; Steven N. Kaplan and Jeremy C. Stein, "The Pricing and Financial Structure of Management Buyouts in the 1980s," Graduate School of Business, University of Chicago, and Sloan School of Management, M.I.T., January 25, 1991; and Long and Ravenscraft in this volume.

39. Likelihood ratio tests for all three kinds of restructuring strongly reject the hypothesis that the coefficients of the model were the same across both periods.

40. The net returns variables are significant at the 80 percent level, however. In the alternative version using the varying-risk premium form of the net returns variable, the results are similar but both the net returns and the cash generation variables are statistically significant at the 90 percent level.

41. For all three types of restructuring activity, the results were qualitatively very similar for alternative regressions using the measure of net returns estimated with a changing risk premium.

42. The magnitude of this effect varied from version to version. In the version with the highest explanatory power, the model suggests that industries whose net return to capital was 1 percentage point lower than the average of 1.2 percent for all industries in 1979–85 would have experienced a rate of private buyout activity in that period that was about 0.2 percentage points higher than the average rate of 1.26 percent during that period. But the variance around that effect was high.

43. Documentation for this master file is available from the authors.

44. Because the beginning of the fiscal year may differ from the beginning of the calendar year, a few transactions were kept if they involved firms that, for example, last reported in Compustat as of fiscal year 1985, but were not bought out until calendar year 1986.

45. One firm, Triangle Pacific Corp., was bought out twice, in 1986 and again in 1988.

46. We wanted transaction values to correspond as closely as possible with data from Compustat on other kinds of transactions and other firm-level measures. Thus the book value of assets from Compustat was the first choice in defining transaction value, even if actual transaction value was reported in the IDD source data.

47. Wigmore described and analyzed the 1980-88 data in "Decline in the Credit Quality of Junk Bond New Issues," pp. 53–62. These data, as well as the 1989 data, were compiled from transactions reported by IDD Information Services of New York. We are grateful to Wigmore and Fridson for use of their data.

48. We required that Compustat have data on the issuing firm for the year of the issue.

49. We chose measures of value that corresponded most closely to other firm-level measures from Compustat and that indicated the amount of assets involved in the deal. Although for PBOs, the book value of assets was most appropriate, for junk bonds the measure of value that comes closest to meeting these criteria was the face value of the bonds.

50. We used an earlier edition of the Compustat PCPlus data base covering 1970–89 for this step. We assumed that the distribution of year-to-year changes we created for 1970–88 applied to 1971–89 as well.

51. Although firms come and go from the Compustat file, the number listed in each year rose from about 5,000 in 1970 to around 7,000 in 1975 and then stabilized at about that level through the end of the 1980s.

52. See Blair and Schary, "Industry-Level Indicators of Free Cash Flow," in this volume for more details.

53. Dennis C. Mueller and Elizabeth Reardon, "Rates of Return on Corporate Investment," University of Maryland, Department of Economics, College Park, 1992.

54. John Hunt Burgess, "Poison Pills and the Market for Corporate Control," Ph.D. dissertation, University of Maryland, College Park, 1992.

Decade of Debt:
Lessons from LBOs in the 1980s

William F. Long and
David J. Ravenscraft

UNDERSTANDING the causes and effects of leveraged buyouts is important for at least four reasons. First, LBOs were a significant part of the 1980s merger wave, the largest and longest in history. Second, firms that have undergone an LBO represent a form of organization distinct from that of traditional publicly held companies. When compared with publicly held firms, their performance can yield important insights into the optimal debt level of a company and, more generally, into the way corporations should be governed. Third, some of the profits from LBOs may come at the expense of employees, bondholders, suppliers, communities, shareholders, or government, making the buyouts a controversial public policy matter. Finally, explaining the cycle of growth and collapse—LBO activity increased steadily in the 1980s and then declined sharply in late 1989—can illuminate the ways capital markets function and financial innovations are diffused.

Previous research on LBOs has focused on three questions. What types of firms undergo an LBO? What determines the premium paid to a target firm's shareholders? And how do LBOs affect the operation of a company after the buyout? Research on the first question has shown that a firm is more likely to undergo an LBO when its free cash flow and management ownership stakes are high. It is less likely to undergo a buyout if its relative value (based on ratios of price to earnings, or price to book value, or Tobin's q) is high or its R&D activity is relatively intense.[1] The findings on the second question complement those on the first. Premiums paid to shareholders rise with increases in a firm's cash flow (especially for firms with low levels of insider ownership) and fall with increases in a firm's relative value. Transfers from bondholders are not an important determinant of the premium, but tax savings can explain a significant portion of the premium paid.[2] With respect to the third question, LBOs improve operating income, save working capital, and increase productivity. However, they also reduce capital expenditures, taxes paid, and employment relative to their industries.[3]

This research paints an attractive picture of LBOs: they target cash-rich underperformers, and after the buyout, operating performance and the management of working capital improve significantly. The main potential drawbacks are reduced tax payments and fewer employees and the long-term effects of decreased capital expenditures. However, if LBOs improve corporate performance, a government tax subsidy may be a good policy and may even increase net tax revenues. The decreases in employment and capital expenditures may simply reflect unprofitably high levels of each before the buyout.

But if LBOs do improve underperformers and release excess cash to shareholders and bondholders, why have many of the firms that have been bought out experienced financial distress, and why has buyout activity plummeted? There are a number of possible answers. The economic downturn at the end of the decade may have increased the cost of capital. Competition may have increased premiums to the point that dealmakers paid too much. More recent LBOs may also have been different from earlier buyouts. Increased buyout activity may have led to more marginal deals for companies that had less room for improvement after the buyout. Alternatively, the methodology or publicly available data employed in the early studies that were done may have resulted in misleading conclusions.

This paper summarizes the findings of a large-scale research project that has extended and revisited previous research to produce a comprehensive, current, integrating study. We began by listing virtually every deal in the 1980s that someone called a leveraged buyout or "going-private" transaction. We collected public information on key characteristics of industries, firms, and deals for each buyout, including data on shareholder premiums from the New York Stock Exchange, American Exchange, and over-the-counter market. We linked the public information file to three confidential Census Bureau data bases—the Quarterly Financial Report (QFR), Longitudinal Research Data (LRD), and the National Science Foundation (NSF) R&D data—containing pre- and post-LBO information on numerous accounting, finance, and production variables at the firm and plant levels.

These data portray the LBO landscape and changes in that landscape during the 1980s. The sample, substantially larger than previous ones, allows less biased and more accurate estimates of the determinants of LBO premiums and postbuyout changes in performance. We also employ a longer time series, balanced before-and-after samples, and specific significance tests for prebuyout and postbuyout trends. The four large data files can be integrated, permitting post-LBO performance to be linked to premiums and changes in R&D. The expanded set of variables measuring LBO characteristics can also help uncover which types of LBOs succeed and which tend to fail. Finally, the study addresses changes in performance that might explain the increased incidence of distressed buyouts and the recent decline in buyout activity.

Data Sources

Our project employs four large data bases: a comprehensive list of LBOs and their characteristics, variables from whole-company balance sheets and income statements from the QFR files, data on individual plants of manufacturing firms from the LRD files, and whole-company R&D data from the National Science Foundation files. We compiled a list of LBOs from public sources and a data base purchased from the ADP M&A Database (now owned by IDD Information Services of New York). The Bureau of the Census collects the other three data bases.

The foundation for our file on LBO characteristics was the M&A Database, which contains data on LBOs completed since January 1981. We augmented this list with the names of companies supplied by other researchers. For each LBO, we searched the *Wall Street Journal* for the three years before and after the buyout announcement and coded information on the announcement and completion date, the value of the transaction, senior management ownership, management participation in the deal, number of bidders, management opposition to bids, acquisition and divestiture activity, and several other items. We obtained additional information on whole company LBOs from Compustat, Moody's, the Center for Research on Security Prices (for stock return data), and *Value Line* (for pre-LBO senior management ownership data). After duplicates and misclassified transactions were eliminated, the file covered 2,324 deals. Of these, 1,396 were buyouts of a division of a company, 821 were whole-company buyouts, and 107 were going-private mergers.[4] In total, we collected 50 variables measuring characteristics on each LBO. However, the number of observations varied widely, with the most comprehensive information on buyouts of large whole companies listed on major stock exchanges.

Our primary source for information on the performance of entire companies before and after LBOs is the QFR data. This previously untapped source contains thirteen income statement variables and thirty-two balance sheet variables for all firms, public or private, in mining, manufacturing, wholesaling, and retailing that have more than $25 million in assets. The QFR also contains a large scientific sample of firms with assets of less than $25 million. The reporting is mandatory and staff accountants carefully audit reports. By the mid-1980s there were 4,000 to 5,000 firms in the sample with assets of $25 million or more and 12,000 to 16,000 smaller firms. Because the smaller firms were included in the sample for eight continuous quarters and then replaced by other firms, they did not have a sufficient time series of data to be included in our pre- and post-LBO analysis.

We retrieved the 1977–88 QFR data from archived tapes, linked them across time, and checked for outliers.[5] Of the 821 whole-company LBOs in the comprehensive list, 550 were found in the QFR data. Most of those not found were either small or not among the industries surveyed by the QFR program. For LBOs between 1981 and 1987, data for the year before and after the buyout existed for 198, and data for three years before and after existed for 94. The number of observations dropped from 550 to 198 for two main reasons. Post-LBO data on 1988 LBOs have not yet been retrieved, and pre-1981 deals were dropped because evidence suggested many were not LBOs.[6] Also, the QFR program sampled many of the 550 firms for only eight quarters because they had assets of less than $25 million. For these companies, the required pre- and postbuyout data do not exist.

The LRD file contains census and annual survey data on manufacturing plants. For census years, there are data for all but the smallest establishments. For other years the LRD file contains data on all manufacturing establishments with more than 250 employees and a large scientific sampling of smaller establishments. In 1985 some 56,000 establishments reported to the annual survey. The LRD data make it possible to expand the QFR analysis to divisional LBOs, whole-company LBOs with extensive divisional sales, and small LBOs. It also allows such additional variables as inventories, employment, and capital expenditures to be analyzed. The disadvantages of the LRD data are that 43 percent of the LBOs have occurred in nonmanufacturing industries, nonplant expenses and balance sheet data are not collected, a complete time series is available only for large plants, and the data cannot be externally validated.

Approximately 6,000 LRD plants have been linked to the whole and divisional LBO list. For 1,637 plants data exist for both one year before and one year after the buyout. For 932 plants there are three years of matched pre- and postbuyout data. Our analysis of these data later in this paper extends the work of Frank Lichtenberg and Donald Siegel in a number of directions.[7] It provides a more comprehensive list of LBOs and employs the full census and annual survey panel, not just those very large plants with complete reporting between 1972 and 1981. It also uses a more accurate methodology for the difficult task of identifying plants undergoing divisional LBOs by employing division names, plant addresses, and changes in status codes and SIC codes, not just product descriptions. There is a separate analysis of whole and divisional LBOs, and we include 1987 census data, allowing for longer post-LBO time series and more recent LBOs. We also use a balanced pre- and post-buyout time series and explicit tests for changes in LBO performance, and an analysis of how LBO characteristics affect performance.

None of these data sets contains information on R&D, a key measure of long-run performance. The detailed company R&D file collected by the Census Bureau for the National Science Foundation fills this gap. It contains primarily whole-company data on a large number of R&D-related variables for all companies spending more than $500,000 on R&D and a scientific sample of smaller companies.[8] But before employing the data, we had to address problems of data quality. The data contained a large number of imputations, errors, and outliers. After correcting them, we found a matched sample of R&D-sales ratios for seventy-two whole companies one year before and after their LBOs. We discuss the impact of LBOs on R&D later in this paper. Drawing policy conclusions from any observed relationship between LBOs and R&D is complicated, since postbuyout declines may simply reflect wasteful pre-buyout R&D expenditures. Sharper conclusions can be drawn by linking the R&D and QFR data. If postbuyout declines in R&D expenditures represent myopic behavior, these declines should lead to a deterioration of longer-run (three to five years after the buyout) profitability.

LBO Characteristics

Table 6-1 presents means for some of the key whole-company LBO descriptive variables. Also included are the correlations of these variables with a linear time trend (the LBO year minus 1975). The means and correlations reveal the typical characteristics of a buyout firm and how these characteristics have changed over time.

The statistics indicate the importance of studying more recent LBOs and nonmanufacturing firms. Almost half the 1980s LBOs occurred be-

Table 6-1. Characteristics of Whole-Company Leveraged Buyouts

Variable	Number of companies[a]	Percent or mean	Time trend[b]
Year of LBO (mean)	821	1985	. . .
Value (millions of dollars)	470	292	.1923*
Manufacturing[c]	747	57	−.0120
Mean number of SICs (maximum 11)	747	2.68	−.0454
Stock market premium paid	297	21	.1225*
Senior management stock ownership[c]	290	30	−.2951*
Management involvement[c]	735	41	−.1172*
Employee stock ownership plan[c]	821	4	−.0122
Single bidder[c]	368	26	.1975*
Hostile bid[c]	368	12	.1794*
Lawsuit from any party[c]	368	24	−.0202
Announced potential credit downgrade[c]	368	8	.1721*
Acquired assets as percent of total assets in 3 preyears	192	7	−.0008
Divested assets as percent of total assets in 3 preyears	192	6	−.0250
Acquired assets as percent of total assets in 3 postyears	192	3	−.2558*
Divested assets as percent of total assets in 3 postyears	192	10	.0255

Source: Authors' calculations. See text.

a. For all but the last four variables, the number given is the number of nonmissing observations. For the last four variables, it is the number of firms for which we found one acquisition or divestiture value.

b. Time trend gives the correlation between the variable and a linear time trend variable. An asterisk indicates the correlation is statistically significant at the 5 percent level or better.

c. For these variables, the number given in the percent or mean column is the percentage of the sample with the variable's characteristic.

tween 1986 and 1988, and 43 percent occurred in nonmanufacturing industries. On average, LBOs pay shareholders a 21 percent premium, which is lower than other tender offers.[9] Firms targeted for buyouts had more incentive to maximize shareholder wealth than most large publicly held firms, since senior management owned an average of 30 percent of the company's shares before the transactions. LBOs are much easier when management already owns a significant equity stake, but the benefits of reduced conflict of interest between shareholders and managers might also be smaller in these cases. Management continued to participate in 41 percent of the postbuyout firms, but labor participation was rare: only 4 percent of the buyouts involved an employee stock option plan.

LBOs are often linked with hostile takeover attempts because a buyout by management or a third party is one of the defenses or alternatives to a hostile threat. However, a hostile threat preceded the LBO in only 12 percent of the buyouts mentioned in the *Wall Street Journal*; for 75 percent no other bidder was evident. This lack of competition raises concerns that management has inside information about the value of the company and may be able to buy the company when the firm is undervalued by the market.[10] The number of lawsuits reveals the controversial nature of LBOs. In almost one-quarter of the buyouts mentioned in the *Wall Street Journal*, shareholders, management, or stakeholders brought lawsuits within one year.

Buyouts are often associated with substantial sales of assets afterward. Divestiture or acquisition activity can distort whole-company data. Therefore, identifying acquisitions and sell-offs within three years of the buyout was a high priority. We tracked asset restructuring by announcements in the *Wall Street Journal* and the ADP M&A Database.[11] The sources were searched using the pre- and postbuyout name of the company for any announcement of an acquisition or divestiture for the three years before and three years after the buyout. We found some evidence of asset restructuring for 192 of the 821 companies. For these 192, pre-LBO acquisition and divestiture activity involved 6 to 7 percent of a company's total assets. In the first three years after the buyout, only 3 percent of a company's assets stemmed from acquisitions. However, divestitures increased to about 10 percent of the assets. Thus although acquisitions and divestitures are important for some LBOs, the great majority are not driven by asset restructuring.

These statistics, however, mask some important changes in the buyout market in the 1980s. A significant time trend—positive or negative—exists for half the variables in table 6-1. The value of the average deal increased substantially during the decade. Premiums also increased in the second half of the 1980s, in part because competition (from both hostile and other bidders) increased. Senior management's equity participation in a company, both before and after the buyout, was greater in the earlier deals than in the later ones. Thus the earlier buyouts tended to be of smaller, closely held companies and to involve smaller premiums and little competitive bidding. Competition for the more recent deals grew along with the premium paid.

Sources of Shareholder Gain

Some of the matters we have raised can be more fully addressed through a specific analysis of the premium paid to the pre-LBO shareholders.[12] What are the main determinants of the shareholder gain? How much have premiums risen? Can other time-related changes in LBO characteristics explain this increase? Are shareholders being taken advantage of in management buyouts, particularly given the typical lack of competition?

To answer these questions, we sought data on stockholder return for the 821 whole companies in our comprehensive list. Using tapes from the Center for Research in Security Prices covering the three major stock exchanges, we found sufficient shareholder return data on 297 companies. The premium paid (or more accurately the abnormal shareholder returns) was measured using standard methodology. The market model was estimated with daily returns for 250 days through the fortieth day before the first bid. The market index used was the NYSE/AMEX or NASDAQ value-weighted index, corresponding to the exchange listing of the firm's common stock. We estimated the cumulative abnormal return of the firm from 20 days before to 5 days after the first bid by anyone, plus 20 days before to 5 days after the first bid by the ultimate acquirer, less any overlap.[13]

Equations 1 and 2 illustrate our analysis of the sources of shareholder gain. The number in parentheses under the coefficient is the t-statistic.

(1)   LBO premium = .1243 + .0092 TIME R^2 = .0150, and
             (2.88)   (2.12)

(2)   LBO premium = − .0515 + .0012 TIME + .0637 MULTI + .0182 MBO
             (−0.73)   (0.26)   (2.38)   (0.82)

   + .0207 LNVALUE − .1089 PREACQ + .0335 POSTDIV R^2 = .0899,
     (2.94)   (−1.57)   (0.62)

where TIME is a linear time trend, MULTI is 1 if there was more than one bidder and zero otherwise, MBO is 1 if the *Wall Street Journal* or *Mergers and Acquisitions Journal* indicated management participation in the deal and zero otherwise, LNVALUE is the natural log of the consideration paid for the LBO company, PREACQ is the percentage of assets acquired in the three years before the LBO, and POSTDIV is the percentage of assets divested in the three years after the LBO.

Equation 1 confirms that the LBO premium rose 1 percentage point a year. LBOs at the end of the decade paid more than half again the premium of those at the beginning. However, equation 2 shows that the relationship between premium and time is complex. When five variables are added to the equation (all of which are significantly correlated with time), the TIME variable becomes insignificant. Further analysis revealed that most of TIME's explanatory power is captured by LNVALUE.

The positive correlation between the LBO premium and the size of the company was unexpected.

Competition increases the prebuyout shareholder return. The entry of a second bidder adds 6 percentage points to the LBO premium. This increase is comparable to the impact of multiple bidders in mergers and tender offers. There is no evidence that management involvement yields a lower return to prebuyout shareholders. In fact, the premium with management involvement is 2 percentage points greater on average, but this increase is not significantly different from zero. The coefficients on preacquisition and postdivestiture activity are both insignificant, providing further evidence that asset restructuring is not a critical motivation for the typical LBO.

Whole-Company LBO Accounting Performance

Although a study of the premium paid to prebuyout shareholders yields some important insights, it has several weaknesses. First, unlike typical mergers, there are no bidder returns from the LBO announcement to make it possible to assess whether the bidder overpaid or earned above average returns. Unless the market for LBO firms is perfectly competitive (implying no abnormal return to the bidder in the long run), target gains yield information only on the bidder's assessment of the LBO gains, not the net value created. Second, the premium paid may reflect transfers from bondholder losses, tax savings, or reduction in employment. Thus the premium does not give an estimate of the operating improvements stemming from the buyout. Third, shareholder returns and postmerger accounting analyses often result in differing conclusions, making it important to pursue both approaches.[14]

Our post-LBO accounting analysis of whole-company LBOs employed the QFR data. We found data for the year before the buyout and the year after on 198 LBOs occurring between 1981 and 1987. We compared the performance of this balanced sample of LBO firms with a balanced control group of firms that did not undergo an LBO.[15] Specifically, we regressed QFR performance variables on an LBO dummy variable with industry-time fixed effects. The fixed effects model employed compares the LBO firms to control group firms in the same industry and data year.[16] Thus general macroeconomic factors and industry differences are eliminated. The control group consisted of 18,992 non-LBO firms.

Table 6-2. Whole-Company, QFR, Matched One-Year Pre- and Postbuyout Sample, 1981–87[a]

	1981–87 LBOs			1981–84 LBOs	1985–87 LBOs
Item	Pre-LBO	Post-LBO	Post − pre	Post − pre	Post − pre
Coefficient	0.17	1.00	0.83	1.99	−0.15
t-statistic	(0.23)	(1.25)	(0.98)	(2.48)	(−0.10)
Percentage impact	2	11	9	23	−2
Number of positives	112	113	111	54	57
Total number of LBOs	198	198	198	91	107
Number in control group	18,992	18,992	18,992	10,628	8,364

Source: Authors' calculations. See text.
a. Dependent variable: post-LBO minus pre-LBO cash flow to sales. Independent variable: LBO dummy variable.

Table 6-2 shows the pre-LBO, post-LBO, and post-LBO minus pre-LBO results for the key variable in our analysis, cash flow to sales. Cash flow was defined as operating income before depreciation. This variable captured operating improvements resulting from the LBO without being affected by asset reevaluations stemming from the purchase accounting used in the buyout. The first row in the table presents the coefficient on a dummy variable that equals one if the firm is in the LBO group and zero if it is in the control group. Specifically, it measures the average difference between the LBO firm's cash flow and that of the control group. The second row presents the t-statistic on the LBO dummy variable. The third row translates the coefficient into a percentage by dividing the coefficient by the average ratio of cash flow to sales for the full sample. The fourth row shows the number of LBOs with the ratio of cash flow to sales superior to their industry counterparts.

There is some weak evidence that buyouts occurring between 1981 and 1987 improved the performance of the firm purchased. The pre-LBO, post-LBO, and post-LBO minus pre-LBO coefficients are all positive, suggesting the firms purchased had above average performance before the transaction and improved on that performance. The LBO increased cash flow–sales ratios by an average 9 percent. However, none of these coefficients is significant at standard levels. The number of firms with above average performance tells a similar story: firms improved on an already above average pre-LBO performance. However, using a z score, all these counts of above average performance are significant at the 10 percent level in a two-tailed test. Fifty-six percent of the buyouts led to increased cash flow–sales ratios.

If LBOs generally improve a firm's operating performance, why have a significant number of buyouts resulted in financial distress and why did buyout activity decline in 1989? Was it primarily a consequence of the rising premiums or did competition and increased LBO activity lead to more marginal deals? To address these questions, we split the sample of LBOs into 91 early ones (1981–84) and 107 more recent ones (1985–87). The early deals showed strong evidence that LBOs can substantially improve operating performance (table 6-2). They raised cash flow–sales ratios by a statistically significant 23 percent, and almost 60 percent of the buyouts led to improved operating performance. For more recent deals, however, the average change in performance was negative and statistically insignificant. Only slightly more than half of the buyouts increased cash flow–sales ratios. Clearly, more marginal deals were pursued as the LBO activity heated up.[17]

Since comparisons of pre- and post-LBO performances of only one year are subject to criticisms that they may not represent longer-run changes, we repeated our analysis using averages of three prebuyout years and three postbuyout years. For 71 LBOs occurring before 1985 the buyout increased the cash flow–sales ratio by 30 percent; 63 percent of the purchased companies improved performance. For 23 LBOs occurring in 1985, the average change in cash flow–sales resulting from the buyout was essentially zero, and only 40 percent of the firms improved performance. The longer time series and averaging strengthens the findings.

We conducted a similar analysis on other financial ratios including income tax to sales, net income to sales, long-term debt to assets, long-term bank debt to assets, long-term other debt to assets, and working capital to assets. LBOs did create large tax savings, with the ratio of income taxes to sales dropping by 50 percent after the buyout. The tax savings resulting from more recent LBOs were slightly higher than for earlier buyouts. Substantial increases in interest payments lowered the postbuyout ratio of net income to sales relative to prebuyout levels, despite the operating improvements and tax savings. A few large losers in the ratio of net income to sales made the average declines of this ratio for more recent LBOs five times as great as for the early ones, but the difference was clearly not statistically significant. Savings in the ratio of working capital to assets were evident in both time periods but were greater after more recent buyouts. However, more work is needed to uncover whether the changes in working capital stem from increases in short-term liabilities or savings in inventories and accounts receivable. Another critical time-related change occurred in long-term debt. The more recent buyouts took on significantly more total long-term debt relative to their assets. Furthermore, the early buyouts mostly increased bank debt; the later ones raised nonbank debt, including junk bonds, which suggests a correlation between the increase in junk bond use and the decrease in LBO performance.

Causes of Differences in Post-LBO Performance

The findings so far lead to two questions. What explains the variation in the performance of firms after a buyout? What factors explain the decline in buyout activity over time? Because the characteristics of buyouts changed dramatically during the 1980s, these questions are related. In this section we focus on four characteristics—management involvement, manufacturing, size of the firm, and use of junk bonds—that might explain the differences in how firms perform after a buyout. The size of the deals and use of junk bonds increased significantly during the decade. A negative correlation between size of the deal or junk bond use and performance would partially explain the decline in performance. Similarly, management involvement decreased, so a positive relationship between this factor and performance would also help explain the decline. The methodology for testing for differences in performance is a straightforward extension of the approach discussed earlier. An interaction term between the LBO characteristic and the LBO dummy variable is added to the fixed-effects regression equation. With the linear LBO dummy variable still included, this interaction term reveals the direction, magnitude, and significance of the effect that increases in the characteristic have on performance.

The industry-adjusted one year post-LBO minus one year pre-LBO ratio of cash flow to sales is 9 percentage points higher for buyouts with management involvement than for others, with a t-statistic on the interaction of .87. The difference between a management buyout and non-management buyout appears to be unimportant for whole-company LBOs. The findings on firm size are even weaker. The coefficient on the interaction between LBO and size indicates a performance improvement of 2 percentage points for an average-size firm ($300 million in sales) relative to one of the smaller firms ($25 million). This economically small difference in performance is not statistically significant ($t = 0.11$).

There is a substantial economic difference between the performances of manufacturing and nonmanufacturing firms. On average, 1981–87 LBOs of nonmanufacturing firms lowered operating performance by 5 percent. LBOs of manufacturing firms improved performance by 15 percent. The t-statistic on the difference between manufacturing and nonmanufacturing LBOs is 1.80 when other variables that are highly correlated with this variable are excluded. This difference suggests the potential importance of investigating more narrowly defined industry categories or specific industry characteristics such as growth, stability, and degree of competition.

Differences in the results of LBOs due to management involvement, firm size, and broad industry class provide little insight into the declines in performance. The effects of management involvement and firm size are economically unimportant. That the industry is in manufacturing is a potentially important factor, but the percentage of LBOs involved in manufacturing is similar for early and late LBOs. We have suggested a correlation between the rise of junk bonds and the decrease in LBO performance. Firms that financed the buyout with all bank debt improved performance by 35 percent more than firms that financed the buyout with only nonbank debt. The t-statistic on the interaction between type of debt and LBO is 2.55. While the type of financing is clearly critical, further work revealed that the difference between early and later buyouts remained even after controlling for the buyout financing.

These preliminary findings do provide some answers to the question posed at the beginning of this section. But further work employing a broader array of LBO characteristics, longer pre- and postbuyout periods, nonlinear relationships, and alternative methodologies is needed to fully understand variations in LBO performance across industries and in the long term.

Plant Productivity, Cash Flow, and Capital Expenditures

Do improvements in profits come from fundamental improvements in plant performance or do they mainly occur in overhead, marketing, or other nonplant operating expenditures? Are there significant cash flow savings through inventory reduction? Does the increased debt lead to cutbacks in capital expenditures? How does performance differ between whole-company and divisional buyouts?

Table 6-3. Whole and Divisional, LRD, Matched One-Year Pre- and Postbuyout Sample[a]

Item	Pre-LBO	Post-LBO	Post − pre
Price-cost margin	.0123	.0114	− .0010
	(3.11)	(2.87)	(−0.25)
	5.88	5.45	−0.48
Total ending inventories	.0098	.0020	− .0078
	(3.74)	(0.77)	(−3.28)
	6.41	1.31	−5.10
Total capital expenditures	− .0042	− .0070	− .0029
	(−4.25)	(−7.19)	(−2.19)
	− 12.54	− 20.90	−8.66

Source: Authors' calculations. See text.
a. The first number is the average difference between an LBO plant and its four-digit industry average. The second number is the t-statistic. The third number is the percentage impact (measured as the first number divided by the overall LRD sample average times 100).

To address these issues, table 6-3 reports the findings on three variables computed from the census plant data: price-cost margins (PCM), the ratio of total ending inventories to value of shipments, and the ratio of total capital expenditures to value of shipments.[18] Because of the size of the LRD file, the plant data methodology differs slightly from the previously discussed whole-company QFR methodology. Instead of using a fixed-effects regression model with an LBO dummy, we simply converted all the LBO plant data into deviation form. We adjusted the data for plants that underwent LBOs by subtracting the mean of that data item for the relevant four-digit industry for the relevant year.[19] The numbers reported in table 6-3 are the average for only the LBO sample plants using the industry-adjusted and time-adjusted data. Data for the LBO plants are averaged over the pre-LBO year, the post-LBO year, and the difference between two. The 1,637 LBO plants represent a sample of whole-company and divisional LBOs with data on at least one year before the buyout and one year after.[20]

The LRD plant performance findings differ substantially from the QFR whole-company findings. There is no evidence of improvements in price-cost margin related to the buyouts. The margin is measured as the value of shipments minus wages minus inventory-adjusted cost of materials, all divided by the value of shipments. In table 6-3, the margin declines slightly after buyouts. The margins for LBO plants tend to be significantly above average before a buyout and remain so afterward. On average, the 587 divisional LBO plants performed better than the 1,050 whole-company LBO plants. For both groups, however, the change in performance was insignificant. This finding suggests that most of the improvements in operating income found in the QFR sample stemmed from savings in nonplant expenditures.

Our findings on price-cost margin contrast with the plant productivity improvements found by Frank Lichtenberg and Donald Siegel. We explored a number of possible explanations for this apparent conflict. The difference in samples does not affect the findings on price-cost margins. When we looked at the intersections of the two samples, the change in the margin was still insignificantly negative. When we switched to the measurement of value added per employee, a crude proxy for total factor productivity used by Lichtenberg and Siegel, the change after the buyout become positive but was still insignificant. For whole-company LBO plants, the improvement in value added per employee is statistically significant. Lichtenberg and Siegel's sample has a larger percentage of whole-company LBO plants than our combined whole-company and division LBO sample. However, an influence diagnostic procedure shows that much of this improvement is due to a few extreme observations.[21] There appeared to be substantial improvement in price-cost margins and value added when we switched to the unbalanced-panel approach used by Lichtenberg and Siegel.[22] For the 25,758 observations in our unbalanced panel spanning nine years before the buyout and six years after, price-cost margins and value added almost doubled in the two years after the buyout. In sum, although there is some evidence of plant performance gains from LBOs, this evidence is sensitive to outliers and to the measure and methodology employed.

LBO firms did clearly find cash flow savings in reduced inventories. These firms cut inventories by a statistically significant 5 percent (table 6-3). LBOs accomplished this reduction by targeting firms with above average inventory levels and bringing the inventories back into line with the industry average. The pre-LBO average ratio of inventories to shipments was a statistically significant 6 percent higher than the industry average. After buyouts the ratio was roughly equal to the industry average. These findings are robust with respect to alternative specifications.

Splitting the sample into plants from whole-company and divisional buyouts did reveal some important differences in inventory behavior. In the one-year matched pre- and postbuyout sample, only plants of divisional buyouts displayed inventory savings. The level on inventories was not significantly different from the industry average, either before or after the buyout, for plants from whole-company LBOs. Plants from divisional buyouts cut inventories from a statistically significant 14 percent above the industry average before the buyout to a statistically insignificant 3 percent above average afterward. At least for divisions selected as buyout candidates, independent ownership coupled with debt created incentives for controlling cash flow that were lacking in large multidivisional organizations.

After buyouts plants also increased the cash available to make interest payments by cutting capital expenditures. The ratio of capital expenditures to shipments dropped by 9 percent. Cuts in capital spending are more controversial than improvements in inventory controls. Those that come from tighter controls on wasteful capital spending are warranted; those that hurt long-run performance may cause concern. The pattern of capital spending before and after LBOs suggests that the concern is warranted. The pre-LBO level of capital expenditures to shipments was 13 percent less than the industry average. This capital deficit occurred in plants with performance significantly above the industry average. After a buyout the ratio of capital expenditure to shipments dropped to 21 percent below average. The capital spending results are robust with respect to alternative specifications.

Whole-company and division buyouts both showed reductions in capital expenditure, but divisions that were bought out were twice as far below average as whole companies both before and after the buyout. A three-year matched pre- and postbuyout sample shows that the reductions were permanent, especially for whole-company LBOs, whose capital expenditures continued to decline slightly in the three post-LBO years. Plants of division LBOs showed some evidence of an improvement in capital expenditures (to 2 percent below the industry average) in the third year after the buyout.

LBOs' Impact on R&D Expenditures

Reductions in capital expenditures suggest that R&D spending may also be reduced by LBOs. Bronwyn Hall and Abbie Smith have contended that this result is less important than other effects of LBOs because companies that were bought out have tended to perform little R&D.[23] Still, a substantial number of firms that underwent LBOs had large R&D expenditures: almost half the manufacturing firms in the QFR whole-company sample were considered large R&D performers ($500,000 to $1 million in R&D) by the National Science Foundation.

Lichtenberg and Siegel investigated the effect of whole-company LBOs on R&D through the R&D survey data collected by the Census Bureau. Using an unbalanced panel, they found that R&D declined after a buyout, but the decline was not statistically significant. However, statistical insignificance does not imply no change, especially when the sample is small and the data are noisy or biased. Although the National Science Foundation survey data are the best for studying R&D, they are far from perfect. We further analyzed the relationship of LBOs and R&D emphasizing the largest clean sample of NSF R&D performers possible. Specifically, we focused on three matters of data quality: imputations, data errors, and survival bias.[24]

The R&D survey draws a new sample every six or seven years. In 1974, 1981, and 1987 all small R&D-performing companies reported data. In 1978, 1983, and 1986 most small companies responded, but a sizable percentage had their data imputed. In other years, all the data for the small companies are imputed. A small, though noticeable percentage of the large R&D-performing companies' data are imputed each year. For most years the electronic files do not give codes indicating whether the data have been imputed. The imputation rates also differ by year, sample and size, and data item. Through a painstaking cross-section and time-series procedure, we identified potential imputed data items and checked them against the hard copy files that contained imputation codes. Twenty percent of the firms in the R&D survey that underwent a buyout had their data imputed in the year before or after the buyout.

We also identified a substantial number of data entry errors in the file and used the original survey forms, when they were available, to make corrections. Even after imputations were eliminated and obvious errors corrected, outliers still existed. In our matched one-year pre- and post-buyout sample, we identified as potential outliers observations that had ratios of R&D to sales of more than 3.5 standard deviations from the industry mean.

After eliminating imputed data, data errors, and outliers, we had pre- and post-LBO data on 53 whole-company buyouts occurring between 1981 and 1987 and 3,348 control-group observations. These firms also reported to the QFR. Using a methodology identical to the earlier QFR analysis, we found that in the year before an LBO the average target firm's R&D-to-sales ratio was 1.56 (or 48 percent) below the overall sample average, with a t-ratio of -2.44. The ratio dropped by 0.55 after the buyout, or almost 35 percent of total R&D. The t-ratio on the decline of R&D to sales was -1.95.

The R&D analysis contained one potentially important bias. For nineteen LBOs with prebuyout data, the postbuyout data are missing because the company was dropped from the survey. A company may have been dropped because it was acquired by another company (sometimes the holding company created for the LBO), it failed to respond to mandatory questions, after changes in the NSF sample in 1981 and 1987 its R&D expenditure was less than the threshold amount needed to be included in the certainty sample, or the company was no longer an R&D performer according to the survey rules. The last reason clearly leads to a survival bias. A bias also exists if the other three reasons are correlated with sharp declines in R&D. To illustrate the maximum potential of a survival bias, we assumed that the LBO firms dropped from the sample performed no postbuyout R&D. Under this assumption, the average LBO firm's ratio of R&D to sales was -1.88 below the overall sample average before the buyout (with a t-ratio of -3.41). The change becomes -0.63 (or 34 percent of total R&D) (with a t-ratio of -2.61). The survival bias is small because most firms that left the sample had low R&D expenditures before the buyout.

Conclusion

LBOs can improve performance. For whole-company buyouts occurring before 1985, the companies increased their ratios of operating income (before depreciation) to sales by 20 to 30 percent. Approximately 60 percent of the companies improved operating performance. Much of this improvement came from savings of nonplant operating expenses (we did not find consistent improvements in plant performance for whole-company or division buyouts). LBOs also led to dramatic improvements in management of working capital at the level both of the plant and higher. Greater than average prebuyout inventory levels were brought into line with the industry average after the buyouts, an inventory savings of 5 percent. These savings were higher for division than for whole-company LBOs. We also found substantial tax savings from whole-company LBOs. These results suggest that leveraged buyouts should continue to be important in revitalizing firms in the 1990s.

Some of the savings related to LBOs, however, can harm companies. LBOs reduced plant capital expenditures by 9 percent and R&D by 40 percent. If these expenditures were abnormally high or wasteful before the buyouts, the cuts were a clear benefit. However, they may sacrifice long-term growth to make short-term interest payments. Some indirect evidence lends weak support for this argument. Before they are bought out, target firms have profits that are superior to the average for their industry, but already have capital and R&D expenditures that are below their industry average. A complete resolution of differing interpretations requires more direct evidence. In future work, we will investigate the link between changes in capital and R&D expenditure and changes in longer-run performance.

More recent LBOs raise the concern that there are significant limits on the conditions under which buyouts can improve performance. As the 1980s wore on, LBOs were hit from three sides—increasing premiums, increasing debt, and declining performance. The premium paid to the shareholders before a buyout increased at a statistically significant rate of roughly 1 percentage point a year. Most of the premium increase went to pay higher prices for increasingly larger deals. As the success of the early deals became apparent, money began pouring into the buyout market. This reduced the amount of equity needed to complete the deals and pushed up debt levels. The long-term ratio of debt to assets was 15 percent higher for more recent LBOs than it was earlier. And the increased LBO activity had another consequence: more marginal firms began to be bought up. On average, an LBO occurring after 1984 failed to improve the operating performance of a company.

The dynamics of the LBO market in the 1980s have at least two important implications. First, the number and type of firms that can be revitalized through LBOs is limited. It is unlikely that leveraged buyouts will replace public corporations as the new corporate form. Second, capital markets can overreact to profitable opportunities, turning innovations into fads. Increasing premiums and reduced operating performance, together with the recent, sharp decline in LBO activity and increased number of distressed LBOs, suggest that the savings in taxes and working capital were insufficient to prevent losses on many of the more recent LBOs. The market may now have swung too far in the other direction by refusing most deals (even with 30 percent or more equity) despite evidence that some buyouts work.

Although public policy cannot directly help identify the good and bad deals, it can increase or decrease certain buyout costs or benefits, thereby affecting the marginal deals. Policymakers can, for example, affect the large postbuyout income tax savings. The savings may have encouraged deals that did not substantially improve operating performance. Tax breaks are more appropriate for investments such as those made in R&D that substantially benefit society, benefits that are not fully captured by the investors. Government must also be careful not to react in ways that make market overreaction worse. The market lags in recognizing excess entry into a profitable area. Because government regulation suffers from

a similar lag, poorly timed regulation can discourage productive investment. For example, banks claim they are unable to make promising new
LBO loans because their stock price will drop and because the regulators
have changed reporting requirements and tightened the definition of a
highly leveraged transaction. For a buyout to gain bank financing in the
early 1990s, it must be structured to avoid the label of highly leveraged
transaction.

Finally, because LBOs are an appropriate solution to corporate governance problems for only some public corporations, government policy
should encourage other means of improving the governance of public
corporations. Various mechanisms that have been suggested include increased competition in markets; higher share ownership and improved
compensation packages for directors and managers; a more efficient market for corporate control, including hostile takeovers; more active, pa-
tient, long-term involvement by banks and institutional investors; and a
more effective proxy system. One of these mechanisms, hostile takeovers,
risks many of the potential debt problems encountered by LBOs. Making
the other corporate control mechanisms more attractive could minimize
the need for constraining managers through high debt.

Perhaps the clearest means of dampening potential market overreaction is to improve public information. If investors can more easily identify,
on a timely basis, the signals that profits are likely to fall, government
intervention will not be needed. Insights into why the performance of
buyouts turned sour are important, not only for obtaining an optimal
proportion of LBOs in the future but also because they may help explain
other markets, such as real estate, that go through similar boom and bust
cycles.

Our project has begun to explore the dynamics of the LBO market.
We have identified a host of LBO characteristics that have changed over
time. The size of the deals, number of bidders, premiums paid, and
hostile pressure have all increased, while the pre- and postmanagement
equity participation in deals has decreased. To the extent these characteristics are related to company performance, the changes may explain
the declines in performance. Preliminary work on four characteristics—
size of the deal, whether management was involved, use of junk bonds,
and whether the company was in manufacturing—reveal that management involvement and size of the deal are not critical for determining
postbuyout performance. The insignificance of these variables, however,
has important implications in light of the other findings in this paper. The
lack of a link between size and performance for LBOs leaves unexplained

why larger firms paid higher premiums. The insignificant correlation between management involvement and performance, combined with an insignificant relationship between management involvement and premiums paid, suggests that current regulations preventing management from unfairly buying out shareholders are effective. Manufacturing LBOs perform substantially better than those in nonmanufacturing sectors. This finding points to the potential importance of industry factors in determining which LBOs succeed and which fail.

Nonbank debt (including junk bonds) had the strongest influence of the four variables considered. The performance of firms after buyouts that relied more heavily on nonbank debt relative to bank debt was dramatically and significantly lower than that of firms financing the buyout primarily through bank debt. This finding adds further evidence to the theory of market overadjustment. The increased availability of capital provided by junk bonds contributed to more competition in the LBO market, leading to higher premiums, increased debt, and more marginal LBO candidates. Junk bonds may also be linked to reduced performance after a buyout because holders tend to be more highly dispersed than holders of bank debt and therefore less effective at monitoring the corporation.

The results reported here represent the findings of an ongoing project. A great deal of additional research needs to be done. The 1989 through 1991 QFR data are available and will substantially increase our sample size and ability to study longer-term LBO performance. Even with the current data, we have not gone beyond the third postbuyout year and have not analyzed trends in pre- or post-LBO performance. Our measure of working capital needs to be refined to isolate inventories, accounts receivable, and accounts payable. Now that the initial analysis has been completed on all four major files, we can turn to integrating them. This integration should lead to new insights into the key determinants of LBO success and to a better understanding of why firms' performance has deteriorated.

Comment by Carl Ferenbach

I have chosen two matters treated by Long and Ravenscraft to discuss: the key events in the leveraged acquisition market during the past ten years and the form of corporate governance employed by Berkshire Partners and other professional owners of corporate properties and how that interacts with management incentives.

In 1982, the Dow Jones industrial average was at 1000, a level that had been its high water mark since the 1960s. The United States was still experiencing high inflation. Balance sheets were fat by today's standards. Management theory held that the good athlete could manage anything, and since managers thought they were good athletes, they commanded diversified corporations in fields with which they often had no experience. The period was characterized by low valuations and excess, redundant, and undermanaged assets that could be bought more cheaply than they could be replaced. Management practices were slack. Today, the Dow Jones is well above 3000. Most managers will tell you that operations are very lean: collections are as up to date as they can be and they schedule inputs for immediate use and manufactures for immediate shipment to keep inventories low. Management theory is focused on what the manager does well and on servicing the customer and providing quality, all at a competitive price.

The early 1980s turned out to be terrific for debt-financed acquisitions. Acquirers bought cheap, leveraged, retired debt from excess assets as they restructured operations, and the improving economy added to equity returns. The early 1990s have offered fewer opportunities for financial leverage because debt must be retired solely from cash flow, requiring reasonable margins for error. The transition from the first period to the second was taking place throughout the decade. At the same time, lenders and financial entrepreneurs were bidding prices to ever higher levels and providing more and more capital to finance acquisitions. Somehow the capital markets managed to overlook what was going on at the level of the operating company. When the economy entered a normal cyclical downturn, all were caught up. While it had momentum, the leveraged acquisition movement was extraordinarily powerful, all but ignoring the market crash in 1987 as well as public opinion and political opposition and nearly surviving the demise of Drexel Burnham Lambert.

One (including one who continues to acquire companies and to use financial leverage to enhance equity returns) is compelled to ask why. Three reasons especially stick out. First, major institutional investors—life insurance companies, private and public employee pension funds, endowments, bank holding companies—placed equity in the hands of financial entrepreneurs through the form of limited partnerships. These funds were for investment in new LBOs. The financial entrepreneurs often were able to cover their own coinvestment commitments out of fees from managing their capital pools and from organizing and financing acquisitions. Their incentives were largely to put the money to work, thereby making available a large and relatively undisciplined underpinning for financing newly acquired leveraged acquisitions.

Second, thinking on valuation evolved in new ways that justified higher prices. Historically, lenders in highly leveraged transactions provided credit based on their evaluation of the companies' assets, advancing funds against a percentage of receivables, a somewhat smaller percentage of inventory, and some part of fixed assets after receiving an appraisal. It was left to those who thought the assets were worth more to take the additional risk if they wanted to supply additional funds. Cash flow was viewed as the second way out of these loans. But in the early 1980s divisions and subsidiaries were successfully sold after acquisition at multiples of cash flow that were higher than the purchaser had paid for the entire company, with the proceeds going to retire debt. Acquisition became a game of risk arbitrage in which the acquirer took advantage of inefficiency between the equity market and the market for control. Lenders adapted by being willing to secure their credits with the stock of the subsidiaries or other assets to be disposed at high prices, justifying the extension of more credit. The buyers of public high-yield debt stepped in for the risks of subordination (generally without the customary equity) in the belief that these value kickers plus the availability of a trading market for their paper limited their potential losses, particularly if they held a diversified portfolio.

As a third reason for the mood of the 1980s, commercial banks and investment banks were faced with the loss of traditional high-margin business from larger and financially stronger corporate credits and securities issuers. Commercial banks lost business to commercial paper markets that provided credit at lower prices. For investment banks, the evolution of shelf registration, by which firms could register a large new issue of stock to be sold to the public over a long period of time, meant that corporate issuers no longer needed the services of the investment banks. This breakdown of relationships led to competitive bidding for the firms' paper at ever lower spreads. Both commercial and investment banks therefore needed to find new, profitable business. Leveraged acquisitions in the end exceeded their wildest expectations. They were highly motivated to keep the business going.

These factors help explain Long's and Ravenscraft's findings about efficiencies in the early part of the decade and fewer gains or a lack of gains in the later part. The factors also imply that high prices, rather than the presence of the junk bonds that helped finance the high prices, influenced later outcomes negatively. Also, while a new-issue market for LBOs evolved in the high-yield market in the mid- and late 1980s, it was limited to those capable of issuing more than $100 million. There remained throughout a vast private placement market for subordinated debt for leveraged acquisitions. This market continues to function, albeit in a far smaller way.

The failure of judgment in the late 1980s should not, however, damn leveraged acquisition. The form has many useful features when well applied. The failures suggest much about how it should be used, and I hope my comments about governance will suggest that it has much to offer.

The starting point on governance is ownership. In the Berkshire model, a fairly common one, management buys common stock (5 to 10 percent) at the founder's price, receives options at the same price for another 5 percent that vest over five years, and can receive additional stock based on exceeding the forecasts that are the basis on which all participants are investing. The standard for performance is a valuation standard five years later, depending on a number of factors in a five-year plan that forms the basis for participating in the deal.

The investor groups with which we are familiar would not invest without this management commitment, a fact that does not fit with Long's and Ravenscraft's data. They would not invest because they depend on management for developing and executing the plan and want management's financial commitment to it. They feel strongly that corporations should be run by people whose interests are made parallel by their equity ownership in the business. The reasons Long's and Ravenscraft's data do not fit, one suspects, are that in most sales of public or private companies, as well as subsidiaries and divisions, particularly beginning in mid-decade, those responsible for the sale did not want management to favor a given buyer. Management was therefore generally excluded as a bidder, meaning that when a transaction was announced management had not been established as a new owner. Typically this takes place after the announcement. The other owners of the company in a leveraged acquisition are the sponsor group, if there is one, and the institutions providing the financing.

Lenders typically do not want to incur conflicts of interest by sitting on boards; so management, the sponsor group, and one or two outsiders who also purchase stock make up the board. This prevailing model also conflicts with Long's and Ravenscraft's findings on management involvement in LBOs. This is also explainable. In the transactions before the mid-1980s, sponsors worried that suppliers and customers would take advantage of the newly leveraged company, as would competitors. Therefore, they tailored press releases to describe the transaction as a management buyout. This was often well received by constituents who did not care much about the debt if they knew management had committed its own funds to the deal. As time passed and LBOs became more common, and as management was increasingly excluded from the initial bidding because of perceived conflicts, sponsors stepped forward as announced buyers.

The form of governance I have described is a professionally owned corporation governed by professional owners and management. The sponsor groups generally are investing their own capital and that from managed pools capitalized by large institutional investors, the same investors who would consider investing in the common stock if the company were to go public. There are, however, some important differences from the public model

—The board of the LBO company is made up only of owners.

—The LBO company is private. The only focus given to quarterly results is to understand their impact on strategy and financial structure issues.

—The LBO company measures its progress against the five-year forecast on the basis of which its owners bought it. The stockholders of public companies are not afforded this opportunity and do not have this tool available for governance. Yes, boards see five-year plans, but they and the other stockholders did not buy the company on the basis of them.

—LBO management focuses on cash flow. So do its owners. Valuations are calculated as multiples of free cash flow.

—Management compensation is driven by equity, not current income. The board has strong incentives to keep it that way.

—Debt is an early warning system that something is wrong and needs to be fixed. The board is usually fully familiar with operating problems when they arise, having extensively analyzed the company before making their investment.

Long and Ravenscraft use operating ratios to measure performance, and so do professional owners. Yet perhaps more relevant is the other set of measures we are bound by, the returns to our investors. The bulk of our compensation depends on this performance, and it is a strong incentive and control on the behavior of the board. Access to this type of information will require the cooperation of the institutions that participate in LBO funds and will require some missionary work.

It is extremely difficult to weigh the importance of governance in directing management decisionmaking versus the importance of the disciplines of the markets in which the company competes. Owners who govern have personal priorities that affect their decisions and commitments to new programs that entail risk. The form of governance I have described is based far more strongly on investors' having greater knowledge of the operations of the corporation and of the human and financial consequences of decisions made than is the governance system of many public companies. It is thereby more financially and socially effective. At Berkshire we believe that our commitment of much of our personal capital to coinvestment with our limited partners in each acquisition has been a deterrent to overreaching (although we have certainly not been error free). Hence, our bias is that cash financial commitments by owners result in the best risk assessment environment for the company.

In the past few months a fresh pattern for leveraged acquisition activity has been established. Middle-market transactions generally valued at less than $75 million are being successfully completed in an environment of highly restricted bank credit. They are typically priced at significantly lower multiples of cash flow than their predecessors, and these are, of course, recession cash flows. Capital structures are far more conservative, consisting of three parts debt and one part equity versus the nine-to-one ratios of the 1980s. Financing is commonly completed without the subordinate debt or high-yield component—or with seller assistance at that level. New equity partnerships are no longer called LBO funds but rather private equity funds; but only those who established solid credentials in the 1980s need apply.

Comment by Frank Lichtenberg

The primary objective of Long's and Ravenscraft's paper, like that of several others that have appeared in the past few years, is to determine the effect of the leveraged buyouts that occurred in the 1980s on the "performance" of the companies involved.[25] The econometric methodology is also similar to that used in earlier studies. Most of this paper's value added consists in the greater size, representativeness, and richness of the data base.

The authors began by collecting a list of virtually every LBO and going-private transaction in the 1980s; there are 2,324 deals on their list. In contrast, Lichtenberg and Siegel started with 244 deals for 1981–86, and Smith analyzed only 58 management buyouts that occurred from 1977 to 1986. But the major advantage of Long's and Ravenscraft's data base is not its size per se but its smaller susceptibility to sample selection bias. Smith, for example, was able to obtain postbuyout operating data only for those companies that offered common stock or had public debt or preferred stock outstanding after the buyout, which may be a biased sample of all buyout firms. Because Long and Ravenscraft had access to the Census Bureau's quarterly financial reports (QFR), which must be filed by privately as well as publicly held companies, their sample is not censored in this respect. Neither was Lichtenberg and Siegel's sample, which was also based on mandatory census data. Their data base, however, excluded many small deals and deals outside manufacturing, although it is not obvious why this would produce biased estimates.

Another virtue of Long's and Ravenscraft's data base is that it includes information on stock ownership by senior management, whether there was a hostile bid or multiple bidders, and even whether the buyout was associated with a lawsuit, and other important attributes of a deal (see table 6-1). The authors have also calculated, whenever possible, the stock market premium paid for the company. Hence they observe both the stock market's forecast of postbuyout earnings, and the realizations of those earnings (at least for a few years after the buyout). The relationship across deals between the two is not directly examined in the paper, however.

The core results of the paper are those presented in table 6-2, which displays estimates of the mean of normalized (by industry and calendar year) profitability (measured as cash flow divided by sales) in year $t-1$ and $t+1$ of companies involved in full-firm LBOs in year t. Although their complete list included 821 full-firm LBOs, only 550 were present in the QFR at all and only 198 had the necessary data for years $t-1$ and $t+1$; only 94 had the necessary data for $t-3$ to $t+3$. Their sample is larger and more comprehensive than that analyzed by anyone else, and probably as complete as can be constructed, but these numbers suggest that even here missing data and sample selection bias may pose potential problems.

The performance measure used by the authors, the ratio of cash flow to sales, is similar (although not identical) to the accounting concept of return on sales or the economic concept of the price-cost margin. The paper contains no justification or even discussion of this measure. There are alternative (in my view, preferable) measures of a firm's performance, such as return on assets and (especially) total factor productivity. Both require reasonable estimates of the firm's real capital stock, and the authors do not have the data necessary to calculate that on a consistent basis before and after the buyout. Moreover, in practice, there is likely to be a reasonably strong positive correlation across firms between pre- and postbuyout changes in these different performance measures.

Table 6-2 may be summarized as follows. Buyouts that occurred between 1981 and 1984 had a large, positive, statistically significant "effect" on profitability. (I place "effect" in quotation marks because neither these authors nor those of previous studies can completely resolve questions about causality. Long and Ravenscraft do not seem to acknowledge this qualification.) Early LBOs were associated with a 23 percent average increase in return on sales, which is very close to the mean 21 percent stock market premium reported in table 6-1, but the latter figure corresponds to the full sample, not just early deals. Buyouts that occurred between 1985 and 1987 had essentially no effect on profitability: the mean change is negative but very small and far from significant. The estimate based on the full sample is close to a weighted (and simple) average of the period-specific estimates: it is positive (implying a 9 percent average increase in profitability) but insignificant ($t = 0.98$).

These are estimates of the change in profitability between $t-1$ and $t+1$. The authors report that estimates of differences between average profitability three years before and three years after are similar: the change in profitability was 30 percent for LBOs from 1981 to 1984 (presumably because ratios of cash flow to sales increased more in $t+2$ and $t+3$ than in $t+1$), and zero for later LBOs. The authors should present separate estimates for each year around the buyout ($t-3, t-2 \ldots t+2, t+3$), so that one can determine, for example, whether performance was improving before the buyout. (Lichtenberg and Siegel found this to be the case for management buyouts.) Because the number of observations for year $t + k$ declines as k moves away from 0 (due to missing data), there are two ways to calculate the time series of year-specific means: using all available data for each year and censoring the sample to include only those firms with complete data for all years as the authors have essentially done. If the data are randomly missing, both procedures are consistent, but the first procedure is more efficient.[26] Otherwise, both procedures yield inconsistent estimates.

The authors also examine whether the change in profitability following the buyout was related to certain buyout attributes (other than the date at which it occurred). They find essentially no difference between buyouts that involve management and those that did not. There is a "substantial economic difference" between the point estimates of the effects of manufacturing (+ 15 percent) and nonmanufacturing (− 5 percent) buyouts on profitability, but this difference is not statistically significant. The authors do not offer any reasons why buyouts should have different effects in the two sectors.

The authors also do not compare their estimates with those provided by earlier studies, such as Kaplan's and Smith's profitability estimates. The three major previous studies all found there to be significant improvements in mean performance for all buyouts in their respective samples. Lichtenberg and Siegel also found that management buyouts had a much larger effect on manufacturing plant productivity than nonmanagement buyouts, and that "late" buyouts had a larger effect than "early" buyouts (although they defined "late" as those that occurred in 1983 or later). Do Long and Ravenscraft believe that their estimates are in fact consistent with earlier ones, which were based entirely or primarily on deals that the present authors classify as "early" (pre-1985)?

The authors also state that "a significant number of buyouts resulted in financial distress." The fact, reported in table 6-1, that only 8 percent of the buyouts in their sample were subject to "potential credit downgrade" does not appear to support this claim.

Long and Ravenscraft have assembled the largest and most complete data base on leveraged buyouts to date, they have linked this to one important Census Bureau file, and they are in the process of linking it to several others. They deserve praise for undertaking this monumental task. In this paper, they have begun to analyze this data set to reexamine the effect of buyouts on firm performance. The major news is that pre-1985 buyouts increased profitability significantly, but that later buyouts had essentially no effect. They infer from this that capital markets can overreact to profitable opportunities, turning innovations into fads. They may be right, but before I accept that conclusion I would like to see additional evidence, such as more detailed pre- and postbuyout trajectories of profitability and of alternative performance indicators, particularly productivity. I am confident that they will produce this sort of evidence as they make further progress on their project.

General Discussion

Martha Schary wondered whether the performance improvements associated with leveraged buyouts that have been observed by other researchers were short term or sustainable over the long term. She noted that Frank Lichtenberg's earlier work suggested that the performance improvements endured.[27] But an important case study on LBOs finds that most improvements in cash flow performance come from savings in working capital, which would boost cash flow only in the short run.[28]

Although Long and Ravenscraft looked at performance for up to three years after the LBOs, they could do that only for buyouts occurring in 1985 or earlier. Some of their key findings do, however, relate to what happened after 1985. Thus the authors indicated that they plan to add data for 1989 and 1990 so that they can track the performance of more transactions for a longer period of time.

Warren Farb and Bronwyn Hall wondered whether Long and Ravenscraft had measured the performance of firms in their sample in absolute terms or relative to some benchmark, and whether they were adjusted for general economic cycles. Long responded that using dummy variables for both time and industry in the regression analysis has the effect of adjusting all the measures of firm performance for both industry-specific and macroeconomic effects. The reported numbers are deviations from industry averages, he said.

Ronald Gilson observed that earlier research by Steven Kaplan had found that the gains from management buyouts (MBOs) are typically split evenly between the buyout team and the target company shareholders. The gains from non-MBO takeovers typically go much more to target company shareholders. Gilson asked whether Long and Ravenscraft's results should be interpreted as implying that a larger share of the gains from management buyouts goes to target company shareholders than Kaplan had found. Ravenscraft responded that they had not explicitly measured the split but had found the premiums paid in MBOs comparable to those paid in non-MBO takeovers and that the posttakeover performance is about the same. Thus they concluded that target company shareholders were no worse off if the takeover team included management. Long cautioned, however, that the variable used to identify transactions as MBOs may be less reliable than most of the other variables used.

Carl Ferenbach also expressed caution about the interpretation of this variable. The MBO variable is picking up information about whether management was officially part of the buyout team at the time the deal was announced. But especially after 1985, boards of directors were careful to avoid appearances of conflict of interest. So they usually insisted that management groups not be allowed to bid. But once a leveraged buyout group bought the company, the group nearly always cut deals for management to stay and become significant owners.

Robert McCauley cautioned Long and Ravenscraft about treating the use of nonbank long-term debt financing as equivalent to using junk bonds, noting that insurance companies and other nonbank financial institutions were also supplying long-term debt to finance buyouts.

Long said that one of the troubling technical problems he and Ravenscraft had was that the data often included a few extreme observations that dramatically affected the results. These problems are ameliorated somewhat by averaging across firms or across several years for each firm. Such techniques reduce the number of observations, Long noted, but the statistical significance of the findings often improved. F. M. Scherer objected that the extreme values are actually quite important, noting that in his earlier work with Ravenscraft on mergers they found that the long-run distribution of returns to investing in conglomerates had neither a finite mean nor a finite variance.[29] "It has always struck me that this may be one of the fundamental explanations of merger activity," he conjectured. "It may well be that at the median you do not do so well, but there are some outliers that do extraordinarily well, and that drives the whole process."

Ravenscraft argued that bad judgment on the part of buyout entrepreneurs toward the end of the 1980s should not be used to condemn leveraged buyouts as a mechanism for influencing corprate governance. He argued that the postbuyout capital structure serves three functions. The concentration of ownership intensifies the monitoring of the firm; the debt service requirements provide an early warning system for cash flow problems; and the debt puts pressure on people to do things they would not otherwise do, such as press suppliers for breaks or eliminate poorly performing people or operations. He doubted that all three functions could be performed without the use of highly-leveraged capital structures.

Notes

1. Rebekah J. Maupin, "Financial and Stock Market Variables as Predictors of Management Buyouts," *Strategic Management Journal*, vol. 8, no. 4 (1987), pp. 319–27; Bronwyn H. Hall, "The Impact of Corporate Restructuring on Industrial Research and Development," *Brookings Papers on Economic Activity, Microeconomics* (1990), pp. 85–124; and Kenneth Lehn, Jeffry Netter, and Annette Poulsen, "Consolidating Corporate Control: Dual-Class Recapitalizations versus Leveraged Buyouts," *Journal of Financial Economics*, vol. 27, no. 3 (1990), pp. 557–80.

2. Larry DeAngelo, Linda DeAngelo, and Edward M. Rice, "Going Private: Minority Freezeouts and Stockholder Wealth," *Journal of Law and Economics*, vol. 27 (April 1984), pp. 367–401; Steven N. Kaplan, "The Effects of Management Buyouts on Operating Performance and Value," *Journal of Financial Economics*, vol. 24, no. 2 (1989), pp. 217–54; Kenneth Lehn and Annette Poulsen, "Free Cash Flow and Stockholder Gain in Going Private Transactions," *Journal of Finance*, vol. 44, no. 3 (1989), pp. 771–87; Laurentius Marais, Katherine Schipper, and Abbie Smith, "Wealth Effects of Going Private for Senior Securities," *Journal of Financial Economics*, vol. 23, no. 1 (1989), pp. 155–91.

3. Ivan Bull, "Management Performance in Leveraged Buyouts: An Empirical Analysis," in Yakov Amihud, ed., *Leveraged Management Buyouts: Causes and Consequences* (Homewood, Ill.: Dow Jones–Irwin, 1989); Kaplan, "Effects of Management Buyouts"; Chris J. Muscarella and Michael R. Vetsuypens, "Efficiency and Organizational Structure: A Study of Reverse LBOs," *Journal of Finance*, vol. 45, no. 5 (1990), pp. 1389–1414; Frank R. Lichtenberg and Donald Siegel, "The Effects of Leveraged Buyouts on Productivity and Related Aspects of Firm Behavior," *Journal of Financial Economics*, vol. 27, no. 1 (1991), pp. 165–94; Abbie Smith, "Corporate Ownership Structure and Performance: The Case of Management Buyouts," vol. 27, no. 1 (1991), pp. 143–64; and Aaron Singh, "Management Buyouts: Distinguishing Characteristics and Operating Changes prior to Public Offering," *Strategic Management Journal*, vol. 11 (1990), pp. 111–29.

4. Several studies from which we obtained data analyzed going-private transactions. A public company may be taken private either through an LBO or by being acquired by a private company. When we discovered that one of the companies on our list had been acquired by a company with existing operations (excluding holding companies), we classified it as a going-private merger.

5. The 1989 and 1990 data are now available, and we hope to include them in later studies. Because there are 15,000 observations each quarter, we screened

for outliers by eliminating any observation more than three and one-half standard deviations from the mean.

6. We eliminated ten pre-1981 observations with data for one year before and after the LBO because, on average, debt did not increase for these companies, indicating a problem with classifying firms as LBOs before 1981.

7. Lichtenberg and Siegel, "Effects of Leveraged Buyouts on Productivity."

8. The cut-off defining a large R&D performer was increased from $500,000 to $1 million in the mid-1980s.

9. In fact, the LBO premiums were statistically indistinguishable from the going-private merger premiums included in our sample.

10. To make matters worse, management involvement and the number of bidders are significantly negatively correlated.

11. This file includes all mergers, acquisitions, and divestitures listed in *Mergers and Acquisitions Journal*. When checking the whole-company QFR data for sensitivity to significant asset restructuring, we added a third source to confirm the restructuring. The LRD data has codes that indicate whether the plant changed ownership that year. We included almost all the substantial restructuring activity found via the LRD data in our list.

12. This section summarizes the results from Shawn Phelps, William F. Long, and David J. Ravenscraft, "Determinants of Whole-Company LBO Premiums," working paper, 1992.

13. We also explored other time lengths. In a few cases with missing data, we substituted shorter times or single announcements for longer times or multiple announcements.

14. This section summarizes some of the main findings in William F. Long and David J. Ravenscraft, "Financial Performance of Whole-Company LBOs," 1992.

15. Since the LBO firms had to have continuous data for one year before and after the year of the buyout, the control group was also required to have data for the year before and the year after the buyout year.

16. The QFR data use a roughly two-digit primary industry classification system.

17. The findings for the more recent LBOs were not affected by the elimination of firms that underwent asset restructuring. Firms were eliminated if acquisitions or divestitures from the year before to the year after the buyout resulted in 20 percent of their assets being restructured. The findings for the earlier LBOs were weakened somewhat by eliminating companies undergoing substantial restructuring. However, the improvement in the ratio of cash flow to sales remained statistically significant.

18. We also investigated the impact of LBOs on a host of other variables compiled from the LRD file. However, because of space limitations, we have focused on only three.

19. As with the QFR data, we eliminated outliers that were more than three standard deviations from the mean. Because extreme observations affected the standard deviation, we repeated this procedure an additional time before converting the data to the deviation form. For further analysis see William F. Long and David J. Ravenscraft, "Plant Performance of Whole versus Divisional LBOs," working paper, 1992.

20. The number of plants in this matched sample is substantially fewer than the approximately 6,000 plants coded as LBOs. Most of the 6,000 coded plants were smaller ones that appear only in census years or only sporadically in other years. We can study differences between these larger and smaller plants by investigating changes between census years, particularly 1982 and 1987. Our matched sample is twice the size of Lichtenberg and Siegel's.

21. David A. Belsley, Edwin Kuh, and Roy E. Welsch, *Regression Diagnostics: Identifying Influential Data and Sources of Collinearity* (John Wiley, 1980).

22. In an unbalanced panel an observation is used no matter how many years it appears in the sample. For example, a plant that appears in the LRD sample only in the year before the buyout would be included in an unbalanced panel. A balanced panel would only include an observation if it appeared consistently in both the pre- and post-LBO period.

23. Hall, "Impact of Corporate Restructuring"; and Smith, "Corporate Ownership Structure and Performance." This section summarizes some of the main findings in William F. Long and David J. Ravenscraft, "LBOs, Debt, and R&D Intensity," *Strategic Management Journal* (forthcoming).

24. None of these issues was discussed by Lichtenberg and Siegel.

25. Kaplan, "Effects of Management Buyouts"; Lichtenberg and Siegel, "Effects of Leveraged Buyouts on Productivity"; and Smith, "Corporate Ownership Structure and Performance."

26. Zvi Griliches, "Economic Data Issues," in Griliches and M. Intriligator, eds., *Handbook of Econometrics*, vol. 3 (Amsterdam: North-Holland, 1984).

27. Lichtenberg and Siegel, "Effects of Leveraged Buyouts on Productivity," pp. 165–94.

28. George Baker and Karen Wruck, "Organizational Change and Value Creation in Leveraged Buyouts: The Case of O. M. Scott & Sons Co.," *Journal of Financial Economics*, vol. 25 (1990), pp. 163–90.

29. David J. Ravenscraft and F. M. Scherer, *Mergers, Sell-Offs, and Economic Efficiency* (Brookings, 1987).

Corporate Restructuring in the Chemicals Industry

Sarah J. Lane

ALTHOUGH the chemicals industry enjoyed a long period of expansion and innovation after World War II, by the early 1980s it was in serious decline. Nevertheless, after a burst of mergers, acquisitions, and other types of restructuring during the decade, the industry rebounded strongly. Its future may still be uncertain, but chemicals is considered a restructuring success story of the decade.[1]

It is the forces behind the extensive restructuring and how the restructuring activity evolved that is the focus of this chapter. A study of a single industry can examine restructuring in unusual detail; it can discuss the experience of individual firms in the context of industrywide changes; and it can consider more types of restructuring, including changes in financial structure, control, and major lines of business. Ultimately, such an investigation may help determine whether the decade of restructuring really benefited the U.S. economy.

The debate on restructuring often makes a distinction between financial restructuring and operational restructuring. The distinction is important in deciding whether the restructuring of the 1980s has weakened or strengthened U.S. firms in general. Critics contend that mergers and leveraged buyouts are mainly financial manipulations that weaken companies, forcing them to pay too much attention to immediate financial constraints and to sacrifice long-term development that would enable them to compete in a global market. Those who approve of restructuring counter that the motivation is to achieve increased operational efficiency

The Boston University Manufacturing Roundtable and the Brookings Institution provided financial support for this project. I thank research assistants Kelly Anson, Igor Dukovich, Nancy Kong, Mary Beth Sigler, Girish Uppal, and Joanne Vo. Thanks also to Jeremy Chantry, Michael Salinger, Martha Schary, John Strudwick, and seminar participants at Harvard, the Brookings Institution, and the University of Illinois, Champaign-Urbana, for their comments on earlier versions of the paper.

239

and better competitiveness from a firm that is not achieving its potential. Obviously, financial and operational motivations are not mutually exclusive and sometimes not easily separable. An ostensibly financial decision to increase leverage to thwart a takeover may result in a future sale of assets. An operational decision to diversify through acquiring other firms may change the capital structure of a company. Distinctions are potentially difficult when financial and operational changes occur close to one another. Nevertheless, the distinction between the two is useful for establishing a primary motivation, for considering whether the types of restructurings changed during the 1980s, and for assessing the effects on the U.S. economy.

Three different types of data—covering all or most of the period from 1979 through 1991—are used in this chapter. Data on corporate acquisitions, divestitures, and other changes of control are compiled at the level of the industrial chemicals industry as a whole and compared with manufacturing as a whole. Data at the plant level on changes in ownership and capacity are compiled for fifty-four major chemical products that represent a subset of the industrial chemicals industry (see appendix for details). Finally, the analyses of these data are supplemented with detailed case studies of eleven large chemical firms that were actively restructuring during the 1980s.

The methodological approach is largely descriptive. No theories of restructuring are rigorously tested, but the findings do shed light on the various motivations for different kinds of restructuring. Three distinct periods of activity are identified. From 1982 to 1984 the industry was shutting down capacity and consolidating through horizontal mergers—apparently in response to the recession that began in 1981. From 1986 to 1987 the falling value of the dollar led U.S. firms to sell off operations to foreign companies. In mid-decade large diversified chemical companies sold off commodity chemical operations to new firms specializing in producing these products. From 1985 to 1989 financial restructuring became paramount as industrial chemicals companies became active in stock repurchases, junk bond issuances, and leverage increases.

The data suggest that mergers and takeovers were not the primary mechanism for reducing capacity during the first period because most of the decrease in production capacity occurred before the big increase in mergers and plant sales. Neither can the restructurings of the first and second periods be explained solely as an effort by chemical firms to "dediversify." Although the data suggest that some firms were selling off unrelated businesses and reducing the number of different chemical products they produced (within the fifty-four-product subset studied), other firms were acquiring new businesses and producing new specialty chemical products outside the subset. Moreover, the units being sold off were not just peripheral businesses acquired in an earlier period, but were often core commodity chemicals businesses, which were in turn acquired by new firms that sprang up during the middle of the decade to specialize in commodity chemicals production. Thus a key motivation for the restructuring was the reorganization of the commodity chemicals business. Indeed, much of the financial restructuring activity of the end of the decade was undertaken by the same firms that were involved in this reorganization.

The Extent and Characteristics of Restructuring

The extensive restructuring in the industrial chemicals industry changed the ownership of more than 2 percent of its assets each year from 1979 to 1987.[2] In manufacturing overall, 1.7 percent of assets changed ownership each of those years. Dow, Du Pont, Monsanto, and Union Carbide, four of the largest manufacturers of industrial chemicals, were each involved in restructuring of one sort or another. In fact, almost every major firm, as well as a large proportion of small firms, was involved in some form of restructuring.

The extent of mergers and acquisitions in the industrial chemicals industry from 1979 to 1987 is presented in table 7-1. Relative to all manufacturing firms, chemical manufacturers were more active as acquirers. Although the industrial chemicals manufacturers accounted for approximately 4.5 percent of the value of all shipments in manufacturing, mergers and acquisitions in which chemical companies were acquirers accounted for 7.9 percent of the value of transactions in which a manufacturing company was the acquirer. Transactions in which chemical companies were targets accounted for 3.5 percent of the value of transactions in which a manufacturing company was the target.

At the industry level the number of mergers and acquisitions was consistently high during the 1980s (table 7-2). In the four years in which the number and total value of acquisitions by chemical companies are highest, the increases can often be explained by a few large transactions.[3] The large increase in the value of acquisitions in 1981 is accounted for by Du Pont's purchase of Conoco. The number of acquisitions increased in 1983; the largest was Diamond Shamrock's purchase of Natomas. The

Table 7-1. Percentage of Mergers and Acquisitions in Industrial Chemicals Manufacturing Relative to All Manufacturing, 1979–87

Ratios	1979	1980	1981	1982	1983	1984	1985	1986	1987	Average
Acquirers										
Acquiring chemical firms as percentage of all acquiring manufacturing firms	3.5	5.3	3.8	3.1	4.5	3.5	5.8	2.2	3.8	3.9
Value of chemical firms' acquisitions as percentage of value of acquisitions by all manufacturing firms	4.0	2.0	29.1	3.7	13.4	0.4	7.8	2.3	8.9	7.9
Targets										
Chemical firms acquired as percentage of all manufacturing firms acquired	2.1	2.1	2.8	3.5	1.9	2.7	2.2	2.7	2.9	2.5
Value of chemical firms acquired as percentage of value of all manufacturing firms acquired	0.2	2.9	4.0	2.9	0.5	1.8	2.3	3.6	13.6	3.5

Source: Author's calculations from data in M&A Database of IDD Information Services of New York (formerly ADP). See Margaret M. Blair, Sarah J. Lane, and Martha A. Schary. "Patterns of Corporate Restructuring, 1955–87," Brookings discussion papers in economics 91-1, January 1991.

Table 7-2. Value of Mergers and Acquisitions in Industrial Chemicals Manufacturing and All Manufacturing, 1979–87
Millions of 1982 dollars unless otherwise specified

Year	Acquisitions[a]		Targets[b]	
	Value	Number	Value	Number
Chemicals				
1979	720 (1)	9	38 (1)	5
1980	266 (1)	11	332 (0)	4
1981	8,098 (2)	14	759 (2)	11
1982	874 (1)	10	678 (8)	14
1983	2,092 (8)	16	79 (6)	8
1984	178 (7)	15	653 (5)	13
1985	3,845 (12)	27	1,293 (4)	12
1986	1,541 (7)	17	2,921 (10)	25
1987	4,075 (8)	19	7,829 (7)	18
Total	16,689 (47)	138	14,582 (43)	110
All manufacturing				
1979	18,162 (51)	258	16,514 (46)	238
1980	13,265 (49)	206	11,543 (47)	189
1981	27,872 (143)	367	18,756 (158)	398
1982	23,442 (130)	325	23,709 (172)	398
1983	15,585 (139)	354	15,060 (185)	423
1984	45,339 (156)	424	35,925 (184)	485
1985	49,549 (167)	466	56,491 (218)	547
1986	67,303 (332)	788	82,180 (380)	916
1987	45,987 (178)	500	57,539 (242)	616
Total	306,504 (2,245)	3,678	317,697 (2,469)	4,210

Source: See table 7-1.

a. A firm in the chemicals industry (based on primary SIC code) buys another firm from any industry. Manufacturing acquisitions are defined similarly. The value is the value of the deal or the value of the assets of the acquired firm if deal value data are missing. The number of missing values is indicated in parentheses. Figures underestimate total value of transactions because of this missing value information.

b. A firm in the chemical industry (based on primary SIC code) is bought by another firm. Manufacturing targets are defined similarly. The value is the value of the deal or the value of the assets of the acquired firm if deal value data are missing. The number of missing values is indicated in parentheses. Figures underestimate total value of transactions because of this missing value information.

peak year for number of acquisitions was 1985, but only Monsanto's acquisition of G.D. Searle was exceptionally large. The final year of high activity, 1987, saw many large acquisitions that involved foreign acquirers (Rhône-Poulenc, Akzo NV, and ICI PLC each bought part of Stauffer Chemical; Henkel KGaA bought a division of Occidental; and Hoescht acquired Celanese).[4]

Target activity measured by number was highest in 1986. Of the twenty-five targets in industrial chemicals, seven were divestitures by Union Carbide. These were part of a massive restructuring the company undertook in 1985, in part to reduce the debt it acquired in fighting off

Table 7-3. Firms, Plants, and Products in Data Set, 1978–88

Year	Firms	Change (percent)	Plants	Change (percent)	Product-plants[a]	Change (percent)
1978	149	. . .	373	. . .	705	. . .
1979	150	0.67	376	0.80	714	1.28
1980	152	1.33	372	−1.06	713	−0.14
1981	153	0.66	372	0	708	−0.71
1982	142	−7.19	351	−5.65	673	−4.94
1983	146	2.82	345	−1.71	648	−3.71
1984	146	0	349	1.16	639	−1.39
1985	140	−4.11	339	−2.87	615	−3.76
1986	142	1.43	331	−2.36	602	−2.11
1987	142	0	338	2.11	603	0.17
1988	146	2.82	340	0.59	605	0.33
Average	146	. . .	353	. . .	657	. . .

Source: Author's calculations.
a. A product-plant is a product produced at a particular plant.

an attempted takeover by GAF Corporation. In fact, divestiture activity accounted for a large proportion of the targets in chemicals. For example, in 1986, twenty-two of the twenty-five targets in chemicals were divestitures.

The extent of restructuring activity evident in the product-level data is also high. The fifty-four products studied were selected with a bias toward segments of the industry that were intensely involved in restructuring activity. In the product-level data set on average, there are 146 companies, 353 plants, and 657 product-plants a year (table 7-3).[5] Of the 240 firms in the data set, 86 were involved in selling plants and 90 in buying; 34 were involved in both. Consequently, more than half the firms in the data set were involved in either the purchase or sale of a plant. Even though the number of firms stayed relatively constant, the ownership changes and number of entries and exits from the market were significant. Of 149 firms producing at least 1 of the 55 products in 1978, only 87 remained in 1988. Of the 240 firms that produced one or more of these products at any time during the period, 153 had exited by the end of 1988.[6] Of these exiting firms, 62 had been in the data set in 1978 and 91 entered and exited during this period.[7] Changes in ownership and entry and exit of firms resulted in similar levels of change in plants. Of the 497 original product-plants in the data set in 1978, only 253 remained in 1988: almost half the plants either changed ownership or shut down production of that product at that plant.

Motivations for Restructuring

Studies have suggested various explanations for the corporate restructuring of the 1980s. Instead of testing one hypothesis against another, I analyze the support for each hypothesis separately because the hypotheses are often not mutually exclusive and some findings can be used to support more than one explanation. Furthermore, the use of three levels of data reveals the complexities, and possible error, inherent in trying to identify only one motivation for the restructuring.

Among the explanations, I consider two of the most dominant in the debate. One suggests that a high level of free cash flow caused by an increase in the real cost of capital resulted in a need to realign managerial incentives to be consistent with those of shareholders. A second states that the activity was primarily a series of divestitures or breakups following the conglomeration during the 1960s.[8] But one can also argue that additional economic forces are driving the need for change. I call one set of these operational and another set financial. An operational force might be a development that would make existing technology obsolete or, as in this case, the simultaneous opening of new plants and an economywide recession, leading to extensive overcapacity. A financial force would be an undervalued stock. Although the distinction may be difficult to make in many cases, in fact, most of the major restructuring events are easily categorized.

The key problems facing the industry during the early 1980s were overcapacity and intense competition. During the 1970s, when demand for bulk commodity chemicals was increasing, chemical companies invested in new plants. By 1982 the industry was overbuilt. Shipments were down, as were the operating rate and the production index, and the ratio of inventory to sales was high (table 7-4). The recession of the early 1980s hit chemicals manufacturers particularly hard. While the real value of GNP fell only 2.5 percent in 1982, the real value of chemicals shipments fell 7 percent and the production index 8 percent. The decline was even greater if compared to 1979, the peak year of production. Falling production, combined with the more than adequate available capacity, made the recession particularly severe.

Because the industry has high fixed costs relative to variable costs, overcapacity seriously limits financial returns. When capacity utilization falls, earnings suffer. Net income as a percentage of sales was low during the early part of the 1980s, and the return on assets was also low. Even

Table 7-4. Indicators of U.S. Chemicals Industry Performance, 1979–90

Billions of 1984 dollars unless otherwise specified

Indicator[a]	1979	1980	1981	1982	1983	1984	1985	1986	1987	1988	1989	1990
General economic conditions												
Shipments	199.9	187.9	188.8	175.6	188.1	198.2	195.9	195.9	221.8	212.8	213.5	218.3
Production index (1987 = 100)	91.3	87.8	89.2	81.8	87.5	91.4	91.4	94.6	100.0	105.4	108.5	110.5
Total assets	126.7	148.9	171.5	182.0	187.6	193.1	205.3	217.2	244.4	277.6	295.5	325.0
New plant and equipment expenditures	13.3	13.4	13.7	13.1	13.3	15.3	16.3	16.6	15.8	17.0	17.0	17.3
New plant and equipment to shipments (percent)	6.6	7.1	7.3	7.4	7.1	7.7	8.3	8.5	7.1	8.0	8.0	7.9
Operating rate (percent)	83.7	78.7	78.3	71.0	75.4	78.0	77.1	78.9	82.0	83.9	83.4	81.7
Inventory to sales (percent)	1.31	1.41	1.4	1.74	1.57	1.54	1.55	1.49	1.37	1.31	1.36	1.32
Producer price index (1984 = 100)	73.9	86.5	95.6	97.2	97.4	100.0	100.7	100.6	103.7	113.0	119.7	120.5
Research and development expenditures												
Research and development	5.0	5.0	5.4	6.4	7.0	7.7	8.2	8.6	9.3	9.4	9.7	10.5
R&D to shipments (percent)	2.5	2.6	2.9	3.6	3.7	3.9	4.2	4.4	4.2	4.4	4.5	4.8
Trade figures												
Exports	23.4	23.9	22.2	20.5	20.5	22.8	21.6	22.4	25.1	28.2	31.4	31.5
Imports	10.1	9.9	9.9	9.8	11.3	13.9	14.6	15.2	15.0	18.0	17.0	18.4
Trade surplus	13.3	14.1	12.2	10.7	9.2	8.9	7.1	7.2	9.2	10.3	14.4	13.1
Financial indicators												
Debt to total assets	0.41	0.49	0.48	0.49	0.52	0.52	0.67	0.61	0.61	0.57	0.62	0.64
Price to earnings	2.81	3.89	2.57	3.61	4.73	3.01	11.5	9.11	7.31	6.30	8.90	7.61
Net income after taxes	14.7	13.6	13.6	10.6	11.9	13.9	9.4	12.8	16.0	21.0	20.7	19.4
Net income to sales (percent)	7.5	7.2	6.9	5.5	5.8	6.6	4.7	6.3	7.4	9.0	8.8	8.2
Net income to assets (percent)	8.6	7.9	7.6	5.7	6.2	7.2	4.6	5.9	6.8	8.5	8.4	7.2

Source: Chemical Manufacturers' Association, *U.S. Chemical Industry Statistical Handbook* (1991), p. 28. Ratios of debt to total assets and price to earnings calculated by author using data from Compustat.

a. Nominal values are deflated by the producer price index (1984 = 100).

though earnings had fallen, the price of chemicals stocks fell further so that the price-earnings ratio fell.

Among manufacturing industries, chemicals has one of the highest levels of foreign imports and of foreign direct investment. In general, there has been an increasing globalization of the industry. The real value of U.S. exports of chemicals has risen 35 percent since 1978, and the real value of imports of chemicals has risen 82 percent. The net effect is measured by the trade surplus, which shows that the U.S. industry fared poorly in the middle of the 1980s but has rebounded. In real terms the trade surplus in 1990 was roughly equal to its level in 1978. Because of this high level of foreign trade and its reliance on petroleum as a major input, the industry is also strongly influenced by the value of the dollar.

Operational Forces
Affecting Restructuring

By the early 1980s chemicals firms felt pressure to cut back capacity, as a response to the increased competition from new capacity and new entrants, and to reduce their exposure to cyclical swings by reducing their manufacture of chemicals with cyclical sales. I discuss each pressure facing the industry and each motivation for restructuring separately. I conclude the section by examining the influence of foreign firms on restructuring.

Contraction of Capacity

The industry expanded in the 1970s, suffered a severe recession in 1982, and faced high oil prices through the early 1980s. After such large changes, some reorganization was inevitable. If excess capacity was expected to persist, one immediate pressure would be to cut it back.

Table 7-5 shows the yearly percentage increases and decreases in capacity by type and direction of change.[9] Incremental capacity increases and decreases are split into capacity changes that occurred during the regular operation of a plant and those that occurred in the first year following the year of new ownership.[10] Total capacity decreased, suggesting that the industry expected long-term pressures. Capacity eliminated through complete shutdown of production capacity of a particular

Table 7-5. **Average Capacity Changes, by Type, 1979–88[a]**
Percent

Year	Total increase	Total decrease	Increases			Decreases			
			Incremental increase in ongoing plants	One year after ownership change	New startup of production capacity[b]	Incremental decrease in ongoing plants	One year after ownership change	Complete shutdown of production capacity	Capacity in plants with ownership change
1979	5.0	1.9	3.4	0	1.6	1.0	0	0.9	1.2
1980	5.5	4.9	3.4	0.2	1.9	1.4	0.1	3.3	3.6
1981	4.3	2.0	3.2	0.2	0.9	1.0	0	1.0	2.2
1982	3.4	6.3	2.0	0	1.4	1.3	0	5.0	0.2
1983	3.6	5.9	1.5	0.3	1.8	1.6	0	4.3	1.5
1984	3.2	12.0	2.3	0.1	0.8	1.3	0	10.7	4.5
1985	3.2	3.4	2.4	0.1	0.7	1.4	0	2.0	2.0
1986	3.1	4.0	2.4	0.1	0.6	1.0	0.2	2.8	4.1
1987	5.8	3.2	2.6	0.6	2.6	1.1	0.3	1.7	10.4
1988	6.6	2.8	5.3	0.2	1.0	1.0	0.3	1.5	3.3
Average	4.36	4.63	2.85	0.19	1.33	1.21	0.10	3.32	3.29
Cumulative change	53.2	56.8	32.4	1.9	14.1	12.8	1.0	38.2	. . .

Source: Author's calculations.

a. Calcuations of actual capacity were made at the plant level by product. For each plant, each type and direction of capacity change from the previous year was calculated. Call this $CCI_{plant, product, year}$. Thus for any one product in any one year, there may be both an increase and a decrease in capacity if one plant increases and another decreases it. CCI_{jit} is the total capacity change of type and direction i for product j in year t. The total percentage of capacity affected at the product level was calculated by dividing the change of each type and direction by the total capcity for that product and year. Therefore, $PCI_{jit} = CCI_{jit}/TCI_{jt}$. Table 7-5 shows the average of these changes across products. A small percentage change in a large product such as ethylene was weighted equally with a small percentage change in a product with small output such as adipic acid, but the percentage change for each product was calculated relative to the product's own capacity.

b. Capacity in plants that did not previously produce the given product.

product far exceeded capacity added through new production capacity.[11] Even though incremental capacity increases in ongoing plants were larger than incremental decreases, the result was a cumulative total decrease of 56.7 percent offset by a cumulative total increase of 53.2 percent between 1979 and 1988.

The response to the recession was further evident in the pattern of changes over time. The greatest contraction in capacity through complete shutdown of production capacity occurred in 1984, the year after the two worst years in the chemicals industry. The highest percentage incremental capacity decrease was in 1983, suggesting that incremental decreases were easier and faster to implement than complete shutdown of capacity. But incremental decreases were much smaller, averaging in the peak year a 1.6 percent decrease of total capacity as against an average 10.7 percent decrease in the peak year for complete shutdown of capacity.[12] Thus capacities were incrementally decreased in the very short term and plant capacity was shut down over a longer period. The decreases and shutdown of capacity were begun fairly rapidly immediately after the recession.

This timing confirms the observation that ownership changes did not precede these capacity reductions. The highest percentage of capacity was sold in 1987, much later than the large decreases in capacity. In the industry-level data, 1987 was also the year of the largest acquisitions of chemical firm targets as measured by value (see table 7-2). The second highest year for capacity sold was 1984, also a year of great activity in the industry-level data, though the percentage of capacity sold was less than half of that sold in 1987. The period of largest ownership change came after the period of capacity reduction.

If mergers and acquisitions facilitate exit from an industry or product, capacity decreases should be greater in plants after ownership change. In table 7-5, changes in ongoing plants were more than ten times as large as in those experiencing ownership changes. Therefore, on an absolute basis the percentage change in capacity after an ownership change is not economically important. However, these percentages were calculated relative to total capacity for production of a given product. Measuring the relative change in plants that were sold shows that the share of capacity changed more in plants that were sold. Approximately 3 percent of ongoing capacity was increased on average, whereas an average 6 percent of capacity sold was increased (table 7-6).[13] The rate of decrease in plants with ownership change was almost three times that of ongoing plants.

Table 7-6. Capacity Changes after Ownership Change, 1979–88
Percent

Year	Capacity sold that then increases[a]	Total incremental capacity increases	Capacity sold that then decreases[a]	Total incremental capacity decreases	Capacity in plants with ownership change
1979	0.1	3.4	2.7	1.0	1.2
1980	6.0	3.6	3.4	1.5	3.6
1981	8.2	3.4	0	1.0	2.2
1982	0	2.0	12.7	1.3	0.2
1983	20.0	1.8	2.1	1.6	1.5
1984	2.3	2.4	0	1.3	4.5
1985	4.8	2.5	0.2	1.4	2.0
1986	2.4	2.5	4.4	1.2	4.1
1987	6.0	3.2	3.1	1.4	10.4
1988	7.6	5.5	9.1	1.3	3.3
Average	5.68	3.04	3.77	1.22	3.29

Source: Author's calculations.
a. Capacity increases in plants in the year after the year of ownership change divided by capacity in plants with an ownership change. Capacity sold that then decreases is defined comparably.

Thus although the total effect of capacity changes in plants experiencing change of ownership was not large, decreases or increases were more prevalent immediately following an ownership change. Furthermore, in plants with ownership change, the ratio of capacity decreases to increases was greater.

Capacity changes after a plant was sold were not uniformly distributed over time. In 1983, the year after the recession, almost one-fifth of the capacity that was sold was increased. In 1983 and 1984 there was very little decrease in plants that were sold. In fact the highest capacity decreases in plants experiencing an ownership change were in the year of the recession and in the last three years in the sample (1986–88).

Thus although various strategies can decrease capacity, the main method was to decrease it in existing plants without ownership changes. Capacity was eliminated by shutting down capacity immediately after the recession but before the peak in ownership changes, and the amount of capacity change in plants that were sold was small. Consequently, the effect of ownership change on the reduction of capacity was small. However, plants with ownership changes had greater increases and decreases than other plants. Furthermore, although increases were more likely than decreases in both types of plants, decreases occurred more often in plants that changed ownership than in ongoing plants.

Reverse Diversification

It has often been suggested that the wave of mergers and acquisitions in the 1980s reversed the 1960s' trend toward diversification as firms divested themselves of unprofitable products.[14] Merger and acquisition activity was consistently high throughout the 1980s. At the aggregate level there does not seem to have been any particular pattern, but investigating the characteristics (horizontal mergers, divestitures, and foreign activity) reveals changing patterns.

At first glance, the industry-level data appear to provide evidence that firms were reversing the 1960s diversification. Relative to manufacturing as a whole, the chemicals industry had a high rate of divestitures (table 7-7). The number was also high between 1981 and 1987 with a peak in 1986. In manufacturing divestitures also increased dramatically in 1986. Overall, divestitures accounted for 69 percent of chemical company targets and a surprising 100 percent of the eight targets in 1983, the year after the recession. Divestitures accounted for a much smaller, though still large, proportion of total targets in manufacturing overall, averaging 37 percent with a high of 54 percent.

Although the idea of reverse diversification is supported by the pattern of asset sales, neither the hypothesis nor the evidence reflects the complexities of the changes occurring in the industry.[15] Firms did divest units, but there was an offsetting trend toward acquiring units in new product areas. The divestment and downsizing by major chemical companies of traditional business operations in commodity chemicals was accompanied by diversification into specialty chemicals and other operations with higher value added, activity that potentially contradicts the hypothesis of reverse diversification. Furthermore, even though the industry-level data show a significant amount of divestment, much of this was due to the consolidation of operations into new firms specializing in commodity chemicals. A large part of the divestiture activity was not the sale of unrelated businesses acquired in the 1960s but rather of core commodity chemical businesses.

There were, of course, exceptions. In 1981 Quantum (formerly National Distillers and Chemicals) sold Beacon Manufacturing, one of the world's largest makers of blankets, so that it could pull back from an earlier diversification strategy and focus on commodity chemicals. In 1986 it purchased a commodity chemical maker and divested its wine and liquor business. In 1988 it sold its oil and natural gas properties. In 1989

Table 7-7. Divestitures in Chemicals Manufacturing and All Manufacturing, 1979–87

Year	Number	Ratio of divestitures to all targets	Value (millions of 1982 dollars)	Percent of transactions for which data exist	Ratio of divestitures' value to value of all targets
Chemicals					
1979	0	0	0	0	0
1980	1	25.0	233	100	70.2
1981	7	63.6	145	71	19.1
1982	12	85.7	320	42	47.2
1983	8	100.0	79	25	100.0
1984	9	69.2	637	67	97.5
1985	7	58.3	148	71	11.4
1986	22	88.0	2,811	55	96.2
1987	10	55.6	2,728	50	34.8
Average	. . .	60.6	. . .	. . .	53.0
Manufacturing					
1979	7	2.9	716	100	0.4
1980	17	9.0	1,001	88	8.7
1981	175	44.0	5,843	53	31.2
1982	188	47.2	4,517	42	19.1
1983	213	50.4	5,011	48	33.3
1984	194	40.0	5,628	60	15.7
1985	217	39.7	12,722	57	22.5
1986	443	48.4	32,805	52	39.9
1987	334	54.2	21,258	57	36.9
Average	. . .	37.3	. . .	. . .	23.1

Source: See table 7-1.

it sold its Brazilian vineyard and winery operation and completed building a new ethylene cracker.

But a more common pattern was exemplified by Monsanto and Dow. Monsanto's major acquisition was G.D. Searle in 1985, which diversified the firm into new products. Monsanto's 1986 annual report noted that although chemicals accounted for 70 percent of sales in 1981, by 1986 they were only 52 percent. Dow became one of the more diversified large chemical companies as a result of acquisitions.

There is, then, little evidence that restructuring was motivated by the desire to divest units acquired earlier. Chemical companies were divesting core businesses, not unrelated ones. Furthermore, they were at the same time diversifying into products with higher value added.

Redistribution of Exposure to Cyclicality

In the 1980s the chemical industry was consolidating production of commodity chemicals in firms specializing in these products. This reorganization was in part driven by two related factors: the movement out of commodity chemicals by the larger diversified firms and the movement by these firms toward acyclical products with higher value added.[16] The rate of horizontal mergers in chemicals was consistent with the move toward consolidation, particularly after 1982, and was comparable to the rate in manufacturing overall (table 7-8).[17] Measured by either number or value, one-quarter of the transactions in both were horizontal. As a percentage of total activity, horizontal transactions were particularly high in 1983 and 1984, involving 60 percent of target industrial chemical firms and representing half the value of all target industrial chemical firms.

Large chemical companies were dropping their less profitable commodity chemical businesses and strengthening their more profitable, less cyclical specialty lines. New undiversified commodities chemical companies were formed. In 1987, for example, Cain Chemical Company bought several plants from Du Pont and others from Corpus Christi Petrochemical and ICI.

The largest firms in the industry undertook some form of restructuring and moved into specialty chemicals.[18] Dow, Du Pont, Monsanto, and Union Carbide produced fewer of the fifty-four products examined in this study and, except for Dow, also decreased the number of plant locations producing them. Although each firm was subject to the same industrywide economic forces, firm-specific differences led to different restructuring responses. Monsanto and Du Pont sold plants; Dow and Union Carbide decreased production capacity. Monsanto and Du Pont were among the top ten sellers of plants; none of the four was among the top ten buyers.[19] Sales of plants were the most frequently made to new companies formed to acquire them. Aristech, Cain Chemical, Georgia-Gulf, Huntsman, and Vista were all created by buying commodity chemical plants of larger diversified chemical companies.

After judging that growth in the 1980s would be much slower than in the 1970s, Dow recognized the need to reduce industry capacity. It began to move into products with higher value added and diversified with numerous acquisitions directed toward specialty products. In the early 1980s it made a number of acquisitions, including Richardson-Merrell, but sold Dow Instruments and Reagents, and Bio-Science Enterprises, its labo-

Table 7-8. Horizontal Mergers and Acquisitions in Industrial Chemicals Manufacturing and All Manufacturing, 1979–87
Percent unless otherwise specified

Year	Number	Ratio of horizontal transactions to total acquisitions	Ratio of horizontal transactions to total targets	Value (millions of 1982 dollars)	Ratio of horizontal transaction value to total value of acquisitions	Ratio of horizontal transaction value to total value of targets
Industrial chemicals						
1979	2	22.2	40.0	6	0.8	15.8
1980	0	0	0	0	0	0
1981	3	21.4	27.3	101	1.2	13.3
1982	0	0	0	0	0	0
1983	6	37.5	75.0	79	3.8	100.0
1984	6	40.0	46.2	120	67.4	18.4
1985	5	18.5	41.7	97	2.5	7.5
1986	6	35.3	24.0	646	41.9	22.1
1987	4	21.1	22.2	3,845	94.4	49.1
Average	. . .	21.8	30.7	. . .	23.6	25.1
All manufacturing						
1979	44	17.1	18.5	2,029	11.2	12.3
1980	51	24.8	27.0	1,870	14.1	16.2
1981	105	28.6	26.4	3,834	13.8	20.4
1982	93	28.6	23.4	3,484	14.9	14.7
1983	119	33.6	28.1	3,306	21.2	22.0
1984	126	29.7	26.0	17,259	38.1	48.0
1985	137	29.4	25.0	7,279	14.7	12.9
1986	258	32.7	28.2	25,831	38.4	31.4
1987	177	35.4	28.7	15,063	32.8	26.2
Average	. . .	28.9	25.7	. . .	22.1	22.7

Source: See table 7-1.

ratory testing unit. Throughout the 1980s it continued to be more an acquirer than divestor, buying a specialty chemical business from Morton Thiokol in 1984, Filmtec in 1985, Essex Chemical Corporation in 1988, and First Brands in 1989. In 1989 Dow continued expanding into pharmaceuticals when it bought Marion Labs. By 1990 Dow was named by *Business Week* as one of the ten companies that made the best acquisitions, that is, gained strategic benefits from the deals and improved its performance during the 1980s.[20] The consequence of this restructuring was that by 1990 basic chemicals represented 48 percent of Dow's revenues—they represented 60 percent in 1980—and revenues from consumer specialties rose from 11 percent to 26 percent of total revenue.

Du Pont, one of the diversified companies among the chemical producers though with a large proportion of its sales in industrial chemicals, was involved in one of the first large transactions of the decade when it acquired Conoco in 1981. This deal increased the company's vulnerability to cycles in commodity markets, but subsequent restructuring was characterized by acquisitions of companies producing high-value-added products and divestitures of others, including producers of commodity chemicals.[21] It sold the commodity chemicals operations acquired from Conoco to Vista Chemical and sold other commodity operations to Cain Chemical. In 1986 it purchased the American Critical Care Unit of Baxter Travenol Laboratories, Shell Agricultural Chemical, Tau Laboratories, and the North American paint operations of Ford.

Meanwhile, Monsanto diversified into high-value-added products when it acquired Searle in 1985. Afterward it announced a restructuring to focus on less cyclical products. It sold its commodity chemicals businesses, decreased its investment in commodity chemicals from 25 percent of total assets in 1980 to less than 5 percent in 1987, and invested in specialized higher-value-added products.

The restructuring of Union Carbide was induced in part by the attempted takeover initiated by GAF in 1985 and by the decline in stock price following the explosion of a Union Carbide chemical plant in Bhopal, India. In 1986, when twenty-five chemical firms or subsidiaries of chemical firms were sold, seven divestitures were by Union Carbide. The company held on to its commodity chemical plants but shut down a significant proportion of its production capacity for the fifty-four products in the data set.

These four companies, Dow, Du Pont, Monsanto, and Union Carbide, then, used various strategies to decrease the commodity-chemicals capacity, the number of commodity chemicals they produced, and the proportion of sales arising from them. Sales of commodity plants were important, but each of the four firms also made acquisitions to move it into specialty areas.

Consolidation of Commodity Chemicals

The overcapacity in the chemical industry arising from the drop in demand was made worse by the number of firms competing in each product group. The consolidation of commodity chemicals production into fewer firms may have resulted from the urge to decrease this competition and thus the threat of overcapacity arising from numerous firms' simultaneously building new capacity.[22] An alternative but complementary hypothesis is that the newly formed firms had some characteristic that either made them better able to deal with the cyclicality of commodity chemicals or that increased their profit margins enough to make the acquisitions worthwhile.[23]

The product-level data show that restructuring consolidated the production of the fifty-four commodity chemicals into fewer, more specialized firms by 1987.[24] The average of all of the three measures—products per plant, products per company, and plants per company—decreased (table 7-9). By 1988 the firms were producing 6 percent fewer products per plant among the fifty-four products studied here and 13 percent fewer products per firm, although maximums stay relatively constant. The decline in average number of products per company again indicates that these firms were becoming less diversified, at least within these commodity chemicals, and that production of these chemicals was becoming more consolidated.[25]

The commodity chemicals plants that the larger chemical companies sold were bought by newly formed firms. From 1983–1987, six commodity chemical firms were founded. Huntsman acquired Shell's polystyrene commodity chemical business in 1983. In 1986 it acquired three more plants from Hoescht. Vista Chemical was formed in 1984 through a leveraged buyout of plants Du Pont had acquired from Conoco. A 1985 leveraged buyout of most of the assets of the chemical division of Georgia-Pacific resulted in the formation of Georgia-Gulf, which went public a year later. After Carl Icahn launched a takeover attack of USX in 1986, the company spun off Aristech. Sterling Chemicals was founded by Gordon Cain in 1986 to acquire Monsanto's petrochemical plants. Cain Chemical, a second company formed in 1987 with the involvement

Table 7-9. Industrial Chemicals Manufacturing Production Trends, 1978–88

	Products per plant		Products per company		Plants per company	
Year	Average	Maximum	Average	Maximum	Average	Maximum
1978	1.90	22	3.36	24	2.52	17
1979	1.90	22	3.37	24	2.52	18
1980	1.92	22	3.30	24	2.46	17
1981	1.90	22	3.26	24	2.45	21
1982	1.92	22	3.31	24	2.49	21
1983	1.88	20	3.15	24	2.38	21
1984	1.83	20	3.09	23	2.41	18
1985	1.81	18	3.13	23	2.44	18
1986	1.82	18	3.04	23	2.35	17
1987	1.78	18	3.00	23	2.40	15
1988	1.78	18	2.93	23	2.34	19

Source: Author's calculations.

of Gordon Cain and financed with $350 million in junk bonds, integrated seven polyethylene plants and pipeline operations on the Gulf Coast. The company was formed through leveraged buyouts of three plants from Du Pont and additional plants from ICI Americas and Corpus Christi Chemical.

Most of these six new companies started with a high amount of leverage and reduced the leverage rapidly during the boom in commodity chemicals in the second half of the 1980s.[26] Half remain independent public companies and half have reverted to ownership by large conglomerates, two foreign and one domestic.

The Foreign Influence

Chemicals is one of the most global industries, with a large percentage of foreign direct investment in the United States, a large percentage of U.S. ownership abroad relative to manufacturing, and a high level of foreign trade and competition. Consequently, foreign influence is important in chemicals restructurings, as is the value of the dollar. On average, 20 percent of the acquisitions in chemicals in the 1980s were made by foreign companies (table 7-10). This was the highest rate of foreign takeover activity of any manufacturing industry, and foreign acquisitions in all of manufacturing amounted to only half this rate.[27]

Foreign firms acquired a large number of U.S. chemical companies of medium size in 1986 and of larger size in the peak year 1987. In 1987 half of all acquisitions of chemical firms in the data set were made by foreign

Table 7-10. Acquisitions by Foreign Firms and Foreign Firms as Targets, U.S. Industrial Chemicals Companies and All Manufacturing Companies, 1979–87

Transaction	1979	1980	1981	1982	1983	1984	1985	1986	1987	Average
Chemicals										
Foreign acquisitions of U.S. targets	0	0	2	2	2	1	4	7	9	...
Ratio of foreign acquisitions to total U.S. targets (percent)	0	0	18.2	14.3	25.0	7.7	33.3	28.0	50.0	19.6
Foreign targets of U.S. acquisitions	2	0	0	2	0	2	1	0	0	...
Ratio of foreign targets to total U.S. acquisitions (percent)	22.2	0	0	20.0	0	13.3	3.7	0	0	6.6
All Manufacturing										
Foreign acquisitions of U.S. targets	39	26	45	32	19	34	55	107	96	...
Ratio of foreign acquisitions to total U.S. targets (percent)	16.4	13.8	11.3	8.0	4.5	7.0	10.1	11.7	15.6	10.9
Foreign targets of U.S. acquisitions	20	8	15	15	20	23	22	34	40	...
Ratio of foreign targets to total U.S. acquisitions (percent)	7.8	3.9	4.1	4.6	5.6	5.4	4.7	4.3	8.0	5.4

Source: See table 7-1.

firms, including the eight largest acquisitions of domestic chemical companies.

An important possible motivation for these foreign acquisitions was the exchange rate. The dollar started low in 1979–80, rose to a peak in 1985, and by 1988 returned to the low of the beginning of the decade. Another motivation may have been the nature of production in the chemicals industry. If foreign firms decide to begin production in the domestic market, they must obviously either build a new plant or acquire an existing operation. Because of the large capital investment and significant technical expertise required, entry into the chemical industry by newly formed firms or new plant construction by existing firms is more difficult than entry by acquisition. For a firm expanding its product line or a firm entering the market, acquisition of existing plants also has a greater chance of success.[28]

Given these conditions, evidence suggests that the decline in the value of the dollar drove foreign acquisitions in 1986–87. But although the value of the dollar had fallen significantly from its peak and continued to fall after 1986–87, acquisitions by foreign firms declined, perhaps in part because those that wanted to enter the domestic market had already done so and because fewer of the right targets at the right price were left.

Summary of Operational Changes

The analysis of restructuring suggests that the increase in activity during 1982–83 was due to the recession and the need to respond to the decline in profitability and the cyclicality of commodity chemicals. The striking feature of the activity in 1986–87 was foreign acquisitions, which were driven partly by the falling value of the dollar.

Some of the evidence indicates that ownership changes were associated with greater changes in capacity, suggesting that this form of restructuring facilitates capacity reductions and reorganization. Nevertheless, most capacity reductions and plant closures took place before the rise in mergers and acquisitions and in plants that did not change owners. Although there was significant divestiture activity, it is unknown whether the divested units had been acquired during the wave of conglomeration in the 1960s. The evidence suggests that at least some of the divestitures were driven by the desire to consolidate commodity chemicals.

The restructuring of chemicals firms resembled the activity occurring in the rest of manufacturing. It was more intense, however, probably because of the greater severity of the recession in chemicals, a greater need for reorganization, and the greater global activity along with the changes in the value of the dollar. Nonetheless, these same factors also probably contributed to increased restructuring throughout manufacturing.

Financial Forces Affecting Restructuring

Three financial forces—growth of cash flow, changes in leverage, and stock repurchases—were prominent features of the 1980s. I will discuss each separately.

Takeovers and Free Cash Flow

Free cash flow is cash from past investments generated at a rate that exceeds what is needed to make new investments. Firms with products in the mature phase of their cycle, for which current returns are high and investment prospects dim, are often considered likely candidates either to be taken over and restructured by new owners or to undertake their own restructuring to increase shareholder payouts and thwart a takeover. According to this theory, when the real cost of capital is high relative to returns from new investment, firms in some industries will find that they have free cash flow and will be under pressure to reduce new investment (at least in that industry) and either reinvest in high-growth endeavors or increase payout to shareholders. Conflicts of interest between managers and shareholders over the choice of strategies may be resolved through takeover, the threat of takeover, or leveraged buyouts or leverage increases. A testable prediction is that restructuring will occur in mature, low-growth industries. In these broad terms chemicals fits the pattern.[29]

This discussion examines the evidence at the more detailed product level for such a sequence of events. At the product level the analogous argument is that investment should be reallocated from products with low growth to those with high growth. Because of conflicts of interest between managers and shareholders, this reallocation will perhaps occur more frequently in conjunction with a sale of a plant. The test therefore is whether sales of plants producing low-growth products occur more frequently than sales of those producing high-growth products.

Even though many of the products studied here are similar, the plants producing them differ significantly in the frequency of ownership change: for some products there was complete turnover of producers; for others all the producers in 1978 were still producing that particular product in

1988. Producers of aniline, methanol, and propylene oxide experienced many plant sales; producers of methyl methacrylate very few. On average 55.3 percent of the firms producing a given product in 1978 still produced it in 1988.

Table 7-11 shows average capacity changes from 1978 to 1988 by product; the four products identified by Marvin Lieberman that had experienced declining production are marked by asterisks.[30] Because the data set is intentionally biased toward products in which restructuring occurred, an overlap of only four products with Leiberman's list of 30 declining products suggests that restructuring due to merger, acquisition, or divestiture was not occurring in declining industries.[31]

As further corroboration, in figures 7-1 and 7-2 capacity changes and turnover of firms are allocated to four groups based on rates of production growth. In addition to the four products in the declining growth group, there are four in the low-growth group and sixteen each in the medium- and high-growth groups. The remaining fourteen products are more specialized and are produced in smaller quantities; there was no production growth information available. The pattern of capacity increases and decreases was approximately as expected. Decreases in capacity in ongoing plants occur more frequently for producers of low-growth products than for producers of high-growth products, and the converse is true for increases. The declining group follows a different pattern. It has the lowest rate of capacity sold and the lowest rate of regular capacity increases. The expected inverse relationship between capacity sold and product growth suggested by the hypothesis holds for the three groups with positive growth. For products experiencing declining growth it does not: the percentage of capacity sold is the lowest of all four groups. However, this result is consistent with the finding that the declining group has a generally different pattern of activity. All types of capacity changes, with the exception of shutdown of production capacity for exiting firms, are low for declining growth products.[32]

Figure 7-2 shows the percentage of the original firms in the data set as of 1978 that were still producers of that product in 1988. The stability of firms increases with product growth.[33] Firms producing declining products again show a higher percentage remaining than those producing lower-growth products. Because relatively few plants producing declining products are sold, the percentage remaining stays high even though their closure rate of production capacity is highest.

The evidence therefore shows that sales occurred more frequently among producers of low-growth products. It also shows that firms pro-

Table 7-11. Percentage Capacity Changes in Chemicals Manufacturing, by Product, 1978–88
Percent unless otherwise specified

| Product | Increases | | | Decreases | | | Capacity sold | 1978 total capacity (millions of pounds) |
	Incremental in ongoing plants	One year after ownership change	New startup of production capacity	Incremental in ongoing plants	One year after ownership change	Shutdown of production capacity		
Acetaldehyde	0	0	0	2.1	0	37.8	20.7	1,205
Acetic acid	48.2	7.6	22.6	27.5	0	25.7	71.2	3,540
Acrylonitrile	20.0	0	18.6	4.7	0	12.6	0	2,145
Adipic acid	9.3	0	0	4.2	0	7.3	0	1,910
Aluminum chloride, anhydrous	2.9	0	4.1	10.3	0	82.7	11.5	243
Aluminum choloride, hydrous	0.4	0	0.3	0.2	0	0.3	0.4	2,009
Aniline	10.5	5.2	17.2	13.1	0	24.1	67.2	1,160
Benzene	34.1	0.8	17.8	18.1	1.8	25.1	46.8	2,190
Bisphenol A	32.6	1.1	0	1.1	0	7.7	15.4	910
Caprolactum	33.3	0	0	0	16.0	0	32.0	1,125
Chlorobenzene, monomer	3.7	0	0	13.6	0	37.1	31.4	700
Cumene	15.4	3.0	8.1	2.0	0	30.2	57.6	4,940
Cyclohexane	34.5	2.0	12.4	6.2	0	25.3	27.3	403
Diethylene glycol	59.5	10.6	8.7	25.3	0	7.6	37.7	462
Dipropylene glycol	23.5	17.3	0	24.7	0	0	53.1	81
Epoxy resins, unmodified	27.4	0	13.7	23.6	0	6.1	4.6	657
Ethyl acetate	14.8	3.7	5.6	14.8	0	37.0	29.6	270
Ethyl chloride	2.7	0	1.3	10.7	0	40.5	0	765
Ethyl ether	4.5	0	0	0	0	21.2	0	66
Ethylbenzene	14.2	4.3	18.7	9.3	0	12.8	57.3	9,440
Ethylene	30.2	3.1	7.6	19.7	0	8.9	41.9	33,720
Ethyleneamines	35.2	0	6.8	0	0	70.5	0	440
Ethylene dichloride	30.7	0.2	28.3	12.7	0.9	32.5	55.6	15,255
Ethylene glycol	30.2	7.1	9.7	14.9	0	32.6	47.9	5,955

Ethylene oxide	35.6	5.5	15.4	0	11.6	22.9	33.8	5,425
Fluorocarbons	58.7	0	0.1	0	26.6	0.1	0	1,090
Maleic anhydride	27.8	2.9	24.8	6.5	13.5	50.5	22.9	525
Methanol	23.2	0.5	46.5	1.2	5.4	27.7	83.1	1,215
Methyl chloride	42.6	0	33.6	0	13.1	46.0	32.8	685
Methyl methacrylate	19.6	0	0	0	6.2	10.7	0	1,125
Pentaerythritol	5.5	0	0	0	5.5	13.7	41.0	183
Phthalic anhydride	20.3	0	15.9	0	15.0	35.6	12.5	1,318
Polybutylene terephthalate resins	29.5	0	42.7	0	1.8	40.9	0	220
Polycarbonate resins	159.1	0	68.2	0	4.5	13.6	0	220
Polyester fibers	19.9	2.0	15.3	0.8	26.2	23.2	67.6	4,665
Polyethylene terephthalate Fil	89.6	0	2.5	0	10.6	2.8	13.9	395
Polyethylene resins, high density	72.9	1.6	45.3	0.2	34.1	17.6	90.5	5,205
Polyethylene resins, low density	65.9	2.7	41.2	12.7	34.8	44.5	52.1	7,970
Polyethylene terephthalate bottle	456.7	13.3	121.7	0	28.3	26.7	46.7	300
Polypropylene resins	67.7	3.2	10.7	0.4	11.0	9.6	78.5	5,145
Polystyrene resins	46.8	3.7	16.8	0	28.0	20.7	49.4	5,358
Polyvinyl chloride resins	56.3	3.4	33.7	0.1	13.5	41.6	77.6	6,817
Propylene	39.2	3.3	9.8	4.7	17.6	6.7	45.3	18,275
Propylene glycol	6.2	8.4	0	0	9.6	0	56.2	890
Propylene oxide	19.3	3.2	0	1.9	4.5	14.6	95.0	3,115
Pyridines, synthetic	0	0	41.7	0	0	41.7	0	60
Sodium chlorate	42.0	1.1	25.3	0	33.8	52.1	18.4	407
Sodium hydroxide	9.8	0.7	9.9	0.6	11.5	12.4	22.9	21,580
Styrene	12.9	0.6	13.3	0	8.1	12.1	56.5	8,428
Terephthalic acid, dimethyl	13.9	0.2	12.3	0	12.7	0	7.7	3,240
Vinyl acetate monomer	33.8	0	21.6	0	4.3	9.2	52.7	1,850
Vinyl chloride monomer	27.2	0.7	18.7	0	13.8	19.8	55.4	8,195
Butadiene (1,3)	23.6	0.3	10.4	7.4	11.8	26.0	56.4	4,308
Butanediol (1,4)	34.2	0	0	0	2.7	0	0	365
Average	38.5	2.3	16.6	1.0	12.6	22.7	34.8	· · ·

Source: Author's calculations.

Figure 7-1. Capacity Changes, 1979–90, by Four Levels of Production Growth, 1979–84[a]

Average percent change, 1979–90

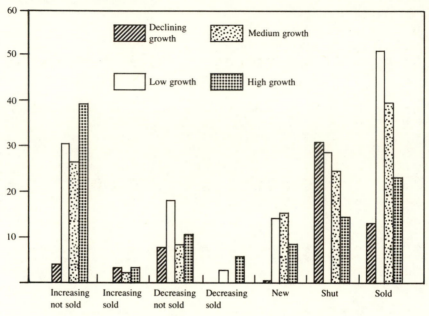

Source: Author's calculations.
a. Production data were collected for 1979–90. Products were grouped based on their growth in production during 1979–84 rather than on the full period because growth behavior before restructuring was expected to be a stronger measure of the pressure to restructure.

ducing declining-growth products are different from those producing low-growth products. The first finding is consistent with the free cash flow hypothesis outlined above, and the second suggests a refinement on the formulation and testing of the hypothesis. Industries in decline should not be lumped with low-growth industries because their restructuring activity will be quantitatively and qualitatively different. Tests that do not differentiate between them potentially will be biased toward finding no effect.

The argument underlying the hypothesis that free cash flow promotes acquisition is that only a takeover or the threat of one can resolve conflicts of interest between managers and shareholders if managers are unwilling to downsize and pay out cash to the shareholders when investment opportunities are diminished. During 1982–83, capacity was relatively more likely to be shut down than sold, and there was little decrease in capacity in the year following the sale of a plant. This suggests that the mecha-

Figure 7-2. Proportion of Firms Producing Product in 1978 That Were Still Producing It in 1988, by Four Levels of Production Growth, 1979–84

Percent

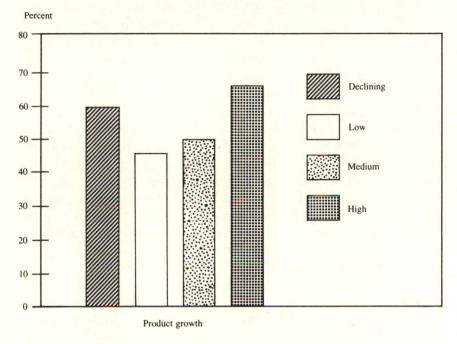

Product growth

Source: Author's calculations.

nisms for reallocating investment in response to the 1982 recession were functioning well without the need for mergers and acquisitions. This finding weakens the case for the connection between free cash flow and high numbers of mergers, acquisitions, and takeovers. But I have so far looked only at takeovers and acquisitions that occurred. It remains possible that fear of takeover may lead companies to restructure before any takeover occurs or even before an imminent threat. In fact, in 1985 the trade press noted widespread restructuring, through mergers, acquisitions, divestitures, changes in financing, and also write-offs, reorganizations, and workforce reductions. Although the restructuring was not obviously motivated by threats of takeover, the plans of many companies had the stated aims of increasing competitiveness and profitability while maximizing shareholder value. Pennwalt, for example, stated that its broad restructuring program was intended to free unproductive or unprofitable assets and to invest more in businesses and assets that were profitable and expected to grow.[34]

Leverage Changes

Although the evidence is not compelling that mergers, acquisitions, and takeovers were necessary to redirect investment from low-growth to high-growth areas, the 1980s did see widespread restructuring of many types and a general concern about maximizing shareholder value. Increased leverage may instead have been the mechanism used to realign the interests of shareholders and managers.

The chemicals industry was not particularly active in leveraged restructurings or issues of junk bonds (figure 7-3).[35] In two respects, however, industry activity was significant. First, the transactions involved most of the firms that were also involved in the reorganization of the commodity chemicals industry. Second, because chemicals is such a large industry with a preponderance of large firms, a low rate of activity in one industry will account for a large share of activity in the economy as a whole. Four of the twenty-five firms with the largest junk bond issues had holdings in commodity chemicals, as had five of the twenty-five largest firms that underwent leveraged restructurings.[36]

The junk bond issues associated with the formation of new commodity chemical companies are by Sterling Chemical in 1986 and Cain Chemical in 1987. Union Carbide also issued junk bonds in 1987 as did Quantum in 1989. The activity was generally greater in the second half of the decade, with a peak in 1986.

The ratio of debt to assets increased strongly for the industry as a whole and for the eleven companies studied in detail (figure 7-4).[37] The ratios for the eleven-company subset, however, did not pull up the industry average, which suggests that some firms must have decreased leverage. The subset had higher debt because of Union Carbide's increase and because many of the newly formed commodity chemical companies had high debt. Thus increased leverage was concentrated among those firms involved in the reorganization of commodity chemicals.

Stock Repurchases

Although mergers, acquisitions, and capacity changes continued at a reduced pace in the late 1980s, stock repurchases, which can dramatically alter a company's capital structure, increased significantly. The undervaluation of chemical stocks had become a common topic in the trade press by the late 1980s.[38] Given the restructurings in the industry and the improvement in profits, executives believed their firms were undervalued

Figure 7-3. Junk Bond Issuances and Leveraged Restructurings, 1980–89

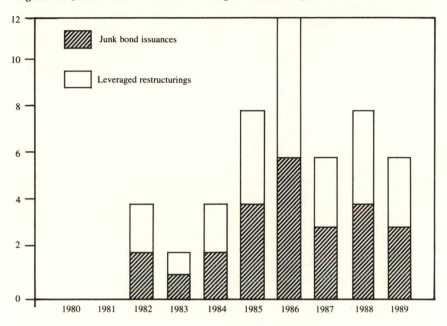

Source: Author's calculations based on data supplied by Margaret Blair and Martha Schary. Data on leverage restructuring and junk bond issues are for all firms listed on Compustat in SIC groups 281, 282, and 286 and those listed that are outside SIC groups 281, 282, or 286 but that own plants producing chemicals in the product-level data base.

and that their stocks should be selling at higher price-earnings ratios.[39] Consequently, companies initiated recapitalizations and stock repurchases in 1988 and 1989.

For example, in 1988 Quantum's concern about its low price-earnings ratio and the possibility of a takeover led it to repurchase 30 percent of its shares and significantly increase its leverage. Its total debt increase was partly paid out to shareholders and partly retained for investment in new plants and R&D. In addition, the stock repurchase was partially funded by the sale of specialty chemicals operations.

Other firms in similar positions, firms with low debt, surplus cash, low price-earnings ratios, high earnings, and large differences between breakup value and current stock price, followed similar strategies. Georgia-Gulf, another commodity chemical manufacturer, repurchased stock in 1988.[40] In 1987 Vista repurchased shares and increased debt. In 1988 Arco Chemical, Aristech, Dow, Du Pont, and Great Lakes Chemical announced share repurchases.[41] Some paid one-time dividends, such as Quantum's $50 a share in December 1988.

Figure 7-4. Industrial Chemical Company Ratios of Long-Term Debt to Total Assets (Book Value), 1979–90

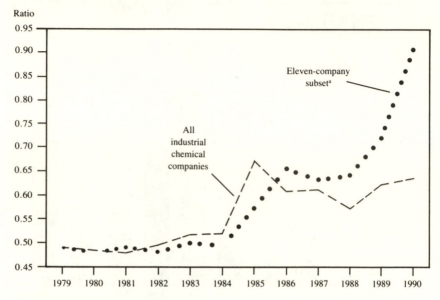

Source: Author's calculations using data from Compustat.
a. Data for some of the eleven companies are missing for some years.

Stock repurchases were, of course, not limited to chemical companies, but the activity in chemicals may have been intensified by its greater sensitivity to the business cycle. Chemical companies are prone to have excess cash at the top of the business cycle and insufficient cash at the bottom of the cycle. Within the industry, commodity chemicals are the most prone to cycles.

Summary of Financial Changes

If 1982–84 and 1986–87 were characterized by operational restructuring, late 1985–89 was characterized by financial restructuring. The sale of plants during the 1980s was more likely for those manufacturing products with slow growth, a finding consistent with the free cash flow hypothesis that these sales helped resolve conflicts of interest between managers and shareholders about changes in operation. However, there seems to be no strong connection between the decrease in production capacity or incremental capacity changes and the sale or takeover of plants.

Most financial restructuring activity in chemicals occurred after 1985.[42] Leveraged restructurings and use of junk bonds increased, as they did in manufacturing overall. The financial restructuring activity in chemicals was neither as large nor as widespread as in some other industries. It does seem to have been associated with firms involved in reorganizing the commodity chemicals part of the industry. Consistent with the increase in leverage was the dramatic increase in stock repurchases. Again the firms engaged in reorganizing commodity chemicals were involved.

Conclusions

There is strong evidence that restructuring activity during 1982–84 differed in many ways from the activity during 1986–87. And although activity in both periods seems to have been operationally driven, additional activity in 1985–89 was financially driven (table 7-12).

Capacity shutdown was highest in 1982–84, and foreign activity and sales of plants peaked in 1986–87. The timing suggests different driving forces for the two types of activity. For capacity shutdown, the 1982 recession was the catalyst; for the sale of plants, it was increased acquisitions by foreign firms and divestitures by U.S. companies. The third period, 1985–89, is the peak for financial restructurings.

Although aggregate industry-level data are extremely useful for understanding general trends and changes, analysis of these data in isolation misses the relationship between merger and acquisition activity and the general level of change and forces for change in an industry. The disaggregated data used in this chapter help show which of the suggested causes of restructuring are most applicable and for which time period. Support for the hypothesis that either mergers and takeovers or the various financial restructurings were motivated by the need to realign shareholder and manager interest is mixed. Much of the operational restructuring in the chemical industry took place before the increase in either mergers and acquisitions or leverage. The two driving forces for the operational restructuring seem to have been the recession and the entry of foreign firms into the domestic market, the latter encouraged in part by the falling value of the dollar.

Comparison with the rest of manufacturing suggests that the chemicals industry was subject to many of the same forces. One question addressed here has been whether the pattern of activity in industrial chemicals is typical of the merger wave of the 1980s. The patterns are similar even though strong differences exist. The unusual features of the chemicals industry were the severity of the recession and the extent of foreign influence, although the effect of the changing value of the dollar also

Table 7-12. Major Restructuring Events, 1979–91

Year	External Shocks	Operational restructuring	Financial restructuring
1979–80	Value of dollar low		
1981		Increase in number and value of acquisitions begins *Du Pont acquires Conoco* *Dow acquires Merrell*	
1982	Overcapacity and recession Oil prices high		
1983		Peak in number of acquisitions 100% of targets are divestitures High level of plant closures Largest incremental capacity decreases	
1984		*Vista Chemical formed through LBO of Du Pont plants*	
1985	Value of dollar high	Restructuring programs announced by 10 major chemical companies *Monsanto acquires G.D. Searle*	*Union Carbide increases debt to fend off takeover attempt by GAF*
1986	Price of oil falls Value of dollar falls	Top eight sales of U.S. chemical firms to foreign buyers Peak of targets and divestitures *Sterling founded by acquisition of Monsanto plants* *Stauffer and Chesebrough-Ponds merge* *Union Carbide divests units to pay off debt*	*IPO[a] of Aristech Chemical, Ausimont, Georgia-Gulf, Vista Chemical[a]* *Sterling Chemical junk bond issue*

Year	Industrywide events	Firm-specific events
1987	Stock market crash	Cain Chemical forms with aid of junk bonds
	Foreign companies acquire 50% of targets in chemicals	IPO[a] of Arco Chemical, Calgon Carbon, Formica, HIMONT, Wellman
	Highest plant sales in product data	
	Hoescht acquires Celanese	
1988	Dollar low	Georgia-Gulf, Dow repurchase shares
	Occidental acquires Cain Chemical	Quantum recapitalization and purchase of shares
		IPO[a] of Sterling
		Aristech repurchases shares
1989	Creation of Marion Merrell Dow with majority ownership by Dow	Quantum junk bond issue
		Du Pont repurchases shares
1990	Management buyout of Aristech financed by Mitsubishi	Georgia-Gulf recapitalizes as part of takeover defense against NL Industries
1991	Vista acquired by German firm	Monsanto repurchases shares

Source: Firm-specific information is from scholarly journals, annual reports, and articles in financial press and trade journals. Industrywide events are from author's calculations.
a. IPO is initial public offering.

affected other industries. This suggests that in general the findings may be applicable to other manufacturing industries.

Appendix

In this study the industrial chemicals industry is defined as industrial inorganic chemicals (SIC 281), plastics and synthetic materials (SIC 282), and industrial organic chemicals (SIC 286). The value of shipments in these groups accounts for 5 percent of the value of shipments in manufacturing overall and 50 percent of the value of shipments of chemicals and allied products (SIC 28). Thus the industry is a significant part of the U.S. economy. Its importance is even greater if one considers the extent to which chemicals are used in downstream production.

The first data set used in this paper is drawn from a data base covering more than 15,000 merger and acquisition transactions from 1955 to 1989.[43] These data are used to compare the restructuring activity in chemicals to that in manufacturing overall and to provide an overview of the characteristic pattern of merger and acquisition activity within the chemicals industry.[44] The chemicals industry was selected for study because an analysis of these data by industry showed that chemicals had a high rate of restructuring activity through the 1980s, both absolutely and relative to the average rate in manufacturing.

The second data set was collected to look not only at the firms undergoing restructuring but at their experience in comparison to those that remain unchanged. This required gathering comparable information on all firms in the industry. Fortunately, in the chemicals industry the product is well defined, and the complete set of manufacturers for any specific product can be easily identified.

Data were collected at the plant level on manufacturers of a well defined subset of products. These data show sales of plants and changes in capacity by product from 1978 to 1988. For this subset all producers were identified, not just the major chemical companies, and comparable data were collected for all firms. (By contrast, in the industry-level data set, firms were assigned to industry categories on the basis of their major product and, consequently, the industry-level data include only companies whose major interest is in chemicals.) The product-plant data set also includes oil companies, natural gas companies, and all other such companies with some part of their production coming from this subset of chemical products. Consequently, all restructuring activity affecting chemicals production is captured in the product-level data set, and restructured firms can be compared with those that were not.

The fifty-four products chosen for this study are listed in table 7-11. Data on the firms that produce these products are from *The Directory of Chemical Producers*, which reports U.S. production by product, firm, and plant observed at the start of each calendar year. In addition, the directory contains nameplate capacity listings for chemicals with comparatively large markets.[45] The products in the sample typically have more producers than an average product listed in the directory and are likely to be commodity-type chemicals.[46]

These fifty-four products were chosen using information on the companies involved in mergers and acquisitions. Those products for which the *Directory* gave capacities were identified for the companies involved in mergers or acquisitions. Of these, chemicals that were frequently named as being produced by firms undergoing restructuring were included in the data base. Thus the sample of products was chosen with an intentional bias: if there were any discernible patterns of restructuring, it would be in this group. Because of the requirement that capacities be listed, the sample also has an unintentional bias toward commodity-type chemicals.

Hundreds of firms produce industrial chemicals, and more than 200 produce the fifty-four products in the subset. From among these firms eleven were chosen for more detailed study. These fall into two groups. The first consists of four of the largest domestic chemical companies: Dow, Du Pont, Monsanto, and Union Carbide. The second is a subset of the firms whose primary products are commodity petrochemicals: Aristech, Cain, Georgia-Gulf, Huntsman, Quantum, Sterling, and Vista. These two groups were chosen because of their unique contributions to the restructuring of the chemical industry in the 1980s. Information on a broader range of firms was also reviewed.

Comment by F. M. Scherer

Discussing conference papers is usually an iterative process. The present case is somewhat more so than usual. Many of the original discussants' comments have been embodied in the revised version of Sarah

Lane's valuable survey, so I am left in general agreement, with only grace notes to add.

On a macroeconomic plane the merger wave surging forward during the early 1980s was unique among America's four great twentieth century merger waves. The previous three rode stock market booms. This one accelerated during a period of depressed stock prices, which in turn resulted from the Federal Reserve Board's efforts to fight inflation through high interest rates. From 1979 to 1982, it may be recalled, the Dow-Jones index averaged 888. For a would-be acquirer who recognized that sooner or later the Federal Reserve had to retreat from its tight money policy, there were bargains everywhere. As stock prices rose rapidly later in the decade, the merger wave acquired more traditional bandwagon characteristics. If you did not buy that target company today, you would have to pay a higher price tomorrow. Relaxed antitrust enforcement and financial innovations contributed to the excitement. Foreign buyers joined in during 1986 and 1987 as the dollar's value plummeted, making U.S. chemical manufacturers particularly attractive to overseas-based multinationals using strong currencies to carry out their acquisitions, especially if earnings were to be repatriated only in the distant future, when the dollar's value moved closer (if it ever does) to purchasing power parity. Previous U.S. merger waves had subsided with stock market crashes, and the wave of the 1980s was no exception. Rather than suggesting once again that there were bargains to be had, the precipitous decline of stock prices in October 1987 and mounting distress of the financial system more generally injected uncertainty into merger makers' calculations and led them to be more cautious.

In addition to the significant role of foreign acquirers, chemical industry mergers had a second special feature. As Lane demonstrates, much of the activity during the early 1980s entailed restructurings in which well-established companies sold divisions to other firms, often newly organized leveraged buyouts, that for some reason believed they could manage the units more effectively. The sell-off movement was not new. In many industries, it was well under way during the 1970s, and what occurred in the 1980s was more a mopping-up exercise. So why did it become so prominent in chemicals during the 1980s? Sell-offs, David Ravenscraft and I found, are commonly precipitated by unsatisfactory divisional financial performance.[47] Relative to the parent population from which they were selected, the merger-prone product lines Lane focuses on had sales concentrated disproportionately in organic chemicals. By my reckoning, fifty of the fifty-four product lines singled out for analysis were organics, while 24 percent of 1977 value added in the three-digit groups from which they were drawn originated in *inorganic* chemical lines. During the mid- and late 1970s, natural gas price controls (from which, to be sure, intrastate gas prices were excluded, although they were still affected by competition from substitutes) and crude oil price controls gave U.S. chemical makers a significant cost advantage over international rivals. Thus at first, American organic chemical producers were somewhat sheltered from the macroeconomic shocks triggered by the first great oil price jumps of 1973–74. But in the early 1980s the U.S. industry was hit by a quadruple whammy. Oil and natural gas prices were decontrolled, eliminating much of the input cost advantage for organic chemical makers; the second (Iranian revolution) oil shock drove feed-stock prices to unprecedently high levels, inducing demand shifts away from petrochemicals; high interest rates raised the dollar's value relative to leading foreign currencies, cheapening competitive imports; and the United States (like other industrialized nations) plunged into a severe recession. Distress led to sell-off, although the exact pattern warrants further investigation.

Lane's analysis reveals that the chemicals industry's restructuring during the 1980s did not follow exactly the "back to basics" pattern observed in other industries. Large chemical companies sold off basic chemical operations, including many in which they had long experience and substantial expertise. This differed from the experience of many 1960s-vintage conglomerates, which had acquired units they understood poorly, got into trouble, and embraced sell-off as a solution. But while simplifying operations by divesting themselves of some units, the leading chemical companies simultaneously complicated operations by acquiring higher-value-added specialty chemical units. Why the concurrent simplification and complication?

Before attempting a speculative answer, I must note a preliminary point. Lane's table 7-9 suggests a net trend toward simplification: the number of products per plant decreased by 6 percent over a ten-year period while the number of products per company decreased 13 percent. But this may be the result of a bias in sample selection. Lane's fifty-four product lines comprise for the most part relatively mature commodities. It seems plausible that the plants in question added other, noncovered products even while dropping products on the list of fifty-four. There are appreciable economies of scope in modern chemical plants. When one has the required infrastructure facilities in place—the power plant, the laboratory, a central office, water treatment facilities—it is relatively inexpensive to add further products. This, I suspect, may have occurred in the group of plants Lane surveys.

On why product proliferation and simplification movements coexisted, I can only speculate. One possibility is that U.S. conglomerate corporations have great difficulty sustaining the delicate balance of decentralized incentives and rich information flows necessary to manage complex, ever-changing product portfolios efficiently. Japanese conglomerates do better in this respect, I believe, because they invest more heavily in the generation and transmission of unbiased information—for example, through employee rotation programs and incessant after-hours executive socializing. Accurate communication is also facilitated by the loss of face that comes when one is discovered lying to one's parent managers. Unable to sustain lean operations in highly competitive basic chemicals lines, the large U.S. chemical companies sold many lines to more simply organized entities with control structures better suited to running a tight ship. With wider profit margins as a consequence of more restricted competition, specialty chemicals may have been seen as a less formidable managerial challenge by the large companies. If this is true, it remains to be explained why those firms were willing to pay the high cost of entering new specialty lines by merger rather than internal development. A stream of generous anticipated quasi rents would have to be capitalized at premium acquisition prices. The answer might be found in the expectational asymmetries that unusually high interest rates evoked. Companies with strong internal cash flow had the means to make acquisitions. If their leaders believed interest rates would fall and stock prices would rise more rapidly than the expectations embodied in the market as a whole, the makings of a deal were present.

To test these and other hypotheses, it would be useful to undertake a much more detailed analysis of individual transactions than has been possible in Lane's necessarily broad survey. Further insights about expectational asymmetries and the success of mergers would undoubtedly emerge. Du Pont's acquisition of Conoco in 1981 was probably not viewed as a chemical company acquisition at all. Rather, Du Pont had been hurt by previous petrochemical feedstock market disequilibria and believed that by integrating vertically with a major petroleum and natural gas producer it could ensure low-cost, reliable feedstock supplies. In this it almost surely erred, since the United States seems to have learned the appropriate lessons about the disruptive effects of petroleum price controls, and petroleum prices, instead of continuing to climb as many expected at the time, peaked in 1981 and then declined sharply. Thus,

Conoco was no bargain. The acquisition of Natomas by Diamond Shamrock in 1983 was even more ill-starred. Diamond Shamrock executives believed they were obtaining Asian crude oil reserves at bargain prices, but oil prices fell in subsequent years. And by purging Natomas executives with strong personal links to Indonesian government officials, Diamond Shamrock undermined a key element of Natomas's reserve-winning success.[48] Failure to foresee the decrease of crude oil and natural gas prices, and hence the resurgence of demand for petrochemical products, may also have made traditional chemical makers more willing to sell off or close down basic lines. Products such as ethylene moved from surplus in the early 1980s to shortage in the late 1980s. Monsanto's timing in its acquisition of Searle was better. Searle's most important asset was the NutraSweet patents and franchise. NutraSweet had been approved by the Food and Drug Administration for some uses in 1981 and for soft drinks in 1983. In 1985, when the acquisition was consummated, diet soft drink sales were soaring, sustaining strong growth into 1992, when the U.S. patent on aspartame expires. An analysis that could dig deeply into the managerial expectations underlying these and other acquisitions might add fascinating new insights on how the merger process works.

Comment by Philip K. Verleger, Jr.

The economic impact of the corporate restructuring of the 1980s has been hotly debated for several years. However, a definitive conclusion to the debate remains elusive, as anyone who has read all the papers in this volume will readily understand. One explanation for the ambiguity is to be found in the use of aggregate data. Data at the national or even at the industry level just do not provide conclusive evidence that can be used to accept or refute the hypothesis that restructuring had beneficial economic effects.

Sarah Lane recognizes this problem. In a valiant attempt to overcome the obstacles associated with aggregate data, she created a new data base consisting of information on the numbers and capacity of plants producing fifty-four different chemicals over a ten-year period. Using this data base she studied changes in ownership, continued operation, and additions to capacity in all of the plants listed for these specific chemicals.

One of Lane's objectives in constructing this specialized data base was apparently to test at the microeconomic level whether investment activity was adversely affected by acquisitions. Presumably, if the answer were yes, one might conclude that merger activity had led to a reduction in investment in the economy and thus had adverse effects on economic growth. Alternatively, if the results showed that the acquired firms achieved higher rates of investment, then one would be forced to conclude that the acquisitions were good for the economy.

Unfortunately, Lane is unable to reach such a conclusion. Further, a careful reader may also be unable to come to a conclusion because the presentation lacks focus. Indeed, Lane's objectives sometimes become lost in the details.

However, buried in the paper are some important findings that suggest the fear of corporate restructuring so fervently fanned by members of Congress, Ralph Nader, and others may be drastically overstated. These opponents of takeovers suggest that acquisitions such as Chevron's purchase of Gulf Oil or GM's purchase of EDS and Hughes Aircraft were unusual and harmful to the economy. Aggregate statistics on a specific industry will tend to confirm such results, even in the chemical industry, where statistics show that 3 percent of chemical firms were sold between 1979 and 1987.

Lane's microeconomic data clearly refute these views. According to her analysis, 240 firms produced 1 or more of the 54 products in her sample from 1979 to 1988. Yet only 149 of these 240 were active at the start of the period and 153 had exited from the business by 1988. In other words, there is a tremendous vitality to the industry below the surface that is not captured in macroeconomic statistics. Further, Lane's data show that 3 percent of the capacity in the industry changed hands every year and that increases in capacity in acquired plants were twice as large as decreases.

Given these findings, one might be tempted to embrace the view that mergers and takeover activity contributed to economic growth. Unfortunately, the judgment would be premature because analysis is still incomplete. I arrive at this conclusion for the following reasons:

First, the chemicals industry was undergoing a wrenching structural change in the 1970s and 1980s. The complicated nature of the change makes it almost impossible to reach any conclusions as to the impact of mergers.

Second, the structure of the industry almost defies the type of analysis Lane performs. Many of the chemicals she studies are intermediate products produced by integrated companies for use elsewhere. Often production will be shut down and a plant modified for a different use when customers downstream choose to alter outputs.

Third, Lane's method of measuring aggregate capacity makes interpretation of her results impossible.

Structural Changes in the Chemical Industry

A principal problem with the study is that Lane has chosen the wrong industry and then picked the wrong segment of the industry. She explains that she selected the chemical industry because it had experienced an unusually large number of takeovers and other restructuring events, both in absolute terms and relative to other industries. The sample of fifty-four chemical products was selected with an eye to including those goods produced by firms undergoing restructuring. This results in a bias toward product lines and plants that are actively being bought and sold. It also results, according to Lane, in a bias toward commodity-type chemicals.

The problem is that U.S. firms in the commodity chemical business suffered a serious decline during the 1980s, when they were being forced by international competition to scale back or terminate activities. Historically these companies had enjoyed unique advantages in world markets and a long period of expansion and innovation after World War II. In particular they had access to low-cost energy because of U.S. price controls on oil and natural gas. Their natural competitors in the Middle East had failed to make use of abundant supplies of natural gas. These advantages ended in the late 1970s and early 1980s as U.S. energy prices rose and new efficient capacity with access to free supplies of natural gas was built in the Middle East. Additional competition came from facilities built in Japan and Korea.

The export focus of the U.S. chemicals industry in the 1960s and 1970s helps explain the structural changes the industry endured between 1982 and 1984, a restructuring that Lane calls "operational." Between 1979 and 1984 the world economy experienced three major blows: the 1979–80 energy crisis, a worldwide recession, and a rapid increase in the value of the dollar. U.S. industry suffered two additional blows. Energy prices were deregulated and new capacity was constructed in a number of countries. Not surprisingly the U.S. chemicals industry suffered and, indeed, Lane finds shutdowns of capacity to be highest during these years. At the same time, new environmental regulations made operating in the

United States progressively more expensive. The facts are that the chemicals industry was probably the most exposed of any industry during this time because of its international focus and its reliance on energy.

Under these circumstances it is not surprising to find that large companies exited from the commodity chemicals business. It was natural to sell off facilities, especially if sale of plants would relieve the selling firm of potential future environmental liabilities.

The question a reader may ask is, "Why under such circumstances would another party purchase such assets—even an LBO operator?" Further, one might also wonder why buyers of these facilities were evidently so successful. Neither question is addressed by Lane.

My very limited examination of the purchases suggests that much of the capacity was acquired cheaply. (Lane cites Dow's write-off of $600 million, for example.) Further, it appears that the buyers were able to avoid many of the potential environmental liabilities, possibly leaving the problem to be handled in the future by the Superfund. However, the most important contributor to the success of the investments was the collapse in energy prices. At the time many of the assets were sold, natural gas—an input critical to many commodity chemical processes—cost more than $2.50 per million cubic feet. By the end of the decade some economists predicted the price might reach $4.00 per mcf. Instead, prices collapsed. Indeed, in February 1992 prices fell below $1.00. The decrease provided a strong boost to many of the investments. Profits were also obviously boosted by general economic growth in the mid- and late 1980s.

Thus the first problem that Lane has not fully addressed is the relationship between these exogenous factors and the restructuring. The industry did face the need to restructure as a result of the strengthening of the dollar, expected increases in energy prices, a weakening economy, and falling foreign demand. Under the circumstances it is hard to know whether asset sales, mergers, and liquidations aided or hindered the adjustment.

Industry Structure Problems

The complicated structure of the chemicals industry makes analysis of the type proposed by Lane almost impossible. Firms produce tens of thousands of products. New products are introduced daily and old products are continually changed. Many are produced from factories or refineries that are themselves constantly being modified. These facilities are decidedly flexible and many can produce very different product lines. Consequently, capacity, output, or utilization is very difficult to measure at any given time, let alone over time.

Analysis of the industry is further complicated because most production is captive and goes to other manufacturing processes at other facilities owned by the same firm or associated through long-term contracts. Thus productive capacity may be increased or decreased depending on a given firm's need for the intermediate output without regard to overall market conditions.

These factors result in entry and exit in Lane's data set. For example, a firm may begin producing one of the fifty-four chemicals at one of its existing plants. Presumably the firm and the plant is then added to the data base. A few years later the firm may decide to stop producing the product, either because the profits are not there or—more likely—because the product is an intermediate input to some other activity that is now being altered. When production stops, the plant and the company are removed from the data base. Lane acknowledges that changes such as these do not necessarily imply that new plants have been opened or existing plants shut down. But she notes that of the 497 "original product-plants" in the data set only 253 were left in 1988 and adds, "This finding means that almost half the plants either changed ownership or shut down production of that product at that plant."

Measurement of Aggregate Capacity

Lane's method of computing capacity changes is also confusing. The definition of industry capacity in Lane's data is explained in the notes to table 7-5—individual indexes of capacity changes were constructed for each of the 54 products and then averaged. Thus a small percentage change in capacity for a product produced in large volumes receives the same weight as a small percentage change in capacity for a product produced in small volumes. These procedures lead to the possibility that Lane's capacity index could decline when productive capacity for a chemical produced in large volumes—benzene or ethylene—had increased by 10 percent while capacity for a chemical produced in very small volumes—adipic acid—had dropped by 50 percent. Under such circumstances it is difficult to know whether mergers really have had an impact.

It would be far preferable if Lane had constructed value-weighted indexes of capacity even though the commodity prices used to compute the value weights would have been approximate. Such indexes would have made it possible to value the increased output that resulted from investment in new facilities as well as to determine the value lost from the closure or downsizing of other facilities.

Conclusion

I would like to conclude that Sarah Lane's paper provides clear and convincing proof that the corporate restructuring did or did not have an impact on the chemical industry. However, it is impossible to make such a conclusion. This comment should not be interpreted, though, to imply that the paper is a failure. It is not. Instead, the author has identified a useful direction that ought to be followed by those attempting to examine the impact of mergers and restructuring. The problem is not in the approach but in the implementation. What is required is either a study that examines all manufacturing capacity in the chemical industry or a very carefully constructed statistical sample that allows the author to state that the number of entrants, departures, and plant closings represents a true random sample of actual activity. Either approach will require a great deal of effort and substantial funding.

Notes

1. Two studies that extensively review restructuring in the chemicals industry are Joseph L. Bower, *When Markets Quake: The Management Challenge of Restructuring Industry* (Harvard Business School Press, 1986); and Kirkor Bozdogan, "The Transformation of the U.S. Chemicals Industry," in *Working Papers of the MIT Commission on Industrial Productivity*, vol. 1 (MIT Press, 1989).

2. Calculations were made using data from the M&A Database and IRS Statistics of Income. See also Margaret M. Blair, Sarah J. Lane, and Martha A. Schary, "Patterns of Corporate Restructuring," Brookings discussion papers in economics 91-1, January 1991.

3. The increases in these years were not only absolute increases but increases relative to manufacturing (see table 7-2).

4. Many of these companies have also been active in related areas. For example, in paints and coatings ICI bought Glidden one year later. Note that Unilever NV's acquisition of Chesebrough-Ponds is also classified as a chemical acquisition in the industry-level data set.

5. A plant is an actual plant at a particular location. At any plant a number of products may be produced. A product produced at a particular plant is designated a product-plant. Since there are 657 product-plants and 353 plants, there are almost 2 products per plant.

6. The data set was checked extensively to clean out all instances of name changes, to ensure that counted exits are real exits.

7. The rate of exit (number of exits divided by number of firms) for those firms in the market in 1978 was lower (42 percent) than it was for new entrants (60 percent). This is consistent with the findings of other scholars regarding the relative survival rates of ongoing firms and new entrants. See Timothy Dunne, Mark Roberts, and Larry Samuelson, "Firm Entry and Post Entry Performance in the U.S. Chemical Industries," *Journal of Law and Economics*, vol. 32 (October 1989), pp. s233–75; and Marvin B. Lieberman, "The Learning Curve, Technology Barriers to Entry, and Competitive Survival in the Chemical Processing Industries," *Strategic Management Journal*, vol. 10 (1989), pp. 431–47.

8. Those hypotheses are summarized in Margaret M. Blair and Robert E. Litan, "Corporate Leverages and Leveraged Buyouts in the Eighties," in John B. Shoven and Joel Waldfogel, eds., *Debt, Taxes, and Corporate Restructuring* (Brookings, 1990), pp. 43–89; Michael C. Jensen, "Takeovers: Their Causes and Consequences," *Journal of Economic Perspectives*, vol. 2, (Winter 1988), pp. 21–48; and F. M. Scherer, "Corporate Takeovers: The Efficiency Arguments," *Journal of Economic Perspectives*, vol. 2 (Winter 1988), pp. 69–82.

9. Capacity increases or decreases are summed across plants for a given product, and the total change is measured as a percentage of total capacity for that product; the percentage changes are then averaged across products. Unweighted averages are used so that changes in large-volume products do not dominate the reported results. My focus is on capacity decreases, but increases are included for two reasons. First, they work as a general check on the validity of the data. Second, decreases are absolute gross decreases because they are calculated at the plant level. Including gross increases allows the calculation of the net change by product.

10. Because the data are annual they did not allow identification of plants that were sold and in which capacity was immediately shut down. Such shutdowns would be attributed to the selling firms. However, for a company to buy a plant and to very quickly shut down its capacity of a particular product within the year is expected to be rare. The capacity changes are calculated for the first full year of new ownership. Capacity changes that occurred during the year of new ownership are included with increases and decreases in ongoing plants.

11. Because of the nature of the chemical production, capacity decreases will more likely occur through complete shutdown of capacity than incremental decreases.

12. These findings are consistent with those of Dunne, Roberts, and Samuelson, "Firm Entry and Post Entry Performance," pp. s233–75; and Marvin B. Lieberman, "Exit from Declining Industries: 'Shakeout' or 'Stakeout'?" *Rand Journal of Economics*, vol. 21 (Winter 1990), pp. 538–54.

13. Because the share of capacity sold and increased in the following year

averaged 0.2 percent of total capacity, and on average 3.2 percent of capacity was sold, approximately 6 percent of capacity sold underwent a capacity increase (0.2/3.2).

14. The generally long time between acquisition and divesture has not been explained. Why did it take so long for these unprofitable units to be divested? Were the acquisitions in fact a wise move in the 1960s and was there then a change in the business environment that made them unprofitable?

15. To test this hypothesis adequately, the divestitures in the 1980s would need to be matched with data from the 1960s to see if they were acquisitions from the earlier period.

16. Christopher Power, "Chemicals," *Forbes*, January 13, 1986, pp. 83–84.

17. Firms were classified into industry groups based on primary SIC. The measure of horizontal (and vertical) transactions will depend on how the industry group is defined. It is difficult to determine the biases caused by the construction of industry groups. However, chemicals is one of the narrowly defined groupings, and consequently there may be a downward bias relative to manufacturing in the measure of horizontal activity.

18. An exception is Occidental Petroleum. In 1988, Occidental acquired Cain Chemical as part of its strategy to expand its commodity chemical business. Langdon Brockinton, "How Cain Chemical Will Mesh with Oxy," *Chemical Week*, April 27, 1988, pp. 9–13.

19. Top acquiring firms were Chevron (nine plants) and Occidental (twenty-seven). Top sellers of plants were Du Pont (ten) and Gulf Oil (nine). Gulf Oil sold its plants to Chevron.

20. Michael Oneal, "The Best and Worst Deals of the '80s," *Business Week*, January 15, 1990, pp. 52–56.

21. Christopher S. Eklund and Alison Leigh, "What's Causing the Scratches on Du Pont's Teflon?" *Business Week*, December 8, 1986, pp. 60–64.

22. A second advantage of concentrating chemical plants in a few hands is that in a time of declining capacity fewer firms may mean faster exit. Exit may be accelerated because multiplant firms may be more willing to close a plant than single plant producers. See Lieberman, "Exit from Declining Industries."

23. I do not answer the question of what the newly formed firms did differently. There were obvious differences between the sellers (large conglomerates) and buyers (newly formed firms), but what led the buyers to believe that they could operate these plants more profitably? One prevalent view is that they were smaller, leaner organizations with less overhead and speedier decisionmaking ability.

24. Many of these products can be and are produced in the same plant in processes that may be linked. As a consequence, the product observations in the sample are not independent.

25. This measure does not contain information about the level of diversification overall because it only reflects the products in the data set. For firms introducing new specialized products in place of commodity products, the measure would decrease even though there would be no change in the total number of products the firm produced.

26. Sterling Chemical, for example, reduced its ratio of debt to equity from sixteen in 1986 to one by 1988, the year it went public.

27. Domestic chemical firms were also more active acquirers of foreign firms than were manufacturing firms overall. In chemicals, 6.6 percent of the number of firms acquired by domestic chemical companies were foreign, whereas 5.4 percent of companies acquired by manufacturing firms overall were foreign.

28. Dunne, Roberts and Samuelson, "Firm Entry and Post Entry Performance," looked at entry from 1967 to 1982 using census data for five-year periods. Their analysis covered all chemicals and allied products (SIC 28) including biological products, fertilizers, pharmaceuticals, and paints. They found that there were a large number of entrants, but the performance of the new firms varied significantly. New single-plant entrants had the most difficulty surviving and gaining market share; multiplant entrants did better. Entrants fared less well in the chemical industry than in the average manufacturing industry, and the surviving firms in manufacturing grew more than in chemicals. The analysis of exit in Lieberman, "Exit from Declining Industries," shows that small plants had higher rates of closure and smaller firms were more likely to exit.

29. Margaret Blair and Martha Schary in this volume test the hypothesis by analyzing whether the characteristics of industries can be used to explain the pattern of restructuring activity.

30. Lieberman, "Exit from Declining Industries." The capacity changes are calculated separately for each plant producing the product. Therefore, in any one year production of a product may increase and decrease. The capacity changes are summed for the eleven years and divided by the total capacity in 1978 to get the total percentage capacity change of each type. Even though these products are all commodity or bulk products, the final column of table 7-11 shows that they still vary from 60 million pounds of nameplate capacity for synthetic pyridines to 33.7 billion pounds for ethylene. The breakdown by product confirms that capacity increases arising from new capacity are relatively small. Instead increases tend to come from changes to existing capacity in plants already producing the product. Capacity decreases, however, arise mainly from complete shutdown of production capacity rather than from incremental changes in existing plants.

31. As would be expected new capacity in three of these four products is zero and in the fourth is very small. There are also many exits and many decreases in capacity, and these four products are below average in sales of capacity.

32. This finding is also consistent with the fact noted earlier that there are only four products in common when the list of fifty-four products in the data set is compared with the thirty declining products identified by Lieberman, "Exit from Declining Industries."

33. The finding would be expected from models of competition and profit-maximizing firms in which attrition is higher for producers of low-growth products, and high growth allows more room for both entry and continued production by existing firms.

34. W. David Gibson, "How Chemical Companies Are Playing the Restructuring Game," *Chemical Week*, January 15, 1986, pp. 20–23.

35. Leveraged restructuring events are large one-year increases in ratios of debt to assets. See Blair and Schary in this volume.

36. Data are from Margaret Blair and Martha Schary.

37. The companies are Aristech, Cain, Dow, Du Pont, Georgia-Gulf, Huntsman, Monsanto, Quantum, Sterling, Union Carbide, and Vista.

38. See, for example, Elizabeth Kiesche, "Investors Take Note: The Push to Enhance Value," *Chemical Week*, February 8, 1989, pp. 21–24; and Karen Heller, "Financial Services: Chemical Deals Get Fewer, Friendlier, and Smaller," *Chemical Week*, May 30, 1990, pp. 17–23.

39. An opposing view contended that the chemical industry typically trades at a low price-earnings ratio at the high point of the cycle in anticipation of a downturn. See Kiesche, "Investors Take Note"; and Floyd Norris, "Market Place: Cyclical Stocks Seem Depressed," *New York Times*, January 13, 1989, p. D3.

40. At least one stock analyst's view of the buyback substantiates the free cash flow hypothesis by suggesting that Georgia-Gulf had excess free cash flow and no remaining investment opportunities with sufficient returns. See Joseph F. Dunphy, "Prosperity Snags a Buyback," *Chemical Week,* October 12, 1988, pp. 9, 12.

41. Company annual reports; and Elizabeth S. Kiesche, "The Spree in Stock Buybacks," *Chemical Week,* November 23, 1988, pp. 18–20.

42. This observation is also found in the writings at the time. For example, Robert Teitelman, "Passing the Parcel," *Financial World*, February 12, 1988, pp. 36–37, suggests that early deals were harder to finance but were based more on fundamentals. Later deals were easier to finance but turned more on money than fundamentals.

43. The data set was designed to cover all merger and acquisition activity meeting certain minimum size criteria during these years. Further details of the construction of the data base and the characteristics of the data are described in Margaret M. Blair, Sarah J. Lane, and Martha A. Schary, "Patterns of Corporate Restructuring: 1955–1987," Brookings discussion papers in economics, 91-1, January 1991.

44. Data from 1988–89 were collected after the original analysis of the industry-level data was completed. While these new data were not explicitly included in this analysis, a review showed that in these two years, the volume of restructuring activity in chemicals was far below that of previous years and that the conclusions about merger and acquisition activity at the industry level can be applied through 1989. The peak years for the operational restructuring activity occur in the earlier years.

45. There are thousands of chemicals; the directory lists nameplate capacities for more than 300. See *The Directory of Chemical Producers* (SRI International, annual).

46. Total sales, price, and production data are available for thirty-nine of the fifty-four products. These thirty-nine account for approximately 20 percent of annual sales in industrial chemicals as a whole. The data base incudes major chemicals such as benzene, ethylene, and propylene, from which many derivatives are produced. Because these are produced in such large quantities, the products

in the data base naturally account for a large proportion of the value of shipments in the market.

47. David J. Ravenscraft and F. M. Scherer, *Mergers, Sell-Offs, and Economic Efficiency* (Brookings, 1987).

48. See Dorman L. Commons, *Tender Offer: The Sneak Attack in Corporate Takeovers* (University of California Press, 1985).

Financing Acquisitions in the Late 1980s: Sources and Forms of Capital

Peter Tufano

DURING the late 1980s, mergers and acquisitions reached historic peaks. Nearly 2,370 firms with an aggregate market value of $860 billion were acquired from 1987 to 1989. Rather than giving securities to shareholders of buyout targets, acquirers typically paid them in cash. They therefore needed to raise massive amounts, estimated at $565 billion to $747 billion, to make these payments (table 8-1). Bidders could obtain the required funds by draining their own cash or marketable assets, siphoning excess cash and marketable assets from the targets, or tapping investors.

This paper studies the third source of funds: the $667 billion supplied to acquirers by outside investors from 1987 to 1989. To put acquirers' financing choices in context, I compare them with the financing decisions made by nonacquirers. Three differences emerge: acquirers, especially firms financing leveraged buyouts, were more likely to tap private financing, to issue debt claims, and to make extensive use of custom-designed securities. The most striking custom-designed securities adopted by acquirers were the class of reduced cash flow (RCF) instruments that lessen or eliminate short-term requirements to pay interest or dividends in cash.

Some observers claim that RCF securities flourished because investors erred in gauging risk and return. Alternatively, the securities may have resulted from rational contracting between wealth-maximizing investors and issuers who faced severe cash flow constraints and who paid for "insurance" against short-term calamities. It is impossible to determine which of these sweeping generalizations more accurately describes why RCF instruments came to be issued. This paper documents that the RCF securities were issued almost exclusively by firms that needed the type of

I wish to thank Gordon Donaldson, Stuart Gilson, Richard Ruback, Erik Sirri, and participants at the Brookings conference. My research was supported by the Harvard Business School Division of Research and the Brookings Institution.

Table 8-1. Mergers, Leveraged Buyouts, and Other Acquisitions Valued at $50 Million and More, 1987–89
Millions of dollars

Transactions	1987	1988	1989	Total
Number	716	904	746	2,366
Value of acquired companies	249,216	371,268	239,449	859,933
Average size of transaction	348.1	410.7	321.0	363.5
Estimated form of consideration[a]				
All cash	151,087	271,678	142,594	565,359
Securities				
All equity	38,408	33,076	34,867	106,351
All debt	11	5,895	1,198	7,104
Combination[b]	59,711	60,619	60,789	181,119
Total	249,217	371,268	239,448	859,933
Minimum cash payments[c]	151,087	271,678	142,594	565,359
Maximum cash payments[d]	210,798	332,297	203,384	746,478

Source: Securities Data Company (SDC) Mergers and Corporate Transactions Database.

a. Merrill Lynch Business Brokerage and Valuation, *Mergerstat Review* (Schaumberg, Ill., 1989), p. 43, shows form of payment by value of deals. These data were applied to the SDC transactions, broken down into the same size categories, to estimate the dollar value using each form of payment method.

b. Includes cash plus securities, or assorted securities.

c. Transactions offering consideration in cash only.

d. Transactions offering consideration in either cash or combination of cash and securities.

cash flow insurance they provided, and not by other firms. Thus while the RCF contracts may have been mispriced, they were not so grossly mispriced as to be attractive to a wider group of issuers seeking to find the lowest cost funding alternatives.

Methodology and Data

This paper examines virtually all security sales (public offerings and private placements) as well as a subset of bank loans in the late 1980s. I identified capital raised to finance leveraged buyouts, other acquisitions, and nonacquisition corporate purposes, an approach that allows explicit comparisons of acquirers' and nonacquirers' external financing activities. Data are taken from commercially available data bases sold by Securities Data Company and widely used by businesses and financial analysts. The data bases claim to include all publicly registered security offerings as well as a broad sample of private placements and many commercial loans. The data on public offerings are taken from SEC filings and include only offerings in exchange for cash.[1] Private placement and loan data are from major financial institutions, which supply the information voluntarily to Securities Data.[2] Although the public, private placement, and loan data bases have information beginning in 1970, 1981, and 1987 respectively, the quality of reporting, especially for some of the variables of interest, improves markedly for more recent transactions. Therefore, this study covers 1985–89 public offerings and 1987–89 private placements and loans.

To identify whether financing is related to an acquisition, I relied on the issuer's or lender's description of the use of the proceeds. For public offerings, registrants must state how they will use the funds raised. I defined as acquisition-related those securities issues for which the primary purpose was to finance future acquisitions, to finance a current acquisition, including a leveraged buyout, or to refinance an earlier acquisition. For private placements and loan commitments, Securities Data solicits similar information from financial institutions.

Participants' assertions about the purpose of financing activities is obviously imperfect, given that cash is fungible. But because, for public offerings, a firm's misrepresentation of how it will use the funds can be a basis for lawsuits, the stated purpose is likely to reflect true use. For loans and private placements, public scrutiny by vendors and users of the commercially available data base provides firms and data vendors with modest incentives to report truthfully the use of the financings.

Trends in Financing Acquisitions

Three broad patterns characterize acquisition financing in the late 1980s. Acquirers were more likely than nonacquirers to seek funds outside public markets, raise funds through debt contracts, and use customized securities rarely used by nonacquirers. These trends were even more pronounced for firms financing leveraged buyouts.

Seeking Funds outside Public Markets

From 1987 to 1989 acquirers raised $73 billion through public offerings and $107 billion through private placements. They also secured $345 billion in bank loans and accepted $142 billion in bridge loans (table 8-2). These private markets (merchant banks, commercial banks, and purchasers of private placements) provided more than $8 of long-term and short-term financing for each $1 acquirers raised through the sale of publicly registered securities ($594 billion to $73 billion).[3]

In part, the small role played by financing raised in the public markets merely reflects the growing importance of institutional investors in the debt and equity markets. However, acquirers were more likely than nonacquirers to seek funds from private sources, as shown by comparing the

Table 8-2. External Financing Supplied to U.S. Acquirers and to All Nonacquirers, 1987–89[a]

Billions of dollars unless otherwise specified

Sources	Acquisition related	Nonacquisition related
Public offerings[b]	73.29	438.11
Private placements	107.05	414.68
Ratio of public offerings to private placement	0.68	1.06
Bank financing[c]	345.41	d
Bridge financing	141.60	d

Sources: Securities Data Company, Corporate New Issues and Commercial Loan data bases.

a. Financing is considered acquisition related if used to finance or refinance a merger, acquisition, or leveraged buyout. All other offerings are nonacquisition related.

b. Includes only offerings for cash; excludes securities offered in consideration to target shareholders.

c. Includes primarily term loans and revolving credit facilities.

d. SDC loan data are "derived from public U.S. Government filings which pertain to large merger and/or acquisition transactions, corporate financial statements of various types, and occasionally the financial press." Securities Data Company, *Commercial Loan Database Users Guide* (New York, 1989). The data base leans heavily toward collection of acquisition-related loans and therefore is not as comprehensive a source for nonacquisition-related loans.

ratio of the dollar volume of public offerings to private placements for acquirers and nonacquirers in 1987–89. Nonacquirers raised slightly more capital from public offerings than from private placements; acquirers raised only two-thirds as much from public offerings as from private placements (see table 8-2).

The preference of acquirers for tapping large pools of private capital likely reflected their need to complete deals quickly in a fast-paced, competitive market for corporate control. Perhaps the epitome of this trend was reflected in the increasing importance of bridge loans, in which bidding firms secure large short-term commitments from a small number of financial advisers. To motivate acquirers to refinance the debt quickly, bridge loans typically contained provisions that increased the interest rate quickly. For example, in 1989 First Boston extended a ninety-day bridge loan to Union Carbide at 11.5 percent. The loan could be extended every three months for up to two years; however, at each extension the interest rate increased by fifty additional basis points.[4] Despite such incentives, acquirers could not always pay off their loans, and investment banks have found themselves unwilling long-term investors: as of early 1991, Salomon Brothers still held a "temporary" bridge loan it made to Grand Union in 1989.[5]

Raising Funds through Debt Contracts

Even ignoring bank debt and bridge loans, in 1987–89 debt securities accounted for 91.2 percent of the dollar volume of all funds raised by

Table 8-3. Loans and Debt Securities Issued to Finance Acquisitions, by Type, 1987–89

	Size of commitment (millions of dollars)		Maturity of commitment (months)[a]	
Type	Mean	Median	Mean	Median
Public offerings (debt only)	165	125	160	120
Private placements (debt only)	102	40	104	96
Bank financing				
Revolving credit facilities	208	50	51	48
Term loans	253	65	66	72
Bridge loans	420	385	11	6

Source: Securities Data Company, Corporate New Issues and Commercial Loan data bases.
a. Months until maturity or, for putable instruments, number of months until investors can demand that the principal be repaid.

acquirers in public offerings and private placements.[6] In contrast, non-acquirers used public offerings or private placements of debt for 80.5 percent of all funds raised in those markets. Thus while the mid-1980s was a period in which firms generally raised funds through debt, acquirers were even more likely to issue debt.

Debt is provided through the four main channels: bridge loans, traditional bank lending, private placements, and public offerings. Bridge loans, typically credit extended by the merchant bank deal makers, are for very large sums and carry extremely short maturities. Traditional senior bank loans, structured as revolving credit and term loans, are much smaller and have longer maturities. Private placements of debt (purchased by insurance companies) and publicly offered junk bonds (bought by thrift institutions, bond mutual funds, pension funds, and insurance companies) have the longest maturity claims, with median maturities of 96 months and 120 months, respectively (table 8-3).[7]

The role of publicly issued high-yield or "junk" bonds in financing takeover contests has been discussed at length in the press. It is easy to see why junk bonds and takeovers have been seen as related phenomena. From 1985 to 1989 junk accounted for 76 percent of all publicly offered debt raised by acquirers but only 15 percent of the debt raised by non-acquirers. Put another way, in this period half of junk bond issues financed acquisitions, while only 6 percent of investment-grade debt issues financed acquisitions.

Furthermore acquisitions accounted for a rising share of the junk bond market. In 1985, only 35 percent of junk bonds were used to finance acquisitions; the rest financed other corporate business. By 1989 these fractions were nearly reversed: 60 percent for acquisitions and 40 percent for other business.[8]

Raising Funds through Tailored Securities

The category of debt instruments—even publicly offered debt instruments—comprises heterogeneous securities, including standard contracts modeled in theoretical analyses of capital structure as well as more innovative contracts. One hallmark of the capital markets of the late 1980s was the prolific pace of innovation, and in the aggregate, acquirers seemed much like nonacquirers in their use of innovative or tailored instruments. Using data collected in an earlier study, I found that for acquirers, 19.8 percent of the dollar volume of all public offerings in 1985–86 could be considered innovative as compared with 17.7 percent of nonacquirers' offerings. Unfortunately, the sample these figures are based on did not include late 1980s issues, and it used a restrictive definition of innovative securities because of the nature of the question addressed.[9] For the current study, I examined a similar but updated and slightly broader sample of innovative or tailored securities listed in table 8-A1. Under this definition, tailoring was much more likely to be used at the end of the decade. In 1985, for example, 20 percent of the value of acquirers' offerings were tailored securities; by 1989 nearly 40 percent were. Tailoring was also more common in the junk bond market than in the investment-grade debt market. Thirty-one percent of junk bond issues by acquirers but only 8 percent of investment-grade issues were tailored.

How often tailored securities were used says something about the vitality of the capital markets in the 1980s and the rapid diffusion of innovation on Wall Street. However, the tailored instruments shown in table 8-4 include a diverse set of securities. Those that reveal most about merger and acquisition transactions are those not widely used, except by acquirers. For example, among acquirers, resorting to standard cumulative, fixed-dividend preferred stock was rare; preferred stocks whose dividends floated with market rates or were reset through auctions were far more common. However, adjustable-rate and auction-rate preferred stocks were also commonly issued by nonacquirers.[10]

The clear difference between the financing choices of acquirers and other firms lay in the issuance of claims that reduced or eliminated cash payments of interest or preferred dividends. These included the following.

—Zero-coupon bonds and original-issue discount (OID) securities, for which cash interest payments are nonexistent or very small and do not change over time.

Table 8-4. Distribution of Acquirers' Public Offerings of Tailored Securities, by Type, 1985–89

Class	Instrument[a]	Percent of dollar volume
Equity	Standard contract	54.7
	Classified common	5.4
	Master limited partnership (MLP)	6.6
	American depository rights	0.7
	Paired common stock	0.4
	Euroequity	32.2
Preferred stock	Standard contract	3.0
	Payment-in-kind (PIK) preferred stock	29.8
	Adjustable-rate preferred stock	18.8
	Auction-rate preferred stock	36.1
	MLP preferred stock	8.4
	Exchangeable (nonadjustable)	3.9
Equity-linked debt	Standard (convertible) contract	66.9
	Zero-coupon convertibles (LYON)	3.2
	Convertible PIKs	1.6
	Zero-step and warrant	7.2
	Reset debt and warrant	0.5
	Straight debt and warrant	8.5
	Exchangeables	2.0
	Debt and contingent payment unit	0.4
	Mandatory capital securities	6.9
	Debt and common units	2.7
Other debt	Standard Contract	76.9
	Zero-coupon bonds	0.5
	Zero-step bonds	7.9
	PIK bonds	3.0
	Increasing-rate bonds	2.3
	Original-issue discount (OID) debt[b]	1.2
	Credit-adjusted reset bonds	3.1
	Floating rate bonds	2.9
	Extendable bonds	1.9
	Indexed bonds	0.1
	Non–U.S. dollar-denominated debt	0.3

Source: Author's calculations.

a. Italicized terms are reduced cash flow (RCF) instruments that eliminate or reduce cash interest or dividend payments in the short run relative to standard contracts.

b. Excludes other discount obligations specifically identified.

—Payment-in-kind (PIK) securities, for which the issuer has the option to pay interest or dividends, in securities or cash, for a specified period of time.

—Increasing-rate securities, for which short-term cash interest payments are set contractually smaller than long-term cash interest payments. The initial interest rate may be set at zero (called a zero-step, or split-coupon, bond) or at a positive but low interest rate.

—Credit-adjusted reset bonds, with interest rates periodically adjusted so that the bonds maintain a minimum market value. Such securities are comparable to the others in that the initial interest rate, set for one to five years, is generally equal to the minimum rate guaranteed in the long term, so that the interest rate can only rise.[11]

Unlike standard, current-pay bonds (or preferred stocks), these reduced cash flow instruments pay little or no interest (or dividends) in cash in the short run. From 1985 to 1989 the most extreme RCF securities (zero-coupons, zero-steps, and PIKs), which require no short-run cash servicing, accounted for 12 percent of acquirers' public debt issues and 30 percent of their preferred stock offerings.[12] In contrast, in the late 1980s nonacquirers chose these three types of securities for only 4 percent of their public debt issues and 2 percent of preferred stock offerings.[13] Among both acquirers and nonacquirers, RCF securities were issued more frequently by firms with lower credit ratings. RCF securities were eleven times more commonly issued by low-credit than by high-credit acquirers (15.7 percent versus 1.4 percent of all public offerings). A similar but smaller difference existed among nonacquirers.

Although RCF securities popularized by acquirers were rarely issued publicly by nonacquirers in the late 1980s, they were often issued in exchanges by financially distressed firms (which are not included in the Securities Data Company data). The early analyses of RCF securities in the mid-1980s explicitly referred to their more typical use in bankruptcy settings.[14] In fact, RCF securities were first popularized in America by distressed railroads in the nineteenth century. Railroad reorganizations produced instruments now known as PIKs, original-issue discount debt, stepped-coupon bonds, and zero-steps.[15]

LBOs and Other Acquisitions

It is misleading to consider all acquisitions in the late 1980s as being identical. Those pursuing LBOs were even more likely than other acquirers to seek nonpublic funds, use debt securities (especially junk

Table 8-5. Financing Characteristics of LBOs and Other Acquisitions, 1985–89

Characteristic	LBOs	Other acquisitions
Publicly raised funds as percentage of funds raised through loans[a]	16	31
Debt issued as percentage of all publicly raised funds	96	82
Junk debt as percentage of all publicly offered debt	100	58
Percentage of public offerings using tailored securities listed in table 8-A1	42	17
Percentage of debt securities publicly offered using zero-coupon, zero-step, or PIK	29	5[b]

Source: Author's calculations.

a. Includes term loans, revolving credit, and bridge loans.

b. For non-LBOs, 6.9 percent of the non-investment-grade debt used these three features, but only 1.4 percent of the investment-grade bonds used them.

bonds), and issue tailored securities, especially RCF instruments (table 8-5). Many, but not all, of the differences between acquisition and non-acquisition financing can be attributed to LBOs. By definition, these transactions are the most leveraged, so their reliance on debt financing is expected, and it is predictable that debt issues would not be rated investment grade. What perhaps is most striking was these acquirers' extensive use of RCF securities to fund nearly a third of the public debt raised, which significantly exceeded the use of this form of debt even by non-investment-grade, non-LBO acquirers.

Summary of Financing Trends

Extensive use of private pools of capital, reliance on debt financing, and widespread use of RCF securities differentiated acquirers' financing choices, especially in LBOs, from those of nonacquirers. These phenomena were related. Raising capital from a small number of investors made tailoring more convenient because the security offered did not need to appeal to many heterogeneous investors. Financing a business heavily with debt made it attractive to issue securities that did not require short-term cash flows.

Why did the 1980s witness the explosive use of RCF securities? Did they make any economic sense? It is easy to concoct stories as to why particular securities came to exist, but much harder to prove or disprove the claims. The most satisfying explanations are those that appeal to simple external forces such as tax or regulatory arbitrage. Unfortunately, neither taxes nor regulation seems to explain why late 1980s acquirers, especially highly leveraged acquirers, chose to issue RCF securities. Most

RCF instruments were unattractive to investors because accrued interest was taxable even if not received in cash. Furthermore, under 1989 tax law, interest paid on high-yielding RCF instruments may not be fully deductible by issuers.[16] This factor, along with the general decline of the junk bond and acquisition markets, may explain why certain types of RCF securities, especially new payment-in-kind issues, disappeared between 1989 and 1991, but it cannot explain their appearance in the first place.[17]

Why then did late 1980s acquirers and investors agree to sell and buy RCF securities and other junk bonds at all? Loosely speaking, the arguments seem to be that either everyone involved was acting rationally or else some or all of the parties acted irrationally.

That everyone was being rational appeals to deal makers and to some economists. RCF securities provided investors—often financial institutions and intermediaries—with attractive, long-duration assets akin to equity and guaranteed issuers valuable cash flow flexibility. The securities helped keep firms undergoing massive organizational change from undergoing temporary but extremely costly financial distress. That selling and buying RCF securities was irrational entails a far simpler explanation. Mutual fund managers, insurance companies, thrifts, and other investors bought RCF securities and junk bonds out of misguided hopes based on their promised returns. One well-known deal maker, after listening to an earlier version of this paper, passed me a note that provided his definitive answer: "Most mergers do not make sense. Therefore you have to use securities that the buyers do not understand and that are different from the last round of bad merger securities." Academics have adopted a similar argument, although in more restrained tones: "the increased involvement of public-subordinated lenders in these (LBO) transactions is puzzling, and would seem to represent either a degree of miscalculation or incentive problems at the institutions making the loans."[18]

My goal in the remainder of this paper is twofold: to restate the arguments underlying the different theories of why RCF securities exist and to introduce new, albeit inconclusive, evidence that questions whether the popularity of the securities was the result of gross miscalculation and improper investor incentives.

Explanations for the Popularity of RCF Securities

It is not difficult to explain why RCF securities could have been attractive to some issuers, even if fairly priced. They provided cash-flow-constrained issuers seeking to issue debt valuable financial slack that current-pay debt could not match. Buying a plant, division, or entire firm creates for the acquirer immediate, nondeferrable needs for capital, major discontinuities in management and strategy, and lower expected short-run cash flows than long-run cash flows (because of expected improvements in operations). Inadequate current cash flow relative to long-run expected cash flow virtually rules out sales of equity: because future cash flows are not known by outsiders but believed by insiders to be high, an informed insider would prefer to avoid selling equity.[19] In addition, if they issue equity, firms forgo the tax advantages of debt and fail to create tight contractual cash flow constraints that some observers believe to be critical in properly motivating managers.[20] Finally, in the case of LBOs, issuing equity would mean allowing outside participation in directing the company, which is contrary to the "going private" nature of the deals.

Issuing extensive current-pay debt to fund immediate capital needs is also not ideal. If current cash flows are smaller than expected long-run cash flows, little long-term current-paying debt can be issued without risking immediate, temporary, and costly financial distress and attendant recontracting of claims.[21] Short-term debt also exposes a cash-short firm to the risk of losing nonassignable rents because of pressure from borrowers to liquidate.[22] Finally, restrictions imposed by preexisting senior debt claims may prevent the firm from gaining access to junior funds.[23]

Thus issuing RCF securities is attractive to acquirers because it allows them to trade future cash flows for short-term cash-flow flexibility, a trade-off crucial to the modeling of the debt-equity choice. As Oliver Hart's paper in this volume makes clear, a key issue in optimal capital structure design is to ensure that inefficient liquidation is avoided. RCF securities permit firms and investors to contract to avoid short-run, inefficient liquidation in firms where long-run cash flows will be strong. In exchange for this flexibility, the issuer promises to make higher cash payments to investors later—if it survives.

From the investors' perspective, RCF securities may be reasonable investments because they satisfy a particular need for long-duration assets and promise greater rewards for bearing greater risk. Investors' liabilities sometimes dictate their preferences in assets. Pension funds with long-duration, fixed-dollar liabilities, for example, fueled the demand for long-duration, fixed-dollar instruments.[24] RCF securities may have provided another means of satisfying this demand, much like the slow-pay tranches of collateralized mortgage obligations. RCF bonds also enable investors to earn higher promised yields than current-pay bonds.

For example, in late 1988 zero-step debt promised 153 basis points more than the next senior cash-pay bonds of the companies, and PIKs promised 225 basis points more.[25]

Investors acted reasonably only if these promised yields were large enough to offset the increased likelihood of distress and default. No academic study has specifically examined the risk and return offered by RCF securities, but researchers have examined broad samples of junk bonds. They have documented realized default rates and returns but could not distinguish bad pricing from bad luck.[26] Studies of cash flow coverage have documented that junk bonds became weaker, but they could not conclude whether later deals were overpriced, earlier deals underpriced, or the fundamental risk-reward relationship had shifted.[27] Other studies have suggested that investments in RCF securities were relatively good deals for investors. One study that used option valuation techniques to analyze a sample of deferred-coupon instruments found that they were underpriced.[28]

In principle, RCF securities may have been issued primarily because they were grossly mispriced. Investors may have been confused, or they may have been operating rationally under perverse accounting and regulatory mandates, such as thrift institutions' apparent risk-taking incentives under the protection of deposit insurance. Alternatively, RCF instruments may have been fairly priced contracts whereby investors agreed to sell issuers valuable and much needed cash flow flexibility. Which of these interpretations is closer to reality depends on whether investors received an appropriate return for purchasing the securities.

Patterns of Usage as Indicators of Mispriced Securities

During the 1980s, chief financial officers and their bankers flocked to issue debt securities that they believed would save even a few basis points in interest. Once the tax advantages of zero-coupon bonds became evident in the early 1980s, scores of firms issued them. In the mid-1980s minor discrepancies in exchange rates, along with an active swap market, induced U.S. firms to issue bonds in foreign currencies to produce modest savings in all-in costs. The firms most likely to take advantage of perceived, temporary market opportunities were drawn from a small roster of large, sophisticated, frequent borrowers. By this logic, if RCF securities in the late 1980s existed because of gross mispricing, opportunities to save even a few basis points would have likely attracted a broad group of sophisticated issuers.

But if RCF securities were not overpriced, if they were costly "disability insurance policies" by which issuers could buy cash flow flexibility before they ran into trouble, most firms would choose not to overinsure and pay premiums for unneeded flexibility. If the insurance was costly, the most likely issuers of RCF securities would have been firms with the tightest short-term cash flow constraints.

By this logic, observing which firms issued RCF securities provides indirect evidence on the degree to which these securities were mispriced. Issuance of RCF securities by disparate issuers would support the contention that issuers capitalized on investors' excessively optimistic valuations. Issues of RCF securities only by firms with little cash flow would be consistent with RCF securities' being costly and not grossly mispriced insurance policies that firms with large cash flows avoided buying.

The discussion earlier in this paper made clear that RCF securities were not randomly issued in the late 1980s. They were more likely to be issued by firms with lower creditworthiness and greater leverage. Yet more to the point, if RCF securities truly were like disability insurance policies rather than grossly mispriced offerings, the acquirers most constrained by cash flow would have been the most likely issuers. A direct test of whether RCF securities were issued primarily by firms with large immediate capital needs and relatively low short-run cash flows requires firm-level, cross-sectional data. Therefore, I collected from the SDC Mergers and Corporate Transactions Database a sample of thirty-two buyouts of firms valued at more than $50 million, announced between 1987 and 1989, that had issued some public debt.[29] I tested whether the issuers of RCF junk bonds had even weaker short-term cash flows relative to their immediate financing needs than did issuers of current-pay junk bonds.

Two variables—bid premiums and cash flow coverage—measured firms' immediate funding needs relative to current cash flow. In a competitive takeover market, prices paid for target firms reflect bidders' expected long-run cash flows from running the target. The prebid price reflects the market's value of the cash flows under existing management. A larger bid premium reflects bidders' expectations of greater increases in the target's cash flow. Thus larger premiums indicate larger immediate needs relative to current or historical levels of cash flow. The second measure compares bidders' valuations of the firm to the target's recent

Table 8-6. Characteristics of Large Firms That Issued Public Debt Securities to Finance an LBO, by Type of Debt, 1987–89

Characteristic	Firms issuing zero-coupon, zero-step, or PIK bonds[a]	Firms issuing only current-pay debt[a]
Value of firms (millions of dollars)		
Mean	3,627.9	751.9
Standard deviation	7,148.8	689.1
Buyout premiums[b]		
Mean (percent)	57.7	37.3
Standard deviation (percent)	30.0	29.1
t-statistic[c]	−1.922[d]	
Buyout cash flow multiple[e]		
Mean	9.57	8.68
Standard deviation	2.40	2.65
t-statistic[c]	−0.949[f]	

Source: Author's claculations based on Securities Data Company data base.

a. Data in each column are for sixteen firms with values of more than $50 million.

b. Stock price paid by acquirer divided by stock price four weeks before buyout announcement.

c. t-statistic of one-tailed test of null hypothesis that the mean value of the variable (buyout premiums, buyout cash flow multiple) for firms issuing RCF securities is no larger than for issuers of current-pay junk debt.

d. Can reject null hypothesis (that firms issuing RCFs pay smaller buyout premiums) at 5 percent level of confidence.

e. Bidder's valuation of target divided by target's historical cash flow. Valuation of firm calculated as market value of equity (calculated at the takeover price) plus assumed debt. Cash flow of target as measured by its earnings before interest, taxes, depreciation, and amortization for the twelve months before the leveraged buyout.

f. Can reject null hypothesis (that firms issuing RCFs pay smaller buyout cash flow multiples) at 20 percent level of confidence.

accounting cash flow. The bidder's valuation was measured by the equity, valued at the price of the stock at takeover, plus assumed debt (at book value). The target's recent cash flow was measured by the previous twelve months' earnings before interest, taxes, depreciation, and amortization (EBITDA). Firms whose bids implied a larger multiple of current cash flow were those whose bids were predicated on larger increases in the target's cash flow.

Table 8-6 compares firms that issued RCF bonds to those that issued only current-pay bonds. The RCF issuers were larger, but more important, they had measurably weaker cash flows relative to immediate cash needs. Issuers of RCF securities paid larger premiums and larger buyout cash flow multiples than did LBO issuers of only current-pay debt. This evidence further documents that the pool of RCF issuers was very limited: not only were RCF issuances drawn almost exclusively from acquirers, especially issuers financing LBOs, but even among LBO issuers, RCF issuance was concentrated among firms with the greatest cash flow constraints. While I do not deny that RCF securities may have been mispriced, this pattern of usage suggests that they were not so grossly mispriced as to attract a wide variety of issuers.

Discussion

The extensive use of RCF securities to support high-priced acquisitions raises three sets of provocative and largely unanswerable questions about how the supply of funds influenced the merger market. The first concerns what the merger market of the late 1980s would have looked like had RCF securities not existed. If investors had not been willing to buy RCF securities, would as many acquisitions have taken place? If so, would acquirers have paid less for their targets? Would they have structured these transactions differently—for example, as stock deals? What types of current-pay debt or equity would have been used instead of the missing RCF securities? Did the availability of RCF securities fuel especially aggressive acquisition activity or did aggressive acquirers demand that financial designers and marketers structure RCF securities?

Most of these questions will remain unanswerable. However, it is certainly true that the existence of available financing in the form of RCF securities, other junk bonds, and bridge loans and an active market for selling assets, divisions, and whole companies facilitated large acquisitions. The financial logic for many deals whose projected cash flow could not meet forecast interest obligations was the hope of quickly selling off assets, reducing debt, and having an interest holiday through RCF borrowings.[30] The existence of willing junk bond buyers, RCF investors, and bridge lenders was a necessary but not sufficient condition for an active merger market. The precise form by which financial support was made available could have been very different. Remember that the market for mergers was very active in the 1960s and earlier, when junk bonds, RCF securities, and bridge loans were not significant forces. Thus one cannot leap to the conclusion that in the absence of RCF securities fewer or different mergers would necessarily have occurred.

The second set of issues concerns the motives of the investors in RCF securities. For observers who believe that acquisitions in the late 1980s were taken to unreasonable limits fueled by easy access to money, it seems puzzling that the capital markets, which academics think of as a disciplining force, bought RCF securities and willfully encouraged bidders, even those with the highest cash flow multiples. Were the RCF securities inherently poor investments dominated by other securities?

First, recall that RCFs were the junk-debt instruments of choice primarily for LBOs, not for other acquisitions; in LBOs, issuers' financial choices were constrained. As a result, investors' choices were also limited. An investor hoping to bet that a firm would succeed could typically not buy stock but could buy one of the firm's bonds. Among these bonds, both current-pay and RCF bonds offered limited upside returns, but the RCF varieties gave investors greater chances of earning higher returns, albeit at higher risk.

For example, consider one particular LBO. In its 1989 acquisition of TW Food Services, TW Holdings issued both discount debentures (in the form of zero-step bonds) and current-pay bonds. The zero-steps were to pay no cash interest until November 1994 and require no sinking funds until 1999. The current-pay bonds were to pay regular cash interest, be subordinated to the discount bonds, and include no mandatory sinking fund. Otherwise the two bonds had the same maturity, optional redemption features, and covenants. Despite their junior status, the current-pay bonds promised a yield 200 basis points lower than the senior, zero-step bonds. If TW does not default, it will pay—and the zero-step investors will receive—200 basis points annually for the cash flow flexibility bought and sold.[31]

According to popular wisdom, the deferral of cash payments in the zero-step "juniorizes" the RCF instrument (despite its legal seniority), and its investors will fare worse if the firm defaults before maturity. [32] This is not necessarily correct. Even if TW defaults, the RCF instruments may produce realized returns superior to the current-pay bond for two reasons: their higher promised return if the firm survives and their higher recovery rate on principal in bankruptcy because of their seniority. Suppose TW defaults in 1993 and both creditors receive $0.32 for each dollar of principal owed.[33] The current-pay holder realizes an annualized return of −0.1 percent and the zero-step holder a return of −4.4 percent. Suppose however that the firm survives five years longer, to 1998, then defaults. The zero-step holder realizes a 5.8 percent return but the current-pay holder a 5.3 percent return. In general, the RCF security produces superior returns the longer the firm survives, and its investors face no reinvestment for the first five years.

Thus if one wants to understand why insurers, pension funds, and mutual funds bought RCF instruments, one must understand this precise pattern of risk and return: RCF bonds threatened bigger losses for early default but smaller losses for later default, larger returns if no default, and lessened reinvestment risk. Furthermore, all other things being equal, firms that issued RCF securities were less likely to default than firms issuing current-pay debt instead. An investor optimistic about TW's future may have preferred to buy equity in the firm or, if forced to buy debt, to buy the RCF securities. For betting on the rising fortunes of this firm, RCF securities apparently offered a useful alternative to current-pay bonds. One cannot easily conclude that these securities were in some sense dominated by other securities available to investors, and thus one cannot conclude that their buyers clearly erred by purchasing them.

The last set of issues about how the supply influenced the merger market concerns the incentive effects of RCF securities. Ultimately, these securities commit managers to make large cash payments. Therefore in the long run they remove cash flow slack. If they work as intended, RCF securities encourage managers to focus on long-run value as opposed to short-run cash flow and avoid costly but needless temporary financial distress and financial recontracting.

However, managers of firms that have been "unlucky" in the short run and that would have been bankrupt if current-pay debt had been issued may have perverse incentives if they issue RCF securities. Until the securities' payback demands begin to mount, managers have freedom and incentives to take on very risky projects. Of course, firms are monitored by bank lenders and by holders of private placements as well as by their equity holders, who are often sophisticated LBO associations with long-run interests in the firm. Holders of RCF junk bonds may ride free on other claimants' monitoring, especially because other claimants tend to hold large illiquid interests in the firm and hence are motivated to watch the actions of management closely. Free riding will protect junk bond holders only if their interests and those of the other monitors are perfectly aligned. But given inevitable conflicts among claimants, their interests are likely to be at odds. Ultimately, whether the structures set up to finance acquisitions provide proper incentives for managers to maximize value is an empirical question that future research must address.

I have attempted to document in clear terms how acquisitions were financed in the late 1980s. The anomaly most striking is the extensive use of instruments that gave issuers much cash flow latitude. It is tempting to look at this practice and claim that stupid money drove bad acquisitions. Perhaps so. However, my view of the firms that did and did not issue RCF securities does not support this conclusion. Although these instruments may have been mispriced, they appear not to have been grossly mispriced, and they had the potential to meet the economic needs of issuers and investors.

Table 8-A1. Standard and Tailored Securities Issued in U.S. Public Markets, 1985–89

Type of contract	Standard forms	Tailored forms
Debt	Fixed-rate coupon	Floating-rate securities Indexed securities Reset securities Increasing rate securities
	Current coupon-paying	Zero-coupon bonds Original-issue discount (OID) bonds Zero-step bonds Payment-in-kind (PIK) bonds
	Fixed-maturity	Extendable debt
	Local currency	Non-U.S. dollar-denominated debt
Equity-linked debt	Convertible debt	Debt plus warrants Mandatory convertibles Exchangeable bonds Debt and stock units Debt and contingent payment units Tailored debt (above) with convertible feature
Preferred stock	Cumulative, nonconvertible, fixed-dividend preferred stock	Adjustable rate preferred stock Auction rate preferred stock PIK preferred stock Exchangeable preferred stock
	Convertible fixed-dividend preferred stock	Master limited partnership preferred stock
Common stock	Single class	Master limited partnership Classified common stock Paired common stock
	Domestically issued	Euroequity American depository rights

Comment by Robert Vishny

Peter Tufano's paper has two goals. The first is descriptive: it documents very precisely how acquisitions in the late 1980s were financed, focusing particularly on ways that financing used by acquirers was different from nonacquirer financing. That is the principal benefit of the paper. The second goal is to say something about capital structure in general and about the unique characteristics of acquisitions that have led to the use of specific kinds of innovative contracts. The paper delivers less on this second theme. What was it about late 1980s acquisitions that made these securities particularly appropriate, and, in general, what does this tell us about optimal capital structure? This second goal is obviously a much more difficult problem, and that is where I will focus most of my comments.

The three principal findings about the pattern of acquisition financing are, first, there was much more use of high-yield, risky debt in acquisitions in the late 1980s than in nonacquisitions, or in acquisitions in the earlier part of the 1980s. Second, there were more private placements, and more of the public issues went to large institutions rather than to small holders. Third, there was more tailoring of securities used in acquisitions, particularly more use of deferred interest and deferred-dividend securities.

The focus of Tufano's paper is on the third, the tailoring of securities to defer interest. Let me note that these contracts are not really that innovative. Take zero-coupon bonds, for example. In leasing markets schedules of lease payments often increase over time. Adjustable-rate home mortgages (ARMs) with teaser rates are common, especially in cases of high inflation because inflation creates a high rate of growth of nominal income over time. The ARM gives the customer a teaser rate and then adjusts it. In effect, the lending is tied to the buyer's growth in money income according to the consumer price index. So these contracts have existed for a long time, as has the theory behind them, first articulated in the tilt model of Modigliani and Lessard.[34] And these contracts have been used in ways other than for acquisitions.

Second, the theory that deals with the problems Tufano addresses is well developed. Myers wrote about the underinvestment problem. And papers by Diamond, Hart and Moore, and Harris and Raviv discuss keeping managers on a tight rein so they do not waste money.[35] These authors also discuss the balance between being able to liquidate the firm when it becomes less efficient and making sure that liquidation does not occur too soon.

Finance theory has also dealt with the problem of lenders who want to be able to pull the rug out from under management to get their money back as a precondition for lending in the first place. The tighter the rein on the manager, the greater the chance that lenders will be able to get their money back at the appropriate time. But inefficient liquidation is more likely when multiple creditors fight with each other.

These issues have been extensively discussed. So we can understand the timing of the required payments in terms of the kind of constraint lenders want to put on management, and also the liquidation value of the firm. Do lenders give management two years to play with the money, because they know that in two years they can fire the management and there will still be substantial collateral left if they need to sell the assets?

Theories that address these issues explain contracts that look like the ones Tufano describes, contracts that give management leeway but retain the right to force a liquidation later.

The new contracts, when viewed as part of a package including bank debt and public debt, may actually be putting management on a much tighter rein, however. The payment-in-kind (PIK) bonds are only part of the total picture. We need to know what the whole structure of the deal looks like, the combination of public and private securities. These deals usually entail a lot of bank debt, and that bank debt had very fast principal repayments in the late 1980s. So it may very well be that when the fast principal repayments on the bank debt are combined with the PIK, the total package has the same structure of payoffs over time—there is just divided labor. The banks have the primary responsibility for carrying the stick, since they are a single party, and they enforce the covenants. The security holders have something more like an equity claim with deferred payments, the PIK bonds.

So it is not clear that PIK bonds, when viewed in the context of the entire deal, have resulted in more slack for the firm. They may for a few years, but in terms of five to seven years, the whole deal is putting management on a tighter rein. The PIKs are used to loosen that rein, and to assign the task of collecting the money quickly to the senior lenders who might be best able to do that.

The other possibility is that the pattern of payments is hump-shaped. For the first couple of years there is very little in the way of required payments because, perhaps, the lenders are counting on asset sales. They give managers a couple of years to do an orderly sale or a couple of years to do well with the assets, but if the managers do not, the lenders can force them to go out and sell the assets.

Then, over five to seven years, the lenders are going to require everything back. The reliance on asset sales in this market may actually encourage leeway at the beginning, but a much more stringent payment schedule over five to seven years.

Finally, I want to go back to the three key facts: lots of risky debt, a smaller number of creditors, and deferred interest. Are these really different facts? Or are they intimately related? Do these things always go together?

One would think that deferring interest and deferring dividends on preferred stock is only a relevant concern for a company that is highly leveraged. If it does not issue junk bonds, it has a low probability of default and does not have to worry about liquidity. Perhaps the reason firms that have been bought out need to have PIK bonds in the first place is simply that they have much riskier debt and are much tighter on their coverage of earnings to interest. It is not so much that the uncertainty of their cash flows has risen, but that a lot more interest is due. They are much closer to the border. This suggests that to understand what is going on one would want to examine data not just by acquisition or nonacquisition or LBO and non-LBO, but in terms of the riskiness of the debt, and then determine the extent to which PIK bonds are used.

Other ways to look at the data would be on the basis of how much bank debt is used or the importance of asset sales. Simply looking at acquisitions and nonacquisitions is too much of an apples and oranges comparison. They differ in so many ways that it is difficult to know what the fundamental differences are that are driving the use of the financial contracts. I am suggesting, then, a cross-sectional analysis that shows how deferred-interest securities are related to characteristics such as high leverage, the reliance on asset sales, the extent of bank debt, and how fast the principal repayment on the bank debt is.

The three facts may be related in other ways. With a small number of investors it is, obviously, much less costly to tailor securities. So perhaps the tailoring has increased because there are fewer investors, and maybe the number of investors is smaller because transactions occur quickly and there is no time for a public issue. It could also be that the number of investors has been reduced to facilitate tailoring.

Tufano still has some work to do to show exactly why it is that these securities were resorted to and what is unique about acquisitions.

Comment by Robert Johnson

Peter Tufano has presented an empirical analysis that encourages hypotheses about the structure of merger and acquisition financing. Detectives Frank Gannon and Joe Friday from "Dragnet" would be very pleased that the paper leads off with, as they used to say, "just the facts." But Tufano also seeks to explain some of what the facts suggest about corporate acquisitions and the structure of the capital market.

The paper is organized into three parts. At the outset Tufano presents aggregate data on the channels of acquisition-related financing and compares them with nonacquisition financing methods. The results are that acquirers rely much more on debt issuance (rather than equity issuance) to raise funds than do firms raising funds for nonacquisition purposes, and acquirers are more likely to draw upon intermediated and privately placed funds than are firms raising funds for nonacquisition purposes.

These two empirical tendencies reflect decisions made by acquiring managers. The choice of debt issuance instead of equity may indicate that the managements of acquiring firms are concerned about losing control of the firms and being thrown out themselves if they offer too much of themselves to the market after a provocative act (such as making an acquisition that the market does not like). A second, widely asserted motivation, is that the managements of acquiring firms may not believe that outside stockholders understand the possibilities in the proposed acquisition, and therefore undervalue the stock of the target company. This may lead to an undervaluation of the stock issuance of the acquiring company as well because the market does not perceive that the company is onto a good thing.

Regarding the second empirical finding, that acquirers were more likely to use intermediated or privately placed funds, I would like to construct two hypotheses. First, the use of these channels of fund raising may have been motivated by the desire for secrecy, to keep other potential acquirers off guard. Public issuance of bonds or stocks, especially in a climate pregnant with the possibility of takeover, signals an impending move and leads to an increase in the price of the target firm or tips off potential targets, which can then begin to plot a counterstrategy. Time may also have been an important consideration in takeover attempts, and bank loans, in particular, may be a slightly more rapid means of arranging funds.

Second, greater reliance on intermediated funds may be related to the demand for strategic advisory services from financial institutions. Although large investment banks could arrange for public offerings of securities or provide the strategic advisory services as stand-alone products for a fee, the complementary nature of the advisory services and capital-raising services may have helped produce this result.

The second section of the paper discusses the use of custom-tailored securities in acquisition financing. Tufano again illustrates that reduced- or deferred-cash-flow instruments are more prevalent as a means to finance acquisitions, particularly leveraged buyouts, than they are in non-acquisition financing, and more prevalent in noninvestment grade than in investment grade financing.

Before presenting his own hypothesis on the motivation behind these results, Tufano considers two possible explanations—tax advantages and the possibility that these securities are a cheaper source of financing. The latter might be true because investors find that they fill a special niche in their investment portfolio. Neither explanation appears to stand up to scrutiny, though the tax argument will be put to a test if and when the grand-fathering provisions of the Revenue Reconciliation Act of 1989 expire.

The third part of the paper attempts to make sense of these facts. The difficult question to answer from the perspective of neoclassical economic theory is, "Why don't they just go to the bank and get a loan if they have temporary adjustment difficulties?" Here the word temporary must be underlined.

Tufano suggests that discontinuous or lump sum financial distress costs may account for the prevalence of deferred cash flow instruments in takeovers. He makes a good case for the possibility that there is a transitory change in business practice during the period immediately following acquisitions, and that these changes could impinge on cash flow. What is difficult to explain is the need to arrange the financing ex ante rather than on the fly. Intertemporal arbitrage would suggest that one should be indifferent between the two methods of avoiding the lump sum distress costs.

I have only two tentative thoughts on this question. The first pertains to the question of priority of claims in the event of a bankruptcy and the second has to do with the market for managers.

When one arranges a large cash-deferred financing, economic theory would suggest that investors look at the probability distribution of returns and then decide on a price for the security that compensates them adequately for the risk. A standard bond must be serviced with interest payments in the period immediately following the acquisition, and failure to make the payment will result in either bankruptcy or another loan. Holders of a second loan will stand in line behind the holders of the debt financing arranged at the time of acquisition. But the marginal lender faces a significantly higher rate of default risk than does the average lender. That is without even drawing any inferences about the likely success of the project based on the information conveyed by the firm seeking additional financing. In practice, that marginal lender is likely to believe that if the company needs to borrow again, this has implications for the probability distribution of success for the firm. That will tend to increase the cost of marginal finance even further.

Now all this could be theoretically computed by the borrowing firm ex ante and would increase its appetite for the cash-deferred instruments. In effect, the borrower figures it will have to pay the lump sum costs associated with a cash flow shortfall in any event. Either the marginal lender gets it or the repo man does. Using backward induction, these possibilities are likely to be reflected in the price of the initial security and would tend to support the idea that the custom tailored instrument would be expensive relative to the debt contract using "fair value approximations."

What I am suggesting is that the borrower and lender are sharing the benefit of avoiding the costly situation that will arise in any event if cash flow cannot meet debt service in the initial stages of business for the newly restructured firm. A sense of proportion is missing here, and without a sense of the magnitude of the lump sum bankruptcy costs or the increase in the cost of borrowing at the margin once a cash flow deficiency arises, it is difficult to know how significant this type of explanation is. I would be curious to learn by how much the instruments using deferred cash flow exceed fair value estimates for a security to see if the differential appears reasonable when compared with bankruptcy costs.

The second hypothesis that I find attractive relates to the fixed costs of bankruptcy from the eyes of the managers. Once again they are the decisionmakers. If an acquisition is flagged as sour by the business press because the firm misses an interest payment, the reputation of the managers might be impaired. If they lose their jobs because of a bankruptcy they will then be associated with a failure. If they stay with a troubled firm, anyone bidding for their services may wonder about their ability. Or potential employers may bid less for them because the bargaining power of these managers has deteriorated. In either case the desire of managers to maximize earnings and avoid sending bad signals about themselves to the market may increase the attractiveness of securities using deferred cash flow to the people making the decisions.

Perhaps the cash flow deficiency is transitory and the manager may be the Babe Ruth of his area. But it is hard for an outsider to discriminate between bad luck and bad ability, and the manager would pay the price.

Although it may be better to be lucky than good, it is better to be good and lucky than just lucky. As baseball team owner Branch Rickey used to say, "Luck is the residue of design." Perhaps the development of the custom tailored securities by acquirers is evidence that they are good, and that they are attempting to design the environment in such a way as to permit them to avoid being unlucky.

General Discussion

Carl Ferenbach noted that it is difficult to make a trading market in public debt issues of less than $100 million. There were plenty of publicly registered high-yield issues that were smaller than that in the 1980s, but markets were not made in these, and investment banks did not like to take the risk of a public distribution of these smaller issues. For firms that could issue debt in large enough quantities, bonds could be issued without covenants, and on a rate-only basis. Thus this was a relatively cheap source of capital, with some issues priced as low as a yield to the purchaser of 13 percent.

By contrast, Ferenbach noted that most debt for acquisitions consisted of smaller, privately placed issues and that much of this debt was bought by insurance companies and later by pension companies. This debt generally had equity that enhanced the return to the purchaser, or conversely, cost the issuer more. The nominal return on these smaller instruments was typically around 25 percent.

Charles Schultze observed that if the purpose behind most LBOs was to put pressure on managers by committing them to pay out cash flows, then it would be important to be able to distinguish effects on cash flow performance that are permanent and those that are transitory. The financial instruments Tufano describes, he said, appear to provide room for transitory slippage in cash flow performance, while still maintaining pressure over the long term.

Schultze also suggested that, to the extent that the success of the transactions was premised on asset sales whose timing was uncertain, the appropriate financing tool would have been medium term financing with call options that would enable the issuers to get out from under the debt as soon as they could sell off the relevant assets. Tufano responded that bridge financing used in many of the transactions actually served this purpose. Although bridge financing instruments had very short-term maturities, they were callable by the firm at any time.

Stephen Roach was also concerned about the distinction between permanent and transitory cash flow fluctuations. Roach claimed that his own work shows that LBOs, mergers, acquisitions, and corporate debt growth in general, were concentrated in industries with good cash flow stability over the long term. In particular, while public utilities, business services, and nondurable goods manufacturing account for only 30 percent of GNP, they accounted for about 70 percent of the overall growth in corporate debt service in the 1980s.[36] Firms in these industries, he argued, are the most capable of servicing high debt in the long term, although they may face short-term cash flow shocks while they go about the business of restructuring through asset sales or other types of consolidation. Sarah Lane added that it would be useful to look at Tufano's data by industry to see whether tailoring was more heavily used in some industries than in others and how those differences relate to other industry characteristics.

Frank Lichtenberg said that, according to his research, firms that are takeover targets typically have declining profitability in the five years before they are taken over. He suggested that it would be interesting to test whether in fact the firms that used deferred interest instruments also tended to have higher growth in cash flow following the acquisition.

Bronwyn Hall commented on the similarity between the forms of contract described by Tufano and the types of mortgages available now, adding that the timing of both financial innovations is roughly contemporaneous. Both are late 1970s and early 1980s innovations. But Martin Lipton pointed out that highly leveraged securities and watered stock were used in the railroad consolidations of the 1870s and again at the turn of the century in the creation of U.S. Steel and other large oligopolistic firms. Again, warrants, various kinds of subordinated instruments, and so-called Chinese paper were used in the merger wave of the 1960s that created the big conglomerates. "Historically in the United States each wave of intense merger activity was essentially accomplished with innovative and highly leveraged securities," he said.

But the unanswered question about the use of these securities, Sidney Winter noted, is whether the fancy securities were an important causal factor, helping to explain the surge in overall merger and takeover activity, or whether they were "a frill on the edge that affected the form the activity took, but not the substance."

Hall proposed a "spread-sheet theory of financial contracts" to explain why these innovations became so popular in the 1980s. "It's just a lot easier to cook these things up," she said. "You could have used a big computer to do it twenty years ago, but most people, especially the customers, didn't have big computers that they could use to analyze the alternatives." Nowadays, she said, it is very easy for a manager to sit at his desk and calculate the expected values of complex financial contracts under different cash flow assumptions or different assumptions about interest rate trends.

Robert Johnson agreed, adding that technology makes it possible for financial managers to explore more possibilities, and "the management above them is comfortable because they can see an eight-and-a-half by eleven page that tells them how it all nets out."

Tufano responded by noting that the total package of financing for merger transactions is usually like a collateralized mortgage obligation and that the difference between these packages and what we normally think of as debt and equity is that the residual claims are divided up in different ways. "Instead of slicing them up into fixed claims and variable claims," he explained, "they are divided up according to when the firm can pay."

Barrie Wigmore expanded on this point, noting that any equity used to finance an acquisition has an option value. In early LBOs, he said, about 30 percent of the capitalization was equity. Since the LBO buyer paid a premium for these shares, he was, in effect, paying a high price for the option value in the equity. Over time, however, the LBO organizers were able to sell securities at higher and higher costs to themselves, but they were able to reduce the amount of equity they bought, and thereby reduce what they were paying for the option. "I think they were also raising the strike price of the option," Wigmore noted, "but mostly they were reducing what they paid for the option itself." In effect, Wigmore argued, "they actually got debt holders to pay option prices for the assets underlying the debt."

Nonetheless, Tufano said he remained puzzled by the question of why these particular forms were chosen. Why didn't firms simply refinance when they got into a cash flow squeeze?

Martha Schary and Wigmore both suggested that many firms in the nonacquisition category in Tufano's data might be undergoing changes that make them more like the acquisition firms than one might at first suspect. Public-company restructurings usually took place because there was an acquisition proposal on the table, and the restructuring was just a way for the target to do the same thing to itself that the acquirer was going to do, Wigmore explained.

Wigmore also noted that there was a severe, broad-based decline in credit quality during the late 1980s. Early in the decade, he said, junk bonds had pro forma interest coverage ratios of 2 or 3, but in the period covered by Tufano's data, the pro forma interest coverage ratio averaged around 0.6. The average cash flow before capital expenditures was slightly over 2 percent of outstanding debt, he added, which was scarcely enough to cover gross capital expenditures necessary to maintain existing equipment. So, he said, "as a starting base, these issuers were logically unable to pay more than about two-thirds of the interest that was due. The cash flow that was available here was very close to zero."

Wigmore observed that the risk aversion of various groups of investors buying these securities "declined almost inexplicably and very dramatically," with yield spreads between junk bonds and AAA-rated securities dropping from around 700 or 800 basis points in more normal times to as low as 200 basis points in the late 1980s.

Paul Francis argued that the reason so much leverage capital was used was very simple: It was "extraordinarily cheap capital, particularly on an after-tax basis, and particularly in the case of junk bonds, where there were virtually no operating restrictions placed on the companies." Noting that he had spent the past five years working for a leveraged buyout company that was adding leverage to companies, Francis said it was economically rational to employ as much of this cheap capital and as much of this leverage as was available. He argued that the demand by leveraged buyout firms such as his own to do deals was just as great in the spring of 1991 as it had been in the late 1980s, but that the absence of supply of this cheap capital from investors has led to a dramatic falloff of leveraged restructuring activity.

Martin Lipton argued that there were four factors driving the use of the securities Tufano describes: "First, you have issuers who are gambling—the LBO sponsors or the highly leveraged takeover players—or who are desperate—the companies that were restructuring in order to avoid a takeover." Second, "you had either callous or crooked intermediaries." Third, "you had compromised or bribed buyers. You had dumb buyers, and you had the 'crammed down' buyers, the shareholders of the restructured company who were issued these securities as dividends." "Finally, they were given credibility by academics who analyzed them as if they made sense."

Johnson acknowledged that the possibility of outright corruption on the part of intermediaries represents a real problem for top management at banks or investment banks who must keep track of what is happening in a number of different business fiefdoms reporting to them. The managers of each have a "real incentive to pad the income statement and get paid a bonus at the end of the year, to devastate the balance sheet, and then quit by the time the day of reckoning comes in." He said he could not tell whether this was caused by corruption or bad incentives within firms, "but it is between the two, and I am sure there is some of both."

Tufano responded that, if all else fails, he would be willing to consider talking about gambling, calloused people, and bribery. However, he said he would find it much more satisfying to look first at a framework that could help explain why certain contracts existed to solve interesting problems that might not have been solvable with other contracts.

Notes

1. Offerings for other than cash, in which target shareholders are given securities in which consideration in a merger, are excluded from the SDC data base and are not considered in this study.

2. Self-reporting can produce systematic bias, but investment banks rely on volume reports by SDC and its rival, IDD Information Services, to measure market share, which figures prominently in marketing literature and advertising. Therefore, it is unlikely that they would systematically underreport their completed deals.

3. This result is consistent with small-sample studies of acquisition financing. An unpublished SEC study apparently found that bank and bridge loans accounted for $32.9 billion, or 63 percent, of $52.2 billion in financing for 150 successful takeovers from June 1987 to June 1988; Thomas E. Ricks, "Bridge Loans Aid Major Takeovers, SEC Study Finds," *Wall Street Journal,* November 2, 1988, p. C18. In a study of 54 hostile and white knight transactions in 1985 and 1986, the General Accounting Office found that 42 percent of the financing came from bank or bridge loans; General Accounting Office, *Financial Markets: Issuers, Purchasers, and Purposes of High-Yield, Non-Investment-Grade Bonds,* GAO/GGD 88-55FS (1988). Steven Kaplan and Jeremy C. Stein, "The Evolution of Buyout Pricing and Financial Structure," working paper 3695, National Bureau of Economic Research, May 1991, contend that bank debt accounted for 57 percent of the total debt in 124 LBOs from 1980 to 1989, or 50 percent of the total post-LBO capital structure.

4. Alan S. Glazer, "Acquisition Bridge Financing by Investment Banks," *Business Horizons,* September–October 1989, pp. 49–53.

5. See Linda Sandler, "Salomon, after Investing Millions of Dollars, Has Little to Show from Foray into LBOs," *Wall Street Journal*, February 25, 1991, p. C2.

6. If bank debt and bridge loans are included, the percentage of all funds raised by acquirers through debt rises to 97.6 percent.

7. Mutual funds, insurance companies, pension funds, and depository institutions held 79 percent of all high-yield bonds; General Accounting Office, *Financial Markets*, app. 2, p. 20.

8. Securities Data Co., Corporate New Issues Database.

9. Results calculated from data in Peter Tufano, "Financial Innovation and the First-Mover Advantages," *Journal of Financial Economics*, vol. 25 (December 1989), pp. 213–40. For the definition of "innovative" and for methodology, see that paper.

10. Tufano, "Financial Innovation and First-Mover Advantages," p. 218.

11. Tom Takacs, "A Primer on High Yield Extendable Resets," *High Performance* (Morgan Stanley Credit Research, December 1988), pp. 9–16.

12. These data underestimate the use of RCF securities because they include cash offerings but exclude the extensive offering of deferred interest or dividend instruments, commonly called cram-down securities, as consideration for either an acquisition or an exchange. For instance, the first two uses of PIK debentures were by BCI, Inc., and Safeway in 1986, both cram-downs in conjunction with LBO financing; see Laurie S. Goodman and Alan H. Cohen, "Pay-In-Kind Debentures: Structure and Valuation," *Financial Strategies Group Report* (Goldman Sachs, November 1987).

13. From March 1981 through June 1982 forty-nine OID debt securities were issued by nonacquirers. From July 1982, when the tax code was revised to eliminate the tax advantages of these securities, to December 1987 only six OID debt securities were issued; Raj Varma and Donald R. Chambers, "The Role of Financial Innovation in Raising Capital: Evidence from Deep Discount Debt Offers," *Journal of Financial Economics*, vol. 26 (August 1990), pp. 289–98. This study, which excludes issues with confounding information such as control changes, confirms that original-issue discount debt was very rarely used by nonacquirers in the late 1980s.

14. See Laura Jereski and Jason Zweig, "Step Right Up, Folks," *Forbes*, March 4, 1991, pp. 74–77; and Mark Walsh, "Zero/Coupon Bonds: Buyouts Spawn a High Yield Specialty," *High Performance* (Morgan Stanley Credit Research, July 1986), pp. 6–11.

15. Peter Tufano, "Business Failure as a Stimulus to Innovation: An Institutional and Historical Perspective," working paper 91-039, Harvard Business School, 1991.

16. The Revenue Reconciliation Act of 1989 limited the deductibility of interest on high-yielding OID and PIK debt issued after July 1989. Both House and Senate legislators clearly stated their intent to discourage use of these instruments and decrease the high level of leverage supporting corporate takeovers and restructurings. See Kathleen E. McKay, "Limitations on the Deductibility of Interest on High-Yielding OID and PIK Instruments," *Journal of Taxation of Investments*, vol. 7 (1990), pp. 267–92.

17. See Floyd Norris, "Del Monte Sells Pay-in-Kind Issue," *New York Times*, September 16, 1991, p. D6.

18. Kaplan and Stein, "Evolution of Buyout Pricing," p. 3.

19. Stewart C. Myers and Nicholas S. Majluf, "Corporate Financing and Investment Decisions When Firms Have Information That Investors Do Not Have," *Journal of Financial Economics*, vol. 13 (June 1984), pp. 187–221. Robert A. Korajczyk, Deborah J. Lucas, and Robert L. McDonald, "Equity Issues with Time-Varying Asymmetric Information," working paper 84, Northwestern University, Kellogg Graduate School of Management, October 1990, extend Myers's and Majluf's result to cases with time-varying asymmetric information and show that, in equilibrium, managers may wait for markets to become better informed before issuing equity. See also Oliver Hart's paper in this volume.

20. Michael C. Jensen, "Agency Costs of Free Cash Flow, Corporate Finance, and Takeovers," *American Economic Review*, vol. 76 (May 1986), pp. 323–29.

21. Bankruptcy entails direct, deadweight costs; see Jerold B. Warner, "Bankruptcy Costs: Some Evidence," *Journal of Finance*, vol. 32 (May 1977), pp. 337–47; and Lawrence A. Weiss, "Bankruptcy Resolution: Direct Costs and Violation of Priority of Claims," *Journal of Financial Economics*, vol. 27 (October 1990), pp. 285–314. It also entails personal costs to directors and managers; see Stuart C. Gilson, John Kose, and Larry H. P. Lang, "Bankruptcy, Boards, Banks, and Blockholders: Evidence on Changes in Corporate Ownership and Control When Firms Default," *Journal of Financial Economics*, vol. 27 (October 1990), pp. 355–87. And it gives rise to strategic costs, an example of which is provided by Carliss Y. Baldwin and Scott P. Mason, "The Resolution of Claims in Financial Distress: The Case of Massey Ferguson," *Journal of Finance*, vol. 38 (May 1983), pp. 505–16.

22. Douglas W. Diamond, "Debt Maturity Structure and Liquidity Risk," *Quarterly Journal of Economics*, vol. 106 (August 1991), pp. 709–37.

23. Stewart C. Myers, "Determinants of Corporate Borrowing," *Journal of Financial Economics*, vol. 5 (November 1977), pp. 147–75.

24. Zvi Bodie, "Pension Funds and Financial Innovation," *Financial Management*, vol. 19 (Autumn 1990), pp. 11–22.

25. First Boston Company, *First Boston High Yield Handbook* (January 1989), p. 24. Also see Tim C. Opler, "Financial Innovation in Leveraged Buyouts: Evidence on the Value of Investor Intermediaries and Strip Finance," University of California, Los Angeles, November 1990. Using a linear bond-valuation methodology, Opler finds that promised debt costs are higher when PIK or OID bonds are used to finance LBOs, which is consistent with RCF investors' receiving higher promised yields for investing in these instruments. His result is apparently not robust; in multivariate specifications, the use of OID and PIK devices does not significantly influence borrowing costs.

26. For default rates see Paul Asquith, David Mullins, Jr., and E. D. Wolf, "Original Issue High Yield Bonds: Aging Analyses of Defaults, Exchanges, and Calls," *Journal of Finance*, vol. 44 (September 1989), pp. 923–52; and Edward I. Altman, "Measuring Corporate Bond Mortality and Performance," *Journal of Finance*, vol. 44 (September 1989), pp. 909–22. For returns see Marshall E. Blume and Donald B. Keim, "Realized Returns and Defaults on Lower-Grade

Bonds: The Cohort of 1977 and 1978," working paper 31-89, Wharton School of the University of Pennsylvania, 1989.

27. Barrie A. Wigmore, "The Decline in Credit Quality of New-Issue Junk Bonds," *Financial Analysts Journal,* vol. 46 (September–October 1990), pp. 53–62; and Kaplan and Stein, "Evolution of Buyout Pricing."

28. Laurie S. Goodman and Alan H. Cohen, "Valuing Deferred Coupon Debentures," *Financial Strategies Group Report* (Goldman Sachs, 1988).

29. For 1987–89, SDC lists 298 LBOs valued at $50 million or more. Of these, 107 reported financial data, which is necessary to measure the degree of cash flow constraints. Of these 107, 32 issued public debt whose terms can be used to identify the presence of RCF securities.

30. Wigmore's "Decline in Credit Quality," which showed that junk bond issuers in the late 1980s had pro forma ratios of EBITDA to interest coverage below 1.0, is consistent with this observation. Interest includes both current-pay and accrued interest.

31. This difference cannot be explained solely as the product of a rising yield curve. The duration of the current-pay bonds is 6.0 years and for discount bonds 9.2 years. In November 1989, when these bonds were issued, the yield curve was fairly flat: six-month yields for Treasury bonds were 7.46 percent and for ten-year bonds 8.03 percent; see *Standard and Poor's Statistical Service, Current Statistics* (S & P Corporation, June 1991). Although comparable yields are not available for high-yield bonds, given this flat-term structure, it is unlikely that a duration difference of 3.2 years would produce a 200-basis-point increase in yields.

32. Kaplan and Stein, "Evolution of Buyout Pricing."

33. I know of no published study that shows the difference in recovery rates between different classes of subordinated debt within the same firm. Edward I. Altman, "Setting the Record Straight on Junk Bonds: A Review of the Research on Default Rates and Returns," *Journal of Applied Corporate Finance,* vol. 3 (Summer 1990), p. 95, gives aggregate data showing that for the late 1980s, recovery rates for senior subordinate debt and subordinated debt were both approximately equal at 32 percent.

34. See Franco Modigliani and Donald Lessard, "Inflation and the Housing Market: Problems and Potential Solutions," *Sloan Management Review,* vol. 17 (Fall 1975), pp. 19–35.

35. See, for example, Douglas W. Diamond, "Debt Maturity Structure and Liquidity Risk," *Quarterly Journal of Economics,* vol. 106 (August 1991); Oliver Hart and John Moore, "Default and Renegotiation: A Dynamic Model of Debt," working paper 520, MIT Department of Economics, 1989; and Milton Harris and Artur Raviv, "The Theory of Capital Structure," *Journal of Finance,* vol. 46 (March 1991), pp. 297–353.

36. The evidence presented by Margaret Blair and Martha Schary in this volume is not consistent with Roach's findings, however. They find that financial restructuring activity was concentrated in durable and nondurable goods manufacturing and wholesale and retail trade, and they find no correlation between the rate of restructuring activity and the stability of cash flows by industry.

Takeover Politics

Mark J. Roe

TAKEOVERS cannot be fully understood without under-
standing the role of American politics in finance. Politics prohibits some
ownership structures and regulates or taxes others, often powerfully influencing corporate governance. Politics' influence on takeovers falls into
two categories. First, politics fragmented American finance, facilitating
the scattering of shareholders of large public companies. This scattering
of shareholders set the stage for takeovers. Second, takeovers created
winners and losers. Those at risk of loss in takeovers had the political
muscle to get state legislatures to pass antitakeover laws.

Financial fragmentation came first. Before the recent takeover wave,
American politics fragmented financial institutions and their portfolios
and weakened coordination among those financial institutions. American
laws generally raised the institutions' cost of entering the corporate
boardroom. Three determinants produced this result: American federalism, popular fear of concentrated economic power, and the power of
interest groups.

Federalism created the states that in the nineteenth century created
their own separate financial systems. State-by-state organization gave
clout in Congress to those—usually smalltown bankers—who wanted to
keep American finance fragmented. Moreover, many lawmakers sincerely
believed that the financial system would be more stable if fragmented.
And the American people historically deeply mistrusted central accu-
mulations of economic power. Thus banks, insurance companies, mutual
funds, and pension funds are either prohibited from controlling large
blocks of stock, regulated so that taking control of them is costly, or

Bernie Black, Michael Fitts, Lou Lowenstein, Todd Mason, Geoffrey Miller,
Roberta Romano, and participants in a workshop at the University of Pennsylvania
Law School made helpful comments on an earlier draft. The Brookings Institution and
the Bradley Foundation supported the research.

structured so that managers of operating companies control their decisionmaking.[1] Until very recently, Congress consistently pursued a policy of keeping financial institutions small and separate.

This fragmentation set the stage for takeovers. In the absence of institutional shareholders controlling large blocks of stock, the shareholders of public firms are scattered and have small investments. None has enough incentive or means to see that the firm is well run or check on what managers are doing. Each small shareholder free-rides, refusing to invest the time or money even to understand the firm enough to cast an informed vote for directors. Managers thus are freer than they would be if they had a boss owning a large portion of the company's stock.

Most managers do their jobs well, but inevitably some mismanage their companies or build personal empires for the prestige, compensation, and fun of running larger enterprises. Shareholders, if they could act collectively at low cost, would stop these derelictions. Many observers believe that the threat of a takeover mitigates this difficulty of collective action. The offering company can make a profit by putting the mismanaged firm back on the right track, and thus the threat acts in the best interests of the shareholders. Of course, the problem of achieving collective action would be less severe if institutions held large blocks of stock. (There would be other problems, yes. The financial institutions would be afflicted with their own agency costs, for example.) Even if operations did not improve, the voting power of the institutions would force managers to share authority with them; institutions might still block takeovers, and we would worry about abuse by financial institutions.

The increase in takeovers and leveraged buyouts in the 1980s thus arose partly because many ownership forms that would have reduced the authority of managers were prohibited. My first claim, then, is that takeovers are made possible by the fragmenting of American finance.

My second claim arises directly from the politics of hostile takeovers. Hostile takeovers weakened managers in the 1970s and 1980s, shifting power from them to shareholders and to the takeover entrepreneurs. When takeovers occur, there are losers—managers and workers in target firms, primarily. But the losers do not sit idly by; they call for political reinforcements, lobbying legislatures to pass laws that prohibit the takeovers, raise their cost, or give target firms room to maneuver. Managers in the 1980s were losing autonomy. But they struck back in the political arena, where they won back the autonomy they had lost.

Many laws validate, explicitly or implicitly, defensive tactics like the poison pill that were questionable before they received judicial approval in the 1980s. The poison pill and antitakeover laws do little that the corporation's shareholders could not do themselves by amending the corporate charter. The implication of this contractual alternative is that managers do not ask shareholders for protection because they fear that shareholders will not give it to them.

Takeovers disrupted the lives of managers and workers; both groups sought to restrict them. Any efficiency gains from takeovers would have been diffusely distributed among shareholders and others who would benefit from a more tightly run enterprise, making gainers less motivated than targets to influence politicians, who respond well to pleas to maintain the status quo. With public opinion dubious about the value of takeovers and with managers lobbying against them, laws restricting them were to be expected.

More difficult to predict would have been where the laws would be made—in Congress or in the states—and how strongly antitakeover they would be. The accidents of law and politics led to the laws' being made in the states, which are even more strongly antitakeover than Congress. In fact, because antitakeover forces in many states had the votes from the very beginning, the real question is why they took so long to win.

Antitakeover laws, now in place in more than forty states, raise the cost of a hostile takeover. Some laws responded to distortions favoring raiders; distortions favoring incumbents went uncorrected or were increased. The laws are the response of local politicians to local business leaders, workers, and public opinion.

Thus a unified story can be told. Federalism long ago influenced politics to favor small financial institutions. In the 1980s it tilted politics to favor managers. Federalism made local politics important, increasing the power of small financial institutions that wanted to fragment Wall Street's power and enhancing the power of managers who wanted to thwart takeovers. The politics of corporate governance are largely determined by these interest groups and a public of bystander-voters that has historically preferred fragmented financial institutions and in modern times has been suspicious of takeovers.

The Legal Framework of
Fragmented Ownership

The structure of the large American public corporation is obvious. Dispersed shareholders trade their stock on the stock exchanges. Dispersion creates free riders lacking incentives to monitor management carefully. Some separation is functional; managers are better informed about a company's business than shareholders are, and dispersion helps shareholders diversify risk. Some separation is dysfunctional; managers can pursue their own agendas: an easier life, a bigger empire. Separation also raises the cost for managers to communicate proprietary or technical information to shareholders. Adaptive mechanisms reduce managerial slack and empire building via proxy contests, a board of directors of outsiders, and incentive compensation.

Unlike small shareholders, large stockholders have the financial motivation to become involved and somewhat informed because they keep a large portion of any gain. (True, they have to overcome their own agency problems: just as industrial managers sometimes do not do the job properly for their organization, financial managers at the institution with a big block might not do the job right for their organization. Although shared authority might improve corporate performance, a shift in power in the large public corporation might just shift the locus and type of poor decisions.) Irrespective of whether intervention by financial institutions is functional, in other countries—Japan with its *keiretsu* and Germany with its universal banking, for example—financial institutions have been more involved with industrial companies than are financial institutions in the United States.[2] Economists suggest that large stockholders arise in firms that should most benefit from monitoring.[3] But American law constrains the supply of large stockholders.

Rules that Fragmented Financial Institutions and Portfolios

Elsewhere I have argued in detail how the fragmentation of finance in America exaggerated the shift of power from shareholders and financiers to managers.[4] In this section I argue that this fragmentation set the stage for takeovers.

Nearly all the institutional financial assets of the United States are in four types of institutions: banks (including bank trust funds and bank holding companies), insurance companies, mutual funds, and pension funds. What rules constrain them from holding large blocks of stock?

BANKS. Until recently American banks have been constrained, mostly by the McFadden Act of 1927, from branching across states. These geographic limits kept them small in relation to the largest industrial companies and reduced their ability to make large investments of any sort. (Banks in Germany and Japan are much larger in relation to those countries' largest industrial companies, giving them the financial muscle to take sizable blocks of stock.)

On top of the size limits are portfolio limits. Banks cannot own stock. The Glass-Steagall Act of 1933 prohibited bank affiliates from owning and dealing in securities, severing commercial banks from investment banks. The prohibitions on dealing in securities are breaking down, but prohibitions on banks' owning equity remain. (The legal restraint on stock ownership is probably no longer the key barrier because banks today lack the financial strength to become large stockholders.) The Bank Holding Company Act of 1956 restricts a holding company to activities related to banking. A bank holding company cannot own more than 5 percent of the voting stock of a nonbanking company, and regulators usually interpret the law as requiring passivity with the stock they do own.

Bank trust departments are commercial banks' remaining direct link to equity. Potential liability under trustee laws encourages bank portfolio fragmentation well beyond the needs of diversification.[5] Other rules make it difficult for trust departments to coordinate their stock with stock held by other institutions.[6]

MUTUAL FUNDS. During the 1930s, Congress, suspicious of mutual funds' potential power to control industrial companies, mandated a review of them by the Securities and Exchange Commission. The SEC declared that "the national public interest . . . is adversely affected . . . when investment companies [have] great size [and] have excessive influence on the national economy." It wanted mutual fund directors and employees off the boards of all companies in which the funds invested. While it had to compromise with the mutual fund industry, the SEC achieved many of its goals when Congress passed tax laws governing mutual funds and the Investment Company Act of 1940.[7] These laws subjected a mutual fund that devotes most of its portfolio to owning blocks of stock greater than 10 percent of a company to regulatory and tax restrictions. A mutual fund with large blocks of stock would be taxed unfavorably on its *entire* portfolio.[8]

INSURANCE COMPANIES. In 1906 New York forbade life insurance companies from buying stock. The prohibition affected most insurance companies because more than half of the industry's assets were in New York insurers.

This prohibition remained in place for nearly a half century and has only been seriously amended in the past decade. Even as amended, insurers cannot easily buy influential blocks.[9] (As with banks, insurers' financial weakness now reduces the impact of the regulatory restrictions.) New York life insurers, for example, cannot put more than 2 percent of their assets into the stock of any single issuer and are encouraged to be passive with the stock they do own. Other restrictions limit the amount of influential or controlling stock they can take in noninsurance firms. Inside coordination by tying financial institutions together is limited: insurance companies cannot own banks. Forty states limit an insurer's investment in common stocks to between 2 percent and 25 percent of its assets.[10]

PENSION FUNDS. Private pension funds are functionally under the control of managers who invest their employees' pension money. If, for example, the managers of the pension fund at General Motors actively oversaw managers of another firm, they could expect the wrath of GM's operating managers, their bosses.[11] Pension financing could be organized differently; but thus far operating managers control private pensions.

Public pension funds are less directly limited and have been active in shareholder proposals (although not in board representation). Yet they too face political constraints. The governor of California sought to restrain its large state pension fund, the most active public pension in the country and one of the most influential. The press reported that managers of public firms prodded the governor to intervene and dampen the pension fund's activity.[12]

Although pension funds are not subject to the strict portfolio restraints that bind banks, insurance companies, and mutual funds, indirect rules are probably just as effective in fragmenting their portfolios. Fiduciary rules foster portfolio hyperfragmentation beyond what financial economists say is needed for diversification.

JOINT VENTURES AND GENERAL RESTRICTIONS ON CONTROL. Thus these restrictions limit the supply of large blocks of stock held by financial intermediaries. And although financial institutions owning small blocks could cooperate to assert authority in the boardroom, laws discourage them. Insurance companies cannot own banks, banks cannot easily get into the insurance business. Commercial banks cannot yet own full-scale investment banks, and vice versa. The Bank Holding Company Act discourages or prohibits groups of banks from owning more than 5 percent each of the stock of an industrial company. Nor does it encourage cross-ownership between groups of banks and groups of industrial companies, a feature of the Japanese keiretsu. In Germany, banks achieve authority in the boardroom through coordinated voting of stock they own directly, stock owned in bank-controlled investment companies, and custodial stock whose vote the bank controls. Such a network or financial supermarket would run into severe problems in America because of the Glass-Steagall Act, the Investment Company Act of 1940, and the Bank Holding Company Act of 1956.

Coordination is made difficult because U.S. financial institutions are segmented functionally, partly fragmented geographically, or have fragmented portfolios. And coordination across portfolios and institutions is made difficult by securities laws. The institutions could vote to elect to the board people beholden to the institutions, but thus far they have not, perhaps because until now the gains from organization, even organization to vote, have been outweighed by the costs of organization.[13]

For example, groups that have 5 percent or more of the vote in a company must, under the Securities Exchange Act of 1934, outline their plans, and reveal their ownership and sources of financing.[14] Although the filings cannot stop group action, academics believe that they raise the cost of such action,[15] because the filings require information that institutions would prefer to keep confidential, can require a statement of intention when the plans are vague (the institution wants to talk with other institutions to form a plan of action), and have been the basis for nasty litigation in the takeover wars as lawyers for managers of target firms seek to wear down the morale of those who would assert control.[16] Institutional investors avoid that kind of litigation and publicity.[17] They have a product to sell—usually related to the securities business—and would like to avoid news stories: "XYZ Mutual Fund Sued for Securities Law Violations," or "XYZ Mutual Fund, ABC Insurance Company, and MNO Bank Sued for Conspiracy under Securities Laws." With a small stake in the enterprise, each institution and its employees see little reason to take on such costs, psychological and financial. Takeover entrepreneurs are not as easily deterred: they typically have a larger economic stake in the target, are less sensitive to the consumer relations costs of a lawsuit, and are psychologically predisposed to such combat.

Group formation also requires communication, which, if it involves enough other institutions, is deemed a proxy solicitation that would have to proceed under the securities laws. The active institution would have to file with the SEC; it would have to give those contacted the information specified in schedule 14A.[18] Some of these rules are breaking down; the SEC now allows some institutions to talk without filing if none is soliciting votes for a proposal.[19] Because some financial institutions have sought changes in the SEC rules, they may now find it worthwhile to incur some costs of organization, and some may find it worthwhile to seek removal of some legal impediments to organization. Whatever may be the future of the SEC rules restricting coordination, they were in place during the 1980s, raising the costs of organization among financial institutions.

Such groups face other problems. If a group member is a lender, it faces the increased risk—small but real—that its loan will not be repaid in a reorganization. The group faces legal risks from the mere fact of control: controlling entities can be liable under securities laws for the misdeeds of the controlled company and can be sued by the controlled company for mismanagement.[20] And members of the controlling group would have to constantly file and update their ownership positions and might have to return to the corporation any profits made on trades of stock held six months or less, irrespective of whether the profits were made on inside information.[21] Thus financial institutions until now considered the costs of control to outweigh the benefits. And the gains from influence probably would not be huge. Most managers do their job anyway, institutional checking will only occasionally improve the results of those who do not, and not all of the social gains will be captured by the group. These positive externalities mean that even a small legal risk could have been enough to deter institutional coordination.

The Politics of Financial Fragmentation

Why did America choose to fragment its financial institutions? American federalism has been the most important political factor. At the beginning of this century the United States had forty-eight banking systems, one for each state and territory. In unit banking states, banks could not do business other than from a single location. Even now, as some states allow interstate banking, the United States still has the most unusual banking system in the world.

The fragmentation of banking affected corporate finance. Few banks were big enough to provide large amounts of equity capital to the big enterprises that became technologically possible at the end of the nineteenth century. And bankers at small banks lacked the staffs to become sufficiently expert in industries so that they could effectively monitor investments. In contrast, at the end of the nineteenth century, Germany had banks large enough to have staffs of industry experts.[22]

The small country banks became an interest group, and an enormously powerful one, as the lobbying that preceded the savings and loan debacle of the late 1980s illustrates. Smalltown bankers have money, importance in their community, and access to members of Congress who want to curry the bankers' favor. Repeatedly, these bankers saw to it that laws denied incipient large financial institutions the scale and sometimes the legal power to become involved in large enterprises.

Federalism is not the only explanation for financial fragmentation. The American public has always mistrusted concentrated economic power and has preferred to disperse it, usually by breaking up any incipient concentration. These anticoncentration emphases can be found from the beginning of the nation in the thought of the Jeffersonians, in the debate swirling around the destruction of the Second Bank of the United States, and in the ideology of the populists of the 1890s. Anticoncentration bias also played a part in creating the Federal Reserve System in 1913 to take power away from J. P. Morgan and in shaping the political rhetoric of the 1930s.

Franklin Roosevelt wanted laws to keep bankers out of industry because "industrial empire building, unfortunately, has evolved into banker control of industry. We oppose that. Such control does not offer safety to the investing public. . . . Interlocking financial controls have taken from American business much of its traditional virility, independence, adaptability, and daring. . . . Men will dare to compete against men but not against giants."[23] Anticoncentration themes also appear in modern debates about financial institutions. In 1986 the chair of the Senate Banking Committee, William Proxmire, said, "The genius of American banking is competition. And the more competition, the better. You look at every other major country, and they only have a handful of banks that account for most of the business."[24]

Anticoncentration sentiment also had positive public-spirited bases: sound policy usually demands that institutions that hold the average person's savings be safe. Safety usually requires diversification. Influence cannot come without a large holding. A large holding cannot be part of a diversified portfolio unless the portfolio, and the institution, is large. But large size was not possible, partly due to the influence of small-town bankers and also because financial institutions' potential for insolvency or for monopoly power was best dealt with, according to some, by fragmenting them.

Perhaps public opinion is now more tolerant of large-scale finance, just as it became more tolerant of large-scale industry in the middle of the twentieth century. Recent Treasury proposals to abolish many restrictions of the Glass-Steagall Act, the Bank Holding Company Act, and the McFadden Act may indicate that there is less popular distrust of private concentrations of financial power. But because banking is weak, voters have no reason to fear immediate concentrations of private economic power. And with the rise of strong regional banks, the anti–Wall Street sentiments have become muted.

Thus the United States entered the 1980s with ownership of the large public firm fragmented, partly because politics pulverized finance. Managers at American industrial firms were freer from institutional influence by large stockholders than those at firms in other countries. There are fewer shareholders in the United States than in Japan that own 5 percent or more of the largest companies. And the American holder of a large block is more likely to be an individual. In Japan the large shareholder is likely to be a financial institution.[25] Banker voting influence in industry in Germany is also very concentrated; three banks control 40 percent of most large firms' stock.[26] (Which system is better is an open question.)

The market experimented with other, perhaps better, forms of monitoring: audit committees of outside directors, incentive compensation, M-form conglomerates. Proxy contests emerged to discipline managers. Why the hostile takeover emerged in the 1980s cannot be tightly tied to legal change. But it did emerge and it threatened managers of large public firms. Takeovers concentrated the disparate owners of the public firm.

Politics and Takeovers

The fragmentation of American finance was a prerequisite for takeovers. Takeovers are difficult if two or three financial institutions control large blocks of stock in industrial companies, as they do in Germany, or if cross-ownership of the largest industrial companies and the largest financial institutions is common, as it is in Japan. This leads to the second political claim I want to advance here. Takeovers are done with dollar votes to buy stock. But ballot box votes elect politicians, and politicians make takeover laws. Tactical success in a takeover need not make for political success. True, views of the "merits" (are takeovers functional) do affect legislators. But factors such as public opinion and political strength affect political outcomes. Neither need be closely related to the merits of takeovers.

Voters and Takeovers

Voters are unsympathetic to hostile takeovers. In a Louis Harris poll, 58 percent of the respondents thought they did more harm than good; only 8 percent thought they were beneficial.[27] The public mistrusts takeovers and financial maneuverings.[28] In popular novels, movies, and the press, Wall Street's greedy investment bankers are shallow yuppies who have no function. In Tom Wolfe's *Bonfire of the Vanities,* a character explains that the job of the investment banker (a bond salesman, to be sure, not a takeover engineer) is to slice and reslice the cake, hoping to keep the crumbs that fall off with each slicing. Although the popular image of parasitic moneychangers is hardly recent, these images have helped shape the political possibilities.

Public hostility or indifference to takeovers makes political action easier for interest groups seeking to restrict them. People potentially affected by takeovers do not sit idly when corporate law is made. Losers in takeovers—managers and workers at target firms—lobby legislatures for protection. But politicians do not always respond to interest group lobbying. Sometimes both sides lobby, canceling one another out. Some seek the public interest or fear association with special interests. But politicians who respond to these interest groups (managers and employees) will not be seen as catering to special interests because the bystanders—other voters—believe takeovers are unproductive and unfair. And some politicians surely share the public's wariness about takeovers.

People sympathize with workers displaced by manipulators from Wall Street. The public lumps takeovers with Ivan Boesky's insider trading and Michael Milken's junk bonds. When the Supreme Court upheld an important state antitakeover statute, the *Wall Street Journal* reported that its "decision came on the heels of Wall Street's insider-trading scandals and amid a national uproar against takeovers. While the justices didn't directly acknowledge that background, their tone indicated that they, too, believed the merger game had gone too far."[29] Managers and workers at firms that are not yet targets sympathize with employees at targets. The losers in a successful takeover know they have lost. For purposes of understanding political preferences, it matters little whether economic studies show increased employment due to takeovers; the prototypical image, not the average economic result, defines the political considerations for the legislator. The winners, other than raiders and some stockholders, are scattered. Any efficiency gains are spread through the economy. Dispersed winners do not even know they have won.

Managers who seek political protection are not climbing uphill; legislators who do managers' bidding do not have to fear reprisal from voters. It is the opposite. Politicians who bash Wall Street and thwart takeovers are rewarded by the average voter.

Corporate Politics in the States and Washington

Public opinion and the interests of managers and employees had to influence the making of takeover law. How influential they would be depended partly on where in American politics that law would be made.

American federalism allows both Washington and state governments to make corporate law. Although Congress has left most matters of corporate governance to the states, it could exercise more authority—in fact all of corporate law could be made in Washington. Congress passed the securities laws in the 1930s, mandating disclosure and prohibiting insider trading. It extended coverage to takeovers in 1968 through the Williams Act, which requires offerers to disclose takeover plans, prohibits fraud and deception in takeovers, and regulates how long bids must be kept open. The threat of further federalization probably affected what states did and did not do in the 1980s. States in general and Delaware in particular were wary of triggering a congressional response; and there were constitutional uncertainties about how far states could go. In this part I develop the argument that only at the end of the 1980s were states free to make stringent antitakeover laws. This makes it important to understand how each state is more likely to respond to the goals of targets than of raiders.

The political balance in the states differs from that in Washington. States will oppose the takeover of local businesses more vociferously than will Washington. Imagine a state, Pennsylvania, with several large public companies that are evenly divided between potential targets and potential offerers. Such a state's political balance will not be an even divide between protakeover and antitakeover legislation; the state will have an antitakeover tilt. To be sure, Delaware, with half the large corporations in the nation, is the state that counts; the import of what the other forty-nine do is mostly in how they affect Delaware. The nondevelopment of federal takeover law in the 1980s freed states to make takeover law, and when they produced persistently antitakeover law, they put pressure on Delaware to produce antitakeover law also.

Managers of Pennsylvania targets will invest heavily in political antitakeover action because if they succeed, they immunize themselves from takeover both by raiders from Pennsylvania and those from out of state. Public choice theory also predicts that people with something to lose will invest heavily in protectionist legislation.[30] And targets are often already organized, in chambers of commerce and industry associations, groups influential in the passage of antitakeover legislation.

Out-of-state raiders will try to block the antitakeover law, but they face organizational problems, and as Mancur Olson observed, focused groups tend to prevail over dispersed, disorganized groups.[31] Raiders look to the other forty-nine states for targets, so they will less intensely oppose their own state's antitakeover law. Out-of-state raiders are less organized than in-state targets; they might sit back or do little. And out-of-state institutions are less influential in a state; politicians respond first to their constituents. (When an offer is launched, the target shareholders are a discrete, focused group. But they have only a few weeks to organize for political action. By the time they do, it will be too late.)

How about the Pennsylvania raiders? A strong antitakeover statute does not prevent raiding. Pennsylvania law deters *only* raids on Pennsylvania corporations. Raiders are free to look for targets in the other states. In-state raiders will invest less in politics than in-state targets.

In national politics the organizational disparities between targets and raiders are smaller. Each has a symmetrical interest in takeover law. In national politics there are no in-state raiders who are only tangentially interested in the legislation. And managers and targets are as geographically dispersed as raiding companies. The president, unlike state politicians (and members of Congress) is the one nationally elected politician. This is not to say that state politics is antitakeover and national politics is protakeover. Public opinion tilts even the national balance, as was reflected in the Williams Act of 1968, the major national takeover law, which was mildly antitakeover. Congress is more likely to preserve the status quo than support a program with diffuse gains that too few voters could recognize. And when in the 1980s raiders were no longer mostly large companies, targets were already organized and ready for political action at state and national political levels—in chambers of commerce, in the business roundtables, in industry associations. But the new raiders were not politically ready and had to form new lobbying organizations. Finally, because managers of target firms have their economic lives on the line, they would lobby more intensely than offerers; targets were defending their "homeland" from invasion.

The SEC and the States

Nevertheless, national politics was less antitakeover during the 1980s than state politics. The 1980s SEC was protakeover, attacking state antitakeover laws as unconstitutional and recommending that Congress overturn them. The FTC supported hostile takeovers. And Congress does not get to items such as takeover policy that are far down its long agenda. This difference in degree between states and nation was strengthened in the 1980s by the free market ideology of the presidency, reflected in appointments to the SEC.[32]

To be sure, the federal result may be that Congress has many reasons not to act. Once it acts, it may act similarly to the states, and because of its "monopoly" position, state-level experimentation with takeover legislation would end. Essentially, the federal legal outputs have higher "variance"; we just have not seen the full range of federal outputs. But this doubt must be qualified; the full range of inputs at the federal level might well have led to different legislation. Federal antitakeover legislation could well have limited poison pills and greenmail in ways that state legal outputs never did.

In the early 1980s it looked as if law covering takeovers would be national law. Although Congress might not have decided to act anew, federal courts and the SEC would interpret and enforce the Williams Act. And the act prohibited states from doing anything important. States, particularly Delaware, were quiet, partly because they had reason to fear national law and partly because they could not do anything important under the Supreme Court's interpretation of the act.

The Federal Punt

Congress could displace the states and enact all corporate law if it wanted. Although it has not done so, fear that it might displace the states has partially motivated states, particularly Delaware. Fearing federal preemption, Delaware probably bends its law to what it expects the federal government wants, to reduce the chance of federal action, but only insofar as the state believes the federal government may act.

National law and state law could conflict in four ways. First, Congress could pass new laws. Second, courts could interpret laws on the books as explicitly displacing state law. If it told firms to "do this" while states said "do not do this," Congress would prevail; its law is "supreme." Third, if Congress and a state pass laws that conflict, courts decide whether the national law preempts the state law. If national law systematically regulates part of commerce, a state cannot intrude, even if its law would not explicitly contradict the national law. Last, if a state tramples on interstate commerce too much, even without trespassing on congressional law, courts will strike down the interfering acts.

FEDERAL PREEMPTION OF STATE LAW. States could not pass laws inconsistent with the Williams Act to require disclosure in takeovers, regulate some of the procedures, and, as it was said, provide a level playing field for takeovers. If courts interpreted the Williams Act as a comprehensive regulatory scheme, all state takeover laws would be struck down. This view was widely believed in legal circles in the 1970s and early 1980s.

By 1982 it was more than widely believed: the Supreme Court declared unconstitutional an Illinois antitakeover statute. Illinois had increased the delay between tender offer and its consummation beyond the time allowed for in the Williams Act, and it allowed state regulators to kill the offer even if the offer complied with the Williams Act. The Supreme Court held in *Edgar* v. *MITE* that the Williams Act balanced the interests of offerers, target companies, and shareholders, preempting state law that upset this balance. And the Court also held that the burden of the Illinois law on interstate commerce was so great as to be unconstitutional.[33] Thirty-seven states had antitakeover laws similar to that of Illinois; *MITE* rendered them all unconstitutional.[34] For the next five years significant state antitakeover activity was dormant.[35]

But how far did the Williams Act go? Did it regulate enough takeover activity so that through judicial interpretation and SEC rulemaking nothing would be left to the states? The act prohibits "fraudulent, deceptive or manipulative acts or practices in connection with any tender offer."[36] Interpreting such a phrase may not interest economists, but it is the lifeblood of lawyers. How wide a grant to courts and the SEC was the wording? Were two-tiered tender offers manipulative? The two tiers—$50 a share if one tenders within twenty days, for example, $30 if one waits—create an incentive to tender. Were "poison pills" manipulative? By diluting the offering company, poison pills encouraged the offerer to withdraw its offer. Was "greenmail" manipulative? Were target firms using a manipulative practice when they gave "crown jewel" options and "lock-up" options to friendly firms? Were all defensive tactics manipulative? If such tactics were manipulative, the federal judiciary and the SEC could control them.

State laws could be displaced by national law as interpreted by the SEC. For example, in its zig-zag between antitakeover and protakeover law in the early and mid-1980s, Delaware allowed a target company to exclude an offering company from the target's self-tender for its own shares.[37] The SEC then promulgated an "all-holders rule," requiring that self-tenders be made to all stockholders.[38] Delaware and its corporate law industry had to fear SEC preemption by regulation.

And then a federal circuit court, the judicial level just below the Supreme Court, decided in *Mobil* v. *Marathon* that Marathon Oil's giving of a crown jewel option to US Steel was manipulative, prohibited by the Williams Act. Mobil had tendered for Marathon Oil; Marathon managers preferred purchase by US Steel. They gave US Steel an option on 17 percent of Marathon's stock and on part of Marathon's huge Yates oil field. A successful offerer would thus see its Marathon stock diluted, and the Yates field bought out from under it.[39] The decision could have been a wedge toward making takeover law national. It attracted academic support.[40]

THE EBBING ASSERTION OF NATIONAL AUTHORITY. But other courts did not follow *Marathon,* and in 1985 the Supreme Court buried it, deciding that "manipulative" included only lying or bid rigging, not most takeover tactics.[41] Moreover, the Court's interpretation also stopped the SEC, whose authority to regulate takeovers comes from the same phrase.[42] After the decision, states no longer found the SEC or the courts determining the legality of takeover tactics. But even if SEC and federal judicial power were modified, states might still not be free to enter the vacuum. *MITE* implied that they could not. The next question was how far could the states go?

Some states passed "control share" statutes, which required that when a shareholder obtained a big block of shares, say 20 percent, the other shareholders can vote on whether the newly controlled shares could vote. Federal courts ruled these statutes unconstitutional.[43] For example, in March 1986 Indiana passed a control share statute. Dynamics Corporation had offered to buy the stock of CTS, an Indiana corporation. In *Dynamics Corporation* v. *CTS Corporation,* Dynamics sought federal courts to declare the Indiana law unconstitutional. This the courts promptly did, holding that the law clashed with the Williams Act by frustrating the purpose of Congress in striking a balance between the investor, management, and the takeover bidder in takeover contests." The law also clashed with the commerce clause because its "substantial interference with interstate commerce . . . outweighs the articulated local benefits."[44] Either way the statute was dead. The court of appeals said, "Even if a corporation's tangible assets are immovable, the efficiency with which they are employed and the proportions in which the earnings they generate are divided between management and shareholders depends on the market for corporate control—an interstate . . . market that the State of Indiana is not authorized to opt out of, as in effect it has done in this statute."[45] Legal commentators questioned whether state court decisions validating the poison pill could continue to stand in the face of *MITE* and the Court of Appeals *CTS* decision.[46]

Having lost in the lower federal courts, CTS appealed to the Supreme Court, hoping it would reverse *MITE* and the lower federal courts' view that Indiana had acted unconstitutionally. The Supreme Court did. Congress surely can preempt state takeover laws, said the Court. But Congress did not say it was preempting the states in the Williams Act; in fact the act has an *anti*preemption clause. It only preempted Indiana if Indiana made compliance with it impossible. Indiana can regulate the internal affairs of corporations having sufficient contact with the state. Five years after the Supreme Court stopped strong state antitakeover laws in *MITE,* it gave states back the constitutional room to maneuver.[47]

An explosion of state antitakeover laws followed, some perhaps overstepping what *CTS* made constitutionally permissible.[48] Delaware did not wait long: three days after the Supreme Court decision, its secretary of state asked the Delaware bar association whether it should consider new takeover legislation. Later that year, the bar produced a takeover statute that it believed would be more effective than the Indiana control-share statute.[49]

CONGRESSIONAL INACTION. Congress held hearings in the 1980s on poison pills, greenmail, golden parachutes, and two-tiered offers but passed no important new takeover law. Had *CTS* not shifted the battleground to the states, managers would have pressed Congress to pass antitakeover laws, as Representative John Dingell, chairman of the House Energy and Commerce Committee, has said they were doing before *CTS*. Perhaps they would have succeeded; business lobbyists won narrow victories in the Senate Banking Committee just after *CTS*, but the bill died. Still, a congressional antitakeover law was likely also to curb managerial defenses like poison pills, as Dingell's bill would have.[50] Regardless, between 1982, when the Supreme Court struck down a state antitakeover law in *MITE*, and 1987, when it held in *CTS* that a new state antitakeover formula was constitutional, managerial pressure on Congress failed. After *CTS*, managers shifted their pressure to the states, where they succeeded.[51]

WHAT THE STATES HAVE DONE. State antitakeover laws are manifold. The pre-*MITE* first generation of statutes required the offerer to file with the state, required it to wait before commencing the offer, and sometimes allowed the state administrator to determine the fairness of the offer and stop it (at least to that state's residents) if it was unfair. After *MITE,* states revised first-generation provisions to keep them constitutional. But what was left had no teeth.

The second-generation laws—found constitutional in *CTS*—deny voting rights to control shares. Once an offerer reaches a specified percentage of target shares—20 percent, 33 percent, 50 percent—it cannot vote. Some control-share statutes require that other shareholders approve the voting rights of the control shareholder. This provision makes the statute less than fully antitakeover because target management usually fears a shareholder vote and scrambles to avoid one. The statutes apply to corporations with some nexus to the state: the state is the state of incorporation, the location of the firm's principal assets, or the residence of some percentage of shareholders.

Third-generation antitakeover laws validate poison pills and expand the corporate constituency to allow—or mandate—directors to consider the effect of a takeover on employees, communities, suppliers, and customers. Most states now have these constituency-expanding statutes.[52]

Other antitakeover laws restrict mergers between a target and an interested shareholder, usually defined as any shareholder owning more than 10 or 15 percent of the target's stock.[53] This can disrupt the offering company's ability to finance the takeover because it often needs to secure its borrowing for the takeover with the assets of the target company, something it cannot do easily until it merges the target into itself. Others require corporations incorporated in the state to have a staggered board, one elected over several years, which prevents a raider from immediately taking control of it. Massachusetts now does this.[54]

Managers are often behind these laws. When a company becomes a target, its managers ask the state legislature to thwart the takeover. Managers could get the same protections via a shareholder vote, but they lack time to get a vote or they know that the shareholders will vote them down. Financial evidence shows that firms with contractual antitakeover devices in place are unaffected by state antitakeover legislation, suggesting that antitakeover laws do no more than what charter amendments could do.[55]

After *CTS* unleashed the states, action was swift, often in response to a real takeover. Asher Edelman bid for Burlington Industries, a North

Carolina company, in 1987. On April 23, 1987, two days after the Supreme Court announced *CTS,* the North Carolina legislature required bidders to get a favorable vote from 95 percent of the stockholders; Burlington's managers controlled more than 5 percent of the stock, making a takeover somewhat difficult without managerial approval.[56] When Dayton Hudson, a Minnesota company, became a target two months later, its managers "got Minnesota to hold a special legislative session. Within hours, the state had a new antitakeover bill."[57] When Citizens & Southern National Bank, a Georgia bank, became a target, the bank's representatives convinced the Georgia legislature that state corporate law ought to allow directors to weigh effects on corporate constituencies.[58] In July 1987 Greyhound, an Arizona company, feared a takeover and got a special session of the Arizona legislature to pass an antitakeover bill. "Greyhound said 'Jump' and we said, 'How high,' " said state representative Jim Skelly.[59]

I do not want to portray the state statutes as absolute show-stoppers. Some present no more than a paper barrier; others raise the cost of takeovers, but do not prevent them. Court decisions that validated the poison pill are more important, because the pill can be a show-stopper. The legislature could have killed the pill—as congressional legislators proposed—but did not.[60] The impact of state legislatures' laws was less in the barriers created than in those left standing. The legislatures' complex impact can be seen by recalling two key Delaware decisions of the 1980s. The first, *Smith* v. *Van Gorkom,* caused a shock in boardrooms. Its antimanagerial tilt came from holding directors liable for failure to review merger terms carefully. *Moran* v. *Household International, Inc.,* validated the poison pill. (*Moran* might have been the Delaware court's way of making amends to managers.) Legislative forces then essentially reversed *Van Gorkom* but preserved *Moran.* Political forces were there, but hidden, because the legislature's key move was to preserve the poison pill by legislative inaction.[61]

The political forces were not hidden in the debate in Pennsylvania before a sweeping antitakeover message passed in 1990. The press reported that "Behind the debate [on the merits] in Pennsylvania is a power struggle between the shareholders . . . and the directors and managers. . . . Pennsylvania business groups supporting the bill are aligned with unions seeking to protect the jobs of their members. . . . The bill's supporters point to a wave of populist revulsion with the takeover boom of the 1980's. . . ."[62] Labor and Pennsylvania's Chamber of Business and Industry lobbied hard:

[The] lobbying effort is the product of teamwork between . . . Pennsylvania labor unions and a coalition of over two dozen corporations working for the passage of the bill under the well-organized direction of the Pennsylvania Chamber of Business and Industry. A hardcore group of a dozen manufacturing concerns, including Armstrong, Scott Paper Company, PPG Industries Inc., The Rorer Group Inc., Aluminum Co. of America, and Consolidated Rail Corporation—along with several banks and utilities—have been the most active supporters.[63]

Institutional investors opposed the law; the Pennsylvania statute would sap investors of $4 billion in value according to a recent estimate.[64] But the best these principally out-of-state forces could muster was a ninety-day opt-out provision. And in New York, Governor Mario Cuomo appointed a business-labor task force, which proposed that New York public pension systems be prohibited from financing hostile takeovers.[65] Politics and not just economics determines the weak ties between shareholders and managers.

Delaware

Thus far I have presented an explanation, not very different from that already in the literature, of why states with target industries would like antitakeover laws.[66] But why should Delaware have also been antitakeover? State corporate law is largely Delaware law, because Delaware is home to half of America's large companies. And it is a small state, not as susceptible to the pressures of managers, workers, and public opinion as larger Rust Belt states. Legal scholars sympathizing with the disciplinary effects of takeovers hoped for a different political balance in Delaware so that it would not become antitakeover.[67] That hope was not misplaced in the mid-1980s.

Delaware is sandwiched between two forces: it does not want the national government to take a greater role in corporate governance, and it does not want to lose incorporation business to other states. In the early 1980s it had to fear that heavy-handed moves to favor managers could lead to federal takeover law. It had little reason to join the antitakeover states when the national government had a good chance of regulating takeovers and when sister states lacked the constitutional authority to make their antitakeover laws stick.[68]

At the beginning of the 1980s these two forces kept Delaware's anti-takeover tendencies mild. Its legislature was not strongly antitakeover.[69] Some Delaware court decisions blocked takeovers; others facilitated them.[70] Even decisions allowing defensive tactics were intermediate: managers could not "qualify for the protections of the business judgment rule simply by pointing to a 'danger to corporate policy' based on a carefully orchestrated record. Defensive tactics [had to] face a proportionality test: They [had to] be shown to be 'reasonable in relation to the threat posed.' "[71]

But by the end of the decade Delaware appeared to have become antitakeover. Delaware politicians believed that their market share was threatened. The governor affirmed his support for antitakeover legislation: the "$188 million annual revenue from corporations—18 percent of the state's total revenues—is in danger because of competition from other states if Delaware does not protect its corporations the way other states have."[72] When targets considered Delaware court opinions insufficiently antitakeover, lawyers sensitive to the state's weak points urged managers to consider reincorporation: "Unless Delaware acts quickly . . . the only avenues open . . . will be [to] leav[e] Delaware for a more hospitable state of incorporation."[73] Mergers and acquisition conferences in 1988 and 1989 were said to abound with dismay at Delaware and threats to move to states with better corporate laws.[74] Because by then federal preemption was no longer a threat and sister states were making antitakeover law, Delaware had reason to stop zig-zagging and to become more clearly antitakeover.

Delaware judges are quite conscious of the SEC breathing down their necks. In *Moran* v. *Household International, Inc.*, the key opinion validating poison pills, the Delaware Supreme Court wasted no time in referring to the SEC's amicus brief opposing validation, but noted that the SEC split 3–2 on whether to intervene.[75] In a 1987 speech a Delaware justice commented that Congress was not doing much to control takeovers, implying that the Delaware judiciary had room to maneuver.[76]

In starkly painting these forces, I do not mean to portray Delaware legislators, judges, and governor as automatons, crudely calculating their (or their state's) advantages and disadvantages every six months. Some judges may never think about keeping business in Delaware. But by the end of the 1980s political and economic forces pressed Delaware to oppose takeovers. Politicians and judges who favored takeovers swam against the tide. Whether the antitakeover legislation and judicial opinions resulted from these forces or would have occurred without them I cannot say.

And there are too few data points: one antitakeover statute, which was far from leakproof, and one major Delaware Supreme Court decision, *Paramount Communications* v. *Time Inc.*, which, given the judiciary's previous indecisiveness about takeovers, does not establish a trend.[77] Although legal commentators think they have seen an antitakeover trend in Delaware and there seems to be one, the paucity of tangible results makes me reluctant to believe firmly that the state shifted.[78]

In the *Time* case, Time's board refused to present a bid from Paramount to Time's shareholders, preferring that the company merge with Warner Communications at a lower price and maintain managerial continuity. One lawyer who often defends management in hostile takeovers hailed the *Time* decision as the all but "explicit recognition that a [board may] 'just say no.'"[79] The Wall Street Journal complained that *Time* showed "how far the law has moved from the notion that corporate boards exist to serve stockholders."[80] That is, with a poison pill in place, the management of a target firm could as a matter of business judgment refuse to pull the pill. It needed little more than a business plan that contemplated the company as an independent firm.

That reading is not the only one that could be given the *Time* opinion. Nevertheless, the opinion seems more antitakeover than, say, *Revlon* v. *MacAndrews and Forbes Holdings,* its previous major takeover decision, which required management to conduct an auction for the target company once it was clear that the company was going to be sold to someone.[81]

Taxes, Lawyers, and Market Share

Law is a product of many things: ideology, public opinion, money, interest groups, reactions to scandal. Delaware corporate law cannot be explained as solely a crude effort to benefit local groups at the expense of those outside the state, but this perspective bears analysis and surely helps explain some results. Delaware's crude public choice goals have been described before.[82] The state wants to maximize its tax revenues. Its lawyers want to maximize lawyers' fees. The means are several: efficient law, managers' law, lawyers' law, and judges' law.

EFFICIENT LAW. Delaware can provide efficient corporate law by providing stable and clear corporate law, a detailed system with answers that promote the efficient operation, financing, and governance of corporations at low legal cost. Stability and detail make it easier for lawyers to operate; lawyers can, more often with Delaware law than the law of other states, give answers to clients.[83] With an economy of scale from having many large companies, Delaware can provide a judiciary that specializes in corporate litigation, astutely filling in the inevitable gaps in the legal system. Corporate litigants know they are likely to get in Delaware a judge sophisticated in corporate matters.

MANAGERS' LAW. Delaware can appeal to managers. If managers and not stockholders make the decisions about where to incorporate, they will choose a state that gives managers free rein. In this view, states "race to the bottom" to provide the law that managers want, and managers go to the state, Delaware in modern times, that allows them the most freedom. William Cary, a former SEC chairman, argued that for this reason Delaware law ought to be replaced by either a national incorporation statute or minimum directorial standards.[84] The existence of a race to the bottom has been hotly contested.[85] State competition should drive out the most inefficient promanagerial corporate law terms.

LAWYERS' LAW. Maximizing tax revenue is not Delaware's only goal. Lawyers are a potent interest group in a small state, and some of the state's laws are not promanager but prolawyer.[86] Suing managers is easy in Delaware, hard elsewhere. The fee-award system to successful attorneys is especially generous.

Lawyers gain by having more corporations inside the state; the companies need legal opinions about Delaware law and need lawyers to litigate disputes. Stability might attract corporations, but lawyers also gain from wobbling, uncertainty, and instability, which enhance the chance, length, and legal fees of a fight.

Lawyers could do best if the state followed a mixed strategy of clearly articulated standards that can only with difficulty be applied to the facts of any specific controversy. Lawyers could articulate a clear rule but would need a court to resolve its uncertain application to the messy facts. For example, a court seeking to maximize lawyers' revenues would validate the poison pill, as it was validated in *Moran,* but then announce a judicially reviewable proportionality standard, under which the courts, aided by lawyers, determine whether a board should yank the pill in the face of a particular offer. This Delaware did.

Invalidating the pill is a clear protakeover standard that does not need much lawyers' work to enforce. Validating the pill in all instances is a clear antitakeover standard that also needs little lawyers' work. Validating the pill but subjecting it to review is neither overwhelmingly pro- nor antitakeover. But it does require a lot of lawyers' work.[87]

In a small state, lawyers and others profiting from corporate business can be politically powerful, as can be seen in the way Delaware's corporate law is produced. Amendments to corporate law first go to the bar association's corporate law committee for approval; then they go to the legislature for passage.[88] True, extreme self-seeking here will not work because businesspeople ultimately control the incorporation decision, and if Delaware acquired a reputation for legal costs exceeding its legal advantages, its reincorporation business would decline.

Nor do I believe that the presence of Machiavellian lawyers explains everything in Delaware. Rather, in a sea of doctrinal uncertainty (should managers' sole duty be to maximize shareholder value?), policy uncertainty (are takeovers good for the country?), and different judges with different answers to these questions, the lawyers' goals have some survival value.

Another way to look at the role of Delaware lawyers does not require one to see only self-interest. First, everyone concedes that lawyers heavily influence the content of the state's corporate law. Second, their clients are primarily managers of large companies. When in the early 1980s takeover offerers became entrepreneurs taking over large and medium-sized companies (and less often large companies taking over small ones), the rhetoric the lawyers heard shifted. Clients complained about the disruption from hostile takeovers, the manipulative tactics used by raiders, and the inability of honest managers to get enough time to mount a defense. A story could be told of the production of Delaware law with lawyers as the conduit, but without lawyers or legislators being conscious of their economic interest in an antitakeover tilt. The arguments they heard were the arguments and woes of the targets, the lawyers' clients and the legislators' constituency, not the abstract arguments about efficiency from financial economists. Even without an active interest group lobbying, one would predict the result to be law with an antitakeover tilt.

JUDGES' LAW.   Are Delaware judges the tools of the legislature and the lawyers, as William Cary, former SEC chairman, asserted?[89] Because the judges have long-term appointments, they do not have to respond to either group. A theory of jurisprudence has vexed scholars for ages; although I am not going to present one here, something useful can be said.

First, there is survivorship. If the legislature dislikes a law made by judges, it can overturn the law. Delaware has done so, overturning rules that would subject corporate directors to intense review, but not overturning court decisions validating antitakeover defenses such as the poison pill.[90] Even if judicial opinions were generated randomly, the opinions surviving would be those that the legislature, and the lawyers that influence the legislature, do not despise. And some argue that the bench actively favors what the legislature and bar want.[91] Selecting judges is a political act; politics will select judges whose theory of the public interest coincides with the needs of Delaware's legislature and its most prominent interest groups.

Second, some judges like being at the center of corporate law. Delaware judges get more attention than those of other states and have a lot of power in the economy. Law that keeps corporations inside Delaware keeps Delaware judges powerful and under the klieg lights. Doctrinal uncertainty in the mid-1980s required that the judges be consulted before major mergers occurred. It is not irrelevant that William Cary suggested a coup d'etat against the Delaware judiciary, proposing that Congress give national courts jurisdiction to hear lawsuits and appeals about critical matters of corporate law.[92] Little else could better sensitize the Delaware judiciary to its precarious position in American life. Nor is the pride that these judges express irrelevant: "With the possible exception of the Supreme Court of the United States, which I mention only out of respect," said a Delaware Supreme Court judge, "I doubt that there is a more exciting appellate court on which to serve."[93]

Third, Delaware judges want respect from the news media and from leading corporate lawyers. Thus the publicized lawyers' meetings in the late 1980s denouncing Delaware's protakeover opinions could have affected the judges. The media did not usually laud heroic protakeover judges, so no countervailing psychological pressure offset criticism from corporate lawyers, making the net audience pressures on judges at the end of the 1980s antitakeover. Alternative psychological pressures could have come from news media views of takeover entrepreneurs as populist folk heroes attacking corporate bureaucracies as elitist sinecures for the rich and ineffective. Indeed, some Reagan-era officials offered such views to the media but drew back, perhaps because the Boesky insider trading scandal hit soon after.[94]

Delaware as an Antitakeover Laggard

Why did it take Delaware so long to join the antitakeover bandwagon?

First, the legislature and the judiciary probably were genuinely uncertain whether takeovers were good for the country. Did takeovers primarily discipline the management of target firms? Or were offering companies building empires, exploiting inefficiencies in the securities markets, and exploiting tax deductions that target firms left unused?[95] Although "good for the country" is not the standard for Delaware corporate law, I have to believe many Delaware lawmakers are public spirited and affected by their conception of the public interest. And neither the news media nor academic commentary created certainty that takeovers were beneficial. However, by the end of the 1980s takeovers were associated with scandal, insider trading indictments, the collapse of the junk bond market, Michael Milken and Ivan Boesky. Analysts might argue that the excesses should be separated from useful disciplinary effects, but neither the public nor, perhaps, many lawmakers seemed likely to do so.

Lawmakers were also uncertain how takeovers fit into corporate law. Sometimes managers had better information than the market and ought to win. And the disruption to workers, community, and suppliers was not always worth the gains, some judges surely believed. Managers could oppose such takeovers. But if other managers just used collateral interests as excuses for self-entrenchment, courts had to intervene to remove takeover defenses from them. Delaware's proportionality standard— case-by-case review of whether defensive tactics were proportionate to the threat to the firm—would require that wise judges sort out the validity of a raider's offer and of management's defense.

Indecision and zig-zagging were also good for the Delaware bar, at least until the state's "market share" became threatened. And Delaware judges are not averse to being at the center of all important corporate transactions. Zig-zagging kept them there. Agonizing over tough issues reveals them to be professionals making difficult and important decisions.

Indecision was further abetted because, before the junk bond takeover started in the 1980s, offerers were America's largest corporations, which are disproportionately Delaware firms. Delaware politicians had to keep them satisfied. The offerers of the mid- and late 1980s were no longer mainly Delaware firms, but outsiders, sometimes without a significant operating firm, just a letter from Drexel Burnham Lambert stating that it could arrange financing. Thus the balance of law in Delaware should, all other things being equal, have shifted to defending targets. (This suggests that there will be less antitakeover pressure on Delaware in the 1990s. With Drexel's demise and a weak junk bond market, raiders will again be large Delaware firms.)[96]

Finally, the potential for federal pressure subsided during the 1980s. Delaware is poised on a political boundary: it cannot offend the federal body politic too much, or Congress, the SEC, or the courts could abolish the state's special advantages. And it cannot be too far out of line with the other states. These pressures changed in the 1980s to push Delaware toward a promanager, antitakeover position.

Competition among States

Two ideas dominate the debate on state competition in corporate law. Do states compete to provide corporate law that promotes efficient economic operation of the corporation at low legal cost? Or do they compete by providing the law that managers prefer, irrespective of efficiency—so-called racing to the bottom? And where does Delaware fit in this tension? Are states that provide an inefficient promanagerial law seriously penalized in capital markets? Some scholars have contended that competition among states induces law fostering efficient economic operation. But even if that is so in other corporate law contexts, the incentive for state legislatures to pass efficiency-enhancing takeover law is weak.

Considerations other than corporate efficiency will dominate state policymaking, particularly in states other than Delaware, discouraging legislators from looking much farther than the next election. If antitakeover law is popular (even if inefficient), legislators have reason to give voters what they want. Senior managers at targets also have a short time frame; raising long-term capital costs is a burden they will allow their stockholders to bear. And states compete in other dimensions. For most other than Delaware, long-term capital costs are not politically significant; they want to avoid disrupting current employment. True, they also want new plants to locate in their state, but antitakeover law need not deter new plants. State legislatures can provide a two-tiered law that protects current employees and allows companies needing new capital to choose not to be bound by that law and to keep their capital costs low.

COMPETITION TO PROVIDE EFFICIENT CORPORATE LAW. Theorists from Louis Brandeis to William Cary have argued that state corporate law is a race to the bottom, as states pander to managers by providing weak, promanagerial, antishareholder corporate law. Those that provide the weakest law will get incorporation business and the related taxes. But in a sharp critique of these theorists, Ralph Winter has contended that state competition should induce efficient corporate law. Capital markets would penalize corporations located in a state lacking efficient law, which would prevent a race to the bottom. The argument consciously echoes Charles Tiebout's concept of efficient outcomes to state competition.[97]

Winter did not argue that law would always appear to favor shareholders. The cost of tracking down minor managerial malfeasance could make for a loose but efficient corporate law. Nor did he argue that analyses of state competition applied to antitakeover law.[98]

Would state competition encourage laws favoring takeovers if takeovers are efficient? Some have so argued, as a derivative of the basic state competition argument.[99] Entrepreneurs will incorporate in states with laws that lower capital costs. States with weak antitakeover laws will increase the cost of capital, and entrepreneurs will avoid them.

The cost of capital does put some lid on the freedom of states to give local managers and workers the takeover protection they want. But it is not a tight-fitting lid. True, studies show declines in share prices of companies in states passing antitakeover laws.[100] But the impact of the decline is limited because although new capital may seek protakeover laws, takeovers address management of existing capital, of which the United States has quite a lot.[101] States can burden existing capital and keep new capital free. The burden on existing capital will make new capital providers nervous, but states that do not import much capital are not powerfully and immediately penalized. And states with sectors that do not need new capital can pass antitakeover laws that permit the capital-importing companies to choose not to be covered.[102]

And for most firms, retained earnings and debt, not new equity, are the primary sources of new capital; antitakeover laws only tangentially burden a company's ability to use debt and retained earnings.[103] Or states can allow out-of-state companies with out-of-state laws favoring takeovers to build new plants in-state. Thus states protecting companies with plants in place do not directly raise the cost of capital for those building new plants.[104] States can compete for new capital and burden old capital. So capital in place gets an antitakeover law from which new capital can opt out, and companies promising to bring new capital to the state for a new factory get new roads, infrastructure, and a ten-year tax holiday. And retained earnings, which incumbent managers control, make up the bulk of new capital.[105] Added up, the number of companies immune from the discipline of seeking new equity capital before their current chief executive officer retires is not small.[106]

Even for firms raising new equity, the impact of antitakeover law is weak. New equity often flows into firms run by founder-shareholders who own enough stock to block an unwanted takeover anyway and provide the discipline that a takeover threat would impose. True, protakeover laws might change expectations about earnings that will come later when the founder will be gone. But delayed legal effects have to be discounted to present value, reduced by the uncertainty of what the legislature will do later, since states can and do change their laws, and are swamped by business uncertainties.[107] What counts more than law is whether the company has a good product, will find oil, will have low production costs.[108] And because the securities analyst usually lacks legal training, paying to assess the law will not be worthwhile unless the analyst thinks the legal effects will be large.[109]

For state competition to induce protakeover laws, states must credibly pass laws with provisions that companies could not themselves establish with equal credibility. But states cannot easily bind themselves not to change legislation in the future. A later legislature can change the rules. To the extent a promise of no legislative change is not credible to capital markets, the protakeover legislation will be discounted in the price of capital.[110]

And it is easier for corporations to bind themselves than it is for legislatures. Managers can use a corporate charter prohibiting themselves and their successors from using current antitakeover techniques or require them to present bona fide, fully financed, all-holders bids to stockholders. Corporations that want protakeover rules do not need protakeover legislation. Takeover law is a ratchet: managers who want protakeover rules for themselves do not need the legislature, but managers who cannot get their shareholders to pass antitakeover charter rules want courts and legislatures that will impose those terms.

Thus although the state competition argument cannot be dismissed summarily at least until there is empirical confirmation, one must doubt its widespread and powerful impact. It will have little effect on states, industry sectors, or companies not soon expecting to raise new capital via stock offerings. Of those expecting to do so, takeover law will have only a small effect, and that effect is subject to offset and reversal by other political factors. Takeover law's primary effect is on capital in place; its effect on new capital can be cordoned off.

LEGISLATIVE MYOPIA.   Public-spirited legislators, even if they believed that takeovers impose discipline, would feel pressure to provide short-run benefits to constituents. Legislators want to win the next election. Their time horizon is even shorter than that of the 58-year-old manager who wants to run the show for a half dozen years. Legislatures should be expected to seek the long-term corporate needs of the state only weakly.

If antitakeover law is popular, then, even if it is inefficient, Rust Belt legislators will have reason to give constituents what they want.

And to the extent states are competing, most other than Delaware are unconcerned with long-term capital costs; they want to avoid disruption of current employment. Even if Delaware wants to compete on capital costs, it could compete by being just a little less protakeover than other states.

COASE AND INCOMMENSURATE VALUES. Even if all legislatures produced antitakeover laws that diminished shareholder wealth more than they enhanced managerial wealth, why don't shareholders buy managers off, paying them to run the firm as it should be, or to sell it to those who would? The transaction cost of organizing shareholders to make the payoff is a standard Coasian answer; legislatures and law could be a means of this organization, instead of the means through which managers defeat shareholders.[111] Perhaps golden parachutes were a means of organization.

There is another response. The matters that Coase would trade are incommensurate in takeovers. Senior managers finally get to run the enterprise when they reach their late fifties, and they expect to have the satisfactions of power and prestige for a half dozen years. They are already financially well-to-do. They cannot easily, or at all, be bought off with money; they want something else entirely: autonomy, power, and prestige, which they will fight to retain.

OUT-MIGRATION FROM DELAWARE? Even if Rust Belt legislators passed antitakeover laws, what was Delaware afraid of? Couldn't it stand pat and let other states pass antitakeover laws? Even if other states considered the cost of capital a goal secondary to protecting current employment and managerial stability, did Delaware have to go along with them?

Maybe the state overreacted, mistakenly fearing that other states would get its corporate business. Delaware did have reason to fear that managers would not ignore such considerations. Martin Lipton, the most prominent defender of target-firm management, recommended that managers consider leaving Delaware for states that were producing "better" antitakeover legislation. And Roberta Romano reported that such threats were not idle: some firms left Delaware in the late 1970s and early 1980s to better insulate managers from a takeover.[112]

But mass migration from Delaware was implausible, because managers usually need approval from shareholders to migrate.[113] A more realistic fear was that firms might stop reincorporating into Delaware, which has had 80 percent of the national reincorporations, perhaps 200 firms a decade.[114]

So Delaware might feel compelled to provide certain promanagerial advantages if other states provide them. One theory of competition suggests that if one is competing against a competitor, or group of competitors with the same location, one should position oneself close to the most significant competitor, to take up all of the competitive space on the other side.[115]

COLLAPSE OF DELAWARE STANDARDIZATION? Delaware has reason to keep as many companies as possible incorporated in the state. If other states systematically have a rule that corporate decisionmakers find beneficial, Delaware has reason to use the same rule. Even if the erosion of Delaware's market share is not massive and immediate, its corporate law business may be fragile. An explanation for the state's persistence is that it provides a standard form of corporate law: because many major companies are governed by Delaware law, other companies find it advantageous to adopt that law also. Legal costs are lower for the additional company that uses Delaware law. Decisionmakers will not be blamed if something goes wrong, in the same way that no one ever got fired for buying IBM.

But to maintain this advantage, Delaware must keep its lead. Were it to lose its lead, it might never regain it, as New Jersey discovered early in the century. Delaware has no reason to test whether alternative theories better explain its persistence. If it is only offering a standard form, then once the standard collapses the network might be rebuilt anywhere (or nowhere).

The collapse of Delaware's advantage could lead to *no* state's picking up the business. At the turn of the century New Jersey and Delaware provided large-scale enterprises with critical legal components that are today unimportant. Large companies had grown out of cartels and needed a corporate law that allowed them to hold stock in other corporations and to merge with other companies. New Jersey first provided this service, then Delaware. Once there was substantial incorporation in Delaware, the state could standardize corporate law terms. But without a catalyst, the opportunity to standardize might never have come about.

So standardization may be strong enough to maintain Delaware's lead but too weak to create a lead.[116] Accordingly, some Delaware actors could conclude that its lead is fragile. Once lost, it may never be regained. So every precaution against losing it must be taken.

THE DIMENSIONS OF STATE COMPETITION. Delaware law is the product of many forces: ideology about what is the best law, interest-group pressures, legislators' fear of losing tax revenues, reaction to scandal, and more. When other states systematically provide antitakeover rules, there is little advantage to Delaware in not providing roughly similar rules, especially when it no longer fears federal preemption. Rust Belt states have little reason to keep the cost of capital a primary consideration in their takeover lawmaking. Legislators look to the next election: if takeovers are unpopular, then no matter what financial economists may say about efficiency, state legislators have reason to pass antitakeover laws, especially laws that allow capital-seeking companies to choose not to be covered. When managers and big labor press for these laws, and only politically weak, primarily out-of-state groups are opposed, state legislators, many of whom share popular mistrust of takeovers, have little reason to resist. Delaware politicians might have been able to resist the rhetoric of reincorporation out of Delaware. They said they wanted to keep companies in the state by providing "good" takeover law. But providing managers with what they wanted might have been necessary only if Delaware's lead depends on providing a standard, which could collapse if reincorporation into the state stopped. This view is not proven, however, and was not articulated. Delaware might have mistakenly overreacted, although when sister states make antitakeover law, Delaware legislators have little reason to resist. Rather than racing to the bottom ahead of the competitive pack, Delaware seems to have been a reluctant (and perhaps unnecessary) follower in the takeover competition.

Conclusion

Politics is one of the determinants of corporate governance. Laws set the rules for takeovers, and politics influences what laws are made. Two types of political moves deeply influenced the takeover boom of the 1980s. The first arose from the politics of financial institutions in America. American politics fragmented financial institutions and their portfolios and severed ties that would allow them to easily coordinate the stock they could hold. Financial intermediaries cannot easily assert authority in industrial boardrooms. Explanations for fragmentation lie in American federalism, the political power of small financial institutions, popular opinion that favored reining in Wall Street, and the public-spirited view that fragmenting finance led to a more stable financial system.

Takeover politics comes in a second, more direct, variety. The takeovers of the early 1980s shifted power from managers to shareholders and takeover entrepreneurs. Managers, losing their autonomy in the economic arena, struck back in the political arena. It is not too much of an exaggeration to say that by calling for political reinforcements, managers won in state-by-state political combat what they could not win in contracts with shareholders. They won freedom, nearly complete, from takeover.

For non-Delaware firms this simple political story explains much; for Delaware the political story is more complex. Part of the public choice story is hidden because key initial antitakeover moves were transactional and then judicial. But legislatures can overturn transactions and court decisions. Roughly simultaneously in the mid-1980s, Delaware courts handed down an antimanagerial decision and a promanagerial poison pill validation. The legislature overturned the first but added to the barriers set up by the second. True, the recent decline in takeovers has additional explanations. The stock market is up, takeover techniques such as junk bonds are less available after the demise of Drexel Burnham Lambert, and takeover activity worldwide is down. Politics is only part of the story. But a mass revival of takeovers will need new takeover technology to overcome the antitakeover laws.

Public opinion made antitakeover law possible by helping to fragment private financial power and then by making it easier for managers to obtain protective legislation. A unified story is available: Contracts that probably would not be written in an unregulated environment (that is, contracts that favor managers) are written in the political environment.

Federalism makes local politics important. Federalism long ago tilted politics to favor small financial institutions; in the 1980s it tilted politics to favor managers. Federalism increased the power of small financial institutions that wanted to restrain Wall Street and enhanced the power of managers who wanted to thwart takeovers. The politics of corporate governance is largely determined by these interest groups and a public of bystander-voters sympathetic to fragmenting financial institutions and suspicious of takeovers.

Comment by Martin Lipton

Mark Roe's paper builds on previous work by Roe and Joseph Grundfest that provides the economic philosophy underlying the implicit assumptions in this essay.[117] The previous articles and the present one attempt to paint a history of takeover legislation and corporate governance that runs (implicitly or explicitly stated) as follows:

—Because of the separation of share ownership and corporate management, there is an agency problem. Left to their own devices, managers will prefer their own interests to those of their principals, the shareholders, and will misbehave and violate their agency relationship.

—The hostile takeover movement of the 1970s and 1980s was beginning to correct this agency dysfunction by moving power away from managers and back toward shareholders.

—Managers struck back in the political arena. They possessed political muscle because of the concentrated nature of their interest group, their wealth, their control over substantial political contributions, and the general public's antipathy toward hostile takeovers (which itself was at least partly a product of managers' being effective at swinging votes in local areas).

—Managers used this political muscle to cause states to enact antitakeover laws.

—State antitakeover laws killed the hostile takeover movement. "By calling for political reinforcements, managers won in state-by-state political combat what they could not win in contract making with shareholders. They won freedom, nearly complete, from takeover."

—The death of hostile takeovers leaves managers once again free of discipline and free to pursue their own selfish agendas, meaning that the interests of stockholders will once again be subordinated to the interests of management and other constituencies.

Boiled down to its basics in this way, it is hard to believe the argument would be taken seriously were it not being advanced by two thoughtful and well-respected academics (and probably accepted by a host of others). It is hard to know where to start in addressing the holes in the story.

To begin with conceptual issues, Roe's work perpetuates the model of the public corporation as no more than a relationship between shareholder-principals and manager-agents. This model, which underlies the view of corporate governance as a means of ensuring that managers carry out the wishes of the shareholders, is a gross oversimplification of modern corporate structure. The model seems to be so embedded in the literature that articles like this accept it without question or examination. Steven Rosenblum and I have examined the agency model in joint work, but much more could be done on the subject.[118] At a minimum, it is necessary to reexamine the blind acceptance of this model.

Second, both Roe and Grundfest evidence an underlying distrust or an antipathy toward corporate managers that is never examined or explained and that is unjustified. Very few of the academic articles espousing this point of view attempt to present concrete examples of managers preferring themselves at the expense of shareholders. Instead, they repeat the same generalities (managers build empires, managers spend lavishly on themselves, and so forth) and recite the same Adam Smith-Berle-Means theoretical model of agency problems. Grundfest's article, for example, does refer in passing to a few concrete examples of management misbehavior, but the examples (pollution of the environment, adulteration of baby food, overcharging the Pentagon) are instances of misbehavior in pursuit of *corporate* profit, not in pursuit of *personal* profit. Indeed, they constitute an effort to enhance corporate profit at the risk of personal *detriment* (including personal criminal sanctions).[119]

Third, these articles accept the idea that the wave of hostile takeovers was a positive development for corporate governance in that it provided a needed mechanism through which to discipline managers. This again is an idea that Rosenblum and I tried to address in our article. That takeovers are a productive disciplinary mechanism is now seriously questioned by a number of economists. Roe (and Grundfest) should take into account some of these questions.

The claim that corporate managers pushed through antitakeover legislation in response to takeover activity that threatened their personal interests is oversimplified. Corporate managers had a role in the enactment of many takeover-related statutes. But the sequencing and causal relationships presented by Roe are fundamentally wrong. States expressed concern about the nature and scope of takeover activity almost from the start of the takeover explosion. State antitakeover legislation started in the 1960s and was prevalent in the 1970s. The second generation of statutes in the 1980s was a legislative response to the Supreme Court's 1982 decision in *MITE* striking down the first generation of statutes (that may have been more antitakeover than the second-generation statutes). They were not primarily the product of the "losers" (managers) of the 1980s takeover activity striking back in the political arena to protect their self-interest. Nor was there an "explosion of state antitakeover moves" following the *CTS* case. In fact, the response began right after *MITE*.

The "protectionist" portrait of takeover legislation is insulting to the wide array of commentators, practitioners, judges, and now some academics, who have expressed sincere (and I believe warranted) concern over the impact of takeover activity on the economy and the ultimate health of corporate enterprises. The legislative response to takeovers goes much further back and is much more widely and deeply rooted than Roe acknowledges.

Second, the idea that the second-generation takeover statutes are responsible for the current slowdown in takeover activity is wrong. The claim that corporate managers have won freedom from takeovers is also wrong. The current slowdown is a product of economic conditions. State statutes may have some impact on the process and negotiating leverage for takeovers. But they can hardly stop takeover activity. Takeovers are only temporarily in abeyance. When economic conditions change, they will come back, unless we change the system more fundamentally in the meantime. And, if the "shareholders' rights" protakeover agenda now being promoted by some academics and groups such as the United Shareholders Association and the Council of Institutional Investors is adopted, they will come back with more vengeance (and more destructive potential) than ever.

Third, Roe's portrait of the Delaware legislature and bar as calculating its legislative responses in terms of maximizing tax revenues and lawyers' fees is overstated. As Roe partially recognizes, these concerns have an impact in a far more complex and subtle picture of interactions.

Some concluding thoughts. Roe's paper and its predecessors suffer from a common malady: an affinity for tidy boxes and explanations. The agency model is an example. So are the ideas that takeovers discipline managers, that managers "struck back" politically in response to that discipline, and that state antitakeover legislation was the cause of the slowdown in takeover activity.

Second, in corporate governance a number of people seem to be sensing the ability to push an agenda based on "shareholders' rights" and a distrust of the incumbents. Roe and his intellectual bedfellows seem to be campaigning, subtly and without explicitly acknowledging it, for legislative action along these lines. The same campaign is going on within the American Law Institute Corporate Governance Project and elsewhere. By creating a story that the status quo is the product of management perfidy, the academics' legislative agenda may become more of a possibility. I believe their legislative agenda is wrong. I also believe they underestimate the potential that they will be used by the corporate raider types, who are not gone but only (for now) forgotten.

I suggest that in considering Roe's arguments it would be worthwhile to weigh them against these counterarguments:

—A free market system must have a well-functioning mechanism for moving assets from poor managers to good managers.

—Since it involves high friction costs and dangerous changes in capital structure, the hostile takeover is a very inefficient means of moving assets into hands that will make more efficient use of them.

—Rather than a market for corporate *control* that involves buying and selling the capital of a company, we need a market for corporate *management* in which the owners of the capital of a corporation can readily and with relatively low-cost change management to deal with failed strategy or incompetent performance.

The quinquennial system of corporate governance proposed by Rosenblum and me eliminates the free-rider problem, avoids the social and economic costs of hostile takeovers, facilitates long-term planning, forces outside directors to monitor management closely and ensure that it is not ignoring shareholder desires, encourages a constructive partnership relationship between management and shareholders, and facilitates relatively inexpensive and nondisruptive changes of management when appropriate. Accordingly, more attention should be paid to obtaining the legislation necessary to achieve it or something similar than to reversing the state takeover legislation of the 1980s.

Comment by Ronald J. Gilson

In his earlier work Mark Roe demonstrated that politics played a central role in shaping the distinctive structure of the modern American corporation.[120] In that vein he now offers a political history of the corporate takeover phenomenon of the 1980s. This is no small achievement, but it is not all he accomplishes. Roe also manages to locate the intersection of two intellectual frameworks that have been contending—often with the intensity of participants in a particularly nasty hostile takeover battle—within the legal academy in recent years. In its pure form, the law and economics movement rests on the proposition that the central normative and positive characteristic of our system is efficiency. The critical legal studies movement, in contrast, treats claims of efficiency as a façade for a system that, in the end, is explainable only by reference to

I am grateful to Joseph Grundfest for comments on an earlier draft of this comment.

power and politics. Roe's perspective spans both views. In a democracy, he argues, politics serves to limit the influence of markets.

I have little quarrel with Roe's description of the takeover politics of the 1980s. It certainly describes my limited and unsuccessful lobbying experience in connection with the most recent Pennsylvania antitakeover statute. The only thing the legislators to whom I spoke thought they needed to know about this radical legislation was that it was backed by both the state chamber of commerce and the AFL-CIO. One does not have to be a weatherman to know which way the wind is blowing.

More important, Roe's observations are entirely consistent with current empirical evidence concerning the impact of state antitakeover legislation on stockholder wealth. Firms that had no company-level defenses experienced statistically significant negative abnormal returns of almost 4 percent when states adopted antitakeover legislation; firms with preexisting defenses were largely unaffected.[121] As Roe suggests, legislation served as a substitute for corporate governance. When shareholders would not give management protection, management turned to the state legislature. Politics trumped markets.

Because I find that Roe's discussion rings true, I want to extend, rather than criticize, his analysis by focusing on the dynamic relation between politics and markets.[122] Just as politics may check the influence of markets in a democracy, so too markets can check the influence of politics in a market-based economy. Roe describes how state-level politics served to rein in the market for corporate control in the 1980s. Markets may ultimately get even in the 1990s.

A Model of the Role of Corporate Takeovers

To contemplate the dynamic between politics and the market for corporate control, consider a very simple model of the role of corporate takeovers. I have in mind a Coasean world in which the efficient boundary of the firm is determined by existing industrial technology.[123] In period 1 the economy is in organizational equilibrium. All assets are owned by the entity that, conditioned on existing and expected industrial technology and the transaction costs associated with shifting assets to a different (or different kind of) entity, can most efficiently use them. In period 2 an unanticipated change in technology occurs—whether one that, for example, creates economies of scope between previously unrelated activities or one that simply reduces the transaction costs of actually combining related activities. The notion is simply a dynamic market in organizational form. When technology changes the efficient boundary of the firm, a response is initiated. From this perspective, the market for corporate control—acquisitions and divestitures—is merely an equilibrating process that reshuffles assets to those who, as a result of the technological change, now value them more highly. A hostile takeover is simply a subclass of transactions in which one side, the acquirer, seeks to extract rents while the other side, target management, seeks to protect them.

For a stylized example of the model that is consistent with the emerging data (and central to the 1980s market for corporate control chronicled in Roe's political history), imagine an equilibrium in which conglomerate organizations survive because of the costs—including costs resulting from management's defense of their empire—of shifting their assets to more focused and efficient uses. A technological change then occurs: financing becomes available to a new class of breakup entrepreneurs who profit by brokering the movement of conglomerate assets to more focused operators.[124]

Management's Political Platform

Roe starkly describes the outcome of management's political counterattack on the hostile takeover: "They won freedom, nearly complete, from takeover." Evaluating this conclusion is complicated. In some respects it may overstate management's success.[125] However, in other important respects Roe may understate the insulation achieved by management. The potential exists for management to protect itself not only from takeovers but also from a means of displacement that most of the state antitakeover statutes still have left untouched: the proxy contest.

This is not the place for an extended discussion of the barriers that can be erected to electoral challenge of corporate management.[126] But their potential can be seen by reference to a leading figure in the annals of defensive tactics: Time, Inc. Not satisfied with having successfully deprived its shareholders of the opportunity to choose between Time's acquisition of Warner and Paramount's acquisition of Time (at $200 a share), Time's managers took a further step to protect themselves against shareholder reprisals. Certain securities offered in connection with the merger between Time and Warner contain terms that would substantially dilute the equity of common shareholders should they be so bold as to replace over management's objection as few as five of Time's twenty-four directors.[127] While the Delaware Supreme Court has in the past counseled disappointed shareholders that if they were "displeased with the actions of their elected representatives [toward a hostile takeover], the powers of corporate democracy are at their disposal to turn the board out," Time's capital structure now eliminates that option.[128]

And that brings us to the current state of (or at least management's political goal for) American corporate governance. The party platform is that managers must be protected against the threat of takeovers because hostile takeovers force managers to focus on the short term.[129] Unless government protects American management from this threat, American companies will be at a continued disadvantage in global competition with German and Japanese companies whose managers are not subject to such distractions. But here is where the potential arises to extend Roe's political analysis: is it possible that markets may constrain politics?

The Potential for Markets to Constrain Politics

Academic inquiry into the structure of American corporate governance has focused on the search for a governance technique that bridges the separation of ownership and management by holding managers accountable for their performance. Accountability, in turn, requires that some agent actually monitor management's performance. The market for corporate control—through takeovers, proxy fights, and the friendly transactions that anticipate them—for a time served indirectly to monitor management in the context of an American political climate that prevented the development of financial intermediaries who might assume a direct monitoring role. As Roe said, American corporate history "can be seen as an effort to find substitutes for the direct monitoring [of management] that politics disallowed."[130]

Management's political objective draws its special irony from its premise that emulating the success of Japanese and German companies requires protecting management from the paralyzing terror of the market for corporate control: "Free us from takeovers; we want to be like Japanese and German management." But freedom from the monitoring role of takeovers does not come free in Japan and Germany. Rather, the intermittent monitoring of the capital market is replaced by the continuous monitoring of a company's main bank. Paul Sheard has described the Japanese main bank structure as a "substitute for the missing take-over market [which] performs a role that closely parallels in its effect the external takeover market: in particular in bringing about the displacement of ineffectual management and the reorganization of corporate assets to improve efficiency."[131]

Thus, if American management seriously wanted to emulate the Japanese and German corporate governance models, they would propose to replace takeovers with some form of continuous monitoring—a means by which the pursuit of long-term profits can be distinguished from creative excuses for current performance. Examples readily come to mind. For companies with appropriate capital structures and in appropriate markets, Michael Jensen's LBO Association behaves somewhat like a Japanese keiretsu.[132] For other companies, the growth of institutional investors makes feasible the election of a core of institutionally designated professional directors who would have the right incentives to undertake the long-term monitoring role assumed by Japanese and German banks.[133]

It appears, however, that American management wants to have its cake and eat it too. The lesson Roe teaches is that American political history has dictated indirect monitoring by the capital market rather than direct monitoring by financial intermediaries. Management's political platform now seeks, and perhaps has achieved, freedom from capital market monitoring. But no meaningful substitute has been offered. Rather than emulating the Japanese and German system of continuous monitoring, American management seeks to create the only major economic system in which management is not monitored at all.

The potential for markets to operate as a check on this political outcome arises if there is a link between corporate governance and corporate performance.[134] Were the United States an autarky, the link would make little difference. Roe explains why. Where those who benefit from restricting the operation of a market are concentrated but those who suffer from it are widely dispersed, market regulation that actually makes the pie smaller is politically feasible. But that result holds only when the relevant market and the relevant regulatory jurisdiction are coterminous. When those subject to the political outcome must compete with those free of it, markets may operate as a check on politics.

By now, the punch line should be apparent. American business must compete with Japanese and German companies not only in the world of managerial rhetoric but in the real world as well. It has become commonplace that most of the revenues of many "American" companies are earned outside the United States. Even in the domestic market, there is increasing international competition: from 1980 to 1989 foreign direct investment in the United States grew at a compound rate of 22.3 percent. And as Joseph Grundfest has stressed, global business competition inevitably results in global regulatory competition.[135] When companies can choose the national regulatory regime that applies—Grundfest had securities regulation regimes in mind—one can imagine the international equivalent of domestic state competition for corporate chartering business. If some companies are irrevocably committed to a particular regime, whether because General Motors cannot practically reincorporate in Panama or because the French government retains a dominant ownership position in a newly privatized company, regulatory competition occurs by proxy through the performance of the competing regime's captive firms. But in either case, the outcome is the same: when the scope of the market is broader than the jurisdiction of the regulation, politics alone will be insufficient to maintain a rent-protecting regime. If a governance system in which management is accountable to no one must compete, market pressure may come to produce political pressure.

Conclusion

Mark Roe's work demonstrates that politics has played a critical role in shaping the structure and operation of the American capital market in general and the outcome of the takeover wave of the 1980s in particular. Those with access to political power may have the ability to overrule market outcomes. I have suggested here that the interaction between politics and markets may operate in both directions and that a critical element defining the direction of the relationships is the extent to which the boundaries of the political jurisdiction and the relevant market are coterminous. Politics shaped the American capital market over a long period when, for practical purposes, that market was autarkic. In the 1980s, when the United States went from being the world's largest creditor to the world's largest debtor, the breadth of the capital market expanded beyond that of the political jurisdiction. The restructuring of past political solutions that we now observe—like the retreat from the Glass-Steagall provisions—marks the market's counterattack. Roe perceptively recognizes the wave of state antitakeover protection during the 1980s as a political attack on a market result. I suggest that we keep an eye out in the 1990s for the market response. International competition may not resurrect hostile takeovers, but it may put an end to what even Peter Drucker has called "management accountable only to itself."[136]

General Discussion

Oliver Hart expressed reservations about the argument that takeovers were needed in the United States because financial institutions are prevented from holding large positions in U.S. companies. In particular, he questioned the implication that the collective-action problems and the principal-agent problems have been effectively solved in Japan and Germany by institutional structures. When banks and large financial institutions take controlling positions in firms, he said, these agency problems are just pushed one step back. "At the very least, one would expect agency problems, perhaps very significant ones, to exist between these institutions and their owners, and one might expect takeovers of financial institutions rather than takeovers of manufacturing companies."

If there is something about the structure of financial institutions that makes the principal-agent problems easier to solve, Hart noted, this has "very interesting implications for the optimal way to organize a society." But he questioned whether this is the case. "The agency problems come from the fact that you have large amounts of financing to be done, but you do not have very rich people. Then the people who are ultimately supplying the capital are going to be little involved in the activities of the companies to whom they are supplying capital." But that is the case whether the ultimate investors are individual shareholders or individual depositors in banks, he said.

Robert McCauley expanded on this point. The appropriate trade-off is not between managerialism and financial institution control, he said, but between managerialism at the corporate level or at the level of the financial institutions. "Who controls the bank managers?" he asked rhetorically. The answers are either no one, or that there is a structure in which some political or bureaucratic institution is at the center of the system. But, he said, "Once you open the possibility that the bureaucrats control the bankers, you have to also consider the possibility that the bankers control the bureaucrats." Fear of the latter, he added, may explain the "sensible undercurrent of populism" that Roe emphasizes.

Roe responded that he agreed, noting that even if financial institutions were allowed to hold large blocks of stock, all that might be accomplished is a shift in the locus of suboptimal decision-making from the boardroom of an industrial company to the boardroom or the portfolio manager of the financial institution. Gilson added that agency costs, "like gravity and friction, do not go away. They just get moved around."

Despite this, Roe contended that there might be room for improvement on the existing structure. "It is not unusual to have agents checking agents and getting superior performance." This could be the result of something as simple as a "second roll of the dice," he said. "The managers at the industrial company roll the dice, and if they win, either because of luck or perspicacity, that is the end of it. If the financial institution is smart enough to do nothing when the managers are winning, that is fine. But if they lose, the financial institution picks up the dice, rolls again, at smaller odds of winning because it is not as good as the industrial company managers on average. But simply the fact that the dice can be rolled again can improve performance."[137]

Frank Lichtenberg pointed out that the empirical literature is mixed on the question of whether concentrated ownership is good or bad for corporate performance. He noted that a study by Harold Demsetz and Kenneth Lehn found no link at all between concentration of ownership at the firm level and the performance of the firm. But he said his own work on Japanese corporations suggests that firms in which financial institutions have a large equity stake tend to have above-average profitability and productivity, while firms that have significant cross-shareholdings tend to have below average profitability and productivity.[138]

Warren Farb questioned the implication by Roe and Gilson that individual shareholders are better off in Germany or Japan where large financial institutions play a heavy monitoring role. He argued that the U.S. system probably gives the most consideration to the short-term interests of shareholders, while in Germany and Japan, the institutional shareholders, who are usually permanent shareholders, tend to have the most influence. If institutional investors were given similar influence over corporate governance in the United States, he said, problems in corporate performance could be compounded unless these institutions were changed in ways that gave them a more long-term focus.

While improved performance from large block holdings is at least a possibility, Roe said he was not trying to argue that it is necessarily so. "I do make the argument that the system is different, and the difference is a result of American politics," he said. Along the same lines, he contended that discussant Martin Lipton's comments support this view. In discussing the political elements of lobbying that result in protakeover moves, Roe said, Lipton was describing organizations that have influence at the national level but that are weak or nonexistent at the state level.

The Securities and Exchange Commission (SEC), for example, has had a free market ideology lately that has encouraged protakeover regulations, Roe said. But "they are a national institution. They are less responsive to the calls of local managers." It is consistent with his arguments, Roe said, that the SEC is not as antitakeover as the states.

A similar point can be made about the role of Drexel Burnham, or the Council of Institutional Investors. "Their successful lobbying was entirely at the national level," Roe asserted. "They just were not influential in state legislatures."

Ronald Daniels was unconvinced by Roe's arguments that a protakeover coalition of consumers, intermediaries, raiders, and shareholders could not have formed at the national level to try to prevent antitakeover legislation from being passed at the state level. "It is not clear to me, when you consider their organizational capacity and their wealth, that they necessarily would have lost," he said. He wondered why the antitakeover lobby did as well as it had and speculated that the answer has to do with "ideology and the role of ideas," especially a widespread popular feeling "that there is something inherently evil about takeovers."

Peg O'Hara said one of the reasons there has not been an effective constituency against state antitakeover laws in the United States is that many of the laws were enacted in one or two days with little or no notice. The press did not cover them, she noted: "We are still finding takeover laws that were passed and nobody even knew they were there." She said the problems of organizing any kind of constituency on the other side "are virtually insurmountable."

Nonetheless, if the evidence is convincing that takeovers enhance the efficiency of firms, Daniels argued, public policy ought to be aimed at ways to compensate those who are disadvantaged by these transactions, so that they would reduce their opposition. The debate should focus on trying to develop a richer array of instruments to deal with the damage done to some constituents and thereby try to attenuate the ideological objections to takeovers.

Gilson argued that a guiding principle in setting institutional arrangements should be "mutability," so that the lowest-cost solution could be allowed to emerge. The problem with a political solution, or any system that fixes the institutional arrangements too securely, is that it creates barriers to changing the system when the world changes.

Daniels suggested that the linkage between fragmentation of ownership and takeovers is not as tight as Roe argued, noting that Canadian corporations are characterized by a very high degree of concentration of share ownership, and yet Canadian firms also experienced a takeover wave during the 1980s. Likewise, Hart pointed out that firms in the United Kingdom also experienced a takeover wave, even though British financial institutions are not subject to the same restrictions on share ownership as are those in the United States.

Robert Taggart suggested that many of the takeover tactics of the 1980s, including junk bond financing and the leveraged buyout form itself, were devices to circumvent earlier antitakeover initiatives. This was reminiscent of the so-called "regulatory dialectic," he said, a model used in the study of regulatory economics in which an effective political coalition forms to force through regulation to benefit itself. Then some sort of change in the economic environment makes it profitable to circumvent the regulation. This, in turn, causes the political interests to try to recoalesce. The lesson from this model, he said, is that the process is continuous, with one wave of institutional change leading to the next.

Mike Scherer commented that the emphasis on the need to monitor management seemed to dismiss the importance of the monitoring that occurs through product-market competition. "If, indeed, the Germans and Japanese have a more effective managerial monitoring system, that makes them more effective competitors in world markets for tradeable goods," and that, in turn, provides a check on managerial performance. But this argument has an ironic twist to it, Scherer noted, because managers of U.S. companies frequently complain that the monitoring they are subjected to by U.S financial markets makes it more difficult for them to compete against Japanese and German companies in product markets.

Notes

1. Mark J. Roe, "Political and Legal Restraints on Ownership and Control of Public Companies," *Journal of Financial Economics,* vol. 27 (September 1990), pp. 7–41; and Roe, "A Political Theory of American Corporate Finance," *Columbia Law Review,* vol. 91 (January 1991), pp. 10–67.

2. See Mark J. Roe, "Some Differences in Corporate Governance in Germany, Japan, and America," *Yale Law Journal,* vol. 102 (forthcoming).

3. Harold Demsetz and Kenneth Lehn, "The Structure of Corporate Ownership: Causes and Consequences," *Journal of Political Economy,* vol. 93 (December 1985), p. 1155.

4. Roe, "Political and Legal Restraints"; and Roe, "A Political Theory." For similar arguments, see Joseph A. Grundfest, "Subordination of American Capital," *Journal of Financial Economics,* vol. 27 (September 1990), pp. 89–114; Michael C. Jensen, "Eclipse of the Public Corporation," *Harvard Business Review,* vol. 67 (September–October 1989), pp. 61, 65; William G. Ouchi, *The M-Form Society: How American Teamwork Can Capture the Competitive Edge* (Addison-Wesley, 1984) pp. 82, 89; and Lester Thurow, *The Zero Sum Solution: Building a World-Class American Economy* (Simon and Schuster, 1985), p. 164.

5. Mark J. Roe, "Institutional Fiduciaries in the Corporate Boardroom," in Arnold Sametz and James L. Bicksler, eds., *Institutional Investing: Challenges and Responsibilities of the 21st Century* (Homewood, Ill.: Business One Irwin, 1991), pp. 292–300.

6. In Germany, for instance, universal banks can perform all financial activities—lending, taking deposits, brokering stock, owning stock directly, and managing investment companies—activities that in the United States are the province of separate financial institutions. German banks own some stock directly and control large blocks through investment companies, trust funds, and brokerage accounts. By putting these voting blocks together, German banks, unlike American banks, can, for better or worse, have substantial influence inside German industrial firms.

7. Hearings on S. 3580 before a Subcommittee on Securities and Exchange of the Senate Committee on Banking and Currency, Investment Trusts and Investment Companies, 76 Cong. 3 sess. (Government Printing Office, 1940), pt. 1, pp. 216–20, 434. See also Mark J. Roe, "Political Elements in the Creation of a Mutual Fund Industry," *University of Pennsylvania Law Review,* vol. 139 (June 1991), pp. 1469–1511.

8. Internal Revenue Code 851(b)(4).

9. *New York Insurance Law* §1405(a)(6) and (8) (McKinney, 1985).

10. *New York Insurance Law* §1701(a); William McCown and Steven Martinie, "State Regulation of Life Insurance Companies," *Association of Life Insurance Counsel Proceedings,* vol. 27 (1988), p. 8.

11. *The Department of Labor's Enforcement of the ERISA,* Senate Committee on Governmental Affairs, 99 Cong. 2 sess. (Government Printing Office, 1986), pp. 53–58; John Pound, "Proxy Contests and the Efficiency of Shareholder Oversight," *Journal of Financial Economics,* vol. 20 (January–March 1988), pp. 237–65. Corporate managers have opposed changes in proxy rules to make proxy contests easier, and pension groups have guardedly backed changes such as confidential voting that would shield the pension managers from corporate managers' ire. James A. White, "Pension Officers Back Proxy-Rule Shifts," *Wall Street Journal,* April 1, 1991, p. C1.

Several forces keep pension managers passive—the manager's control, fiduciary restraints, and a culture of investment passivity. Thus several forces, each too weak to determine the result by itself, point in the same direction. See Mark J. Roe, "The Modern Corporation and Private Pensions: ERISA's Errors," working paper, September 1992.

12. Judith H. Dobrzynski, "Is Pete Wilson Trying to Mute a Shareholder Activist?" *Business Week,* July 1, 1991, p. 29.

13. Ronald J. Gilson and Reinier Kraakman, "Reinventing the Outside Director: An Agenda for Institutional Investors," *Stanford Law Review,* vol. 43 (April 1991), pp. 863–906.

14. SEC Rules 13d-1 and 13d-5(b)(1), 17 Code of Federal Regulations para. 240.13d-1 and 5(b)(1) (1990).

15. Bernard S. Black, "Shareholder Passivity Reexamined," *Michigan Law Review,* vol. 89 (December 1990), pp. 520–608; and Alfred F. Conard, "Beyond Managerialism: Investor Capitalism?" *Michigan Journal of Law Reform,* vol. 22 (Fall 1988), pp. 117, 162.

16. For example, *GAF Corp.* v. *Milstein,* 453 F.2d 709, 720-21 (2d Cir. 1971), *cert. denied,* 406 U.S. 910 (1972). See generally Jonathan R. Macey and Jeffry M. Netter, "Regulation 13D and the Regulatory Process," *Washington University Law Quarterly,* vol. 65, no. 1 (1987), pp. 131–61 (discussing dozens of lawsuits under the filing requirements).

17. Conard, "Beyond Managerialism," p. 162.

18. Black, "Shareholder Passivity Reexamined;" and 17 C.F.R. 240.14a-1(l) (1990).

19. "SEC Proposed Rules Regarding Securityholder Communications," SEC release 34-29315, IC-18201, June 17, 1991, reprinted in Bureau of National Affairs, *BNA's Corporate Counsel Weekly,* supp. to vol. 6 (June 26, 1991). The SEC adopted a modified proposal on October 15, 1992.

20. See *State National Bank of El Paso* v. *Farah Mfg. Co. Inc.,* 678 S.W.2d 661 (Tex. Ct. App. 1984).

21. Securities Exchange Act of 1934, 15 U.S.C. 78 (1982). See *Feder* v. *Martin-Marietta Corp.,* 406 F.2d 260 (2d Cir. 1969), *cert. denied,* 396 U.S. 1036 (1970) (deputized director triggers principal's 16(b) liability). A group of institutions with 10 percent or more of the stock of an industrial company is subject to Section 16. Rule 16a-1(a)(1) under the Securities Exchange Act of 1934, promulgated in "Ownership Reports and Trading by Officers, Directors and Principal Security Holders," SEC release 34-28869, February 27, 1991, I.3. and II.B.3., to be codified at 17 C.F.R. §240.16a-1(a)(1) (1991) (all voting groups must file an update for changes in positions; pecuniary interest needed for liability).

22. Alfred Chandler and Takashi Hikino, *Scale and Scope—The Dynamics of Industrial Capitalism* (Cambridge, Mass.: Belknap Press, 1990), pp. 144–45, 398, 417–18.

23. Quoted in Vincent P. Carosso, *Investment Banking in America—A History* (Harvard University Press, 1970).

24. Quoted in Bartlett Naylor, "Proxmire to Seek Bank Size Limits," *American Banker,* December 10, 1986, p. 1.

25. John Scott, *Capitalist Property and Financial Power: A Comparative Study of Britain, the United States and Japan* (New York University Press, 1986), pp. 178–80; and Ouchi, *The M-Form Society,* pp. 65–81.

26. Hermann Kallfass, "The American Corporation and the Institutional Investor: Are There Lessons from Abroad?—The German Experience," *Columbia Business Law Review,* vol. 3 (1988), pp. 775–91.

27. "Who Likes Takeovers?" *Forbes,* May 18, 1987, pp. 12–13. The best analysis of the relation between public opinion and antitakeover law is Roberta Romano, "The Future of Hostile Takeovers: Legislation and Public Opinion," *University of Cincinnati Law Review,* vol. 57, no. 2 (1988), pp. 457–505.

28. Jeffrey Gordon, "Corporations, Markets, and Courts," *Columbia Law Review,* vol. 91 (December 1991).

29. Michael W. Miller, "Safe at Home: How Indiana Shielded a Firm and Changed the Takeover Business," *Wall Street Journal,* July 1, 1987, p. 12.

30. Russell Hardin, *Collective Action* (Johns Hopkins University Press, 1982), pp. 82–83. This is just a corollary of diminishing marginal utility. All other things being equal, losses are more strongly felt than gains.

31. Mancur Olson, *The Logic of Collective Action: Public Goods and the Theory of Groups* (Harvard University Press, 1965).

32. Roberta S. Karmel reports, "The SEC's tilt has been to foster takeovers. This is because takeovers are perceived as a corporate governance mechanism and also because investors appear to benefit from takeovers, at least in the short term. Also relevant are the fees takeovers generate for the securities industry." "Do the Capital Markets Need So Many Regulators?" *New York Law Journal,* vol. 204 (October 18, 1990), p. 3. See also Martin Lipton, "A Long-Term Cure for Takeover Madness," *Manhattan Lawyer,* vol. 3 (March 1990), p. 15; and "Hostile Takeovers Get Backing," *Chicago Tribune,* February 21, 1988, p. 13A. Even the SEC's tilt is contingent on politics. Before the Reagan era SEC commissioners were more hostile to takeovers.

To speak of free market ideology here is peculiar. Mergers are highly regulated and subject to large influences from small changes in tax law or antitrust law. Free market ideology is really a hesitancy to add more regulation or to change existing regulations. And the free market ideology emphasizes the importance of takeovers' disciplinary effects on management.

33. *Edgar* v. *MITE Corp.,* 457 U.S. 624 at 643-46 (1982).

34. Roberta Romano, "The Political Economy of Takeover Statutes," *Virginia Law Review,* vol. 73 (February 1987), pp. 111, 113, 121–22, 138–41.

35. Ellen Lieberman and Jeffrey B. Bartell, "The Rise in State Antitakeover Laws," *Review of Securities & Commodities Regulation,* vol. 23 (September 5, 1990), p. 149. Some states found it politically expedient to pass antitakeover laws as symbolic presents to local managers and workers. So states passed antitakeover laws of dubious constitutionality. Of course, with turnover on the Supreme Court and with the justices going in different directions in *MITE,* it was possible that the Court would reverse itself.

36. Williams Act, 82 Stat. 454, as amended; Securities Exchange Act, 14(e), as amended, 15 U.S.C. 78n(e) (1988).

37. *Unocal Corp.* v. *Mesa Petroleum Co.,* 493 A.2d 946 (Del. 1985).

38. 1934 Act Rules, 17 C.F.R. 240.13e-4 (1990); Exchange Act Release 34-22199 (July 1, 1985). More precisely, the SEC reacted directly to a federal court that viewed the discriminatory self-tender as permissible in *Unocal Corp.* v.

Pickens, 608 F.Supp. 1081 (C.D. Cal. 1985). But in doing so, the commission explicitly stated that it was preempting state law, such as Delaware's, if to the contrary. SEC Release 33-6653, reprinted in *Federal Register,* vol. 51 (July 17, 1986), pp. 25873, 25876.

39. *Mobil Corp.* v. *Marathon Oil Co.,* 669 F.2d 366 (6th Cir. 1981), *cert. denied,* 455 U.S. 982 (1982).

40. Ronald J. Gilson, *The Law and Finance of Corporate Acquisitions* (Mineola, N.Y.: Foundation Press, 1986 and 1990 supp.), p. 1043; James J. Junewicz, "The Appropriate Limits of Section 14(e) of the Securities Exchange Act of 1934," *Texas Law Review,* vol. 62 (April 1984), pp. 1171–1205; Mark J. Loewenstein, "Section 14(e) of the Williams Act and the Rule 10b-5 Comparisons," *Georgetown Law Journal,* vol. 71 (June 1983), pp. 1311–57; and Elliot Weiss, "Defensive Responses to Tender Offers and the Williams Act's Prohibition Against Manipulation," *Vanderbilt Law Review,* vol. 35 (October 1982), pp. 1087–1129.

41. *Schreiber* v. *Burlington Northern, Inc.,* 472 U.S. 1 (1985).

42. The story is more complicated. The Court said that the SEC could prohibit tender offer activities that were not themselves deceptive if the prohibition was to stop steps leading to deceptive tender offer actions. Courts later restricted the SEC's range of action. In *Business Roundtable* v. *SEC,* 905 F.2d 406 (D.C. Cir., 1990), the District of Columbia Circuit Court held that the SEC lacked authority to promulgate a one-share, one-vote rule. Voting rules were a corporate governance matter for the states, a matter on which the SEC could not regulate.

43. Gilson, *Law and Finance of Corporate Acquisitions,* p. 529.

44. *Dynamics Corp.* v. *CTS Corp.,* 637 F.Supp. 389 at 399, 406 (N.D. Ill 1986).

45. *Dynamics Corp.* v. *CTS Corp.,* 794 F.2d 250 at 264 (7th Cir. 1986).

46. John C. Coffee, "The Future of Corporate Federalism: State Competition and the New Trend toward De Facto Federal Minimum Standards," *Cardozo Law Review,* vol. 8 (March 1987), pp. 759, 762.

47. *CTS Corp.* v. *Dynamics Corp. of America,* 481 U.S. 69 (1987).

48. Lieberman and Bartell, "Rise in State Antitakeover Laws."

49. Gilson, *Law and Finance of Corporate Acquisitons* (1990 Supp.), p. 559.

50. Vicky Cahan, "States vs. Raiders: Will Washington Step In?" *Business Week,* August 31, 1987, p. 56.

51. *Securities Regulation & Law Report,* vol. 20 (March 11, 1988), p. 368; *CQ Almanac,* vol. 40 (1984), pp. 298, 353; and *CQ Almanac,* vol. 41 (1985), p. 282.

52. Lieberman and Bartell, "Rise in State Antitakeover Laws," pp. 152, 154.

53. Del. Code Ann. tit. 8, 203 (Supp. 1990); and N.Y. Bus. Corp. Law 912 (McKinney 1986 and Supp. 1990).

54. Mass. Gen. Laws Ann., chap. 156B, 50A (West Supp. 1990).

55. Jonathan M. Karpoff and Paul H. Malatesta, "The Wealth Effects of Second-Generation State Takeover Legislation," *Journal of Financial Economics,* vol. 25 (December 1989), pp. 291–322.

56. N.C. Sess. Laws, 88, 1 (April 23, 1987), codified at *N.C. Gen. Statutes,* 55-9-02 (1990).

57. "Expropriation at Home," *Wall Street Journal,* October 9, 1987, p. A24; and Minn. Stat. Ann. 80B.01(9) (West 1986 and Supp. West 1990) (law passed June 25, 1987, effective retroactively to June 1, 1987).

58. William Carney, "Does Defining Constituencies Matter?" working paper (Emory Law School, 1991), p. 83, note 155; and Ga. L. 1989, p. 946, §10, codified at Ga. Code Ann. §14-2-202(b)(5) (1989) (enacted April 10, 1989).

59. Paul Richter, "States Act to Stem Tide of Takeovers," *Los Angeles Times,* September 15, 1987, p. 2. See also "Expropriation at Home," *Wall Street Journal,* October 9, 1987, p. A24; and 1987 *Ariz. Sess. Laws* 3d. ss., chaps. 3 (enacted July 20, 1987, effective July 22, 1987), codified at *Ariz. Revised Stat. Ann.,* paras. 10-028, 10-1201 to 10-1223 (West 1990 and West Supp. 1990).

60. To be sure, the pill was justified as preventing shareholder coercion arising from two-tier and partial tender offers. But the pill goes much further, preventing all offers until the board yanks the pill. The pills could have been written, or enforced, to prevent *only* two-tier and partial tender offers. See generally Lucian Bebchuck, "Toward Undistorted Choice and Equal Treatment in Corporate Takeovers," *Harvard Law Review,* vol. 98 (1985), p. 1693.

61. *Moran* v. *Household International, Inc.,* 500 A. 2d 1346 (Del. 1985) was critical. It might be explained as part of Delaware's zig-zagging on takeovers; it might also be explained as zig-zagging on whether to be pro- or antimanagerial. *Smith* v. *Van Gorkom,* 488 A. 2d. 858 (Del. 1985), was repealed by 65 Del. Laws 289 (1986).

62. Leslie Wayne, "Takeovers Face New Obstacles," *New York Times,* April 19, 1990, p. D1.

63. "Management and Labor Join Forces to Stiff-Arm Raiders in Pennsylvania," *Corporate Control Alert,* vol. 7 (January 1990), pp. 1, 8.

64. Samuel Szewczyk and George Tsetsekos, "State Intervention in the market for Corporate Control—The Case of Pennsylvania Senate Bill 1310," *Journal of Financial Economics,* vol. 31 (1992), p. 3.

65. *Our Money's Worth: Report of the Governor's Task Force on Pension Fund Investment* (Albany, N.Y., June 1989).

66. Romano provides the most complete analysis in "Political Economy of Takeover Statutes." See also Lyman Johnson and David Millon, "Missing the Point about State Takeover Statutes," *Michigan Law Review,* vol. 87 (February 1989), pp. 846–57.

67. Romano, "Political Economy of Takeover Statutes"; and Coffee, "Future of Corporate Federalism."

68. Other forces are relevant. More often than in the 1980s, takeovers in the 1970s were of large companies taking over smaller companies; Delaware did not know which to satisfy, large raiders or small targets, both of which were constituents. In the 1980s junk bonds allowed takeover entrepreneurs to buy larger companies. The larger companies were a Delaware constituency, the takeover entrepreneurs were not. The shift in acquirers from large companies to entrepreneurs, however, does not neatly coincide with the timing of the other shifts, because it occurred at the beginning of the 1980s.

69. Delaware had a first-generation antitakeover statute on its books, but it

did little more than track the Williams Act. Del. Code Ann. tit. 8, para. 203 (repealed 1987).

70. A blocking decision was *Moran* v. *Household International, Inc.*, 500 A.2d 1346 (Del. 1985), which validated the poison pill in 1985. Among facilitating decisions were *City Capital Associates* v. *Interco, Inc.*, 551 A.2d 787 (Del. Ch. 1988); *Grand Metropolitan PLC* v. *The Pillsbury Co.*, [1989 Transfer Binder] Fed. Sec. L. Rep. (CCH) ¶94,104 (Del. Ch. 1988); *Robert M. Bass Group, Inc.* v. *Evans*, 552 A.2d 1227 (Del. Ch. 1988). Inconveniently for the chronology I offer, these decisions occurred after *CTS*. However, they preceded the Pennsylvania law that became prominent takeover news.

71. Gilson, *Law and Finance of Corporate Acquisitions* (Supp. 1990), pp. 203–04, 211; and *AC Acquisitions Corp.* v. *Anderson, Clayton & Co.*, 519 A.2d 103 (Del. 1986).

72. Paraphrased in Tom Troy, "Gov. Throws Support behind Takeover Bill," United Press International, January 12, 1988.

73. Wachtell, Lipton, Rosen and Katz, "You Can't Just Say No in Delaware No More," December 17, 1988, memo to clients. See also Wachtell, Lipton memo to clients, November 3, 1988: "New Jersey, Ohio and Pennsylvania, among others, are far more desirable states for incorporation than Delaware in this takeover era. Perhaps it is time to migrate out of Delaware."

74. See Gordon, "Corporations, Markets and Courts," p. 33.

75. *Moran* v. *Household International, Inc.*, 500 A.2d 1346 (Del. 1985).

76. Justice Andrew G.T. Moore II, "State Competition: Panel Response," *Cardozo Law Review*, vol. 8 (March 1987), p. 779.

77. *Paramount Communications* v. *Time Inc.*, 571 A.2d 1140 (Del. 1990). The statute was a moratorium rule prohibiting many offerers from merging with the target for three years after buying a stake. Del. Code Ann. tit. 8, para. 203(a) (1990).

78. "Law Firm View on Impact of Paramount/Time Decision," *Prentice-Hall Law and Business, Insights*, vol. 4 (May 1990), p. 34.

79. Lipton, "Long-Term Cure for Takeover Madness." For assessments similar to Lipton's, see also Barbara Franklin, "Tough Takeover Statute—Critics Say Pennsylvania's New Law is Extreme," *New York Law Journal*, May 3, 1990, p. 5; "The 'Buzz-Off' Defense: A Play on the Time Ruling," *Mergers and Acquisitions* (March-April 1990), p. 7 ("As soon as the ink dried on the Time-Warner decision, companies under siege were using its key provisions to tell hostile buyers to get lost"); *Corporate Counsel Weekly*, October 17, 1990, pp. 6, 8; *Prentice-Hall Law and Business Insights* (1990), p. 34. *Shamrock Holdings, Inc.* v. *Polaroid Corp.*, 559 A.2d 257 (Del. Ch. 1989), was also an antitakeover decision.

80. L. Gordon Crovitz, "Can Takeover Targets Just Say No to Stockholders?" *Wall Street Journal*, March 7, 1990, p. 19.

81. *Revlon, Inc.* v. *MacAndrews & Forbes Holdings, Inc.*, 506 A.2d 173 (Del. 1986).

82. William Cary, "Federalism and Corporate Law: Reflections upon Delaware," *Yale Law Journal*, vol. 83 (March 1974), pp. 663–705; Roberta Romano, "Law as a Product: Some Pieces of the Incorporation Puzzle," *Journal of Law, Economics and Organization*, vol. 1 (Fall 1985), pp. 225–83; and Jonathan R.

Macey and Geoffrey P. Miller, "Toward an Interest-Group Theory of Delaware Corporate Law," *Texas Law Review,* vol. 65 (February 1987), pp. 469–523.

83. Romano, "Law as a Product." This may not necessarily be efficient, but if lawyers are key decisionmakers in picking a state for incorporation, they may prefer Delaware to other states.

84. Cary, "Federalism and Corporate Law."

85. First in Ralph K. Winter, Jr., "State Law, Shareholder Protection, and the Theory of the Corporation," *Journal of Legal Studies,* vol. 6 (June 1977), pp. 251–92; and later, with new arguments by Romano, "Law as a Product," and Macey and Miller, "Toward an Interest-Group Theory."

86. Romano, "Law as a Product," pp. 273–79; Coffee, "Future of Corporate Federalism," pp. 759, 762; and Macey and Miller, "Toward an Interest-Group Theory."

87. Charles M. Yablon, "Poison Pills and Litigation Uncertainty," *Duke Law Journal* (February 1989), pp. 54–91.

88. Moore, "State Competition."

89. Cary, "Federalism and Corporate Law."

90. *Smith* v. *Van Gorkom,* 488 A.2d 858 (Del. 1985); 65 Del. Laws 289 (1986), codified at Del. Code Ann. tit. 8, §102(b)(7) (1990).

91. Cary, "Federalism and Corporate Law," p. 692; and Macey and Miller, "Toward an Interest-Group Theory," p. 502.

92. Cary, "Federalism and Corporate Law," pp. 704–05.

93. Moore, "State Competition."

94. Peter T. Kilborn, "Treasury Official Assails 'Inefficient' Big Business," *New York Times,* November 8, 1986, p. A1. Ivan Boesky was charged with insider trading one week after the speech by Treasury Officer Richard Darman that offered takeovers as part of the cure for corpocracy. The public's association of the insider trading scandals with takeovers made bashing big business politically difficult.

95. Bernard S. Black, "Bidder Overpayment in Takeovers," *Stanford Law Review,* vol. 41 (February 1989) pp. 597–660.

96. Randall Smith, "The Corporate Raider of the '90s: Big Business," *Wall Street Journal,* December 4, 1990, p. C1.

97. Winter, "State Law and Shareholder Protection"; and Charles M. Tiebout, "A Pure Theory of Local Expenditures," *Journal of Political Economy,* vol. 64 (October 1956), pp. 416–24.

98. Winter, "State Law and Shareholder Protection." He argued that the takeover discourages states from passing other seriously inefficient corporate law, because if they did, their companies' share prices would fall and the companies would become attractive takeover targets. The core contention is that competition, with takeovers as the enforcement mechanism, discourages states from passing seriously inefficient nontakeover corporate law. The core argument does not imply that states compete to produce efficient takeover law. See also Daniel R. Fischel, "The 'Race to the Bottom' Revisited: Reflections on Recent Developments in Delaware's Corporation Law," *Northwestern Law Review,* vol. 76 (February 1982), pp. 913, 919.

99. Daniel R. Fischel, "From MITE to CTS: State Antitakeover Statutes,

the Williams Act, the Commerce Clause, and Insider Trading," *Supreme Court Review,* vol. 47 (1987), pp. 74–84; and *Amanda Acquisition Corp.* v. *Universal Foods Corp.,* 877 F.2d 496 (7th Cir. 1989) (opinion of Judge Easterbrook), *cert. denied,* 110 S.Ct. 367.

100. Jonathan M. Karpoff and Paul H. Malatesta, "[Pennsylvania] Law: State Antitakeover Laws and Stock Prices," *Financial Analysts Journal* (July-August 1990), pp. 8–10; and Karpoff and Malatesta, "Wealth Effects of Second-Generation State Takeover Legislation."

101. Competition in product markets magnifies the effect of state competition. Entrepreneurs with a beachhead affect their competitors in product markets. A few efficient companies incorporate in states with "good" corporate law. These companies invigorate product competition, forcing the old companies to be more efficient. But some dying industries will not attract new entry, and because they will not need new capital, they will lack effective capital market competition. Without the disciplinary effects of takeover threats, managers there will have a lot of slack to dissipate.

102. Two-thirds of Pennsylvania's largest companies opted out from coverage by the Pennsylvania antitakeover law, at least partially; *Corporation,* vol. 61 (Prentice-Hall, December 26, 1990), p. 2. John Pound, "On the Motives for Choosing a Corporate Governance Structure," Harvard University, December 1990, roughly confirms this dichotomy: the stock market had put a premium on those firms that opted out.

103. In fact, one significant theory of takeovers is that they primarily address the misuse of retained earnings when companies with poor prospects retain cash and invest it low-yielding projects. Michael C. Jensen, "Agency Costs of Free Cash Flow, Corporate Finance, and Takeovers," *American Economic Review,* vol. 76 (May 1986, *Papers and Proceedings 1985*), pp. 323–29.

104. But spillover effects will induce those providing capital for a new plant, owned by a company unprotected *currently* by an antitakeover law, to fear that law will change later to cover their new plant.

105. In the mid-1980s the annual gross proceeds from initial public offerings were only about $15 billion. Roger G. Ibbotson, Jody L. Sindelar, and Jay R. Ritter, "Initial Public Offerings," *Journal of Applied Corporate Finance,* vol. 1 (Summer 1988), p. 37. Or, as a proxy for capital formation, consider GNP growth. At its recent rate of 2 percent per year, in about forty years half of the GNP of the year 2030 will represent post-1990 growth. The time new entrepreneurs need to replace incumbents is quite long.

106. The people who find state competition sufficient are unconcerned about antitakeover law because they believe it is enough if state competition provides good takeover law somewhere. There are other reasons not to be overly concerned about the potential demise of takeovers. What if takeovers and LBOs fall into two categories: empire building of offerers and discipline of targets? The empire-building takeovers are not socially useful. And what if the disciplinary portion is itself divided: operating improvement and tax improvement (by leveraging for the interest deduction, not to get better managerial performance). Buyouts to improve a firm's tax standing are also not socially useful. Empire building and tax motivations underlie a large enough portion of restructurings to

offset a chunk of the gains from operating discipline. Black, "Bidder Overpayment"; William Long and David Ravenscraft, in this volume; and Steven Kaplan, "Management Buyouts: Evidence on Taxes as a Source of Value," *Journal of Finance,* vol. 44 (July 1989), pp. 611–32. Ancillary effects count too: many are good, as managers operate firms better to avoid takeover. Some are not, as managers recapitalize with debt to avoid the tax collector or invest heavily in takeover defenses. But evidence indicates that the stock market mistrusts managers at firms that refused to opt out of Pennsylvania's antitakeover law, suggesting that antitakeover law has its largest effect in undermining the disciplinary effects. See Pound, "On the Motives for Choosing a Corporate Governance Structure," p. 13. Antitakeover law seems to raise the cost of the most useful takeovers.

Potentially more significant than direct state competition is pressure from existing shareholders to avoid antishareholder takeover law, putting some limit on the impact of antitakeover law. For example, Investor Responsibility Research Center, *Corporate Governance Highlights,* vol. 33 (November 23, 1990), reports unsuccessful institutional investor pressure on Pennsylvania companies to reincorporate out of Pennsylvania.

107. While the founder is on the scene, interim dividends and the prospect that the founder will sell the company reduce the sum that eventually could be affected by the absence of takeover discipline.

108. See Oskar Morgenstern, *On the Accuracy of Economic Observations,* 2d ed. (Princeton University Press, 1963).

109. This "bounded rationality" suggests that the only way for takeover law to have an impact on the analyst of primary stock offerings would be for the state to get a reputation that requires the analyst to invest little in assessing takeover law.

110. Is reputation relevant? That is, even for new, capital-raising companies, should investors fear that later, when the company no longer needs the capital markets, the state will pass antitakeover laws for managers? States have reason to develop a reputation that they will not pass that legislation later, so that entrepreneurs can more easily raise capital now.

In politics the reputational argument is weak. While the state might have an interest in a good reputation, state legislators generally do not. They want to win the next election and only weakly seek a better state later on. Moreover, since legislatures have trouble binding themselves to future action, they can do little to help their entrepreneurs from fears of the future that imperil capital raising today. And managers at a firm with capital already sunk have short time horizons. They want peace during the half dozen years until retirement; they will pay handsomely for that freedom.

111. Ronald H. Coase, "The Problem of Social Cost," *Journal of Law and Economics,* vol. 3 (October 1960), pp. 1–44.

112. Lipton, "Long-Term Cure for Takeover Madness," p. 15; and Romano, "Law as a Product."

113. Reincorporation is usually uncontroversial and the easiest way to reincorporate requires shareholder approval. But managers might try to reincorporate without direct shareholder approval. And managers have agenda control and

could embed reincorporation in a complex package with some proshareholder features; reincorporation would be the "price" managers ask for tasks they would otherwise forgo but that were beneficial to shareholders. But with agenda control, managers should get shareholders to approve charter amendments that would do exactly what the sister state legislation would do. Managers' central purpose in getting antitakeover legislation is to get what shareholders will not give managers in a charter amendment. Mass migration is not impossible, but it is implausible.

114. Romano, "Law as a Product," p. 245 (data for 1961 to 1983). But companies reincorporating are often growing and do not want Pennsylvania-type statutes. Firms often reincorporate when going public, and the controlling owners are managers unlikely to fear a takeover because they control enough stock to defeat one. Yet they will have successors. Presumably the controlling group's stock would sell at a higher price if it could guarantee that it would not insulate successors from takeover. So this argument must depend on a portion of reincorporations by firms that are already dominated by managers.

115. Harold Hotelling, "Stability in Competition," *Economic Journal,* vol. 39 (March 1929), pp. 41–57.

116. Canada has a similar federal system but no Delaware resulted, although provinces have tried. Ronald J. Daniels, "Should Provinces Compete? The Case for a Competitive Corporate Law Market," *McGill Law Journal,* vol. 36 (1991), p. 130. Canada without a Delaware suggests that without a catalyst—the turn-of-the-century antitrust mergers—no network might have emerged. Firms would incorporate locally and stay there, as they do in Canada. Other explanations for Canada—fewer public firms, for example—might also explain the difference.

117. See Roe, "Political and Legal Restraints," pp. 7–41; and Grundfest, "Subordination of American Capital," pp. 89–114.

118. See Martin Lipton and Steven A. Rosenblum, "A New System of Corporate Governance: The Quinquennial Election of Directors," *University of Chicago Law Review* (Winter 1991), pp. 187–253.

119. The issue of why managers would risk personal disadvantage to seek to improve corporate profit is underexplored. That there are many examples of their so doing supports my view that managers define themselves in terms of the success of their corporate enterprise much more than in terms of their personal wealth. If this is true, the whole academic notion of managers preferring their own interests to the interests of stockholders is misguided.

120. Roe, "Political Theory of American Corporate Finance," pp. 10–67; and Roe, "Political and Legal Restraints," pp. 7–41.

121. Jonathan M. Karpoff and Paul H. Malatesta, "The Wealth Effects of Second Generation State Takeover Legislation," *Journal of Financial Economics,* vol. 25 (December 1990), pp. 291–322. Preliminary evidence gathered by Karpoff with respect to the recent Pennsylvania statute shows an even more dramatic difference between unprotected and protected firms. This approach helpfully explains earlier studies, which reported a negative but surprisingly small effect associated with the adoption of particular state antitakeover statutes. The reported returns found in the earlier studies represented the average samples containing both unprotected and protected companies.

122. I have one nit to pick, but only because my correction strengthens Roe's

argument. Roe describes workers as the losers from takeovers. He is only half right. Managers, especially middle-level managers, also lose. Empirical evidence demonstrates a drop in white-collar employment following takeovers; see Frank R. Lichtenberg and Donald Siegel, "The Effects of Ownership Changes on the Employment and Wages of Central Office and Other Personnel," *Journal of Law and Economics*, vol. 33 (October 1990), pp. 383–408. Workers, however, do not lose. Lichtenberg and Siegel find that employment of production workers increases following takeovers. See Steven Kaplan, "The Effects of Management Buyouts on Operating Performance and Value," *Journal of Financial Economics*, vol. 24 (October 1989), pp. 217–54; Sanjai Bhagat, Andrei Shleifer, and Robert W. Vishny, "Hostile Takeovers in the 1980s: The Return to Corporate Specialization," *Brookings Papers on Economic Activity, Microeconomics* (1990), pp. 1–84; and Amar Bhide, "The Causes and Consequences of Hostile Takeovers," *Journal of Applied Corporate Finance*, vol. 2 (Summer 1989), pp. 36–59. The political story Roe tells is one in which well-connected corporate managers persuade state legislatures to protect managers' rents. That their political activities do not appear to benefit blue-collar workers only adds irony to Roe's account. As Joseph Grundfest has argued, managers who are themselves protected from takeovers remain free to lay off production workers. Joseph Grundfest, "Job Loss and Takeovers," address to the 1988 annual Colloquium on Corporate Law and Social Policy, University of Toledo College of Law.

123. This model draws on that offered in Ronald J. Gilson, "The Political Ecology of Takeovers: Thoughts on Harmonizing the European Corporate Governance Environment," *Fordham Law Review*, vol. 61 (October 1992), pp. 161–92.

124. See Randall Morck, Andrei Shleifer, and Robert W. Vishny, "Do Managerial Objectives Drive Bad Acquisitions?" *Journal of Finance*, vol. 45 (March 1990): evidence "that the source of bust-up gains in the 1980s is the reversal of the unrelated diversification of the 1960s and the 1970s. Hostile bust-up takeovers simply undo past conglomeration." See also Bhide, "Causes and Consequences of Hostile Takeovers," p. 52 ("real source of gains in hostile takeovers lies in splitting up diversified companies"); and Bhagat, Shleifer, and Vishny, "Hostile Takeovers."

125. An assessment of just how much takeover protection management has achieved is complicated by three uncertainties. The first, which Roe discusses, is how to interpret the Delaware Supreme Court's unusually opaque opinion in *Paramount Communications* v. *Time, Inc.*, 571 A.2d 1140 (Del. 1990). Two interpretations are possible. The first, favored by protakeover forces and finding support in the court's language, allows targets to pursue preexisting business plans but not to protect those plans by declining to redeem a poison pill. The critical aspect of this reading is that merely carrying out a business plan typically will not defeat an offer. Thus the recognition of a target's interest in its long-term business plan is a hollow victory for promanagement forces unless there is some way, necessarily artificial, to protect that plan.

An alternative interpretation, favored by antitakeover forces, builds less on the Delaware Supreme Court's lyrics than on its melody. It claims the central issue is whether the target has a justifiable interest in pursuing its business plan. If so, then the particular manner in which it protects that plan should be irrelevant; if merely pursuing the business plan will not be effective, then reliance on a poison pill should be equally appropriate. See Ronald J. Gilson and Bernard S. Black, 1991 supplement to Gilson, *The Law and Finance of Corporate Acquisitions* (Foundation Press, 1991), pp. 421–24.

While some have lamented the fact that six years after the Delaware Supreme Court commenced its current effort at rationalizing the law of defensive tactics, there is still no clear articulation of whether and under what circumstances a target can just say no (see Gilson and Black, 1991 supplement, pp. 423–24). Roe points out that maintaining ambiguity may be Delaware's dominant strategy.

The second uncertainty concerns the recent judicial decision invalidating the employee stock option plan hastily contrived by NCR in what turned out to be a futile effort to defeat the hostile offer by AT&T. See *NCR Corp.* v. *American Telephone and Telegraph Co.*, 761 F. Supp. 475 (S.D. Ohio 1991). Some commentators think the outcome illustrates that "whatever the direction of the law on takeovers and proxy contests, strong, careful judges . . . can still find that American corporate law affords them sufficient discretion to reach the right result." See John C. Coffee, Jr., "How Not to Stuff a Ballot Box: The Lessons of the *NCR* Case," *M&A and Corporate Governance Law Reporter*, vol. 6 (April 1991), pp. 229s–229ee. Others think that the *NCR* result reflected only extremely poor planning and can easily be avoided. See letter from Wachtell, Lipton, Rosen, and Katz, counsel to AT&T in the *NCR* litigation, March 22, 1991.

The final uncertainty concerns whether the various state antitakeover laws have as significant an impact as is commonly assumed. The Delaware law, for example, does not preclude bust-up takeovers unless the asset sale is to the acquirer. Leo Herzel, "Corporate Governance through Statistical Eyes," *Journal of Financial Economics*, vol. 27 (October 1990), pp. 581–93, argues that the principal impact of the Delaware statute is on the kind of financing that can be used in an acquisition.

126. For a careful description of the regulatory and incentive barriers to proxy contests, see Bernard S. Black, "Shareholder Passivity Reexamined," *Michigan Law Review*, vol. 89 (December 1990), pp. 520–608.

127. The dilution results from a change in the conversion rates of various securities that is triggered if a specified percentage of board members are elected without the approval of the preelection board. The provisions are described in Joseph Grundfest, "The Catch-22 in *Time*," *M&A and Corporate Governance Law Reporter*, vol. 6 (March 1991), p. 1–10.

128. *Unocal Corp.* v. *Mesa Petroleum Co.*, 193 A.2d 946 (Del. 1985).

129. Peter F. Drucker has voiced the link between hostile takeovers and short-term management most consistently. See "Corporate Takeovers—What Is To Be Done?" *Public Interest*, vol. 82 (Winter 1986), p. 12. As is usually the case in the polemical literature, the link is asserted rather than established. See also Lipton and Rosenblum, "Proposal for a New System of Corporate Governance," pp. 187–253. Compare Su Han Chan, John D. Martin, and John W. Kensinger, "Corporate Research and Development Expenditures and Share Value, *Journal of Financial Economics*, vol. 26 (August 1990), pp. 255–76.

130. Roe, "Political and Legal Restraints," p. 35.

131. Paul Sheard, "The Main Bank System and Corporate Monitoring and Control in Japan," *Journal of Economic Behavior and Organization*, vol. 11 (May 1989), p. 409. Masahiko Aoki, "Toward an Economic Model of the Japanese Firm," *Journal of Economic Literature*, vol. 28 (March 1990), p. 15, makes a similar point. For the German experience, see John Cable, "Capital Market Information and Industrial Performance: The Role of West German Banks," *Economic Journal*, vol. 95 (1985), p. 129 ("West German banks provide industry with substantial long-term finance, have extensive control over shareholders' voting rights and are widely represented on company boards"); and Louis Lowenstein and Ira Milstein, "The American Corporation and the Institutional Investor: Are There Lessons from Abroad?" *Columbia Business Law Review*, vol. 3 (Fall 1988), p. 747 ("On one end of the spectrum is the German experience, where there is substantial concentration of voting rights in a relatively small number of large banks. It is through the exercise of those voting rights that large banks directly influence the selection of corporate executives and managing boards and indirectly influence all fundamental business decisions").

132. Michael C. Jensen, "Eclipse of the Public Corporation," *Harvard Business Review*, vol. 67 (September–October 1989), p. 73.

133. See Ronald J. Gilson and Reinier Kraakman, "Reinventing the Outside Director: An Agenda for Institutional Investors," *Stanford Law Review*, vol. 43 (April 1991), pp. 863–906. The *Economist* has recently endorsed this approach to revitalizing Anglo-American corporate governance. See "Redirecting Directors," *Economist*, November 17, 1990, pp. 19–20.

134. Aoki, "Toward an Economic Model of the Japanese Firm," explores this link in the context of the structure of Japanese corporations. For an interesting effort to link conceptually organizational structure and the technological character of the manufacturing process, see Michael Piore, "Corporate Reform in American Manufacturing and the Challenge to Economic Theory," working paper 533, Massachusetts Institute of Technology, January 1989. See Stuart Rosenstein and Jeffrey G. Wyatt, "Outside Directors, Board Independence, and Shareholder Wealth," *Journal of Financial Economics*, vol. 26 (August 1990), pp. 173–91; and Lilli A. Gordon and John Pound, "Governance Matters: An Empirical Study of the Relationship between Corporate Governance and Corporate Performance," Kennedy School of Public Policy, June 1991, for recent additions to the small empirical literature.

The link between corporate governance and corporate performance should not strike the managerialists as surprising. It is, after all, at the core of their short-termism argument.

135. Joseph A. Grundfest, "Internationalization of the World's Securities Markets: Economic Causes and Regulatory Consequences," *Journal of Financial Services Research*, vol. 4 (December 1990), pp. 349–78.

136. Drucker, "Corporate Takeovers—What Is To Be Done?" p. 6. As the simple model set out earlier suggests, international competition need not result in takeovers. From my perspective, corporate acquisitions are an equilibrating mechanism that becomes important only following a change in technology, and hostile takeovers become important only when some managers resist the change. Consistent with this analysis, the current effort on the part of the European

Community to reduce the barriers to takeovers is openly instrumental. Takeovers are to be encouraged because in the view of the Community, a technological change has increased the efficient scale of enterprise: "Enabling EC companies to build the necessary scale in their new 'home market' is in many industries essential to assure EC industry competitiveness in an increasingly global environment." Booz-Allen Acquisition Services, "Executive Summary," *Study on Obstacles to Takeover Bids in the European Community,* December 1989.

137. See Roe, "Some Differences in Corporate Governance in Germany, Japan, and America," for an elaboration of this argument.

138. Frank Lichtenberg and George Pushner, "Ownership Structure and Corporate Performance in Japan," working paper 4092, National Bureau of Economic Research, June 1992; and Demsetz and Lehn, "Structure of Corporate Ownership," p. 1155.

Conference Participants

Carliss Y. Baldwin
Graduate School of Business
Harvard University

Margaret M. Blair
The Brookings Institution

John C. Coffee, Jr.
Columbia University Law School

Ronald Daniels
Faculty of Law
University of Toronto

Richard D'Entremont
School of Management
Boston University

Gordon Donaldson
Graduate School of Business
Harvard University

Warren E. Farb
U.S. Department of Commerce

Paul E. Francis
Merrill Lynch

Carl Ferenbach
Bershire Partners

Darius W. Gaskins, Jr.
High Street Associates

Ronald J. Gilson
Stanford University Law School

Bronwyn Hall
Department of Economics
University of California, Berkeley

Oliver D. Hart
Massachusetts Institute of Technology

George Hatsopoulos
Thermo-Electron Corporation

Jean Helwege
Federal Reserve Board

Max Holland
Woodrow Wilson International Center

Kent Hughes
Council on Competitiveness

Robert W. Johnson
Soros Fund Management

Sarah J. Lane
School of Management
Boston University

Kenneth Lehn
Katz Graduate School of Business
University of Pittsburgh

Frank Lichtenberg
Graduate School of Business
Columbia University

Martin Lipton
Wachtell, Lipton, Rosen and Katz

William F. Long
Business Performance Research Associates

M. Laurentius Marais
William Wecker Associates

Robert N. McCauley
Federal Reserve Bank of New York

Robert H. McGuckin
Bureau of Census

Robert A. G. Monks
The Lens Fund

Dennis Mueller
Department of Economics
University of Maryland

Stewart C. Myers
Sloan School of Management
Massachusetts Institute of Technology

Peg O'Hara
Investors Responsibility Research Center

David J. Ravenscraft
School of Business Administration
University of North Carolina
  at Chapel Hill

Mark J. Roe
Columbia University Law School

Stephen S. Roach
Morgan Stanley

Paul R. Samuelson
Colonial Investment Management Services

Ralph S. Saul
CIGNA

Martha A. Schary
School of Management
Boston University

F. M. Scherer
Kennedy School of Government
Harvard University

Charles Schultze
The Brookings Institution

Steven A. Sharpe
Federal Reserve Board

Robert A. Taggart, Jr.
School of Management
Boston College

Peter Tufano
Graduate School of Business
Harvard University

Girish Uppal
The Brookings Institution

Philip K. Verleger
Institute for International Economics

Robert W. Vishny
Graduate School of Business
University of Chicago

Mark J. Warshawsky
Federal Reserve Board

Barrie A. Wigmore
Goldman Sachs

Sidney G. Winter
U.S. General Accounting Office

Steven A. Zimmer
J. P. Morgan Investment Management

Index

Acquisitions. *See* Mergers and acquisitions
Adjustable-rate home mortgages (ARMs), 307
Agency problem. *See* Conflicts of interest
American Law Institute, Corporate Governance Project, 356
Antitakeover legislation, 14, 330–40; competition among states, 347–52; Delaware, 332, 340–52; hostile takeovers and, 354
Antitrust policy, 59
Aristech, 253, 267, 273
Arizona, antitakeover laws, 339
ARMs. *See* Adjustable-rate home mortgages
Assets growth, restructuring and, 169–70, 175–83
Assets, unconventional, 10–11, 55–97, 89; cash flow and, 63–72; coordination, 61–62; expectations, 74–78; implicit contracts, 74–78; interest rates and, 64–72, 75–78, 90–91; reputation of companies, 62–63, 75, 85; R&D, 71–72, 85; strategic choices and, 64–72; unconventional liabilities and, 84–85; valuation of firm and, 62–72

Bank Holding Company Act of *1956*, 325, 326, 327, 329
Bankruptcy, 59, 312; optimal capital structure and, 23, 29–34, 43
Bankruptcy Reform Act of *1978*, 59
Banks: federalism and, 328–30; leveraged buyouts and, 227; management corruption and, 317; stock ownership and, 324–25
BEA. *See* Bureau of Economic Analysis
Beatrice Companies, 157–58
Berkshire Partners model, 226, 228–30
Berle, Adolph, 58
Bhagat, Sanjai, 75
Boesky, Ivan, 331, 346
Book industry, 121

Brandeis, Louis, 347
Bridge loans, 292, 293
Brooks, Stephen H., 115
Bureau of the Census, 12, 233; data bases, 206–09
Bureau of Economic Analysis (BEA), 125–26, 134–35
Burgess, John, 195
Burlington Holdings, 159
Burlington Industries, 338–39

Cain Chemical Co., 253, 255, 256–57, 266, 273
Cain, Gordon, 256–57
Capacity changes in chemicals industry, 245, 247–50, 253, 255, 261–65, 269, 281–82
Capital asset pricing model (CAPM), 106–07, 109–11, 139
Capital cost. *See* Cost of capital
Capital expenditures, leveraged buyouts and, 217–20
Capital markets, 15, 80
Capital return, 183, 188; cost of capital and, 151
Cary, William, 343, 344, 347
Cash flow, 3, 55–97; debt and, 36–37; investments and, 151; leveraged buyouts and, 217–20, 314; rate, 99–100, 104, 110–11, 116–17, 124–25, 188; sales and, 232; unconventional assets and, 63–64; variance of, 187
Cash generation, 11, 13; rate of, 99–100, 104, 110–11, 116–17, 124–25, 188; restructuring and, 171, 175–83
Center for Research on Security Prices, 207, 212
Chemicals industry, 12–13, 241; capacity, 247–51, 253, 255, 261–65, 269, 281–82; consolidation, 256–57; cyclicality, 253–56; data sets, 244, 272–73; financial forces af-

fecting restructuring, 260–71; foreign influence, 243, 247, 257–59; free cash flow and, 104–11, 260–65; junk bonds, 266, 267; leverage changes, 266; operational changes, 247–60, 270–71, 279–80; performance indicators, 246; production, 13, 253–56, 257, 264–65, 275, 281; restructurings, 239–87; reverse diversification, 251–52; stock repurchases, 266–68; structural changes, 279–80

Citizens & Southern National Bank, 339

Coase, Ronald, 350, 358

Competition, corporate law and, 347–49

Compustat, 126, 130–133, 150, 152–55, 184–88, 207

Conflicts of interest, 27–28, 100, 228–29; management and shareholders, 8, 19, 57–58, 194, 260, 354–55

Conglomerates, 87–88, 89, 90, 245, 275, 276; chemicals industry, 13

Congress: financial systems and, 321–22; takeover legislation, 334, 337

Conoco, 241, 255, 256, 276–77

Continuation value, 63–72

Control share statutes, 336–38

Corpus Christi Petrochemical, 253, 257

Cosmetics industry, 85–86

Cost of capital, 73, 127, 188; aggregate, 3–4, 111–15; as cause of investment slowdown, 100–01; calculation methodology, 128–35; chemicals industry and, 104–11; derivation of, 102–03; free cash flow and, 5, 11; increases, 60, 138; industry analysis, 116–28; marginal return on investment and, 91–92, 195–96; restructuring and, 171–72, 175–83; return to capital and, 151. *See also* Investment opportunities quality; Squeeze on capital

Council of Institutional Investors, 356, 365

Credit-adjusted reset bonds, 296

CTS Corp., 336–39, 355

Cuomo, Mario, 340

Cyclicality, chemicals industry, 251–56

Dayton Hudson, 339

Debt, 310: capacity level, 172, 175–83, 197; cash flow and, 36–37; increases, 1, 6, 150; junior debt, 8–9, 44–47; long-term debt yield, 132; market value and, 188; measurement, 195; profitability and, 35–36; restructuring patterns and, 172, 175–83; senior debt, 8, 19, 22–23, 31–32, 43–47; share-

holders and creditors and, 27; tangible assets and, 36; tax law changes and, 59

Debt-for-equity swaps, 37–39

Debt overhang problem, 22–23

Debt securities, 292–93

Debt-to-assets ratios, 150, 154–55, 172; chemicals industry, 266, 268; restructuring and, 156–59, 186–87

Delaware: corporate law, 14, 342–45; federal preemption of state law, 334, 335–36; state supreme court, 360; takeover laws, 332, 339–52

Demsetz, Harold, 364

Depreciation: cost of capital and, 109, 133–34; fadeaway strategy, 10–11; tax shields, 133–34, 135

Diamond, Douglas W., 307

Diamond Shamrock, 241, 277

Dingell, John, 337

Discounted cash flow (DCF) model, 139

Discount rates, fadeaway strategy and, 10–11

Diversification, reverse, 251–53

Divestitures, chemicals industry, 251–53

Dow Chemical Co., 241, 252, 253, 255–56, 267, 273

Dow Jones industrial average, 226

Drexel Burnham Lambert, 226, 346, 353, 365

Drucker, Peter, 363

Drug industry, 119, 121

Du Pont, 241, 253, 255–56, 267, 273, 276

Dynamics Corporation v. *CTS Corporation*, 336–39, 355

Economic depreciation rates, 133

Edelman, Asher, 338–39

Edgar v. *MITE*, 335–38, 355

Efficiency gains, 80

Employees, effect of restructuring on, 58, 74–75, 82

Equity-for-debt swaps, 39–40

Equity prices, 39–40

Fadeaway strategy, 10–11, 66–72, 90, 91

Federalism: banks and, 328–30; financial fragmentation and, 321–23

Federal preemption of state law, 334, 335–37

Federal Reserve System, 329

Federal Trade Commission, 334

Financial fragmentation: sources in U.S., 328–30; takeovers and, 321–30

Financial institutions, foreign, 324–25, 326–27, 330

Financing of acquisitions: bridge loans, 292, 293; data, 290–91; debt securities, 292–93; leveraged buyouts, 296–98; private placements, 291–92; tailored securities, 9–10, 294–96, 306, 307, 311; trends, 291–98. *See also* Junk bonds; Reduced cash flow (RCF) securities

Foreign investment and chemicals industry, 13, 243, 247, 257–59, 274

Free cash flow, 82, 151, 195, 196–97; aggregate data, 111–15; calculation of, 72–74; chemicals industry, 101–11, 260–65; cost of capital and, 245; debt-equity composition and, 8–9; definition, 72, 99, 100; empirical analysis of, 101–15, 116–28

rationale, 3, 5, 12; restructuring patterns and, 11, 12, 168–72, 175–83; social costs, 140–41; theory, 28, 138

Fridson, Martin, 185

Fullerton, Don, 109

GAF Corp., 244

G. D. Searle, 243, 252, 255, 277

Georgia-Gulf, 253, 267, 273

Georgia, takeover laws, 339

Germany: corporate governance, 364; financial institutions, 324–25, 330; product markets, 366

Glass-Steagall Act of *1933*, 325, 327, 329, 362

Grand Union, 292

Greed and financial excesses theory, 173–75

Greyhound, 339

Growth rate of assets, 183, 187

Grundfest, Joseph, 353, 355, 362, 363

Hall, Robert, 102, 103

Harris, Milton, 307

Harris, Robert, 139

High-technology industries, leveraged restructuring and, 151–52

Horizontal mergers, 75, 240

Hostile takeovers, 37–42, 195–96, 322, 354; effect on employees, 74–75; FTC and, 334; junk bonds and, 58–59; leveraged buyouts and, 210–11, 224; management response, 7, 8; Revlon, 85–86; shareholders and, 4; voter attitude toward, 330–31

Huntsman, 256, 273

Icahn, Carl, 74–75, 256

ICI Americas, 253, 257

IDD M & A Database, 207

Incomplete markets, capital structure and, 24–25

Increasing-rate securities, 296

Indiana, control share statute, 336–37

Industrial chemicals industry. *See* Chemicals industry

Institutional investors, effect on restructurings, 15

Insurance companies, stock ownership and, 325–26

Interest rates, 81, 82; capital return and, 15; changes, 3, 10, 79; chemicals industry and, 107, 109; corporate change and, 15, 56, 59–60; cost of capital and, 101, 118, 138; effects of increase in, 10; free cash flow and, 169–70; management choices and, 64–72; restructuring and, 59–60, 91; takeovers and, 87; unconventional assets and, 61–72, 75–79, 83, 90–91

Internal Revenue Service, debt treatment, 23–24

Investment Company Act of *1940*, 325, 327

Investment, 5, 80–81; as unconventional assets, 10–11; cash flow and, 151; debt and, 8–9; free cash flow and, 73–74; neoclassical firms and, 193–94; quality of opportunities, 99–101; rates, 91, 362

Investment opportunities quality, 103, 121, 128–29, 164; definition, 99–100; restructuring and, 171–72, 175–83; tax policy and, 101. *See also* Cost of capital

Investment return, 5, 103–04; cost of capital and, 195–96; *1980s*, 3, 60

Japan: corporate governance in, 360–63; 366; financial institutions, 324–25, 360–61; product markets, 366

Jensen, Michael C., 19, 27–28, 72, 99, 100, 137

Joint ventures, corporate control, 326–28

Jorgenson, Dale, 102, 103, 129, 130

J. P. Morgan, 329

Junk bonds, 12, 89, 150, 151, 313, 316; chemicals industry, 266, 267; company characteristics and, 155–60; company growth and, 160–63; data, 153–54, 185; financing acquisitions and, 293; hostile takeovers and, 58–59; industry-level determinants, 175–84; industry patterns and, 166; leveraged buyouts and, 216–17, 225; Michael Milken and, 331; pricing studies, 300; restructuring rates, 168

Kaplan, Steve, 233
Kester, Carl W., 100–01, 106, 114
King, Mervyn, 109
Kreps, David, 62, 75

Lazard, Donald, 307
LBO Association, 361
Leurhman, Timothy, 101, 106, 114
Leveraged buyouts (LBOs), 5, 86, 141, 179,
    194, 274, 296–98; banks and, 227; capital
    expenditures and, 217–20; cash flow and,
    217–20, 314; causes of, 137; characteristics
    of, 209–11; commodity companies, 13;
    company performance and, 213–17, 222–25,
    231–33; corporate governance and, 235;
    government policy and, 223–24; hostile
    takeovers and, 210–11, 224; increase, 322;
    junk bonds and, 216–17, 225; option value
    and, 315–16; overview, 205–07; plant pro-
    ductivity and, 217–20; postbuyout perfor-
    mance, 216–17; profitability and, 231–33;
    public debt securities and, 300; purpose,
    226–27, 313; reduced cash flow and, 304;
    R&D and, 220–21, 222–23; Safeway, 75,
    82, 157–58; shareholders and, 211–13; taxes
    and, 223; TW Holdings, 304; value, 290
Leveraged restructurings (LRS), 151; com-
    pany characteristics, 155–60; company
    growth and, 160–63; data, 154–55, 186–87;
    industry-level determinants, 175–84; indus-
    try patterns, 167; restructuring rates, 168
Liabilities, unconventional, 84–85
Lichtenberg, Frank, 209
Lieberman, Marvin, 261
Lipton, Martin, 350
Liquidations, 36–37, 60, 61
Longitudinal Research Data (LRD), 206–09,
    218

MacAndrews and Forbes Holdings, 342
McCauley, Robert N., 114–15
McFadden Act of 1927, 324, 325, 329
Majluf, Nicholas S., 25–26
Malkiel, Burton G., 106
Management, 193–96; autonomy, 14; motives,
    197; public corporations, 28–39; response
    to takeovers, 5–7, 11; shareownership and,
    354. See also Conflicts of interest
Management buyouts, 234–35

Managerial discretion: capital structure and,
    19–53; restraint on, 55–56; restructuring
    and, 57
Marathon Oil, 336
Marris, Robin, 72
Marston, Felicia, 139
Massachusetts, antitakeover laws, 338
Means, Gardiner, 58
Meckling, William M., 19, 27–28
Mergers and acquisitions, 235, 274: by foreign
    firms, 257–59; capacity changes and, 249–
    50; chemicals industry, 241–45, 269, 272; fi-
    nancing, 289–320; horizontal mergers, 75,
    240; leveraged securities and, 314; restruc-
    turing firms, 159–60. See also Hostile take-
    overs; Leveraged buyouts; Management
    buyouts; Private buyouts
Merrill Lynch, 126, 130, 131, 185
M-form companies, 84, 87, 90, 330
Milken, Michael, 331, 346
Miller, Merton H., 129
Minnesota, antitakeover laws, 339
Mobile v. Marathon, 336
Modigliani, Franco, 129, 307
Modigliani-Miller theorem, 19, 20
Monsanto, 241, 243, 252, 253, 255–56, 273
Moore, John, 307
Moran v. Household International, Inc., 339,
    341, 343
Mortensen, Dale, 63
Mutual funds, stock ownership and, 325
Myers, Stewart C., 20, 25–26, 307

National Science Foundation (NSF) data,
    220–21
Natomas, 241, 277
Nelson, Richard, 56
Net returns, 4
New York, takeover laws, 340
Nonbank long-term debt financing, 235
North Carolina, takeover laws, 339

Olson, Mancur, 333
Operating profit rate, 3–4, 127
Operational restructuring and financial re-
    structuring, 239–40
Original-issue discount securities, 294
Original-issue, high-yield bonds. See Junk
    bonds

Paramount Communications v. *Time Inc.,* 14, 342

Payment-in-kind (PIK) securities, 9, 296, 308–09; optimal capital structure and, 23

PBOs. *See* Private buyouts (PBOs)

Pennsylvania, antitakeover laws, 332–33, 339–40

Pennwalt, 265

Pension funds, stock ownership and, 326

Perelman, Ronald, 85–86

Phelps, E. S., 62

PIK. *See* Payment-in-kind (PIK) securities

Plant productivity, leveraged buyouts and, 217–20

Poison pills, 195–96, 322–23, 335, 338, 339, 341, 342

Price-cost margins, 219

Price-earnings ratios, 60, 114–15, 267

Private buyouts (PBOs), 150, 151; company characteristics, 155–60; company growth and, 160–63; Compustat data, 152–53; industry-level determinants, 175–84; industry patterns, 165; restructuring rates, 168

Private placement, 291–92, 310, 313

Procter & Gamble, 86

Production: capacity, 240–41; functions, 61; increase in *1980s,* 1. *See also* Capacity changes in chemicals industry

Profitability: debt and, 35–36; leveraged buyouts and, 231–32

Proxmire, William, 329

Public corporations, management and, 28–39

Public debt securities, 302

Quantum, 251–52, 266, 267, 273

Quarterly Financial Report (QFR), 206–09, 213–14, 218–19, 220–21, 231

Radio and television broadcasting industry, 121

Raviv, Artur, 307

Reagan administration, antitrust policy, 59

Recapitalization, 37–42

Reduced cash flow (RCF) securities, 9–10, 289–90, 296; effect on management, 305; influence on merger market, 303–06; investor motives, 303–05; leveraged buyouts and, 297–98, 304; mispriced indicators, 300–03; use, 298–303

Reputation of companies, 62–63, 75–76, 85

Research and development, 196; as unconventional asset, 71–72; leveraged buyouts and, 220–23; restructuring and, 169, 175–83; sales and, 187

Revenue Reconciliation Act of *1989,* 311

Revlon, 85–86, 342

Revlon v. *MacAndrews and Forbes Holdings,* 342

R. H. Macy, 157–58

Risk aversion, optimal capital structure and, 24–25

Romano, Roberta, 350

Roosevelt, Franklin D., 329

Rosenblum, Steven, 354, 355, 357

Safeway, 75, 82, 157–59

Scavenger bait companies, 89

SDC mergers and Corporate Transactions Database, 301

Second Bank of the United States, 329

Securities and Exchange Commission, 325, 327–28, 365; Delaware takeover laws and, 341; takeovers and, 14, 333–34, 341; Williams Act and, 335–36

Securities Exchange Act of *1934,* 327

Securities offerings, 9, 13, 86, 290–91; bridge loans, 292, 293; debt securities, 292–93; private placements, 210, 291–92, 313. *See also* Junk bonds; Tailored securities; *and under names of specific securities*

Shareholders: corporate strategy and, 56; evolution of, 81; hostile takeovers and, 74; legal framework for, 323–30; leveraged buyouts and, 211–13; problem of collective action, 322. *See also* Conflicts of interest

Share prices, debt-for-equity swaps and, 37–39

Sheard, Paul, 360–61

Shleifer, Andrei, 74–77, 82, 85

Siegel, Donald, 209, 219, 220–21, 231–33

Smith, Abbie, 220, 231, 233

Smith v. *Van Gorkom,* 339

Salomon Brothers, 292

Southland Corporation, 159

Squeeze on capital, 103–04, 110, 127, 136–37; average versus marginal returns, 139–40; chemicals industry and, 104–11; variance, 118, 121–22

Sterling Chemical, 256, 266, 273

Stock ownership, legal framework for, 323–30

Stock repurchases, 266–68

Summers, Lawrence, 74, 75, 76, 77, 82
Supreme Court, U.S.: antitakeover law, 335;
  Dynamics Corporation v. *CTS Corporation,*
  337; *Mobile* v. *Marathon,* 336; takeovers
  and, 14

Tailored securities, 9–10, 294–96, 306, 307,
  311. *See also* Junk bonds; *and under names
  of specific securities*
Tajika, Eiji, 114
Taxes: changes in *1980s,* 59; cost of capital
  and, 101, 102–03, 109–10; industry differ-
  ences, 124; leveraged buyouts and, 223; op-
  timal capital structure and, 22–24; restruc-
  turings and, 15, 173–83, 223
Tax Reform Act of *1981,* 151
Tax Reform Act of *1986,* 110, 116, 151
Tiebout, Charles, 347
Time Inc., 14, 342, 359–60
Treasury bonds, 106, 107, 118
TWA, 74–78
TW Holdings, 304
Two-tiered offers, 335, 337

Union Carbide, 241, 243, 253, 255–56, 266,
  273; bridge loans, 292
United Shareholders Association, 356
US Steel, 336

Valuation of companies, 83, 227; unconventional assets and, 63–72
Vista, 253, 267, 273
von Neumann-Morgenstern utility functions,
  24

Wigmore, Barrie, 132, 179, 185
Williams Act of *1968,* 332, 333, 334, 335;
  control share statutes and, 336; federal
  preemption and, 337
Winter, Ralph, 347, 348
Wolfe, Tom, 331

Yui, Yji, 114

Zero-coupon bonds, 9, 294, 300, 307
Zero growth, 78, 88
Zero-step bonds, 307